Three Graves North

including *Seven Graves, One Winter,*
Blood Floe and *We Shall Be Monsters*

by Christoffer Petersen

Three Graves North

Published by Aarluuk Press

Copyright © Christoffer Petersen 2019

ISBN: 978-87-93680-21-0

www.christoffer-petersen.com

Seven Graves, One Winter

~ Book 1 in *The Greenland Crime* series ~

— Ah, it has hardened
Hundreds of Hearts
Bound for the Pole
of unnameable Pain

Author's translation from
NORDPOLEN
by
LUDVIG MYLIUS-ERICHSEN (1872-1907)

— Aa, der er stivnet
Hundreder Hjærter
paa Vej mod Polen,
af navnløse Smærter

Note to the Reader

Seven Graves, One Winter introduces the main character of Constable David Maratse from the east coast of Greenland. This story, the first in a series, takes place after the events described in book two of The Greenland Trilogy: *In the Shadow of the Mountain*. While some reference is made to that book, it is not necessary to read *In the Shadow of the Mountain* before reading this book. I lay all blame for any confusion firmly at the feet of Constable Maratse, as he was quite insistent, in his own quiet manner, for a story of his own. The characters of Petra Jensen and Gaba Alatak have also appeared in short stories featuring Maratse. It is not necessary to read these stories before reading *Seven Graves, One Winter*.

Once again, it is Maratse's fault.

The people of Greenland speak Greenlandic – including at least four dialects, Danish, and English. In many aspects of daily life, West Greenlandic and Danish are the working languages. *Seven Graves, One Winter* is written in British English with the use of some Greenlandic and Danish words used where appropriate, including:

East Greenlandic / West Greenlandic / English

iiji / aap / yes

eeqqi / naamik / no

qujanaq/ qujanaraali / qujanaq / thank you

Sapaat

SUNDAY

Chapter 1

They dug the graves on the mountain's knee, in the stubborn earth pinched between boulders of granite. The graveyard was small, but large enough to accommodate the mothers, fathers, sons and daughters of Inussuk, from the time when the first grave replaced the last cairn, and babies that succumbed to the winter were no longer mummified. The winters were just as dark, the summers just as bright, but the deaths had slowed, and food, from the sea or the store, was easier to come by. But still they dug the graves each long summer, in anticipation of each dark winter when tuberculosis might take a grandparent or a grandchild, when a winter storm might take a hunter, or a depression might force someone to take their own life. They dug two graves for suicide, hoping they were two too many. They dug one for a drunken brawl, one for a fishing accident, one for the stillborn child they knew was waiting in the tiny morgue of the medical centre, one terrible boat ride away. They dug a sixth grave for old age. The seventh they dug for cancer. Even in the Arctic, always cancer.

The men climbed out of the suicide graves and leaned on their shovels for a moment, gazing out at the icebergs in the fjord. The graveyard commanded the best view of the mountains in the distance and the settlement nestled in the lap of the mountain below them. Inussuk was trapped between two beaches, one black and soft, the other shingle, shell and stone. The black beach faced south and east, breaking the waves and absorbing the energy of each storm, littered and glittered as it was with gobs of ice the size of the gravediggers' hands, hearts and heads. The larger ice debris – growlers – studded the beach, and diverted the water running off the mountain and streaming into the sea. It was between two floating growlers that the girl's body would be found a short distance from the beach that autumn, but, at that moment, the gravediggers knew nothing.

They shifted their gaze from the beach to the settlement, picking out the blistered red wood walls of the general store, and the fresh green paint of the house owned by the nature commission, currently occupied by two Danish artists and one small child. One of the men nodded in the direction of the house as the girl played in the sand and dirt beneath the deck. The forty-three adult residents of Inussuk thought the two artists were lovers. The twelve children were too young to care, content with a new playmate, a girl with blonde hair.

"Fifty-eight residents," said the older of the two gravediggers. He reached into the satchel at his feet and pulled out a thermos. A lick of wind off the fjord chased the steam from the mouth of the flask as the man unscrewed the lid. He poured coffee into an enamel cup for the younger man, filling the lid of the flask for himself.

"*Aap*," said the younger man, as he lifted the cup to his lips. He looked down at the settlement, watched the girl playing in the dirt, and then flicked his gaze to his son waving from the dock. The small boy's lips moved and his chest heaved as he shouted and the man waved, reminded as he was every time he saw Qaleraq that the boy was healthy, curious, hellish to teach, but desperate to learn. Qaleraq would see many more winters, unlike his sister's son. They would dig the last grave for his stillborn nephew, the heavy jabs of the spade penetrating as deep as they could dig, to the permafrost if they had the energy for it, so that the boy might rest right down in the earth.

He finished his coffee, flicked the dregs into the grave, and tossed the cup into his partner's satchel. He climbed into the grave and began to dig. The older man poured another half cup into the lid of the thermos, looking around the graveyard as he drank. The antenna mast cast a thin shadow on the graves of his mother and father, the plastic wreaths parched in the polar sun. He made a promise to replace them, the same promise he made the previous summer when they had dug the seven graves, and an eighth in September, just before the first snow of winter. Pneumonia had surprised an elderly couple, the man, Aput, succumbing just a week after his wife, Margrethe. The gravedigger let his gaze wander down the path as he remembered carrying the coffins, one after the other, from the couple's house to the graveyard, before catching his breath during the service and lowering his parents' closest friends into adjacent graves. The path was steep and he knew every turn, boulder and buckle. He had stubbed his toes on rocks, slipped on loose stones, and dug steps alongside the younger man for the better part of six years.

Six years and seven graves each year.

Inussuk was shrinking as the graveyard swelled. The young and educated left the settlement in favour of the larger villages and towns on the west coast of Greenland. The children left for the school in Uummannaq, returning aged fifteen and sixteen after their tenth grade, only to grow bored by the quiet life between the two beaches, and frustrated by the lack of jobs and money. Just one boy had returned to fish the same waters as his father, while his sister and her friend left to study at the Further Education college in Aasiaat, further down the coast.

"Hey," the older man said, as he finished his coffee.

"What?"

"Did you hear about the policeman?"

"Policeman?" The younger man leaned his shovel against the wall of earth and climbed out of the grave.

"He's coming next week."

"Coming here?"

"*Aap*," the older man said and pointed at the dark blue house behind the general store. "He bought Aput's house." He paused. "You didn't know?"

"*Naamik*," said the younger man, and then, "Maybe."

"You should listen to your wife, Edvard. My wife told her."

"Sure."

The older man caught Edvard's eye. "Is something wrong?"

Edvard shrugged. "The baby," he said and glanced to where his son was now playing with the Danish girl. "We want another child, but she is worried that what happened to her sister might happen to her. She says it could be the water."

"The water?"

"Metal, from the mine. It will be in the fish."

"There's no metal in this water."

"You don't know that, Karl."

"No," Karl said and sighed, "I don't." He screwed the lid onto the thermos and pushed it inside the satchel. He gripped his shovel and moved to jump into the grave. Edvard stopped him with a cough. "What?"

"You were telling me about the policeman?"

"*Aap*, he is moving here."

"To work?"

"To live."

Edvard shook his head and said, "You said that already, but will he be working here? As a policeman."

"We have never had a policeman in Inussuk."

"Which is why I want to know."

Karl laughed. "Are you worried about your home brew? If he finds it, maybe there will be more yeast in the store, and I can get fresh bread for a change."

"Maybe," Edvard said and smiled, "but where would you get your booze then, old man?"

"From Uummannaq, like everyone else."

"Suit yourself." Edvard thought for a moment. "But why is he coming here, if not to work?"

"Buuti said he is retiring, something about an early pension."

"He must be ill," Edvard said and glanced at the two graves they had nearly finished.

"Infirm, invalided," Karl said. "I heard he walks with a stick, maybe two."

"So he is moving here from Nuuk?"

"*Naamik*, he is from Ittoqqortoormiit."

"Tunu? East Greenland?"

"*Aap.*"

"Why is he coming here?"

"I don't know. You can ask him next week."

Edvard grunted and jumped into the grave. He picked up his shovel and started to dig as Karl did the same in the grave next to him. They worked for another two hours, finishing the graves at the same time, as they always did, although Karl suspected Edvard slowed each time he was almost done, scraping at the edges instead of digging, waiting until the older man was finished.

Karl was the first to climb out of the grave, and he gave Edvard his hand to help the younger man up, a small token of thanks in return for the respect he showed for his elders. They walked to the other end of the graveyard, closer to the edge that reached down the knee of the mountain and to the waves lapping at the dark, wet rock below. They traced the shape of the two graves they would dig here, as close to the edge as they dared, as close as was considered respectful, without condemning the occupants to an eternity of vertigo.

Edvard paused at the furthest corner and looked out to sea. He prodded Karl's shoulder and pointed at a medium-sized motorboat with a flash of lightning stencilled along the hull, bobbing in the shadow of a large iceberg, too close to escape the wave and debris should it begin to roll or calve. Karl sucked at his teeth and Edvard shrugged. Neither man recognised the boat. Even at this distance it would be strange not to know the shape of a local hull, or the curve of its bow.

"Do you know who that is?"

"*Naamik*," said Edvard. "Maybe it's from Disco Island?"

"Maybe."

The two gravediggers rested on their shovels and watched as the boat drifted away from the iceberg and out of view. They waited until the stern disappeared behind the iceberg. Only then did they make the first cut of the new graves. If they could see through or around the iceberg, they would have seen a man struggle into view from the cabin of the boat, dragging a naked girl by her long black hair. They would have seen him slap her twice in the face. If the wind had been blowing in the right direction, they might even have heard her scream.

She was young with soft curves that defined her sex. Her skin was darker than her European friends, lighter than the Greenlanders. She was bruised. Her nose was bloody. The man wiped her blood from his hand on her stomach, before he dragged her across the deck and shoved her onto the floor. She thrashed her legs like a bloody fish, and he hit her again, this time with the back of his hand, slamming the back of her head against the side of the boat. The boat dipped with the impact and her legs went limp as her brown eyes widened and she stared at the man. The girl's hair flowed onto the seat moulded into the hull and the man squirmed the sole of his boot onto the seat, clamping her in place. He reached over the girl and grabbed a bag from the seat opposite, unzipped it, and spilled winter clothes onto her stomach.

"Get dressed," he said. He tossed the bag towards the cabin and leaned on his knee. The girl held her breath, struggling with the overtrousers and socks, as she stared at the man. He removed his foot from her hair and told her to sit up and put on the fleece sweater, and a large, thick, *Canada Goose* winter jacket. As she dressed, his gaze lingered over the dark areolae of her breasts. He dragged her to her feet and across the deck. He reached for a pair of hiking boots beneath the steering column. "Boots," he said, as he threw them to her. He spun the chair in front of the wheel and pushed her hard into it. She bit her lip and he grabbed her by the hair, eliciting a sob as he tugged once and waited for her to pull on the boots and tie the laces.

When she was done he pulled her to her feet and marched her to the port side of the boat, the one closest to the iceberg.

The girl gripped the rail along the side, her body shaking as she sobbed. The man released her and returned to the wheel, applying a little thrust to manoeuvre closer to the iceberg. He cranked the engine out of gear and let it idle. A pall of grey smoke drifted across the girl's face and she coughed.

"What's that?" he said.

"I coughed," the girl said in Danish. She could taste tears on her lips, salt like the sea.

"What did you say?" The man gripped her by the hair.

"I said nothing," she said, as he twisted her face to look at him. "Nothing," she sobbed.

"Speak Greenlandic, bitch," he said and jerked her head downwards, smiling as another sob caught in her throat.

"I can't."

"Exactly."

The man pushed her toward the railing. The girl cried out as she slipped to her knees. Strands of her hair caught in the fur ruff of the jacket's hood as the man changed his grip, and jammed his hands under her arms.

"Get off my boat," he said and lifted her up. She screamed, her hands flailing at the railing, desperate for a grip as the man heaved her over the side and her legs slid into the water. He grunted with the sudden weight, his feet sliding along the deck as her fingers caught around the railing and she clung to it. The man kicked at her knuckles until she screamed and let go, palms slipping down the hull of the boat as the air inside the jacket swelled on contact with the water. The cold pressed the air from her lungs and she started to convulse, as she fought for her last breath.

As soon as he heard her splash into the water, the man moved back to the throttle, put the boat in gear, and powered away from the girl. Her eyes bulged as she watched him turn a short distance away, before correcting his course and leaning out over the side of the boat to stare at her. She heard the engine roar as he opened the throttle and sped towards her.

With what little strength she had left, the girl splashed at the water with stiff fingers, as she tried to swim away from the boat. The man corrected course and she caught the stiff hull of the boat on her cheek as the man powered past her. Her head dipped under the water, her hair flat on the surface like tendrils and nerves, plugged into the water, tuning into her death, as the man checked his speed, turned the boat, and accelerated towards her one last time. The keel of the boat clipped her head, the vibration knocking along the hull.

The man smiled, and made a slow circle of the girl's last known position. He settled on the seat behind the wheel and reached into his pocket for a packet of mints, frowning as his fingers caught on the girl's topaz panties. He stuffed them back into his pocket and set a course for the mouth of the fjord, as the gravediggers dug deep into the mountain above Inussuk.

Marlunngorneq

TUESDAY

Chapter 2

Constable David Maratse grunted as another rod of pain shot through his legs and lit his lower back in what he imagined to be a wall of fire. It was the same every time he lifted his left foot, with another flaming rod of pain pressing through his nerves when he placed his sole flat on the treadmill. Maratse paused to catch his breath, white-knuckling the handrails as the physiotherapist made another note on his clipboard.

"It's not getting better, is it?" he asked.

"*Eeqqi*," Maratse said, and shook his head. He took a breath, breathed out, once, twice, three times until the pain subsided. "Again," he said, and lifted his foot.

"You're sure?"

"*Iiji*," he said. "Yes, I'm sure." His nerves flamed and Maratse crumpled, cursing as he fell onto the treadmill's rough rubber surface. The physio turned the machine off and helped Maratse onto his feet.

"Let's get you sat down," he said.

"I've been sitting down for a week."

"And before that you were lying down," the physio said, as he helped Maratse into a chair, "for three weeks. This is progress. You have to take it slow."

"Progress?" Maratse grunted. He patted the pockets of his jogging bottoms, and then realised his cigarettes were in his jacket pocket, beside his hospital bed.

"Smoking won't help."

"It helps me."

"Seriously," the physio said, "with the damage your nerves have been exposed to…"

"Smoking helps," Maratse said, and dared the physio to suggest otherwise. The young man shrugged and made more notes on his pad. Maratse thought about nerve damage. He could almost smell his own charred flesh, as the Chinaman had pressed the ends of his improvised torture device into Maratse's chest, his legs, his testicles. Maratse shoved the image from his mind and calculated the distance to his bed. "I need a smoke."

"I'll have someone take you back to your ward," the physio said. He put down his pad and walked across the training room to where Maratse's wheelchair was parked alongside the wall. He started to push it across the floor, stopping when the door opened. He smiled at the policewoman as she entered the room, let go of the wheelchair, and said, "He's all yours."

"He's done?" she said, and brushed a loose strand of long black hair behind her ear. The movement reminded Maratse of another woman who did the same, a Danish Konstabel in the Sirius Patrol, the same woman who had rescued him from the Chinaman.

"I need a smoke," Maratse said and nodded at the wheelchair. "One of you needs to help me."

"Still grumpy, eh?" The policewoman said. She sighed and tucked the envelope in her hand inside her jacket, gripped the handles of the wheelchair, and positioned it alongside Maratse's chair. The physio helped her lift Maratse onto his feet, switching the chairs as the woman supported Maratse. She smiled and caught Maratse's eye. "Forgotten my name again?"

"Hello, Piitalaat."

"My name is Petra," she said. "Constable Petra Jensen." Maratse winced as he felt the physio push the seat of the chair against the back of his legs. Petra helped him sit. "Why do you insist on calling me that?"

"I like it," Maratse gripped the circular bars on each side of the wheels. He backed away from Petra and nodded at the door. "I need a smoke, Constable."

"I heard you the first time," she said. "Oh, and it won't be Constable for much longer."

Maratse turned at the door. "Sergeant's exam?"

"Yes," she said. "It went well. I should get the official confirmation by the end of the week."

"Is that what's in the envelope?"

"No." Petra's lips flattened, and she brushed at an imaginary strand of hair. "That's something else."

"For me?"

"I'm afraid so."

Maratse sighed and nodded at the door. "Let's go," he said.

Petra opened the envelope as she walked beside Maratse towards the elevators. "Do you want me to read it?"

"*Iiji*," he said and let the rubber tyres scuff his palms, "but just the highlights."

"All right," Petra said. She traced her finger along the closely-spaced print. "They are going to give you early retirement, on a full pension." She paused as Maratse grunted. "But you won't be a police officer anymore. I'm sorry."

"It's okay," Maratse said. He stopped at the elevators and pressed the call button. He had expected as much, and the morning session of physiotherapy had confirmed what he already knew, he would never be a policeman again.

"Are you still going to Inussuk?"

"*Iji.*"

Petra folded the letter as the elevator doors opened. "I don't understand why. You could go home."

Maratse went into the elevator first, turned, and waited for Petra to enter and push the button for the first floor. "I'll always be the policeman," he said. "It's better to start somewhere new."

"Retired," Petra said.

"Same thing. It won't make a difference."

"So, you're going to give up the bright lights of the city, and leave me all alone in Nuuk?" Petra leaned against the side of the elevator and composed her best pout. Maratse almost laughed, and she seemed content with the wrinkle of skin around his eyes. Petra straightened her back as the elevator slowed to a stop. Maratse waited for her to get out before following her into the corridor.

"What about Gaba?"

"We don't talk about him," she said.

"Since when?"

"Since last Saturday night." Petra walked behind Maratse and gripped the handles of the wheelchair.

"What happened?" he said and let go of the wheels. He caught the smell of alcohol gel as an orderly cleaned his hands outside the men's bathroom, but it was soon gone as Petra picked up speed.

"I don't want to talk about it."

"Okay." Maratse took a breath as Petra spun him around to back into his room. She wheeled him to the bed and Maratse reached for his jacket. Petra walked to the window, leaned against it, folded her arms and glared at Maratse. "What?" he said, pausing as he pulled the packet of cigarettes from his jacket pocket.

"You didn't ask me."

"You said you didn't want to talk about it."

"I don't." Petra turned away and then pointed at the cover of the newspaper on the bedside table. "That doesn't help."

"I haven't read it."

"That idiot from *Seqinnersoq* is mouthing off again. Using Greenlandic as a campaign promise, as a weapon. It's the only qualification he has." Petra picked up the paper.

"When is the election?"

"Next May." She frowned. "You don't watch the news?"

Maratse shrugged. "I don't vote." He pulled a cigarette from the packet and stuffed it into the gap between his teeth. He gripped the lighter in his fist. "I'm going outside."

Petra turned the cover of the paper towards Maratse and stabbed her finger on the photo. "She wasn't much older than her."

"Who?"

"The *girl* Gaba slept with Saturday night." Petra held the paper to one side and stared at the image of Malik Uutaaq, standing beside his wife, with a *gymnasium*-aged girl in the background. "The girl Gaba slept with is about her age, about seventeen or eighteen."

Maratse grunted and wheeled himself to the door. He heard the thwack of the newspaper landing on the bed as he turned into the corridor and continued on to the elevators. Petra followed him. She didn't say a word until they were huddled in the shed for smokers outside the main entrance to Dronning Ingrid's Infirmary. She waited until Maratse had lit his cigarette and then said, "Why don't you vote?"

Maratse took a long drag on his cigarette and then nodded at the front page of the same newspaper a patient was reading while she smoked. He lowered his voice, and said, "I don't trust politicians."

"But you are employed by the government – a government of politicians. We still have self-rule," she said. "You should have a say in who gets to employ you."

"You're forgetting something, Piitalaat," Maratse said. Petra frowned and he continued, "The Greenlandic police force answers directly to Denmark. They," he said and nodded at the newspaper, "don't tell us what to do. Besides, I'm retired." Maratse raised his eyebrows and took another drag on the cigarette. He imagined his nerves relaxing as the smoke filled his lungs. For a moment, at least, he thought he had found peace.

"I hate it when you call me that. It's like you have to remind me I am Greenlandic."

"You are Greenlandic."

"I know."

Maratse puffed a cloud of smoke towards the ceiling of the shed. "I call you that because I like the name."

Maratse finished his cigarette and reached for another. He sighed when he realised he had left his jacket in his room, again. He rested his hands on his thighs and closed his eyes, opening them for a moment when the patient got up to leave. He nodded at her and closed his eyes once more. Petra sat down on the bench beside him.

"What will you do in Inussuk?" she said.

"Fish and hunt." Maratse opened one eye as Petra took his hand.

"But you can't even walk."

"Not yet," he said, and closed his eyes.

Petra squeezed his hand and he curled his fingers into hers, listening to the wind licking at the dust along the street, the caw of the raven scratching on the hospital roof, and the distant peel of a church bell. Maratse felt the wind prickle at the thin hairs on his arms and he was suddenly grateful that the Chinaman had only scarred the skin he did not show, and that the pain was hidden on the inside of his body. He almost laughed at the thought, wondering at the sudden twinge of vanity, curious if it had anything to do with his thirty-nine years and the twenty-something who was holding his hand.

"Maybe I will visit," she said, and squeezed his hand once more, "if I may?"

"*Iiji,*" he said, and opened his eyes.

"Will you be all right?"

"I will."

"And you'll stay out of trouble?"

Maratse thought for a moment before answering. From a career point-of-view he had emerged unscathed from his involvement with Konstabel Brongaard and the collateral damage she incurred in her private war with the international intelligence community. It was a wonder he was alive, and he wondered if she was. He admired her guts, her drive, and her moral code, and, for a while at least, he had enjoyed the excitement, the rush of adrenalin so different from his normal policing duties. It had nearly killed him, a fact he was all too aware of, but in the moment – some of the moments – it had fulfilled him somehow. And now, he just had to stay out of trouble.

"I will be good," he said, and let go of her hand.

"Okay," Petra said, and stood up. She tugged a strand of hair from the Velcro at her collar, reached inside her jacket, and gave Maratse his discharge papers. "I'd better go."

"Thanks for coming."

"Anytime."

"Tomorrow?"

"Let me guess, you need a ride to the airport?"

Maratse raised his eyebrows, *yes*.

She nodded and looked at the door. "Can you make your own way back?"

"I can."

"Okay." Petra brushed the tips of her fingers across Maratse's shoulder, turned and walked away. He waited until she had turned the corner before stuffing the envelope under his leg and wheeling himself out of the smoker's shed and along the side of the hospital to the ambulance workshop. He nodded at the mechanic working on one of Nuuk's three ambulances and stopped beside a long, rusted bar, screwed at hip-height into the garage wall. Maratse applied the brakes to the wheelchair, reached for the bar, and pulled himself onto his feet. The mechanic looked up as Maratse cursed the bar to hell and back, before cursing his feet, one after the other, as he inched his way along the wall, and back again.

When the pain was at its worst, just when he thought he might faint, he pictured the Chinaman and his electroshock paddle, and he spat at the wall and cursed the man beyond the white man's hell, and into the frost-burning realm of Greenland's darkest spirits, where seared flesh was a delicacy, and pierced eyes nothing more than an inconvenience before the real torment began.

Maratse paused to pick the flakes of rusted metal from his orange-stained palms, and then gripped the bar again, heaving himself along the wall, spitting at the Chinaman, and cursing the fire in his spine, and the white-hot nails in the soles of his feet.

"I will walk again," he said, and took another step.

He heard the crash of metal as the mechanic downed his tools, and he watched as the man wiped his hands with an oily rag and walked across the workshop to stand behind Maratse's wheelchair.

Maratse gritted his teeth and said, "Just one more."

The mechanic nodded and walked to the row of lockers at the back of the workshop. He returned with a bottle of vodka and two dirty shot glasses, placing them on an upturned barrel as Maratse slumped into his wheelchair. The mechanic poured two glasses and gave one to Maratse.

"*Skål*," the mechanic said and clinked his glass against Maratse's. He waited until Maratse had downed the first glass, before exchanging his full glass for Maratse's empty one.

"*Qujanaq*," Maratse said and downed the second glass of vodka. "Thank you."

The mechanic took the empty glasses and placed them by the side of the vodka. He reached for the cap and screwed it back onto the bottle when Maratse shook his head.

"You push yourself too hard," the mechanic said.

"Maybe."

"Yeah, you do." The mechanic cocked his head and stared at Maratse. "Why?"

Maratse pulled the envelope out from beneath his leg and gave it to the mechanic. He wiped the sweat from his brow as the man opened the letter and read it.

"That's why," Maratse said as the man whistled.

"They're going to give you a full pension."

"I don't want it."

"You don't have to work again." The mechanic waited as Maratse took a deep breath. When he exhaled he said, "You want to be a policeman?"

"You want to be a mechanic?" Maratse said and looked around the workshop. He gestured at the man's oily hands, sniffed at the heavy taint of diesel.

The mechanic shrugged and said, "I'm good at it."

"So am I," said Maratse. He nodded at the bottle. "Will you leave that when you go?"

"Sure."

Maratse nodded. He turned away from the mechanic, reached out for the bar, and pulled himself to his feet. The pain lit his spine like a firework and he cursed and spat, until the flame became a rod of lightning, as Maratse raged back and forth along the bar until the sun dipped low in the late autumn sky, and all the vodka was gone.

Chapter 3

Malik Uutaaq pushed one leg out from under the duvet of his son's bed and groaned as he propped himself up on his elbows and blinked at the sunlight streaming through the curtains. He swung his legs over the side of the bed and flinched at the sharp corner of the LEGO brick pressing into his foot. Sipu had forgotten to tidy up his room before leaving for football camp. Malik brushed the brick to one side and stood up, the duvet slipped from his body and he staggered across the room to the door, groaning as he heard the bathroom door shut and the sound of his daughter, Pipaluk, running the shower. He straightened the twist of his boxer shorts, bent down to pick up the t-shirt on the floor, and dressed as he climbed down the stairs on his way to the kitchen. His wife ignored him as he opened the fridge and took out a carton of milk.

"Sleep well?" he asked. She sneered and turned back to her cereal. He opened the milk and drank, pressing his lips into the soft cardboard lip, dribbling milk onto the stubble of his chin. Malik slapped the carton onto the kitchen counter and said, "You have to talk to me sometime, Naala."

His wife dropped her spoon into the bowl and turned slowly to stare at him. She pressed her finger onto the counter and said, "When you stop screwing around, we can talk. How about that?"

"Screwing around?"

"Don't," she said, and held up her hand.

"You think that's why I came home late?" Malik laughed. "Jesus. Jealousy doesn't become you. But if that's what you want to think I was doing…"

Naala folded her arms across her chest and glared at her husband. She started to speak, but Malik stopped her with a laugh.

"Of course, if you lost a few kilos, maybe I would come home more often."

"You bastard."

Naala picked up the bowl of cereal and threw it at her husband's head. Malik dodged to one side as the bowl splintered against the fridge. Milk splattered across his thick black hair, and he flicked a flake of cereal from his shoulder as his wife shoved past him and left the kitchen. Malik smiled, filled the kettle with water and let it boil as he turned on the radio.

He made coffee with a spoonful of instant granules as the presenter started the news. Malik stirred milk into his coffee, pausing at the mention of his political party *Seqinnersoq*, the sunshine party.

"Plenty of that around here," he said, and took a sip of coffee. He listened again as the radio cut to a quote from the party's communications chief Aarni Aviki. Malik smiled at Aarni's nasal twang as he stumbled over a string of points at the top of *Seqinnersoq*'s agenda. The media had already picked up on the communications chief's struggle with the Greenlandic language, exposed the Danish roots of his name, and called him *Arne* at every opportunity. Malik was amazed at the control his friend exercised when they pressed him as they did in every interview. But he knew that there was no better poster-boy for the party than a mixed-blood Greenlander making a significant effort to master the language of the people. Malik took another sip of coffee and smiled at the simplicity of it all. The other parties were forced to comment on healthcare, the economy, and social issues of unemployment and housing, but Malik had managed to keep the narrative on language alone, thanks to the dogged determination of his communications chief.

The water pipes creaked and Malik looked up as he heard his daughter turn off the shower. He switched off the radio, finished his coffee and jogged up the stairs to use the bathroom before his wife. He winked at her as he slipped into the bathroom and locked the door, smiling as he heard her curse before slamming the bedroom door.

Pipaluk was waiting in the car when Malik walked out of the house. He put his briefcase on the backseat and took a step back to admire the American import, a Dodge RAM, the fruits of his labours, and one of the many benefits of not paying VAT on international goods. The morning sun shone on the black bodywork, and Malik smiled at his reflection in the door panel. He waved at Pipaluk in the passenger seat and got in.

"You're so vain, daddy," she said, as he buckled his seatbelt.

"And you're not, princess?" Malik tickled his daughter's ear and flicked the long earring dangling from her lobe. "I thought we said they were for special occasions, only."

"They match my outfit."

"But the teachers don't like them," Malik said and started the car.

"They don't say anything anymore, not since you started your campaign."

"No," Malik said, "I bet they don't."

Malik pulled out of the driveway and turned onto the main road, slowing at the junction. He glanced at Pipaluk as she checked her social media.

"Remember to bring your winter clothes home today," he said and accelerated up the hill towards Qinngorput.

"I left them on the hook in the cloakroom last year."

"Yes, and your mother wants to check that they still fit."

"She said that to you?" Pipaluk said, and looked at her father. "I didn't think you were talking to each other."

"She said it." He glanced at Pipaluk. "What? You don't believe me?" Pipaluk shook her head and focussed on her smartphone. They drove the rest of the way in silence.

It took barely five minutes to drive his daughter to the new school in Qinngorput, less if he hadn't stopped to chat with one of the young mothers dropping off her son in the kindergarten class. Malik had noticed her before, the soft tone of her skin, the way she wore her make-up, the cut of her clothes. The boy tugging at the woman's hand was a brat, and Malik decided it wasn't worth the hassle, especially as he knew the boy's father. He wished the mother a good day, waved goodbye to Pipaluk, and drove into the centre of town.

"More like a city," he thought to himself, as he waited in a short queue of cars at the roundabout. Fifteen thousand people lived in Nuuk. It had an airport, a hospital, courthouse, an international harbour, and a university. "That makes it a city," he said, as the traffic began to move. "And, boy, do I have plans for my city." Malik glanced at his reflection in the rear-view mirror and smiled.

According to the media and the polls his party had paid for, *Seqinnersoq* had a favourable lead on all the other parties, and was gaining popular appeal, especially in the settlements and villages along the coast. Even on the east coast, one of the poorest parts of the country but regionally linked to Nuuk, the people were responding to Malik's call for a renewed national identity, starting with the language. *Seqinnersoq* wanted Greenlandic as a first language, English second, and the eradication of Danish as a working language.

It was that simple.

But Malik knew that Danish roots were long and stubborn. Thin enough to creep into the seams of bedrock, beneath the ice, like a pervasive wire that could not be pulled out without pulling a huge chunk of Greenlandic history and culture with it. Malik didn't care much for history, and the Greenlandic culture was strong, as was the language, for which he might grudgingly accept that Denmark had played a certain supportive role, especially when one looked at the current status of Inuktitut, the language of the Canadian Inuit.

"But we don't have to mention that," he said, and glanced in the mirror. "Do we?"

Malik's focus was the future independence of Greenland. He felt stifled by the Danish influence on his country. He ignored the hypocrisy of sending his children to Danish institutes of Higher and Further education. It was free, after all. But every time he looked at a world map and saw Denmark written beneath Greenland on the world's largest island, he could taste bile in the back of his throat, and he wanted to be sick.

He took a deep breath and sighed as he parked in front of the Katuaq Cultural Centre, the wave form of the building capturing the curve of the Northern Lights he loved and longed for each autumn and winter. Malik turned off the engine and, though the heart of the American beast was still, his own heart beat to a rhythm that made him sweat and he wiped his brow before getting out of the car. He took another breath of fresh air as he picked up his briefcase from the backseat and locked the door.

Aarni Aviki waved at him from his seat in the café. Malik nodded at him, as he crossed the car park and entered the cultural centre. He paused to order a cappuccino and a breakfast pastry and then made his way to Aarni at the table furthest from the door.

"I heard you on the radio this morning," Malik said, as he sat down.

Aarni folded his newspaper and tucked it into his briefcase at his feet. "Can we speak Danish?" he said, in a whisper. "I have another interview scheduled just before lunch, and I need to just relax for a bit."

"Of course," Malik said. He smiled as the waitress brought his coffee and pastry, waiting for her to walk away before speaking. "I've said it many times, you need to relax more."

"That's rich." Aarni looked away for a moment. "These assholes want my blood," he said, and turned to look at Malik. "Constantly."

"You're an easy target. It makes sense for them to go after you. Besides," he said, "it keeps the heat off me." Malik winked. "Perhaps we should raise your salary, again."

"Sure, that would be nice."

"And," Malik said. He paused to spoon the froth from the rim of his cup. "Perhaps more money would mean more social life? A girl, for example? Something else for the media to talk about. To save them speculating about other things."

"Like me being gay? Is that what you mean?"

Malik shrugged. "Your sexual persuasion is your own business, Arne…"

"Don't call me that." Aarni looked around Malik's shoulder. "If people hear you call me that."

"Relax, *Arne*," Malik said. He took a sip of coffee, licking the froth from his lips as he lowered the cup to the saucer. "I'm just saying you're an interesting guy. But you don't need to be *too* interesting. Greenland is a small country, and a little diversion is healthy in certain situations."

"A diversion?"

"Yes."

Aarni leaned over the table. "You're saying I should be more like you?"

"A little more like me, yes."

"Then you haven't read the paper this morning, have you?" Aarni said and leaned back. He reached for the newspaper and handed it to Malik. "Luckily for you, you're not the only one."

Malik frowned as he took the newspaper. He pushed his chair back to make room to turn the pages, and then studied the front page. "This isn't *Sermitsiaq*."

"No. It's yesterday's *Politiken*, from Denmark. Someone left it on my desk last night."

"Last night?"

"I went back to the office after dinner, to pick up some papers. I found it then. Page seventeen."

The newspaper crackled as Malik turned the pages. He paused to study the page, his eyes flicking from one article to the next until he found one, circled in blue ink. Malik lowered the newspaper and said, "Did you put a ring around it?"

"No," Aarni said. He turned his cup on the saucer, pushed back his chair, and stood up. "I'm going to have another. Do you want something?" He waited for Malik to answer, noticed the wrinkles on his boss's brow, and decided to leave him to the article. When Aarni came back, the newspaper was folded on the table.

Malik looked out of the window. "Who put a circle around that article?"

"I don't know," Aarni said, and sat down.

"You need to find out."

"Obviously."

Malik turned at the sound of the waitress returning with Aarni's coffee. He crossed one leg over the other and waited for her to leave before saying, "It doesn't mention my name, at least."

"You would have been called for a comment if it did."

"But someone…"

"Wait a second," Aarni said, and held up his hand. If he was enjoying the shift in the balance of power at the breakfast table, he was smart enough not to show it. "Let's talk about diversions, shall we?" Aarni waited as Malik took a long breath. "I have been your shield for a long time now. I think we both know that's why you hired me."

Malik glanced at Aarni, nodded, and looked away.

"But just because the media has their attention laser-focused on me, that doesn't make you immune." Aarni tapped the newspaper with his finger. "The party-culture of Greenlandic politics that *Politiken* has so eloquently encapsulated, is, fortunately for you, largely historical. But parties are not your problem, Malik."

"No?" Malik looked at Aarni.

"Your problem is your exotic taste in women."

"Exotic?"

"Mixed-blood, to be blunt. You like your coffee medium-roasted, not dark. You never drink it black, you want it with cream…"

"I get the point, Aarni," Malik said. He pursed his lips and said, "Spell it out for me, politically."

"Is that necessary?"

"Suppose that it is."

"All right." Aarni nodded. "Let's put it in perspective. The media comes after me because I struggle to speak Greenlandic. They are probing, waiting for me to trip up, and to speak Danish. They will nail me for that, but that's all they have. Being gay would be a minor issue. Sure, I would lose all credibility, and, given the taboos surrounding homosexuality in this country, my political career would be ruined. But not my career. This campaign has put me in the spotlight…"

"I put you in the spotlight," Malik said and stabbed the table with his knuckle.

"You did, and I am grateful, and I will show you just how grateful I am, and…" He paused as a text message vibrated into his smartphone. Aarni read the message, nodded once, and finished his sentence, "loyal," Aarni said and smiled as Malik looked at him. He closed the message screen on his phone and slipped it into his pocket. "But the political fallout for you will be far greater. You have made it no secret that Greenland is for Greenlanders, and that means speaking the language."

"The people expect that."

"Sure, and you get a charge from that, a buzz. It makes you feel powerful."

Malik snorted. "You forgot *omnipotent*."

"However it makes you feel, it is also your Achilles heel. Your weakness. Your lust makes you weak…"

"Weak?"

"Yes, because your taste in young Greenlandic women of mixed blood makes you the biggest political hypocrite Greenland politics has ever seen," Aarni said, waving off Malik's response. It was his turn to rap his knuckle on the table. "Greenlanders might denounce and raise a ruckus about political misappropriation of funds, nepotism, and under-the-table deals, but they will forgive and forget when they take everything into consideration – when they are reminded about just how many things a politician has to be good at today, how many skills they need to master, how complicated and complex our society has become. But you…" Aarni paused to lean back in his chair, "when it comes to you they will say *he had one job*. Just one job. Greenland for Greenlanders, speaking the language of their country. If you screw just one more Danish-speaking girl, they will find out, and that will be the end of your career – political or otherwise."

Malik pushed the handle of his cup with his finger, turning the cup on the saucer until the handle pointed at Aarni. He looked his communications chief in the eye and said, "You said you were grateful, and loyal."

"I did. I am," he said. "I have been."

"Have been? Have been loyal, you mean?"

"I mean that when the time comes, you will be able to see the depths of my loyalty. Without a doubt. It's the least I can do. My career is set," Aarni said, and smiled. "For that, I am grateful."

"Then I need you to do something."

"Anything."

Malik nodded at the newspaper. "Find whoever put a ring around that article. Find out what they know, and what they want. Do that for me."

Chapter 4

Nivi Winther's office was on the second floor of the government building beside the police station in Nuuk. As Greenland's First Minister and party leader for the Greenlandic social democrats, she was accustomed to a busier schedule than the members of Greenland's minority parties, but she often longed for the slower pace of the small settlement where she was born. Even Ilulissat, the largest town in the north of Greenland, was more relaxed than the capital, and she looked forward to her visit scheduled for the weekend. Nivi leaned forwards at her desk and tapped the photo of her daughter, Tinka, arms wrapped around her father, Nivi's ex-husband, Martin. People said Nivi and Tinka looked like sisters. She smiled at the thought, and then glanced at the image of Martin, the tall Dane from West Jutland.

"That's who you get your long legs from, Tinka," she whispered, just a moment before her assistant knocked on the door and walked into her office.

Daniel Tukku walked across the pine floor to Nivi's desk, arranged three thin folders in front of her, and tapped each one in turn. "Unemployment. Housing. Culture and identity," he said. "You have ten minutes before the interview."

"And he is only going to ask me about these three topics?" Nivi said and reached for the first folder. She flicked it open with a long nail, smooth with a clear varnish.

"That's what we agreed." Daniel tapped the third folder. "But this is the one."

"Culture and identity?"

"And language."

Nivi looked away and sighed. "Story of my week."

"And every week from now until the election. You had better get used to it."

"They can't move on, can they?"

"Malik Uutaaq doesn't want to move on." Daniel shrugged. "He's got you where he wants you, and the whole country is watching."

"But they don't all agree with him."

"Outside Nuuk? Maybe they do."

Nivi pushed her chair back and stood up. She padded to the

window in bare feet, looked out at the sea, squinting at the hazy horizon. "How do we change the narrative?"

"Honestly, I don't think you can. It's personal. He wants it to be personal. And if I was him…"

"You would do the same. I know," she said and turned around. "Remind me again why you chose to work for me."

"Because you can make a difference. Because you won't let language interfere with identity."

"I speak Greenlandic."

"And so do I, but Danish is convenient." The corner of Daniel's mouth twitched. "Should we switch to Greenlandic?"

"Will that make me more appealing to the voters?"

"Malik's voters? No. They listen to him. And each time you beat him in the polls…"

"He reminds the nation that I married a Dane, and have a daughter who only speaks Danish." Nivi shook her head. "It's not fair, Daniel."

"You're right. It's not. Which is why," he said and gestured at the folders on her desk, "I arranged the interview."

"That I have to give in Danish."

"Because the journalist is deaf, Nivi. That's why."

"You couldn't have found another?"

"Qitu couldn't be more Greenlandic. The people listen to him. He has the sympathy vote. Something I will exploit quite happily if it helps us."

"But he does speak Greenlandic?"

"Yes, but it's easier for him to lip read in Danish. Greenlandic dialects can be a problem."

"Remind me again how he lost his hearing?"

"Jumping between the ice floes in the harbour as a child. He fell in the water." Daniel smiled at the memory of a similar experience. "What could be more Greenlandic than that?"

"Sure, you're right." Nivi sat down at her desk. "How long do I have?"

Daniel looked at his watch, and said, "Five minutes. Ten if I offer him coffee."

"Do that," Nivi said, as she opened each folder in front of her. She started to read as Daniel left the office. He closed her door with a soft click.

Nivi skimmed the memo on housing, nodding at each of the bullet points. There was nothing new. Unemployment was another matter, and the promise of jobs in mining and oil was a constant source of optimism in the media, second only to the debate on identity. But Nivi found it difficult to be optimistic when Greenland was dependent on foreign skills and technology. She wanted to boost tourism, but there were only so many jobs the tourist industry could support.

"These are the issues we should be debating," she said, surprising herself at the sound of her own voice. She looked up, half expecting Daniel to nod and agree with her. But she was alone, and the last folder tugged at her conscience. She looked at it, and then picked up her smartphone from the desk. She thumbed through her messages, and then checked her daughter's Facebook page. There were no new updates. Nivi resisted the urge to call Tinka, just to check in. She put her phone down and picked up the last folder, skimmed the notes and stood up. Daniel knocked on her door a second later.

"Ready?" he said, as he leaned around the door.

"Sure." Nivi pulled on her boots and zipped them to her calves, slipped her smartphone into the back pocket of her jeans, and collected the folders into a pile. She gave them to Daniel on her way out of her office. "Where is he?" she asked.

"Conference room."

"What's his last name?" she said as they walked.

"Kalia."

"Okay." Nivi paused at the door to the conference room, teased her fringe with long fingers, and took a breath. She smiled at Daniel, and then opened the door.

"Qitu," she said, as she strode into the room and shook the journalist's hand. "I'm so pleased you could come. She waved at Daniel to close the door and then sat down.

Qitu brushed pastry crumbs from his shirt and sat opposite Nivi. He pushed his coffee and plate to one side and opened his notepad. Nivi caught herself looking for the tape recorder journalists usually had with them. She stopped, leaned back in her seat, and waited. Qitu's voice, when he spoke, was deeper than she had expected. Nivi looked at his mouth, noticed the clean cut of his jaw, and then she saw his eyes, and for the second time found that the journalist had surprised her. She was off-guard, and Qitu's opening question put her on the defensive.

"Tell me about your daughter," he said, his pen poised above the notepad, his dark brown eyes focussed on her mouth.

"My daughter?"

"Yes. Tell me about her."

"You don't want to talk about housing? Unemployment?"

He shook his head. "This is a personal piece. Your assistant said Greenland needs to get to know you. That's why I am here."

Nivi turned to look at the door, but Daniel had closed it. She looked at Qitu, thought for a moment, and said, "All right. What do you want to know?" She paused as Qitu took a sip of coffee.

"Tell me about your daughter."

"Tinka?" Nivi smiled. "She's seventeen. She's in her second year of *gymnasium*, high school."

Nivi watched as Qitu made notes with barely a glance at the notepad. She felt, for the first time in her life, that she truly had someone's attention, as Qitu focussed on her, on what she was saying. Nivi began to relax. She poured herself a cup of coffee, warming her hands around the base of the cup. She took a sip and then started to speak.

"I said she was seventeen, but Tinka acts like she is in her twenties." Nivi smiled at the memory of the thousands of disagreements they had had on a Friday night in Ilulissat, before Tinka had moved to Aasiaat to study, and Nivi had moved to Nuuk. "I have to remember that she is a young woman, and not my little girl."

"When did you last see her?"

"When?" Nivi frowned and leaned forwards. "In the summer, before school started. We spent two weeks in Greece, and then a weekend in Nuuk."

Qitu made another note. "When did you last speak to her?"

"Hey," Nivi said, and put her cup on the table, "what is this about?"

"I am just asking about your daughter. When you last spoke to her."

"Thursday night. Why?"

"Before the weekend?"

"Yes. That's where Thursdays are, every week." Nivi turned as Daniel opened the door.

"Everything all right?" he asked.

"What's going on, Daniel?"

"What do you mean?"

"He wants to know when I last spoke with Tinka." The rubber feet on the legs of her chair burred across the pine floor as Nivi stood up. She pulled her smartphone from her pocket and dialled her daughter's number, glaring at Qitu as she waited for Tinka to answer. Nivi started to tap her foot, pressing redial when Tinka didn't answer the first time.

"She's probably in class," Daniel said when Nivi lowered her phone.

Nivi stared at Qitu. His eyes had lost their initial appeal, and she found herself far less impressed by his note-taking skills, and far more concerned with his motives. Daniel approached the table. She ignored him, folded her arms across her chest.

"Tell me why you want to know," she said.

Qitu stared at her, and then glanced at Daniel.

Nivi tucked her hands around her ribs. She could feel the edges of the smartphone pressing into her skin. She glared at Qitu. "Tell me."

"I'm working on a story."

"About Tinka?" Nivi took a step towards the table.

"Nivi," Daniel said, his voice soft, but urgent.

"Close the door," she said. She waited until she heard the door click closed. "Tell me about the story."

Qitu reached into the satchel at his feet and pulled out a copy of the Danish newspaper, *Politiken*. He laid it on the table, opened it, and tapped an article with his finger. Nivi leaned over the table and started to read. Daniel waited until she was finished and then turned the newspaper so that he could read the article.

"Parties?" said Nivi. "You're writing a story about parties with politicians in Greenland?"

"Yes," Qitu said.

"And," Daniel said, with a glance at Nivi, "you think Tinka has been to one of these parties?"

"Not just one."

Nivi turned away from the table and dialled Tinka's number again. She gave up on the third try and called another number, turning to stare at Daniel as she waited. "*You* arranged this interview," she said.

"I know."

"So she goes to parties. She's a young woman." Nivi tapped her foot. "What's your point?"

"I know. I'm sorry. Shall I ask Qitu to leave?"

Nivi raised her hand and started to speak into the phone. "Martin? Hi. Listen, I need to speak to Tinka." She waited for a moment, nodded, and then said, "Okay, get back to me with Kaka's number, will you? Thanks." Nivi ended the call and looked at Qitu. "She's been with a friend all weekend."

Qitu nodded, folded the newspaper, and closed his notepad. He stood up, slung his satchel over his shoulder, and slipped his notepad inside it. "You can keep the paper," he said, and walked towards the door. He reached for the handle and stopped to turn around. "I'm sorry."

"For what? Accusing my daughter of partying with politicians? That's hardly a crime."

"You're right. It's not."

"Then why are you so interested?" Nivi frowned and tugged at her lip. She lowered her hand and pointed at Qitu. "There's more to this, isn't there?" She took a step forwards. "What are you not telling me?"

Qitu glanced at Daniel, and waited for him to nod. He looked at Nivi. "I'm doing a story about Malik Uutaaq."

"And?" she said. "Don't look at Daniel. Tell me what this has to do with my daughter."

"Uutaaq was in Ilulissat last weekend," Daniel said.

"That's not unusual," Nivi said. "He has a schedule like the rest of us. He was at a meeting. At Hotel Arctic. You told me, Daniel. You were at the same meeting."

"I did. He was. But he stayed over the weekend."

"And went to a party with my daughter?"

"Maybe, I don't know. But if he..."

"If he *what?*" Nivi said, her voice quavering as her heart started to pound in her chest.

Daniel swallowed and looked at Nivi. "If he was there," he said, "and if your daughter was there too, then," he paused for a breath, "we could use this."

"Use this? Use what?" She looked at Qitu. "Are you writing a story about Malik Uutaaq and my daughter?"

Qitu nodded. "Yes," he said.

"Why? Because you think…" Nivi stopped as she realised what it was that the two men were thinking. She felt the colour drain from her face and then swiped at the screen on her smartphone.

"Nivi, wait," Daniel said, and took a step towards her. She raised her hand, her finger extended, a warning. He stopped. Nivi placed her phone to her ear and waited, lowering it again when Tinka didn't answer.

"Okay," she said, and took a long breath. "Okay. You want to tell me something difficult, so tell me."

"Tell you what?" Daniel said.

"You know what."

Qitu walked to the table and sat down, twisting his satchel into his lap like a shield. "We think your daughter had sex with Malik Uutaaq." He waited for Nivi to respond. She pursed her lips and nodded for him to continue. "More than once," he said.

"And you want to use this," she said and looked at Daniel, "because he had sex with my daughter?"

"No," Daniel said and shook his head. "I'm sorry it was your daughter, but that's not why we want to use this."

"Then why? I don't understand."

Daniel sat down at the table and beckoned for Nivi to do the same. She placed her phone on the surface, stared at it, and then turned it face down to hide the screen.

"Nivi," Daniel said.

"Yes?"

"Malik has the popular vote. He has taken the perceived moral high ground."

"In his position on language and identity? It's pathetic."

"And anti-Danish, anti-colonial."

"We are not a colony," Nivi said.

"That depends on how you view our relationship with Denmark," Qitu said.

"Denmark is a long way from the settlements," Daniel said.

"So is Nuuk," Nivi said.

"True, but Nuuk is still Greenland."

"And you think that the election will come down to that? A choice between pro-Danish parties and the popular nationalist vote?"

"Think about it, Nivi," Daniel said. "You know it will."

"Malik's policy is based purely on the language he speaks. He's in it for the power. He doesn't have an ounce of leadership skills, or the experience to balance a simple budget."

"None of that will matter, if the people think he wants only what is best for Greenland."

"You mean independence."

"Yes. I do. And we're not ready. You know that. There's no oil, and the Chinese want our mines for themselves. There are no jobs." Daniel paused. "We have to stop him, Nivi. We have to discredit him."

"With my daughter, Daniel. You are going to use her?" She snorted. "Have you thought, even for a second, how that reflects on me? It makes him look strong. If he can sleep with his opponent's daughter, he can do anything."

"I don't think he knows who she is," Qitu said.

"What?"

"He didn't sleep with her because she was your daughter. He slept with her because he finds her attractive."

"Lots of girls are attractive."

"But Malik Uutaaq only sleeps with a certain kind." Qitu waited for Nivi to ask what kind, but it wasn't necessary. He realised, as he caught the flicker of recognition in her eyes, and the twitch of a muscle in her cheek.

Nivi thought of her daughter's long legs, her pale cream skin, her long, soft black hair, and her thin European eyebrows. She nodded, and said, "He likes Danish girls."

"No," Daniel said, "he likes half and half, the very people he says are not Greenlandic, because they either have mixed parents, or…"

"They speak Danish." Nivi looked at Daniel and Qitu. "I understand," she said. Nivi stood up, picked up her phone and walked to the door.

"Nivi?" Daniel said. He gestured at Qitu. "The article?"

She shook her head, and left the room.

Pingasunngorneq

WEDNESDAY

Chapter 5

The garage doors of the workshop squealed as the mechanic opened them. He beckoned to Petra, stepped to one side for her to pass, and pointed at the railing on the wall in the corner of the workshop.

"That's where I left him," he said. He pointed at the empty bottle of vodka discarded on the floor. "Looks like he finished it."

"Looks like it," Petra said. She peered into the gloom and looked around for a light switch. The mechanic turned on the lights and she nodded her thanks. She found Maratse's empty wheelchair, and walked to the front of the ambulances to find Maratse lying face down on a pile of jackets and boots. Petra knelt beside him. "Hey," she said. "Time to wake up." She curled her fingers around his shoulder. Maratse grunted and tried to roll away, but Petra held on. "Come on. You've got a plane to catch."

Petra examined Maratse as she might a drunk on the street. She took his hands, turning them gently towards the light, before picking at the bloody flakes of rust in his palms. Maratse opened his eyes and watched her.

"You could have used the gym in the hospital," she said, with a glance at the bar on the wall.

"I like it here," he said.

"You like sleeping here too?"

"It's quieter than the ward."

Maratse started to sit up and Petra helped him. He pressed his hand to his head and shut his eyes for a moment. Petra smiled when he opened them.

"Breakfast will help your head."

"You think so?"

"Yeah, I do. My treat," she said, and stood up to get Maratse's wheelchair. He glared at it as she pushed it towards him.

"I need my sticks."

"Which are in your room, on the ward." Petra helped Maratse into the chair. "The sister thought you had discharged yourself, until she found your jacket. She figured you wouldn't have left without your cigarettes."

"Hmm," Maratse said. He flexed his hands around the wheels, and then placed them in his lap. "You drive."

Maratse nodded at the mechanic as Petra wheeled him out of the workshop and onto the road. She turned into a shaft of sunlight stretching between the buildings and Maratse squinted in the glare. Petra turned again, and then pushed him inside the hospital all the way to the elevator. She let go of the chair, pressed the button for the first floor and leaned against the side. Maratse glanced at her and then looked away.

"Your hands are a mess," she said. "Do you want someone to look at them?"

"*Eeqqi.*"

"What about your legs? Are you in pain?"

"No more than usual."

"When did you last take your tablets?"

Maratse shrugged. "Before the vodka."

"I didn't think you drank."

"I wasn't drinking."

"No?"

"I was medicating."

"That's what the tablets are for," Petra said, as the elevator doors opened. She pushed him into the corridor, onto the ward and into his room. "I can wait while you shower." She leaned against the windowsill and the sun caught the loose strands of her hair escaping the ponytail pinched tight at the back of her head.

"Why are you here, Petra?"

"To take you to the airport. Like we agreed."

"That's this afternoon."

"I know."

"Then why are you here?"

Petra stuffed her hands inside the deep pockets of her police jacket. She fidgeted for a moment, as if unwilling to speak. "The Commissioner asked me to look out for you. He knows we've worked together in the past. I told him we were friends, and that I would like to help you."

"Hmm."

"You were tortured, David. It's okay to have a little help."

Maratse lowered his head and studied his palms. He picked at the flakes of rust in the blood lining the creases in his skin. "He asked you?"

"Yes." Petra paused. "After I suggested it."

"You suggested I needed looking after?" Maratse said and looked at Petra.

"Don't you?"

Maratse shrugged, and said, "Maybe."

"Then let me help you. At least until your flight."

"Okay, but no shower."

"I'm not helping you in the shower." She laughed.

"I didn't ask you to. I just don't want a shower."

"You stink, David."

Maratse grunted and wheeled himself to the chair by his bed. He pressed the brakes into position on the chair and reached for the sticks leaning against the wall. He heard Petra move to help him. She stopped when he shook his head. "I have to do it on my own," he said, and struggled to stand up. After wobbling for a moment, Maratse found his balance, pulled on his police jacket and took a cigarette from the packet in his pocket. He rolled it into the gap between his teeth and grinned at Petra. "Ready?" he said.

"Just waiting for you, old man."

"*Iiji*," he said and grabbed his walking sticks. He pinched the cigarette between his teeth and hobbled towards the door. Petra followed, moving to walk by his side as they walked down the corridor and into the elevator.

"What about checking out?" she said. "Do you want to do that later?"

"I just did," he said, as the elevator doors opened. He walked inside and leaned against the rear wall. Petra shook her head and followed him inside.

"Are you always this difficult, or is it because you woke up beside an ambulance?"

"Always," he said, as the doors closed.

Maratse found a rhythm as they walked to Petra's police Toyota. She opened the door to the passenger side and he grunted as he climbed up and onto the seat, stuffing his sticks beside his right leg as Petra shut the door.

"I'm amazed," she said, as she climbed in behind the steering wheel. "You haven't lit that yet."

"Can't," he said.

"Why not?"

"Too much vodka."

Petra laughed as she started the engine. "You're impossible."

Petra drove through town and parked outside a café by the water. Small boulders of ice stranded on the rocks at low tide shone in the sun, as Petra helped Maratse out of the car and into the café. They sat at a table in the window and ordered breakfast.

Maratse stuffed his cigarette into his pocket and drank black coffee as they waited for their order. He was quiet, content to listen to Petra talk about the Sergeant's exam, as he watched the gulls and ravens fighting over the remains of a seal carcass on the rocks. He looked up when their food arrived and Petra stared at him.

"What?" he said.

"I asked you where you are going to live in Inussuk?"

"I'm renting a house. The grandparents of one of the nurses' died last winter. The house is empty."

"Just like that?"

"*Iiji*." Maratse frowned. "What is the problem?"

"You have no things."

"The house is furnished."

"But your clothes, other stuff."

Maratse shrugged. "What do I need?"

"Won't you miss anything?"

"Maybe," he said, and finished his coffee. He refilled the mug from the cafetière on the table.

"Like what?"

"A book."

"Just one?"

"Books. I like science fiction."

"Really?" Petra laughed. "You should read crime. All police officers read crime novels."

"I'm not a policeman anymore." Maratse looked out of the window, sipped his coffee, and said nothing more until Petra said it was time to leave. She paid for breakfast and followed Maratse out of the café. He walked past the police car towards the water, stepping over the salty beam of wood separating the wooden jetty from the concrete and asphalt parking area. Petra followed him to the end of the jetty, standing quietly beside him as he looked out to sea.

"If things were different," she said.

"They are not."

"No, but if they were, would you stay in Nuuk?"

"And do what?" Maratse turned his head towards the sun and

closed his eyes.

"I don't know. Work in the library, maybe, or in the bookshop."

Maratse opened his eyes and looked at Petra. He nodded at the icebergs further out to sea, and the fine mist of a humpback whale blowing air out of its lungs at the surface. "I can't work in the city," he said. "I need to be out there."

"At sea?"

"At sea. On the ice."

"But the sea is here, too. We just a saw a whale."

Maratse pulled the cigarette from his pocket, tucked it between his lips and lit it. He rolled the filter into the gap and flicked at it with his tongue. Petra moved to one side to escape the cloud of smoke he puffed from his lungs. Maratse grinned and pointed towards the land and the buildings rising up from the street.

"I don't want to live here," he said.

Petra opened her mouth to speak, only to stop as her phone began to ring. She answered the call, nodded, and then slipped the phone back into her pocket.

"They need me at the station. A missing person's case," she said. "I won't be long. Do you want to wait here?"

"I can wait," he said and nodded. He watched Petra jog back to the police car, then turned back to hunt for the whale between the icebergs.

The whale dived deep, blowing circles of air in front of it as it swam for the surface, mouth open, closing its massive jaws on a bounty of tiny shrimps, krill from the bottom of the iceberg. Maratse watched the whale feed three more times before flicking the butt of his cigarette into the sea and grabbing his sticks. He hobbled back to the car park and then struggled along the shore in the direction of the statue of *Sassuma Arnaanut*, Sedna, the mother of the sea. Petra found him an hour later on a bench beside a rack of skin-on-frame kayaks, the Greenlandic *qajaq*, as the tide turned and lapped at the base of the ice boulders surrounding Sedna. She had a package in her hand and gave it to Maratse.

"What's this?" he said and unwrapped the paper.

"A book." Petra bit her lip and wrinkled her brow. "In English. I'm sorry. They didn't have anything else." She sat down on the bench beside him. "Can you read it?"

"I'm a little rusty."

"I'm sorry," she said, and reached for the book. "I can take it back."

"*Eeqqi*." He smiled. "I have time." He fanned the pages and laughed. "A lot of time, luckily. *Qujanaq*."

"You're welcome."

"What about the missing person?"

"You want to know?"

Maratse shrugged. "*Iiji*."

"It's interesting, actually. You know Nivi Winther? The politician? It's her daughter. She hasn't heard from her in a few days, and neither has the father." Petra stood up. "I have to work on this now, so…"

"You need to take me to the airport?"

"Yes. I'm sorry."

Maratse handed her the book as he grabbed his sticks and stood up.

"Do you have everything you need?"

He checked his pockets. "Wallet, cigarettes…" Maratse paused to nod at the book. "Something to read. *Iiji*," he said, "I have everything."

"Okay," Petra said. She walked beside Maratse to the car, opened the door and waited for him to get in. Neither spoke on the way to the airport, and, as Petra slowed to a stop outside the door to the airport building, her phone vibrated. She ignored it, searching for something to say to Maratse, until the phone stopped vibrating and he opened the passenger door. "Wait, I'll help you," she said, and opened the driver door. She jogged around the front of the Toyota as Maratse found his balance on his sticks.

"I'm okay," he said.

"I know. But I want to help."

"You don't need to."

"I want to," Petra said, and she tilted her head to catch Maratse's eye. "If you stayed…"

"I would get bored."

"With me?" Petra whispered, and for a moment she thought Maratse had not heard her. He leaned against the car, let go of one of his sticks and took Petra's hand.

"*Eeqqi*, not you. Nuuk." He squeezed her hand. "Thank you, Piitalaat."

"I'm getting used to you calling me that," she said, and let go of his hand to hug him. "The only one I'll allow." Petra's hair caught in the light stubble on Maratse's cheeks. When she let go and took a step back, her hair lingered, until a light wind flicked her hair from his face and severed the connection. Maratse grinned and stuck a cigarette between his teeth.

"Goodbye," he said. He reached inside the police car and tucked the book under his arm.

"I hope you enjoy it," Petra said, with a glance at the book. Her phone began to vibrate, and she pulled it out of her pocket with one hand, waving with the other. Maratse closed the passenger door and waited for her to drive away. He walked to the side of the building and joined the other passengers having a last smoke before their flight.

Maratse leaned against the wall and looked at the book in his hands. It was heavy. The pages spanned the width of his four fingers. He whistled at the page numbers, over a thousand, and then laughed at the name: *The Neutronium Alchemist*. Maratse wrestled his lips around the title, and then read the subtitle: *Volume 2*. He laughed again, flicked through the pages, and found Petra's note, her phone number, and a tight sprawl of words that he decided he would read later. Once he had finished his cigarette he passed through the airport doors to find a seat.

He was halfway into the first chapter when they called his flight. Maratse found the ticket from his wallet and hobbled to the check-in desk. For the first time in his life, he was given priority boarding, but he refused help to climb the steps at the back of the de Havilland Dash 7. He slumped down onto the grey faux-leather cushions of his seat and buckled the belt at his waist. The stewardess took his sticks to stow away. There was a wait while they finished loading the baggage and the other passengers boarded. Maratse pushed the tray table into position and lost himself in the book until the captain announced they were ready for take-off.

Maratse read until the last moment before take-off, when the thrust of the four turbo-prop engines pushed him back into his seat. He slipped Petra's note between the pages as a bookmark, and closed his eyes. He didn't open them again until they landed in Qaarsut, the gravel-strip airport on the Uummannaq peninsula.

He was the last to leave the aircraft, but the first to leave the airport. The gravedigger met him at the door.

"David Maratse?"

"*Iiji*," Maratse said, and shook the man's hand.

"I'm Karl Nielsen. I'm going to take you to Inussuk."

"On that?" Maratse said, and nodded at the quad bike parked behind Karl.

"*Naamik*, that's just to get down to the beach. I have a boat."

Maratse raised his eyebrows and smiled. He handed Karl his book as he climbed onto the quad bike. Maratse rested his sticks across his lap.

"Is this all you have?" Karl said and handed the book back to Maratse.

"It's all I need," he said.

Karl shrugged and shuffled into position, started the engine and clicked the bike into gear. Maratse flinched as they lurched forwards. He grabbed Karl's waist and held on as they raced down to the beach.

The icebergs in the bay were the size of villages. They reminded Maratse of the bergs in Ittoqqortoormiit, the place he used to call home. Karl slowed as they approached the beach, and Maratse smiled at the brown and bloody stains streaking the side of the small fibreglass dinghy at the water's edge. Karl waited for Maratse to get off, parked the quad beside the sledges and fishing boxes above the high water mark, and walked down to boat. He lit a cigarette as he walked and offered another to Maratse. Karl pushed the boat into the water and helped Maratse over the side. He pushed it further until the boat bobbed and the stern was deep enough that Karl could lower the propeller shaft and start the outboard motor. The fumes from the four-stroke engine tickled Maratse's nostrils and he drank it in, along with the smoke from his cigarette and the crisp air of autumn in the north.

"This is home," he whispered, before gripping the sides of the boat as Karl increased the throttle and they powered in a north-westerly direction along the peninsula towards Inussuk.

Chapter 6

The tide was out when Maratse arrived at his new home. Karl powered the fibreglass dinghy up the beach, cut the engine, and lifted the propeller shaft clear of the water and the lumps of ice in the shallow surf. He climbed over the side and helped Maratse out of the dinghy. Maratse took a deep breath and caught the whiff of dried fish lingering between the houses, salt and seaweed exposed on the rocks, together with a variety of cooking smells. Karl picked up Maratse's book, touched his elbow and pointed up the beach in the direction of the general store.

"Your house is over there. The dark blue one between the store, and the green house to the right."

"Who lives in the green house?"

"At the moment? A lesbian couple and their daughter." Karl waited for Maratse to react, and, when he didn't, he shrugged and said, "Follow me."

The shingle and coarse sand frustrated Maratse as he made his way from the boat to the steps of his new home. Karl waited and watched, but offered no help, for which Maratse was grateful. Visions of the rusty bar in the workshop flashed through Maratse's mind. He gritted his teeth and kept going. Just a few metres from the steps, a sledge dog puppy, barely three months old, toppled Maratse onto the beach as it slalomed between his sticks and legs. Maratse cursed and threw a small rock in the direction of the puppy, and it skittered after it as if it was a ball, biting at it with spiny teeth. Karl laughed when the puppy spat out the rock and bounced back to within a metre of Maratse.

Maratse held out his hand to Karl, and said, "Give me a lift up." He clasped the gravedigger's hand and pushed off the beach as Karl helped him onto his feet. The puppy flopped onto its belly, rested its head on its legs and stared at Maratse. "Who's is it?" he asked.

"Nikki, my son's," said Karl. "Do you want it?"

"No," Maratse said, as he hobbled the last few metres to the steps of the house. He tucked his sticks under his arm and pulled himself up the steps with the thick wooden railings on either side. Karl opened the door and the puppy bounced up the steps and skittered around the deck. Maratse ignored it and followed Karl inside the house.

"There's no key," Karl said, as he kicked off his shoes and walked from the tiny hall into the living room, "and it smells like fish." The sofa separated the kitchen from the living area, and Karl pointed out the electric stove, fridge and kettle. He opened a cupboard and pointed at a selection of cups and glasses, plates and bowls. Maratse nodded and flopped onto the sofa. Karl placed Maratse's book on the coffee table and walked to the door. "My wife has made dinner for you. Come when you're hungry. It's the yellow house on the other side of the store."

"*Qujanaq*," Maratse said. He moved his sticks to one side as Karl pushed his feet inside his shoes.

"There's no TV," he said.

Maratse pointed at the book, and said, "I'll be fine."

"But there's a phone over there, by the window." He opened the door and kicked at the puppy as it tried to come in. He turned, and said, "Are you sure you don't want it?"

"Sure."

"Okay." Karl waved. "Yellow house," he said, and closed the door behind him.

Maratse heard Karl clump down the four steps to the beach, and then closed his eyes. The smell of fish lingered. Maratse rubbed at his nose, yawned and opened his eyes. The walls were patched with shadows of picture frames, the white window sills flecked with brown spots of fly shit, and the floor was gritty beneath his feet. Maratse grunted as he removed his boots. He leaned back on the sofa and patted his jacket pocket. He pulled out the packet of cigarettes, tipped the last two into his hand, and stuck one of them between his teeth. He found his lighter, and then stuffed it back in his pocket. Maratse closed his eyes for a second, reached for his sticks, and pushed himself onto his feet. He staggered to the door, opened it, and stepped out onto the deck. The puppy lifted its head, watching Maratse as he crossed the deck to the railing, leaned against it, and lit his cigarette.

"*Eeqqi*," he said, as the puppy belly-crawled towards him. He lifted his finger and the puppy stopped. Despite himself, Maratse studied the pup's large paws, the shape of its head, and its bright brown eyes. It was mostly white with a grey mask, accentuated with white fur flaring to both sides of its muzzle. Maratse pictured the puppy in the winter, when its tail had dropped, and it was ready for harness. He grunted, finished his cigarette, and shuffled back inside the house. The telephone rang as he shut the door.

"Maratse," he said, as he lifted the receiver and answered the call.

"It's Petra. I found your number."

"*Iiji.*"

"Are you settling in?"

"I just arrived."

"I know. I just thought…"

Maratse watched the puppy through the window, as it curled into a ball outside the door. "How is the case?" he asked.

"Developing. We contacted the girl's friend in Aasiaat. It turns out they made a deal that Kaka would say Tinka stayed with her, but she was actually with a man."

"Man?"

"Yes. Older."

"Tinka is the missing girl?"

"Yes. Nivi Winther's daughter."

"The politician?"

"Yes." Petra paused. "You're interested, aren't you?"

"*Eeqqi,*" Maratse said. "Just making conversation."

"How's the book?"

"Difficult, but good."

"I'm sorry. There was nothing else."

"I like it. Thank you, Piitalaat." Maratse felt the pain burning through the nerves in his legs. He turned to look at the sofa. "I have to go," he said.

"That's okay. Can I call again?"

"*Iiji.* You can tell me about the case."

"I'll keep you posted. Enjoy your first night in your new home."

"I will." Maratse ended the call, frowning as he realised he had no bedding to speak of, and the bedroom was up a flight of steep stairs. He looked at the sofa again, and grabbed his sticks. *If I sit down, I won't get up again.* Maratse's stomach growled. He shuffled over to his boots, grimaced as he pressed his feet inside them, and then walked to the door, the ends of the laces tapping softly with each step. He opened the door, making the puppy slide along the deck.

Navigating the steps was more difficult on the way down, and complicated by the puppy weaving up and down between Maratse's legs. He stumbled and fell at the bottom when the puppy pounced on

Maratse's laces. It recoiled several metres at the string of curses Maratse hurled at it, and further still as Maratse swore at each stage of getting to his feet. The ends of the sticks dug into the soft surface of the beach, and Maratse's trousers and jacket were dusted with fine black sand and plastered with tiny shell fragments. He dusted himself off and took the first few steps towards Karl's house. The puppy appeared in front of him a second later. Maratse cursed, and it recoiled. He took a step, and, as the dance continued, Maratse became aware of the small audience of children creeping out from beneath the decks of their houses to watch his progress. The puppy only had eyes for Maratse, its over-sized paws leaving pad prints along the beach, alongside the round imprints from the tip of Maratse's sticks.

They passed the store, and Maratse began to anticipate the puppy's movements. It was only when he reached the steps of the house, that he realised his focus had been on the puppy at his feet, not the pain in his legs. He paused at the bottom of the steps, nodding at Karl as he opened the door.

"Everything all right?"

"*Iiji*," Maratse said, tucking the sticks under his arm and climbing the steps to the house.

"Puppy bothering you?"

Maratse raised his eyebrows, *yes*.

"I'll get Nikki to put it on a chain tomorrow." Karl stood to one side as Maratse leaned on the wall to remove his boots. He hung his jacket on a peg, and walked into the living room. The smell of musk-ox stew made his stomach growl, and he smiled at Karl's wife as she guided him to a chair at the head of the small dining table. The television was on, and the news anchor from *Qanorooq* was halfway through the story of the missing girl.

"She's from here," said Karl.

"Who?"

"The mother, Nivi Winther. She grew up in Inussuk," Karl's wife said. "I used to play with her, when she was a child. I'm Buuti."

Maratse shook her hand and sat down. He looked at the television as Petra appeared, reading a statement from the police. He smiled as he listened to her appealing for people to come forward if they had any information concerning the whereabouts of Tinka Winther. She looked good, brushing loose strands of hair behind her ear as the wind picked up outside the police station. The image cut to a pre-recorded tape of Nivi Winther at a press conference, and the voice of the news anchor saying that Greenland's First Minister was not available to comment. Karl turned down the volume at a word from Buuti, as she served a generous helping of rice and stew on Maratse's plate. The thick dark sauce sank through the grains of rice and Maratse felt his stomach rumble at the sight of traditional Greenlandic food.

"I shot that one," Karl said. "On Svartenhuk."

"To the north?"

"*Aap*," he said, and nodded. "There's a small herd. But healthy. There's trout up there too. We can go this winter." Karl paused and glanced at Maratse's legs.

"I'd like that," Maratse said, and started to eat.

Buuti fussed over Maratse with another helping, followed by coffee and mint chocolate cake for dessert. The coffee settled the rich food in his stomach, and Maratse gestured that they go outside for a smoke. Karl followed him to the deck surrounding the house as Buuti cleared the table. The puppy lay on the beach below the house, pricking its ears as Maratse stepped onto the deck. It stood up, only to flop down again at a single word from Karl.

"Did you have dogs in Ittoqqortoormiit?" he asked.

"*Iiji*," Maratse said. "I had dogs."

"Do you miss it?"

"The dogs?"

"Being a policeman."

Maratse smoked for a moment before answering. He listened to the sea surfing gently up the beach, imagining the crackle and pop of air escaping from the clumps of ice in the water. He looked at the rock face on each side of the settlement, the wooden jetty stretching out from the concrete harbour, and the path zigzagging up the mountain knoll towering above Inussuk on the right. He could just see the radio mast and antenna. Karl's question hung in the air between them, unanswered. Maratse coughed, and picked a fleck of meat from his teeth.

"I do," he said. "But I am not a policeman anymore."

"What happened?"

"Lots of things," Maratse said, and an image of the Chinaman appeared before him, along with the smell, and the sound of the generator as it chugged with the effort of torture.

"I understand," Karl said. "I won't ask again."

Maratse nodded, finished his cigarette, and stubbed it out in an upturned plant pot. Buuti walked onto the deck with a pile of sheets in her arms. She pressed them into Maratse's arms and nodded in the direction of his house.

"You can use these until you get some of your own. There's a duvet and pillow upstairs," she said. Maratse caught her looking at his legs, and he smiled.

"I'll sleep on the sofa tonight," he said.

Buuti nodded, wished him a good night and disappeared inside the house. Karl finished his cigarette and offered to carry the sheets over to the house.

"I'll manage," Maratse said. He shook Karl's hand, tucked the sheets inside his jacket, and grabbed his sticks. The puppy was waiting for him at the bottom of the steps.

Maratse didn't fall on the walk back along the beach. But neither did he notice the children, or the fishermen waving from the dinghy just beyond the surf. Maratse was focussed on the puppy, and not falling on top of it. He let it bound up the steps in front of him, brushing it to one side with his stick as he opened the door.

The fish smell caught in his nose as he removed his boots. It was stronger than the smell of fish drying on the racks. He tossed the sheets on the sofa and walked into the kitchen. Maratse opened the fridge, and wrinkled his nose at the sight of a fillet of halibut sealed in a plastic bag. He took it out, closed the fridge door, and carried the fish to the deck. Maratse opened the bag and spilled the fish onto the deck in front of the puppy. The puppy seized the prize between its sharp milk teeth and scampered down the steps to tear into the fish on the beach. Maratse tossed the bag in the rubbish bin attached to the railing, closed the door and walked to the sofa. He sat down, let his sticks slide to the floor, and lifted his legs so that he could stretch on the sofa. Maratse reached for his book and propped it on his chest.

Soft cries and shouts carried on the wind as the children of Inussuk chased each other beneath the decks of the houses. Sledge dogs howled, and, if he hadn't been concentrating on the book, Maratse would have heard dog chains rattling across the rocks as they moved, the clap of a rubbish bin lid as Buuti got rid of the kitchen waste, and the occasional burr of a fishing dinghy as it motored past the rocks sheltering the beach.

The sirens of Nuuk were gone, as were the sounds of refuse trucks, a stream of traffic, shouts of greeting and drunken arguments on the steps outside the supermarket. The buzz of movement was gone, only the feet of the children, and the pads of the puppies on the beach remained. Maratse sank further into the sofa. He forgot about his legs, forgot about the Chinaman, and had no thoughts for the missing girl, not yet. He picked up his book and started the process of adjusting to his new life. There were no shifts, no paperwork, not even the chatter and static of the police radio. All he had left was his jacket, stained and patched as it was. He didn't think to remove it. On his first night in Inussuk, he didn't think at all.

Sisamanngorneq

THURSDAY

Chapter 7

Aarni Aviki parked next to Malik's huge Dodge RAM and walked up to the door. He let himself in and kicked off his shoes. Malik handed him a mug of coffee and nodded at the kitchen table.

"Let's sit over there," he said, and sat down by the window.

Aarni put his mug down on the table and opened his briefcase. Malik watched him as he pulled out a copy of *Sermitsiaq*. He dropped the newspaper on the table and sat down. "I take it you've read the article online?"

Malik nodded, and pulled the newspaper closer to him. "This is the girl?" he said, and tapped the photo on the front page. "Nivi Winther's daughter?"

"Yes." Aarni took a sip of coffee. "Her name is Tinka. She's seventeen." Aarni waited as Malik read the article, anticipating his reaction when he reached the penultimate paragraph. "Last seen with a middle-aged man at a party."

Malik turned the first page of the newspaper and pinched his chin. He was silent for a moment, and then said, "How bad is this?"

"That depends."

"On what?"

"Do you recognise her?"

Malik nodded.

"Are you that man?"

"Probably," Malik said. "Was I the last man? I don't know. She was pretty drunk." Malik rubbed his eyes, shook his head and took a long, slow breath. "She really is Nivi's daughter?"

"You know that." Aarni put down his coffee and leaned back in his chair.

Malik looked out the window and started to speak. "Sipu comes home tonight. He has been away at football camp. That means I have to find somewhere to sleep." He looked at Aarni. "Naala won't have me in our bed." He nodded in the direction of the living room. "The sofa is too small." Malik sighed, and continued, "Pipaluk's grades have improved, including mathematics."

"That's good."

"It's good?" Malik said and laughed. "It's embarrassing. She is lousy at maths. Not particularly good at languages either. The teachers are grading her according to my popularity."

"Which is soaring," Aarni said, and reached into his briefcase. He pulled out a copy of the polls from the previous month, pointing at the annotations in pencil in the margins. "This was August. Projections have you much higher in October. But, you can expect to slip a little, because of this."

"Because I slept with the girl?" Malik said. He leaned forwards, reaching for the newspaper.

"Because she is missing. No-one knows you slept with her. This is a sympathy response. Nivi will get a spike in support, but it won't last. You have the popular vote."

"Until they find out I was that man."

"They won't."

"When they find the girl, they will. It's just a matter of time."

"No it isn't." Aarni said and shrugged. "It's taken care of."

"Taken care of?"

"It's done."

"What is done? What are you talking about?"

"I told you I was loyal, and now I need you to trust me."

Malik shook his head. "I don't understand. What exactly have you done?"

"*I* have done nothing. I'm just saying that you don't have to worry about the girl recognising you."

"Huh," Malik said. He took a sip of coffee, and stared at his communications chief over the lip of the mug. "What about the reporter? Is it the same one?" Malik peeled back the front page of the newspaper. "Qitu Kalia?"

"I presume so," Aarni said. He looked at his watch. "We agreed you would work at home today. You need to prepare for the debate. I have the notes in my briefcase."

"You think it's necessary? You don't think she'll cancel?"

"That's my next meeting." Aarni placed a sheaf of papers in a folder in front of Malik. "I am meeting with Daniel Tukku."

"Nivi's assistant."

"I think he likes to be called Chief of Staff, even though she doesn't." Aarni laughed. "I like to needle him about that." He stood up. "Don't answer any calls. Okay?"

"You said no-one knows. You said I shouldn't worry about it."

"But the smart move is to be unavailable. You don't need to comment on the opposition leader's poor parenting skills. I mean, she doesn't know where her daughter is."

"That's harsh, Aarni. I thought I was the cynical one."

"It doesn't matter. You have a perfectly good excuse – preparing for the debate – use it. Any comments from you might be twisted, and then there's the chance of you saying something unfortunate. We don't want that. This is the time when she can leap ahead of you. And, if the girl is found…"

"If?"

"Yes," Aarni shrugged. "No-one knows where she is. She might be in Denmark for all we know." Aarni looked at Malik and frowned. "What's wrong?"

"I was thinking of Pipaluk. How I would feel if she was missing."

"Well, she's not. Stop thinking about that." Aarni gestured at the notes. "Concentrate on the debate." He looked at his watch. "I have to go."

Aarni left Malik with the notes and the newspaper. He backed his car out of the drive and continued into the centre of town, parking at the rear of Hotel Hans Egede. He found Nivi's assistant waiting in the lobby café. The cut of the man's suit suggested it was expensive. Aarni tugged at the fit of his own suit, as the top button strained at the end of a short length of cotton. He unbuttoned his jacket, shook Daniel's hand, and sat down.

"Do you want something to drink?" Daniel asked in Greenlandic. "I could do with another latté."

"Sounds good." Aarni fiddled with the contents of his briefcase. He pulled out a single sheet of bullet points and placed it on the table between them. "They are in Danish. I thought the meeting could be in Danish."

Daniel laughed. "Of course." He twisted in his seat and ordered two lattés. He switched to Danish, and said, "Politics aside, I have been impressed with the way you have handled the press. They have been merciless."

"Thank you." The waiter brought their coffee. Aarni unwrapped the Italian biscuit placed by the side of the glass, dipping it in the frothed milk at the top. "It has been a challenge, but if they focus on the language…"

"You don't have to answer to anything else," Daniel said. "Yes, very smart."

"I thought so," Aarni said, and ate the biscuit.

"And what about Malik Uutaaq? Was it his strategy?"

"Mine." Aarni brushed biscuit crumbs from his lips. "And I don't mind admitting it."

"It's certainly working. I have to give you credit for that." He paused for a moment, studying his counterpart as he spooned the frothed milk from the lip of the glass. "Is this a candid meeting? I mean, can we be candid with one another, off the record?"

"I don't see why not," Aarni said. The spoon clinked against the glass as he placed it on the saucer. "Are you thinking about the debate?"

"The debate, policy, the polls. Although, we have been sidetracked this morning. You've seen the news?"

"Tinka Winther?"

"Yes."

"It's a real shame. Nivi must be quite distracted." Aarni nodded at the paper on the table. "Do you want to postpone the debate?"

"Today is Thursday. The debate is scheduled for Sunday night. I imagine this will be cleared up by then. Greenland is a small place after all."

"The largest small place in the world."

"Of course, but where can she go? If she hasn't drowned, that is." Daniel caught Aarni's eye as he reached for his latté. "She will turn up, I am sure."

"Well, we certainly hope so. Please pass on our sympathies to Nivi."

"I will." Daniel put his coffee on the table. "There is another matter I would like to discuss, before we get into the nitty gritty of the debate." Aarni waited as Daniel tugged a piece of paper from a folder tucked between him and the arm of his chair. He showed it to Aarni, and said, "It's a photocopy of a recent article in *Politiken*. You might have seen it."

"No," Aarni said. "It's new to me." He plucked the paper from Daniel's hand and pretended to skim read it.

"It's about the party culture of Greenlandic politics. It's a salacious read, more suited to American and British politics, but no less interesting."

"Why are you showing this to me?" Aarni laid the paper on top of the debate notes.

"You said we could be candid?"

"I did."

"Then what would your boss think of such an article? Would he say there was an element of truth to the story?"

"You would have to ask him."

"Yes, but I am asking you."

Daniel laced his fingers in his lap and waited, as Aarni made a show of stirring the remaining froth of steamed milk into his latté. The waiter visited their table and asked if they needed anything else.

"What do you want, Daniel?" Aarni asked, once the waiter had moved away.

"I want you to change the narrative. Stop talking about language, and start talking about housing, unemployment. Engage us on the grounds of governing, and there will be no need to talk about anything as sordid as booze and bad behaviour."

"And if we don't?"

"Then I see no reason why we can't circulate a story about the inappropriate desires and actions of married party leaders in the media. Do you?"

"Qitu Kalia."

"I'm sorry. What did you say?"

"Qitu Kalia. That's the name of your journalist."

"Possibly."

"Of course it is," Aarni said, and sighed. "I thought dirty campaigns were reserved for the American elections and Hollywood."

"Ah, Aarni, it's all about the news cycle, even here, especially here. For the voters outside of Nuuk," Daniel said, counting the larger Greenlandic towns on his fingers, "Sisimiut, Maniitsoq, Ilulissat and Qaqortoq, items of news tend to have a long shelf-life. And May is not so very far away, when you think about it. And what will your voters think about during the long, hard winter in the north, on the east coast, and even south of here? Do you really think your candidate can afford to lose popularity? It is the popular vote that is keeping him in the game."

"Ahead of the game," Aarni said. "As Nivi Winther's *assistant* I thought you would be more aware of her position in the polls." Aarni leaned forwards. "Behind Malik Uutaaq."

"And yet," Daniel said, the beginnings of a sly grin twitching at the corners of his mouth, "with this bump of sympathy, who knows what might happen. I mean, we all want Tinka to be found safe and sound, as soon as possible, but…"

"But?"

"If her body is found…" Daniel paused. "No matter how tragic the circumstances, that sympathy vote might just topple your lead."

Aarni swallowed as a bout of indigestion collected in his throat. He reached for the glass of coffee, and drained the last third with one gulp, aware of Daniel's eyes following his every move. He took a breath, placed the glass on the table, and leaned back in his chair, brushing at imaginary biscuit crumbs on his jacket.

"The sympathy vote," he said.

"Yes."

"That can go both ways." Aarni felt a renewed injection of confidence. He considered switching to Greenlandic, but decided not to push it. "In the event of such a tragedy, one might question how fit a grieving mother was to lead the country."

"There's that possibility."

"There is, and here is another. Who do you have in your party that could replace Nivi Winther, if she was forced to withdraw?"

"Forced? That's a strong word."

"Compelled is another. What if she was compelled to stand down, due to family matters?"

"Like the loss of her daughter."

"For example, yes. Who would take her place?"

In the silence that stretched across the low table between them, Aarni realised that Daniel had already considered the future implications of Tinka Winther's disappearance, and even her death. He appreciated in that moment, that Daniel was negotiating not on behalf of his leader, but himself. He allowed himself a smile over the text message he received earlier, confirming a loose end now secured. Then he tried to force the contents of his message as far from his mind as possible. He decided to wait for Daniel to speak. He didn't have to wait long.

"We have a number of suitable candidates."

"No you don't," Aarni said.

"We have one suitable candidate," Daniel said.

"Huh." Aarni tapped his fingers on his knee. "If I was to help you, by changing the narrative, what's in it for me? Because the minute I expose Malik Uutaaq to questions beyond language and identity ..."

"Is the very minute when we begin to campaign on an equal footing. That's all I ask. In the event that a change is necessary, it's all I can ask."

"This would be out of sympathy," Aarni said.

"I understand."

"And, in return, you will stop the publication of any salacious material that might implicate my boss?"

"I will."

Aarni took a long breath. "Well then, shall we discuss the questions for the debate?"

"I'm not sure that will be necessary. Nivi is far too preoccupied."

"Then you are going to cancel?"

"Oh, I wouldn't say that. I think we should continue regardless. It's important to show a strong leadership, even in times of duress, especially so, don't you think?"

"Then who will you send in her place?"

Daniel gestured lazily with his hand, and said, "We have a few possibilities, but, if necessary, I can always stand in for our leader. Just this once, you understand?"

"Oh, I think I understand," Aarni said. "Perfectly."

Daniel stood up, fastened the top button of his jacket and slipped the folder into his briefcase. He nodded at the bar. "I've already paid, but feel free to have another coffee on my tab, if you want to stay and mull things over for a while. You've got a few busy days ahead of you if you are going to have your candidate ready by Sunday night. Good luck." He waved as he walked away from the table.

Aarni watched him leave. He glanced at the customers sitting at the tables by the window, and then beckoned to the waiter that he would like another drink.

"Another latté?"

"No," Aarni said in Danish, "I'll have whisky. A double."

It was going to be a long weekend.

Chapter 8

The tramp of boots up the steps and onto the deck, followed by a heavy knock on the door forced Maratse to open his eyes and start a new day in Inussuk. He lifted his legs over the side of the sofa and wiped the sleep from his eyes and the dried saliva from the corner of his mouth, as Karl opened the door and kicked off his rubber boots in the hall. Maratse could hardly see Karl's face for all the things he carried in his arms. Karl dumped the gear on the coffee table and wished Maratse a good morning.

"Coffee?" Karl said.

"I haven't got any."

"I have." Karl picked up the plastic bag that was laying on top of the pile of clothes and walked into the kitchen. "Get dressed," he said.

"Where are we going?"

"Fishing."

Maratse reached out to tug at the pile of clothes, separating warm layers from a tough quilted overall that was greasy to the touch. "I need a shower," he said.

"When you get back." Karl filled the kettle, spooning two heaps of instant coffee into two mugs, as the water boiled. Maratse began to dress, exchanging the layers of clothing on the pile for his own sweaty shirt and police jogging trousers. He lifted his legs into his overalls, pulling them slowly up to his knees. "Need help?" Karl asked, as he put the mugs of coffee on the table in front of the sofa.

"*Iiji.*" Maratse pushed himself into a standing position. He held onto Karl's shoulder with one hand and pulled the overalls into position with the other. "Where are we going?"

"I have a long fishing line running deep from the coast just north of Inussuk. I want to check it."

"Okay."

"I can show you a couple of good places along the way. For your own line."

"I need a boat."

"Edvard has a boat he wants to sell."

"And fishing line, gear?"

"I have enough for both of us."

Karl walked to the window and tapped the glass with his cracked thumbnail and smiled as the puppy lifted its head.

"It's been there all night," Maratse said.

"And been sick on the steps."

"That would be the fish." Maratse zipped the overalls to the collar and then back down to the waist. "I need to pee," he said.

"Edvard empties the buckets twice a week, but you'll have to register with the council."

Maratse nodded. "So, I have to register before I can pee?"

"Yes," Karl said and laughed, and then, "Pee outside, before we get in the boat." He handed Maratse a coffee, and pulled a packet of biscuits from the deep pocket of his overalls.

"What else do you have?" Maratse asked, as he took a handful of biscuits.

"Coffee and cigarettes."

Maratse grunted, dunked the biscuits in the coffee, and ate as Karl leaned against the window. The temptation to sit down nagged at Maratse, but he decided that now he was up he should stay up. He gauged the distance to the hall, looked for his sticks, and then decided to shuffle to the door without them. He put the mug down on the table and moved his right leg. A burst of pain streaked down his leg only to disappear a second later. Maratse gritted his teeth and ignored the pain in his legs, as he worked his way to the hall, shaking his head as Karl offered to help.

"Your boots are the ones with orange caps," Karl said, as Maratse rested against the door.

Maratse nodded, placed his hand against the door and grabbed a fistful of overall, lifting his leg and pushing his foot into the rubber boot. He rested for a second and then pushed his other foot into the second boot.

"Ready?" Karl asked, as he pulled on his own boots.

"*Iiji*," Maratse said and opened the door. The puppy bounded to its feet and nearly pushed Maratse off balance. He growled a quick command and the puppy retreated. Karl laughed as he closed the door behind them. "I used to have dogs," Maratse said.

"You will again," Karl said. "Starting with that one."

"We'll see."

Maratse used the railings to climb down each of the four steps to his house. He moved slowly, deliberately, and, when both his feet were on the beach, he shuffled towards the waterline, and Karl's dinghy, which was tethered through the eye of a large rusty piece of iron drilled into a boulder on the beach. The puppy danced just half a metre in front of Maratse, all the way to the dinghy, acting as the carrot leading the way, as well as the role of the stick that could trip Maratse onto the beach. If he had thought about it, Maratse might have given the puppy some credit for encouraging him to walk without help. But Maratse was preoccupied with reaching the dinghy. Once there he leaned against the gunwales, lowered his hand, whistled once, and made a fuss of the puppy as it bounded towards him. The puppy's soft fur tickling the coarse skin of Maratse's hand made him smile, and he thought about other dogs and teams that he had run on the east coast, before he met Konstabel Fenna Brongaard, before the Chinaman.

Maratse looked along the beach and waved at the fishermen preparing their gear, fixing lines, and stripping outboards. Just four men and not one of them younger than Karl. All of them were at least ten or fifteen years older than Maratse.

"Where are the young men?"

"At school, or in town," Karl said and waved in the direction of Uummannaq. "Inussuk is dying," he said. "We get a little trade each summer, when the cruise ships send passengers in to visit and buy cakes, and try Greenlandic food. But people are leaving Inussuk. One day it will be no more."

Maratse waved at the fishermen one more time and then shooed the puppy away. He used the gunwale to push himself to his feet as Karl pushed the dinghy down the beach and into the water. Maratse shuffled in his wake, following the shallow trench in the sand from the dinghy's hull. The sea lapped at his boots, as he clambered over the gunwales. Karl grabbed his arm and helped him onto the seat spanning the centre of the dinghy. Maratse zipped the overall to the collar and watched the puppy fret at the water's edge, as Karl lowered the outboard motor, pumped fuel from the plastic petrol can into the engine, and pulled the starter handle. Maratse felt the weight of the boat shift as Karl sat down, and again when he handed Maratse a lit cigarette. Maratse rolled it into the gap between his teeth, tugged the collar of the overalls around his neck, and puffed a cloud of smoke into the wind, as Karl increased the throttle and they motored along the coast. Small clumps of ice skidded against the hull, thumping along each side until they were clear of the debris field from a small iceberg calving close to shore.

Karl slowed at various points along the way to his long line, pointing out rocks that were good for attaching one end of the line, high water marks, and the spots that he had used to place stone traps to catch Arctic foxes.

"Buuti cleans the pelts," he said, "and then sells them to the tourists."

"Are they allowed to buy them?"

"Maybe?" Karl said, and shrugged. "We don't ask, and neither do they."

Karl slowed as they neared a point on the peninsula that opened into a large bay. He steered the dinghy at a right angle to the point, and tapped Maratse on the shoulder. A large cube of polystyrene, with a faded flag pressed through the centre bobbed a hundred metres in front of them. Karl let the motor idle, and then clicked it out of gear. He cut the motor a second later and they drifted onto the fishing marker. Karl snagged the thick rope attached to a plastic buoy, hidden behind the marker, and tied a line from the dinghy through the buoy. He sat down and tapped Maratse on the back, gesturing for him to turn around.

"Coffee," Karl said, as he pulled a thermos flask from the satchel at his feet.

"*Iiji,*" Maratse said, and grinned. "You think of everything."

"I think of the essentials," Karl said, and handed Maratse a packet of cigarettes.

"You've been generous."

Karl shrugged. "You're my neighbour. You can bring cigarettes next time."

Maratse nodded and leaned forwards to reach the flame from Karl's lighter. For the next ten minutes they didn't speak, just enjoyed bobbing in the swell of the water, their eyes cruising the surface of the sea in anticipation of a seal coming up for air. Maratse cast a glance at the ropes and gear strewn about the dinghy, spotted the rusted barrel of the Sako .22 and smiled. Karl patted the breast pocket of his overalls and lifted the flap to reveal a plastic box of ammunition.

The trick, Maratse knew, was to startle the seal with the first shot, pushing it back under the water with little or no air in its lungs, while speeding towards its last location, and then firing again, and again, until the hunter could shoot the seal in the head, or the eye, and hook it with a gaff on a stick before the seal sank. The seal would supply meat for Karl's family for a few weeks, and the skin, depending on the time of year, could be sold for a little money, or sewn into gloves or a smock to be sold to the tourists for a lot more. The blubber was for the dogs over the winter, and the bones were a treat for the pack as soon as the carcass was stripped of everything else.

Maratse caught himself salivating at the thought of seal meat on the bone, sizzling in its own fat on a flat rock on the mountainside, with a fire of twigs and driftwood beneath it.

"Ready?" Karl asked, as he stood up. He placed his hand on Maratse's shoulder as he clambered over the centre seat and lifted a wooden stand from the bow of the dinghy. He slotted the base of the stand into two rectangular holes made of fibreglass fixed in position at the bow of the boat. Karl lifted a wooden wheel of fishing line into position. A length of wire with a metal clasp was tucked into a cut in the wood. Karl took it and reached over the gunwales for the fishing marker. He lifted the marker, snapped the clasp onto another clasp attached to the bottom of the flag, and released the marker, letting it bob at the end of a short line attached to the buoy. Karl straightened and slapped his hand on the wheel. "You or me?"

"Me," Maratse said, and prepared to move to the bow of the boat. He waited until Karl sat down on the stern seat. Maratse gritted his teeth and moved forwards, kneeling on two coils of rope in front of the wheel. He gripped the handles on both sides and began to turn. Behind him, Karl pulled a shallow plastic box from beneath the centre seat. He placed it in front of him and hooked the gaff around the fishing line as Maratse reeled it in from the depths of the sea. The boat turned and Karl let the line glide through the rubber glove he was wearing. When the first flat halibut broke the surface, Karl called for Maratse to stop, as he unhooked the fish and tossed it into the plastic box at his feet.

They continued like this for another five minutes, and seven fish, until the handles slipped out of Maratse's hands. The line started to sink back into the sea. Maratse stood up, ignoring the pain in his legs, gripped the handles and slowed the unravelling of the line. He grunted at the weight of the line as he began to turn the handles. He stopped to unzip his jacket with one hand, the fishing line trembled through the handle and into the palm of his other hand. The abrasions in the creases of his palms from the rusted bar of the ambulance workshop opened, and a smear of blood coated the handles as Maratse sweated with the weight.

"A shark, maybe?" Karl said. He peered over the side of the dinghy, as Maratse turned the handles, one slow revolution after another.

"Can you see it?" Maratse said during another pause.

"I can see something." The dinghy dipped to the port side as Karl gripped the fishing line and tugged at it. "Just a little more, and I can get it with the gaff." Maratse turned the wheel another three full turns until he heard Karl gasp.

"Can you see it now?" Maratse waited for a response, but Karl said nothing. He found a length of rope with a loop at one end. It was attached to the legs of the fishing wheel, and Maratse hooked the loop around the opposite handle, locking the wheel in position. He turned around as Karl retched over the side, spilling the coffee from his guts into the water. Maratse stared beyond the contents of Karl's stomach floating on the surface, and saw the slow twists and curls of long black hair moving in the water with the current.

"Do you have a mobile, Karl?"

"Yes," Karl said and tugged his mobile from his pocket. He handed it to Maratse and then moved along the stern seat to the starboard side of the dinghy.

Maratse crawled over the centre seat, ignoring the trim of the boat as he leaned over the side and stared into the glacial white face of a dead girl at the end of the line. He reached into the water and turned her head upwards. The eyes were gone, and the girl's skull felt soft on one side. She was young, Maratse reckoned, and dressed in winter clothes, which was strange, he realised, as the body was well-preserved and perhaps only a week or two old. Despite the damage, she looked familiar, and he remembered the photo he had seen on the news the night before. He let go of the girl's head, and worked his way onto the centre seat.

"Karl?" he said. "Have a cigarette." Karl nodded as Maratse unlocked the keypad on the mobile and dialled the police station in Nuuk.

Chapter 9

Petra noticed the Police Commissioner the minute he walked through the door and onto the first floor office area where she had her desk. He towered above the majority of the police officers in Nuuk. People said he was tall, even for a Dane. Petra was in her second year of training when Lars Andersen had been appointed Commissioner for the police in Greenland. Prior to his arrival, it was rumoured that he didn't tolerate fools or foolish behaviour. It was known that he had an impressive record for policing in Denmark, including a short period overseas, in Nicaragua. But it was a secret, between Petra and the Commissioner that he was mildly dyslexic. Cadets spent their second year of training at the police academy in Nuuk stationed around the country on a practical placement, under the supervision of a mentor. Petra had been in Nuuk, and had surprised the Commissioner one day when he was struggling to work his way through a pile of detailed reports. She offered to help, and he was impressed by the speed at which she read and her flare for Danish grammar.

As the Commissioner made his way along the floor towards her desk, she smiled at the memory of how grateful he had been for her help.

The Commissioner did not smile as he approached Petra's desk. He nodded hello and borrowed a chair from the adjacent desk, and sat down. He crossed one long leg over the other and said, "I need an update on the Tinka Winther case."

"Okay," Petra said, and flipped open her notebook. She scanned her notes and said, "The last person to see Tinka was her father, Martin Winther. I spoke to him yesterday. He said she was staying with a friend, Kaka Satorana, but the girl admitted it was a cover story."

"Covering for Tinka?"

"Yes, the truth was that Tinka was planning to go to a party. Kaka said Tinka was excited about meeting a particular man."

"Older?"

Petra nodded. "Kaka said the man was older, yes."

"Any leads on the man?"

"No, but…" Petra closed her notebook.

"But? You have a hunch?"

"Sort of." She opened the first drawer of her desk and placed a photocopy of a newspaper article on the desk in front of the Commissioner. "Someone left this on my desk last night."

"Give me the gist of it," the Commissioner said, his voice low as he studied the article.

"It's about the party culture of politicians in Greenland."

"A party culture?"

"Amongst some politicians, yes." Petra paused. "It is suggestive, but mentions no current names, only those from the past, before the millennium."

"And your hunch is that Tinka was meeting a politician?"

"I think that's why someone left this on my desk."

"Any idea who?"

"Who left the article?"

"Yes, or the politician. Your best guess."

Petra looked over the Commissioner's shoulders. Three of her colleagues were working at their desks, and a fourth police officer walked through the door with a report in one hand and a coffee in the other. Petra felt a twinge in her stomach.

"Petra?"

"Can we..." Petra started, and then nodded at the glass-walled meeting room to her left. She stood up and gestured for the Commissioner to follow her. Petra imagined a lull in the activity at her colleagues' desks, as she opened the door to the meeting room. She closed it behind the Commissioner, pressed her hands together, and tapped her lips with her fingertips.

"Well, now we have the attention of the entire office, Petra. Are you sure this is necessary? Bear in mind that this is Greenland, Constable, not Hollywood," the Commissioner said, and sat on the table. "However," he said, as he stretched his legs in front of him, "this is political, so you are probably right to be cautious."

"Thank you."

"Do you have a name?"

"I have a name, and a date, and a location."

The Commissioner raised his eyebrows. "Go on."

"It's all supposition, of course," Petra said. The Commissioner made a spinning gesture with his finger, and she continued. "Malik Uutaaq was in Ilulissat for a meeting last weekend. I confirmed this with his secretary."

"Tinka is a high school student in Aasiaat. Am I right?"

"She's a second year student. She has been sick, and was at home in Ilulissat with her father."

"So she was in Ilulissat at the same time as Malik Uutaaq?"

"Yes."

"He's married, isn't he?" he said, and Petra nodded. The Commissioner stood up. "As evidence goes, that's pretty thin."

"I said it was a hunch, based on someone leaving the article on my desk."

"And who was that I wonder?"

"I have no idea."

"All right, if this develops, I think you should talk to Uutaaq's wife." The Commissioner sighed. He walked to the office window and looked out at the sea. The clouds were the same colour as the water, and swathes of rain were storming towards the land. "We have a meeting next door," he said, "in the government building. You and I are going to meet with Nivi Winther and her assistant. I think his name is Daniel."

"Tukku," Petra said.

"That's right. We're a little late, but I wanted to talk to you first." He walked to the door and opened it. "Oh, and I asked Gaba Alatak to meet us there."

"Why?" Petra said. She paused at the door as the twinge in her stomach developed into a queasy feeling.

"Because he is an impressive figure, leader of the Special Response Unit, and I want the minister to feel that we are putting our best people on this. That includes you, Constable."

"Yes, sir," Petra whispered, as she followed the Commissioner out of the meeting room and along the office floor to the stairs. "But did it have to be Gaba?"

"Am I missing something?" the Commissioner asked, as he strode down the stairs. Petra hurried to keep up, despite the feeling of lead in her stomach.

"We were dating," she said, "until he decided younger girls were more interesting."

"That seems to be popular at the moment."

"Yes, sir."

The Commissioner stopped to shake hands with a young police officer, newly returned from paternity leave. Petra waited as the proud father produced a photograph from his wallet. The Commissioner smiled, patted the man on the back, and wished him well. He beckoned to Petra and they walked out of the main door and into the rain.

"I've been meaning to ask you something," he said, as they jogged through the rain the short distance to the government offices. "How is Constable Maratse?" The Commissioner stopped at the door, opened it, and waited for Petra to go inside.

Petra smoothed the rain from her hair, then wiped her hands on her jacket and nodded. "He's okay, all things considered. He flew to Inussuk yesterday."

"Where's that?" the Commissioner asked as he led the way to the elevator.

"In Uummannaq fjord, just up the coast from Ilulissat."

"And what is he going to do?"

"He says he is going to fish and hunt," Petra said, as the elevator arrived. She paused before walking inside.

"You're not so sure, are you?"

"No, sir. He's in a lot of pain. According to the doctors, he suffered a lot of nerve damage when they tortured him."

"Constable," the Commissioner said quietly, as the doors closed, "that is classified information. I told you because I needed someone to take care of Maratse."

"I know, sir."

"Then I expect us to talk about Maratse without mentioning what actually happened, especially inside this building."

"Yes, sir. Sorry, sir."

"So, we understand each other. Good. Now," he said, "compose yourself, I'm about to present you to the First Minister as one of Greenland's brightest police officers."

"Thank you," she said, and then, as the doors opened, she asked, "And Gaba?"

"Purely decoration. Unless we need the services of his team. He will have no say in the case. It's yours, and you report to me, directly."

"But I'm only a Constable," Petra said, as they walked out of the elevator and along the hall.

"Not anymore," the Commissioner said, as they stopped outside Nivi Winther's office. "Congratulations, Sergeant," he said and shook her hand. "Your results came in early this morning. The official papers will be on your desk by the end of the day." The Commissioner winked as he knocked on the door and opened it.

Petra's stomach wrestled with conflicting emotions, as she tried to process everything the Commissioner had told her since he sat down at her desk only a short while ago. She knew she had done well in the Sergeant's exam, but having things confirmed by the Commissioner made it suddenly real. Petra allowed herself a brief smile before entering the room. She glanced at Gaba looking impressive, and then at the First Minister. Nivi Winther had obviously decided not to wear make-up, and, at the sight of tears welling in her eyes, Petra believed the decision had been wise.

"This is Sergeant Jensen," the Commissioner said, and beckoned Petra towards the desk. She shook Nivi's hand, and nodded at her assistant, Daniel, as he stood behind the First Minister. "Petra handles missing person's cases, and, on this matter, she will be reporting to me directly."

"And him?" Daniel said with a nod towards Gaba.

"Gaba is here at my request. I want him to be fully informed in the event that we need him."

"Why would we need him?" said Nivi. "What does he do?"

Gaba took a step forwards. "I lead the Special Response Unit. If we find your daughter, we might need my team."

"If?" Nivi said. "I don't understand."

"This is a high-profile case, First Minister," said the Commissioner. "If we were in America, and the first daughter went missing, well, I think we can all imagine how they would react over there."

"And over here?" said Daniel.

"This is Greenland," the Commissioner said. "We don't have a precedent for such situations, but I want to assure you, that we are taking this seriously, and we are doing everything we can to find the First Minister's daughter."

"You are doing everything you can?"

"Yes, we are."

"Daniel, don't," said Nivi.

"It's all right, Nivi," he said. "I just want to be sure that they really are doing everything they can. I want to know if you have any leads?"

"I can assure you that we are actively investigating Tinka's disappearance."

"And do you have any suspects?"

"Daniel," Nivi said, "stop."

He turned to Nivi, and said, "This is important. I have to ask."

"And I said I didn't want you to."

Petra watched as the First Minister fought to control her breathing. She looked at the Commissioner, opened her mouth to speak, and shut it again when he urged caution with a subtle wave of his hand.

"This is not about an article, Nivi, this is about your daughter." Daniel took a step towards her and placed his hand on her shoulder. He looked at the Commissioner. "What about Malik Uutaaq?"

"What about him?"

"There has been some suggestion that Tinka may have met Malik at a party, and that they may have…" He paused to squeeze Nivi's shoulder, mouthing the words I'm sorry. She nodded, and he continued, "They may have spent some time together. They may have been intimate."

The Commissioner nodded. He turned to look at his officers. Petra took a step forwards and he stood to one side, gesturing for her to approach the desk.

"Do you have a witness who can confirm that Malik Uutaaq was with your daughter, Ms Winther?" Petra waited as Nivi looked at Daniel.

"We know he was in Ilulissat at the same time as Tinka," he said.

"Yes, we have also confirmed that."

"Then you have spoken to Malik?" said Daniel.

"No."

Daniel let go of Nivi's shoulder and walked to the window and Gaba took a step back to give him room. The rain intensified, making it difficult to see the gentle curves of the Katuaq Cultural Centre, inspired as they were by the Northern Lights. Daniel looked at Petra. "Why not?"

"Being a man in Ilulissat does not make Malik Uutaaq a suspect. He is also a politician. If we questioned him without just cause, then we could make this situation worse."

"How could it possibly be worse?" Nivi said. "My daughter is missing. No-one has seen her since the weekend, perhaps as late as

Friday night."

"I understand," Petra said, "but unless we have a witness, or some evidence linking your daughter and Malik Uutaaq, we risk creating a media storm, and you will be accused of using your daughter's disappearance to discredit a political opponent."

"That's quite the political insight, Sergeant," said Daniel. "Thank you. But when we want your political opinion we will ask you for it, not before. I suggest you concentrate on police duties, rather than your evident passion for political commentary."

Petra could feel her cheeks begin to redden, and looked at the Commissioner for support, but it was Gaba that defused the situation and put the First Minister's assistant firmly in his place.

"Sergeant Jensen is doing her job. She is considering all eventualities, and focussing on the one person she is accountable to in this investigation: Tinka Winther. I suggest you let her do her job, or provide her with the evidence necessary to pursue the line of inquiry you suggest." Gaba looked at Petra and gave her the briefest of smiles. He looked at Daniel and waited.

"Nivi?" Daniel said.

"Yes," she said and nodded.

"Thank you Sergeant Alatak. I can assure you I have every confidence in Sergeant Jensen's ability to conduct the investigation, and on that note, to further her lines of inquiry, as you so eloquently put it, might I suggest that she speak with Aarni Aviki, the Communications Chief for *Seqinnersoq*." Daniel turned to Petra. "I think he will give you the necessary just cause to talk with Malik Uutaaq, without unleashing a political storm, although I do appreciate your concern."

"Thank you," Petra said. She looked at Nivi, intending to reassure her when her phone vibrated in her pocket. Nivi nodded that she should answer the call, and Petra swiped her thumb across the screen.

"Piitalaat," said Maratse, his words crackling in the wind, "I have found something."

Chapter 10

Malik Uutaaq turned on the television and surfed to the Teletext channel of Greenland's official television station, *Kalaallit Nunaata Radioa*. As the channel cycled through pages of brief text in Greenlandic and then Danish, he turned on the radio, checked his watch, and waited for the hourly news broadcast. Aarni said he should be prepared for some disturbing news, and that he was on his way over. Malik saw the Danish version of the news about a girl's body being found in Uummannaq fjord just before the hour. He turned on the radio and caught the presenter's last words about the girl, Nivi Winther's daughter, before the station switched to a telephone interview with the local Chief of Police in Uummannaq.

When he arrived, Aarni found Malik with his head in his hands, sitting on the edge of the sofa. The news broadcast was over, and so it seemed was Malik's interest in a political career.

"I'm pulling out," he said, as Aarni came into the living room.

"You can't. The country needs a strong leader. It should be you."

"A strong leader?" Malik looked up. "And what happens when someone tells the country that their leader was the last person to see Tinka Winther alive? Eh? What happens then?"

"It won't happen."

"You know, you say that every time, Aarni. I think you should explain yourself."

"All right," Aarni said. He walked into the hall and looked up the stairs. When he returned he closed the living room door. "We're alone?"

"Yeah," Malik said and stood up. "The kids are at school. Naala is at work."

"Turn off your phone."

"What?"

"Just turn it off," Aarni said. He found the landline in the kitchen, traced the lead to the wall, and pulled it out of the socket."

"What are you doing?"

"Precautions. That's all."

Aarni pushed an armchair closer to the coffee table and gestured for Malik to sit on the sofa. The shadow of a delivery van passed the window, and Aarni stood up to draw the blinds. Malik watched him as he walked back to the chair and sat down.

"What did you do?" Malik said.

"Just wait." Aarni took a breath and loosened the tie around his neck. He looked at Malik, and said, "This is all happening quickly. I'm trying to keep ahead of it, but you have to understand…"

"Just talk. Right now."

"Fine, okay." Aarni wiped his hand with his face. "All right. This is what happened. You went to Ilulissat as planned, last week."

"I came back Saturday afternoon."

"Right, after the party on Friday night. Where you met Tinka Winther."

"I didn't know it was her, Aarni, I swear."

"Sure, but you met her, and someone saw you with her. I know because I got a call around lunchtime on Saturday, before you landed in Nuuk."

Malik stood up and walked to the window. He leaned against the wall by the side of the blinds, and peered through the gap at the street. He tapped his fingers against his leg as Aarni talked.

"The call was from a man, but the line was distorted – but he spoke in Danish, good Danish."

"What did he want?"

"He said he could fix the problem, but it wouldn't be cheap."

"Aarni," Malik said, and looked at his communications chief, "did you pay someone to kill Tinka Winther?"

"No," Aarni said and shook his head. "No way." He pointed at Malik, and said, "*We* paid someone to fix your sexual indiscretions. That's what *we* did. That's all we did."

"You keep saying *we*, Aarni. Do you mean the party? Because I don't remember giving you any money to fix anything. And I will say that in court if I have to."

"You won't have to," Aarni said, his voice louder than he expected. He took a breath and spoke quietly, his words measured and spaced. "The party has attracted foreign interest. We had an injection of funds at the end of last week, and I used a portion of that to clean up your mess. *We*, the party, are in this together."

"When were you going to tell me about the investor?"

"I would have told you on Monday, but I was dealing with this," he said, and waved at the text page on the television. "I received a text when we drank coffee the other morning confirming that it was done. Fixed."

"Confirming that Tinka was dead?"

"No. I never expected it to come to that."

"Just what did you expect?"

"I don't know," Aarni said, aware once again that he had raised his voice. "Money, maybe. A threat. Blackmail, perhaps. That's what I imagined. I didn't expect anything, other than the problem would go away, and that we could move on."

"And you didn't know it was Tinka Winther?"

"Okay, that I knew. That's what the man told me. That's why I had to fix this. The other girls," Aarni said, as Malik opened the drinks cabinet beside the television, "didn't matter. They were either too drunk or too stoned to remember who you were."

"You asked them?" Malik took two glasses and a bottle of gin from the cabinet. He put them on the coffee table and filled each glass to the brim. Aarni shook his head as Malik pushed the glass across the table with two fingers. Malik shrugged and drained both glasses.

"Yes, Malik, I asked them. I have cleaned up after all your indiscretions. I even talked with your wife."

"You did what?" Malik spluttered the last of the gin from his lips.

"I talked with Naala. We agreed you were a bastard. But we also agreed that you could be the next leader of Greenland, and that she could expect things to get better, financially, and at home. We agreed it was better for your kids that she put up with you screwing around, rather than dragging them through a messy divorce."

"You've been busy, Aarni." Malik reached for the bottle of gin, and then pushed it away. He collapsed against the cushions and leaned his head back over the back of the sofa. "And now I am chief suspect in a murder investigation."

"You don't know that."

"Come on, Aarni. It's just a matter of time." Malik flicked his hand towards the television. "Your mystery guy will demand more money. That's how this works. Don't you watch television?"

Aarni leaned his elbow on the arm of the chair and rested his hand in his palm.

"There's more," said Malik, "isn't there?"

"Daniel Tukku knows you were with Tinka."

"What?" Malik lifted his head and stared at Aarni. "I thought you said we were going to be all right."

"I did, and we are."

"Not if Nivi Winther's assistant knows I was with her daughter we're not."

"We are, because I made a deal with him, yesterday."

"What deal?"

"I agreed that we would ease up on Greenlandic as the first language, and instead we would debate topics like housing and unemployment on Sunday."

"You really think the debate is still on? With everything that has happened? Nivi is in no position to debate. They will cancel. *I* would cancel if it was Pipaluk's body they dragged out of the sea." The thought of his daughter sobered Malik, and he pushed himself up and off the sofa. Without a word, he capped the gin bottle and put it back in the cabinet. He picked the glasses off the coffee table and took them into the kitchen. He filled the kettle and switched it on, hunting through the cupboard for two clean mugs until Aarni interrupted him.

"There will be a debate, and you will be there. I made a deal with Tukku that he would keep quiet in return for an open debate, one that allowed for other agendas than our own."

"You agreed to that?"

"Yes," Aarni said.

"Then you just lost the election for us. As soon as I go off message, I will be challenged on topics I haven't prepared."

"Maybe you would be prepared, if you spent less time screwing around."

Malik raised his finger, and then lowered it. "You're right," he said, and leaned against the kitchen counter. "I accept that. Anyway, Nivi is hardly likely to comment, if she even turns up."

"I don't think she will," Aarni said. He waited for a moment. "I think Daniel Tukku will stand in for her. I think he is ready to take advantage of the sympathy vote, and the potential vacuum this creates in the party. I think he plans to step in for Nivi on Sunday, and maybe in the future too."

"That's pretty heartless."

"No," Aarni said, "it's just politics." He took his keys out of his pocket and nodded at the kettle steaming by the side of the hob. "I don't want coffee. I'm going back to the office. Keep your phone turned off. I'll send you an email if I need to contact you."

"And what are you going to do?"

"I'm going to write a press release expressing our condolences to Nivi Winther and her family, and then I'm going to talk to Tukku, about the debate."

"Just like that?"

"Yes. It's business as usual, Malik. Remember that."

Aarni left the kitchen and walked out of the house. He shut the front door behind him and got into his car. The day was overcast like the one before it, but no rain. Aarni started the car and backed out of the drive. When he slowed at the first roundabout on his way into town, he noticed a police car in the mirror. Aarni accelerated, the tyres screeching into the bend as he turned onto the road leading up a small rise before dropping down a curve towards the centre of Nuuk. He glanced at the mirror again, increased speed, and gripped the wheel as the blue lights on the roof of the police car began to spin, followed by the blare of the siren.

The curve in the road was sharper than Aarni remembered. He struggled to negotiate the turn, overcompensating as the steering wheel grew heavy and slippery from his sweaty palms. The police car dropped back a little, as Aarni drifted into the opposite lane. The driver of the first car in a line of three heading towards Aarni braked, as Aarni clipped the side of the car with the bumper and screeched to a halt. He tried to open the driver's door but managed only a few centimetres before hitting the side panel of the other car. Aarni began to clamber over the handbrake to the passenger's side of his car, only to stop when the seatbelt locked, and a tall policeman peered through the glass of the passenger door. Aarni didn't recognise the face of Gaba Alatak. Gaba adjusted the arms of the Oakley sunglasses he wore around the back of his head. He knocked on the window, and gestured for Aarni to roll it down.

"That," Gaba said, as Aarni pressed the window button behind the handbrake, "was stupid."

"I know," Aarni said. He tried to shrug but the seatbelt tightened, forcing him back into his seat.

"You are Aarni Aviki?"

"Yes."

"I've been looking for you. Why don't you answer your phone?"

"I turned it off."

"Really?" Gaba said, and nodded. "Now, that's interesting. A communications chief with no means of communicating." He looked at the line of oncoming traffic, and glanced at his partner who was talking with the driver of the other vehicle. "How about we fix this mess, and then we can talk?"

"Yes," Aarni said. He watched as Gaba directed the traffic around the collision in the centre of the road. His partner took a statement from the driver of the other vehicle, stood back to take a few photos with his smartphone, and then waved the driver on. The man tapped on Aarni's window, told him to get out of the car. He drove the damaged car onto a patch of gravel by the side of a grill bar, while Gaba beckoned to Aarni to join him in the police car.

"Right," Gaba said, as Aarni climbed into the back of the Toyota and closed the rear passenger door, "that's sorted. We'll leave the rest to your insurance companies."

"Okay," Aarni said.

The second policeman opened the driver's door and got behind the wheel, nodding when Gaba told him to take them back to the station.

"I'm not the investigating officer," Gaba said, as his partner pulled out and away from the side of the road. "But before you meet her, I'd just like to tell you who I am." Gaba dipped his head and caught Aarni's eye. "I'm the guy they send in when the situation demands a more physical response. If you understand what I mean?"

"I'm not sure I do." Aarni's voice faltered as Gaba tilted his head and smirked.

Gaba turned to his partner, and said, "He doesn't understand."

The policeman shook his head. "Better tell him straight, boss," he said.

"Really? You think a more direct approach would be better?"

"I do."

The policeman slowed at the entrance to the police station. He found a parking spot opposite the main entrance and turned off the engine. He waited as Gaba got out of the car, opened the rear passenger door, and slid onto the seat beside Aarni.

"My partner thinks I need to be more direct. So, how about we try this," he said, and prodded Aarni's chest with his knuckle. "I'm the one they send in to arrest people who have done unspeakable things." He lowered his knuckle as Aarni gasped for breath. "Arrests like that can be messy. It's not always easy to maintain control over a situation like that. Things can get out of hand quickly." He looked at Aarni. "People can get hurt."

"I think," Aarni said, his words stumbling out of his mouth, "I think I understand now."

"Good," Gaba said, and patted Aarni on the chest with a large, flat palm. "Just remember that, if you see me again. Okay?" Gaba got out of the car, opened Aarni's door, and escorted him inside the police station. Petra was waiting at the door.

"What was all that about?" she asked with a glance at Aarni.

"That?" Gaba said, and shrugged. "I don't know what you're talking about. What about you, Miki?" he said to his partner.

"Nope. No idea, boss." Miki turned to Petra, and said, "He's all yours."

Chapter 11

The hotel boat chartered by the Uummannaq police department dipped, as the Chief of Police, Torben Simonsen, and his assistant Constable Danielsen, heaved Tinka Winther's body over the railings and onto the deck. The girl's flesh sagged as water pooled out from her clothes, exiting her body from the open wound in her skull. Simonsen waved at Maratse, beckoning for him to come alongside. Karl started the outboard motor, and edged the dinghy along the hull of the hotel boat, until Maratse was positioned opposite the gap in the railings. Simonsen helped him onboard and Karl pulled away from the boat, searching for a comfortable distance between him and the dead girl.

"Constable," Simonsen said, as he waited for Maratse to find his balance. "We've never met, but we have a mutual acquaintance."

"We do?"

"Fenna Brongaard," he said with a nod towards Danielsen. "I don't like to admit it, but she pistol-whipped the two of us earlier in the year. Followed by a shoot-out in the old schoolhouse in Uummannatsiaq." Simonsen nodded to the tip of an island barely visible between the icebergs in the distance. He frowned at Maratse's grip on the railing and said, "Looks like I got off lightly."

"Hmm," Maratse said. He stifled a grimace and started walking along the railing towards the bow.

"You don't like to talk about it, Constable?"

"I'm not a Constable."

"Not anymore, maybe," Simonsen said, as he stood to one side of Maratse. They looked down at the body. "You know who she is?"

"*Iiji*," Maratse said. "Tinka Winther, the First Minister's daughter."

"Local politician. She's from Inussuk."

"I know." Maratse shuffled forwards, gritting his teeth as he knelt beside Tinka's body. He leaned over her head and pressed his face close to the open wound in her skull, then, working downwards, he examined the length of her body, without touching her.

"A boating accident would do that," Simonsen said, and tapped a cigarette from a packet into his hand. He offered one to Maratse.

"It could," he said, and rolled the unlit cigarette between the gap in his teeth. Maratse stared at the girl's clothes, peeled back the waterlogged *Canada Goose* jacket and tugged at the fleece she wore beneath it. He used the railings to pull himself onto his feet, and said, "No underwear."

"No?"

"And her clothes are too small."

"The jacket fits," Simonsen said. He handed Maratse his lighter as he knelt beside the girl's head. There was a tag, just visible inside the hood, and he moved Tinka's head to read it. "Pipaluk Uutaaq," he said, and looked at Danielsen. "Write that down."

"Got it," Danielsen said, and flashed the page of his notebook at his chief.

"Uutaaq. Does the name mean anything to you? It seems familiar."

"The politician," Maratse said, as he remembered Petra's outburst at the article in the newspaper.

"Malik Uutaaq?"

"*Iiji.*"

Simonsen stood up, leaned against the railings, and tapped the ash from his cigarette into the sea. He looked at Maratse and took his lighter when Maratse was finished with it. "What do you think?" he asked.

"I'm not a policeman. I shouldn't say."

"You were, and I'm asking. You found her," Simonsen said, "and I found out your first call was to Nuuk, not to me." He stared at Maratse as he took a drag on his cigarette. "Would you mind telling me what's going on, *Constable*?"

Maratse stuck his hands in the pockets of the overalls and puffed a cloud of smoke from his lungs. He remembered telling Petra that he couldn't go back to Ittoqqortoormiit because he would always be a policeman, and would be treated as such. It seemed that moving to Inussuk had not changed anything. He was still a policeman, albeit unofficially. He flicked at the filter of the cigarette and shrugged.

"I called Petra Jensen."

"In Nuuk?"

"*Iiji.*"

"Why?"

"She is looking for a missing girl," Maratse said and dipped his head towards Tinka's body. "Her."

"And you are sure this is Tinka Winther?"

"It's the same girl from the news."

"Write that down too," Simonsen said with a nod at Danielsen. "It's curious that you are so sure it is her."

"I saw her on the news."

"So did I, but I don't recognise her." Simonsen took a last drag on his cigarette and flicked the butt into the water. "Lucky for us, and you, that Nivi Winther, is flying here tomorrow."

"Hmm."

"Constable Maratse," Simonsen said as he pushed away from the railings, "if you're going to live here and get involved in my investigations, I would appreciate you being more cooperative."

"I am cooperating."

"And going over my head."

"I explained that."

"You did." Simonsen tucked his hands into his belt. "But this is my jurisdiction. And, as you said, you're not with the police anymore. So," he said, and leaned forwards, "you might want to think about your priorities. Otherwise, I might be inspired to consider other aspects of this case."

"Such as?"

"How convenient it is that it was you that found the girl…"

"She's been dead for a few days."

Simonsen ignored Maratse, and continued "…on your very first day in Inussuk."

Maratse leaned against the railing, as the boat rose on the shallow crest of a wave. He stared at the Chief of Police through a cloud of cigarette smoke. "Is this really about me?"

"I don't want it to be," Simonsen said, "but you know as well as I do that investigations can take many turns before they are resolved."

"And you want to investigate me?" Maratse shook his head. "Because I called Nuuk first?"

"You have a mysterious past, Constable, with a lot of blank spaces that no-one seems to want to talk about. You were involved with a person of interest…"

"Fenna Brongaard…"

"That's right. From the little I heard, you might even have broken some laws in helping her."

"And that ties me to this girl?" Maratse said, with a nod towards the body on the deck. "That's pretty thin."

"And yet," Simonsen said, and smiled, "it's all I have right now."

"I think I should go." Maratse waved for Karl to come back.

"We can take you back to Inussuk. It's quite a drop into Karl's boat."

"I can manage."

"I'm sure you can." Simonsen waited as Maratse made his way along the railings. "Just remember our little chat, Constable. Remember your priorities."

"I will." Maratse nodded at Karl, as he clicked the outboard out of gear and bumped the side of the boat. He took a last look at Tinka's body before Danielsen covered it with a plastic tarpaulin. The driver of the hotel boat looked relieved when Maratse caught his eye.

Maratse lowered himself to the deck and lifted his legs over the side. As soon as he was seated Karl clicked the motor into reverse, and edged away from the hotel boat as Simonsen lit another cigarette.

"I'll call if I need you," he shouted.

Maratse held on to the seat, as Karl turned the dinghy in a tight arc and pointed the bow towards Inussuk. When the boat levelled out, he plucked the cigarette butt from his teeth and flicked it into the water. Karl was silent as they motored towards the settlement, turning once in a while to avoid growlers of ice, or to go around a large iceberg. The air was chill on Maratse's cheek, and he looked at the thick grey clouds above them, and imagined that the first snow of the year would soon fall. He said as much to Karl, but the older man just shrugged, focussing on getting home. Just ten minutes later he bumped the hull of the dinghy onto the beach.

"Leave the fish and the gear to me, I'll sort it," Karl said as Maratse tried to help. "Maybe we can talk later."

Maratse nodded and left him alone, shuffling up the beach as the puppy bounded towards him from where it was sleeping on the sand beneath the deck of Maratse's house. The Danish girl was playing in the sand. She said hello as he reached the steps. Maratse shooed the puppy from his feet and smiled.

"My name is Nanna," she said. "Mummy is inside. She made a cake."

"Hmm," Maratse said. He started to climb the steps, slowly, gritting his teeth and lifting each leg, and planting the sole of the heavy fishing boots on each step, before repeating the process. He had reached halfway when the girl's mother opened the door of their house and waved.

"Did Nanna invite you for cake?" she asked.

"*Iiji*," Maratse said.

"Will you come?"

"I need a shower," he said.

"Okay, maybe after your shower? It's good cake," she said, and smiled. Maratse noticed flour on her cheeks and trousers. She brushed at it when he nodded. "Great. I'll make fresh coffee."

Maratse waved and continued up the steps. The puppy worried at the heels of his boots as Maratse leaned against the railings to pull them off, tossing them halfway along the deck to distract the puppy as he opened the door and walked into his house. Maratse looked up at the stairs leading to the first floor and the bathroom, frowning at the flimsy banister. He unzipped the overalls and shrugged his way out of them, stealing himself for the climb only to stop when the phone rang. Maratse lifted his legs out of the overalls and hobbled into the living room. He picked up the telephone and leaned on the window sill.

"Piitalaat," he said.

"You knew it was me."

"You're the only one who has my number." Maratse thought for a moment. "I don't even know it." He smiled when he heard Petra laugh.

"I'm calling because of work."

"*Iiji*."

"I'm just about to talk to Aarni Aviki."

"Who's he?"

"He's Uutaaq's communications chief. We think he can confirm that Malik was with Tinka just before she went missing."

"Piitalaat."

"Yes?"

"Why are you telling me?"

"Because…" Petra was quiet for a moment, and Maratse imagined her asking herself the same question. He heard her sigh, and then she said, "I trust you, and I need someone to talk to."

"Are you all right?"

"Yes," she said, and paused. "But the press is going to go nuts when they hear about the dead girl, especially if it is Tinka Winther's body that you fished out of the sea."

"It is," Maratse said.

"You're positive?"

"*Iiji.*"

Petra was quiet for a long time. Maratse waited. He glanced at the puppy chewing at the collar of one of Karl's boots on the deck. Maratse knocked on the window and growled. The puppy looked up, smoothing the expression on its face into one of pure innocence, with wide eyes, and a slight tilt of its head. Maratse growled again, and the puppy picked itself up and loped to the other end of the deck.

"David?" Petra said. "Did you just growl?"

"I have a puppy."

"That was fast."

"It wasn't my decision," he said, frowning as he realised he would have to feed it soon.

"But you're settling in. I mean, you're fishing and…"

"You're going to be okay, Piitalaat," Maratse said.

"I know but, I miss not having you here."

"We'll talk soon." Maratse waited for Petra to say goodbye and then placed the telephone on the cradle. It was an old model he realised. "Like I feel," he grunted, and looked towards the stairs, contemplating how old he would feel as he climbed them. He lifted the collar of his shirt, took a sniff, and decided he had to try.

Images of Tinka's body nagged at Maratse, as he climbed the stairs. He chewed over the details, pleased to have something to occupy his thoughts as he climbed, and again as he fiddled with an unfamiliar shower, and dried himself on the hand towel. Buuti's spare bath towels were still on the coffee table in the living room.

It was Tinka's clothes that bothered Maratse most. The fact that she was wearing winter clothes, and yet, according to Petra, she had only been missing for a few days. The name tag was another curious detail, one that Maratse chose to think about as he climbed down the stairs, naked but for the hand towel around his neck. He rested against the wall in the hall, before walking into the living room and collapsing on the sofa. He pulled on his sweaty shirt and jogging trousers, and made a mental note to visit the store the next morning to buy what they had of clothes. The thought of fresh coffee encouraged Maratse to forget about Tinka for a while, and to get to know his neighbours. He made his way to the door, pushed his bare feet into his boots, and left the house. He growled once at the puppy for good measure, allowing himself a little smile as it retreated to the far end of the deck.

It was just one step from the beach onto the neighbour's deck, a detail not wasted on Maratse. He knocked on the door, and smiled as the little girl opened it.

"Hello," he said, and walked in as she pushed the door wide, and leaned against it.

"Don't get in the way, Nanna," her mother called from the kitchen. The house was the same type as Maratse's, but, unlike his house, the windowsills were overflowing with wings, bones, shells, stones, and skulls. He stared at the collection as Nanna guided him to a seat at the table by the window. She began handing him different things, and explaining what they were, when and where they had found them, and what her mother and her friend were going to do with them.

"Mummy is an artist," she said, as she placed a raven claw in Maratse's palm.

"Hmm," Maratse said, as he pushed the skin of his thumb against the claws.

"I'm afraid it's true." Nanna's mother placed a large cake on a plate on the table, before returning to the kitchen for the coffee, mugs, and plates. She told Nanna to get the milk from the fridge, and gave her a gentle bump on her bottom with her foot as she passed. "I think that's everything," she said, as she sat down. She smiled at Maratse, held out her hand, and said, "I'm Sisse. My partner, Klara, is tramping along the beach somewhere."

"Maratse."

Sisse frowned, and said, "Just *Maratse*?"

"David," he said.

"Are you a policeman, David?" Sisse watched, as Nanna put the milk on the table. She pulled out a chair and helped her daughter sit down. "That's what we heard."

"I was."

"And now?"

"Retired," he said, and nodded when Sisse started to pour the coffee.

"What made you choose to move to Inussuk? Family?"

"Convenience. A nurse told me the house was available."

"A nurse? Have you been in hospital?"

"*Iiji.*" Maratse put the raven claw back on the windowsill.

"Is that East Greenlandic?" Sisse asked, and tried to repeat what Maratse had said.

"It means *yes* on the east coast."

"How interesting." Sisse helped Nanna pour milk into her mug and smoothed her hand through her daughter's hair. "It seems that every time we hear the news – in Danish – it is about language, and how you can never truly be a Greenlander if you don't speak the language. What do you think about that, David?"

Maratse sipped at his coffee, as Sisse cut three slices of cake. He thought about Petra, and how the current debate was chipping away at her identity. A good officer, a good person, a good *Greenlander*, forced to consider her place in her own culture and country, for every day of the campaign until the elections, and maybe for the rest of her life. Sisse lifted a slice of cake onto a small plate and pushed it across the table to Maratse. She offered him a teaspoon, and then tried to catch his eye, in anticipation of his response.

"I don't like politics," he said.

"But it's all they talk about at the moment; on the radio, and the television. You can't escape it."

Maratse shrugged. "I don't listen to the radio. I don't have a television."

"What do you do for entertainment?"

Maratse cut a piece of cake, thumbing it onto the teaspoon when it slipped off. He nodded at the window and used the tip of the spoon to point at the icebergs, the mountains, and the sea. "And when it is dark," he said, and popped the cake into his mouth, "I read."

Nanna spilt some milk and made a fuss of getting a cloth from the kitchen to clean it up. Maratse ate his cake, pleased at the distraction, and content to look out of the window. Sisse helped her daughter to wipe the milk from the table, and Maratse sipped at his coffee, searching for a little patch of quiet in the storm of words that Danes seemed to need when eating a meal in company. But even when Nanna dragged her mother into the kitchen to clean the cloth, Maratse wasn't alone at the table, as images of Tinka occupied his thoughts, and he wondered if that part of his brain, the part that would always remain a policeman, would ever find peace, even in a place as small and secluded as Inussuk.

Chapter 12

Petra slipped her phone into her pocket and walked into the meeting room. She closed the door and offered Aarni Aviki a hot drink. When he declined, she poured a cup of coffee from the thermos and sat down at the table. She glanced at his hands as she arranged her notebook and a small digital Dictaphone that she placed between them. The communications chief for *Seqinnersoq* began to pick at his thumbnail. Petra watched, sipped her coffee, and waited. It was Aarni who spoke first, in Greenlandic.

"I want an interpreter," he said.

Petra turned on the Dictaphone, and said, "Can you repeat that, in Danish?"

"I asked for an interpreter."

"But your Danish is perfect, Mr Aviki."

"I have the right to an interpreter."

Petra pushed her coffee to one side and made a note on her pad. "I'm surprised you haven't asked for a lawyer," she said, and looked up. "Perhaps that would be more appropriate?"

Aarni stopped picking at his nail and sneered. "You're one of them," he said, switching to Danish, "the Danish-speaking Greenlanders."

Petra gripped the pen between her fingers and took a breath. "Lots of Greenlanders speak Danish, Mr Aviki."

"Yes, but they are from mixed parents. What's your excuse?"

"I didn't think I needed one," Petra said. She paused for a moment to take a breath. If she wasn't careful, she realised, this man could easily take her off-topic.

"I heard you grew up in the children's home, here in Nuuk," he said.

"Mr Aviki," Petra said, tapping her pencil on the table, "I would like to ask you some questions about your relationship to Tinka Winther."

"Your parents spoke Greenlandic," Aarni said, and leaned back in his chair. "Why don't you?"

Petra leaned over the Dictaphone and said, "Let the record show that Mr Aviki is evading the question." Petra paused to catch Aarni's eye. "And obstructing the investigation."

"Wait," Aarni said, "I'm not obstructing anything."

"Then answer the question, if you will. What is your relationship to Tinka Winther?"

"I don't have one. We have never met."

"But you know who she is?"

"After last night's news on television, doesn't everyone?"

"I'd like to hear you say it."

"Yes, I know who she is."

Petra made a note, scrawling a quick question beneath it. She reached for her coffee, took a sip, and then placed it on the table. "And Malik Uutaaq, do you know him?"

"Of course I do. He is the leader of my party, my boss." Aarni laughed. "That's a ridiculous question, Sergeant."

Petra ignored him, and made another note. She drew a line between the two. "What is Mr Uutaaq's relationship to Tinka Winther?"

Aarni glanced at the Dictaphone, and then at Petra's notes, squinting for a moment, as if he was trying to read them. He drummed his fingers on the table and looked around the room. He nodded at the thermos flask of coffee and Petra waited as he pushed back his chair and left the table. She noticed sweat on his brow when he returned. The surface of the coffee vibrated ever so slightly as he held the plastic cup in his hand. Petra repeated the question, as Aarni took a sip of coffee.

"Is this on record?" he asked, and glanced at the Dictaphone.

"I'm not a journalist," Petra said. "Everything is on record. Of course," she said, and pushed the notepad in front of Aarni, "if you wanted to write a statement instead…"

"No," he said, and put the cup down on the table.

Petra studied the man's eyes, and if she could see what Aarni was seeing, as he weighed his career against his political allegiance, she might have had some pity for the man's turmoil, as he considered his next move. As it was, she found only contempt for the man who had forced her to consider her own identity, and her place in the country of her birth. She enjoyed seeing him squirm, but still, his answer surprised her.

"No," he said. "Malik has no relationship with Tinka Winther, at least not that I am aware of."

"They have never met?"

"No."

"Perhaps in passing, at a party, for example?"

"Sergeant," Aarni said, and Petra could feel a renewed confidence in the man's demeanour, as if he had gained strength and a sense of peace with his decision to remain loyal to his boss, "I think we both know that Malik Uutaaq has a reputation for enjoying a good party. And why shouldn't he? What he does in his own time, is his own business."

"But when a girl goes missing, and his name is linked to her disappearance…"

"By whom, Sergeant? Who has linked Malik Uutaaq with the girl's disappearance?"

"That's not important. I am just following a lead."

"A lead?" Aarni stared at Petra. "And how many *leads* do you have?" Petra reached for the notepad and began to pull it across the table towards her. Aarni stopped her when he pressed his hand on the top page. "How many, Sergeant?"

"The way this works, Mr Aviki, is that I ask the questions, not you."

"And yet, you are suggesting my boss is involved in the disappearance of the daughter of his political opponent." Aarni let go of the notepad. "I am the communications chief for *Seqinnersoq*, and questions such as these, ones that have a direct influence on the party, are my domain. So, I ask you again, Sergeant, what leads do you have? How many are you pursuing?"

The sweat on Aarni's brow had evaporated. It seemed that the media onslaught since the beginning of the campaign had toughened Aarni Aviki's skin. Any sign of his earlier discomfort had disappeared, and Petra decided she needed to take a new tack, if she was going to get any useful information out of him. A shadow at the window, and a knock at the door caught them both by surprise, as did the identity of the person to enter the room.

"Ms Winther," Petra said, and stood up as Greenland's First Minister entered the room. "I'm sorry, but this is a private interview, and I am going to have to ask you to leave." She looked at Nivi's assistant as he appeared in the doorway.

Daniel Tukku nodded. "I'll handle this. Nivi?" he said. "We have to go. Your flight leaves in forty minutes."

Nivi ignored him and took a step closer to Aarni. She shook as she spoke, her lips trembling. "I have to fly to Uummannaq, to identify the body of a girl that could be my daughter. I heard that you know something," she said and glanced at Petra, "that you have information that might help the police find who did this to my daughter…"

"Nivi," Daniel said, as he placed a hand on her shoulder. He pulled her slowly away from the table, and towards the door.

"If you know anything," Nivi said, "you have to tell them. Because if you hide something, anything…" Nivi's voice grew stronger, as she straightened her back and took a breath. "I will make sure you are finished in Greenland, and I will expose you to the world."

"We have to go," Daniel said. He glanced at Aarni, and Petra caught the briefest of nods as Daniel guided Nivi out of the meeting room and along the office floor to the stairs. Petra closed the door. When she returned to the table, she picked up the Dictaphone, and turned it off. Aarni pointed at it.

"You have it on tape. She threatened me."

"She is upset."

"She was out of line. I could end her career with that tape."

"Police property," Petra said, and slipped the Dictaphone into her pocket. She looked at Aarni. "If you have nothing more to add, then you are free to go." She gestured at the door. "I think you know the way out."

Aarni pushed back his chair, and stood up. He finished his coffee, straightened his jacket and tie, and walked to the door.

"Just one thing," Petra said, as he closed his fingers around the door handle, "off the record."

Aarni looked at her, and said, "I thought everything was on the record, Sergeant."

"You're right, but this is personal."

"Go on."

"You think you're better than me, because you speak Greenlandic and I don't, but you're forgetting something, *Arne*." Petra waited for a second, as he registered her use of his Danish name. "Your mother is Danish. Your skin is lighter than mine. You had an excuse for not speaking Greenlandic in school. I didn't. And every time I tried, they told me that if I couldn't speak proper Greenlandic, then I shouldn't bother. And then they would hit me."

"Are you looking for sympathy, Sergeant?"

"No, not for me, but for the children, the coming generation. You're older than me. You were born after the first school reform, when Danish was prioritised."

The muscles in Aarni's face tightened. He glared at Petra. "That reform cursed me, and has cursed me my whole life. Me and my generation."

"That's right, it did," Petra said. "Just like you and your language extremism is cursing a whole new generation of Greenlanders. It cursed Tinka Winther, and now she is missing, and likely dead."

"You don't know that."

"That she is dead, or cursed? Does it matter?" Petra shrugged. "I know she couldn't speak Greenlandic. Her mother made no secret of that in the press."

"I don't know what you want to achieve with this little off-the-record chat, Sergeant, but I think we are done for the day." Aarni took his smartphone from his pocket and stepped out of the meeting room. Petra followed him.

"I have no more questions for you today, but you would be mistaken to think we are done. If the First Minister makes a positive identification of her daughter in Uummannaq, then this investigation changes gear again. If we discover that you withheld information, and this becomes an investigation of a suspicious death, perhaps even a murder, well..." Petra shrugged as Aarni stared at her. "Your reluctance to help and your lack of cooperation might just put you at the top of the list of people we would want to question, again, under less comfortable circumstances."

Aarni glanced at the screen of his phone, and slipped it back inside his pocket, wiping his hand on his trousers afterwards. Petra tapped the end of the pen against her chin.

"Have you just remembered something, Mr Aviki?"

"No," he whispered, and again, louder, "nothing."

"If you're sure?"

"Yes, I'm sure." Aarni looked around the office, and then glanced out of the window at the parking area. "I don't have a car," he said.

"I'm sure you'll manage."

Petra watched Aarni Aviki all the way to the door. As soon as he was gone, she walked across to the window, leaned against the wall beside her colleague's desk, and tilted her head for a better view of the main entrance below.

"That, Sergeant, might be considered stalking," the policeman said, and continued typing his report on the computer.

"It might."

"You wouldn't want that to come back and haunt you," he said, and laughed.

"Hush," she said. "I am looking out of the window. That's hardly stalking."

"He is Malik Uutaaq's spin doctor. If he sees you, he can choose to call it what he wants." Petra slapped her colleague on his shoulder with the notepad. He laughed again. "You just upgraded to abuse."

Petra ignored him as she watched Aarni. The glow from the screen of his smartphone lit his face as he began to punch in what she presumed was the number of a taxi service. He never made the call. A flash of headlights from a car parked opposite the main entrance caught Aarni's attention, and he put the phone back in his pocket. Petra watched him walk to the car and peer in through the driver's window. She couldn't see the driver, and the shadow cast by the police minibus parked nearby made it difficult to see if it was a man or a woman sitting in the driver's seat. Aarni stepped back and waited for the car to pull out before getting into the passenger seat. Petra switched her attention to the number plate, but it was obscured with dirt. She reached out and grabbed her colleague by the shoulder.

"Quick," she said, "see if you can read the number of that car."

The police officer pushed back his chair and stood up, pressing his face to the window as the car below them pulled out of the car park and into the street.

"Sorry," he said. "I didn't see it."

"A black Suzuki," Petra said, and made a note on her pad.

"Do you think it's important?"

"Who knows, but right now, it's all in the details."

She walked back to her desk and sat down on the office chair, dropping her pad beside the computer keyboard as she moved backwards and forwards in the chair, tapping her chin with the end of the pen. Whoever was in the car was waiting for Aarni, but Petra couldn't recall him calling anyone, or sending a text message during her brief interview. Gaba had him too spooked to call anyone on the ride to the station. Petra smiled at the thought – Gaba had that effect on people. No, she decided, whoever was waiting for Aarni had discovered he was at the police station without him contacting anyone. Petra just didn't know if it was important.

"Another small detail," she whispered to herself.

Petra wheeled the chair to the desk and moved the computer mouse to refresh the screen. She typed in her password and checked her intranet messages. There was nothing new. She typed up her notes and thought about what the First Minister had said about flying to Uummannaq. A positive identification would take the case in a new direction, and create a potential frenzy in the media, both in Greenland, and likely in Denmark too.

Petra finished with her notes and leaned back in the chair. She checked her watch, and then looked at the clock on the wall. She had ten minutes before her shift ended. The convenient arrival of someone to give Aarni Aviki a lift from the station intrigued her, but it was something that could wait until tomorrow.

Tallimanngorneq

FRIDAY

Chapter 13

Maratse watched the hotel boat moor at the jetty. There was a small buzz of people waiting for Nivi Winther and her ex-husband to arrive, Karl and his wife, Buuti, among them. The news of Nivi's positive identification of her daughter's body had spread quickly, and the preparations for her funeral had been arranged shortly afterwards.

Maratse sipped at his coffee as Karl and Edvard helped Martin Winther, and three other men, lift the coffin containing Tinka Winther from the deck, and carry it along the jetty to the beach. Nivi walked behind the men carrying her daughter to the graveyard overlooking the fjord and the people of Inussuk followed. There were at least three reporters among the mourners, and it surprised Maratse that Nivi seemed not to notice when they took her picture at various points along the way. But then, her level of grief was probably such that she didn't care, certainly not before the pictures were on the front pages of the newspapers, at which time it would already be too late. Maratse finished his coffee and straightened the black tie he had borrowed from Karl.

He walked to the hall, pleased that he had learned to ignore the pain in his legs. He slipped his feet inside his boots. It was still a trial to tie his own laces, but the stairs were useful. When he was finished with his boots, he heaved himself onto his feet with one hand on the banister and the other on the windowsill. When he walked out onto the deck the puppy looked up from where it guarded the seal bone Maratse had given it, something to occupy it while he was away.

"Is that the First Minister?" Sisse asked, from where she stood on the deck of her house.

"*Iiji*," Maratse said, and walked down the steps to the beach.

"Do you think I can go up there?" Sisse pointed at the procession of family and mourners following the men carrying Tinka Winther up the steep side of the mountain. "Or would it be inappropriate?"

"I'm going," Maratse said. "You can come with me."

Sisse reached inside the door of her house and grabbed her jacket. Her partner offered to keep an eye on Nanna while she was away. She pulled on her jacket and jogged to catch up with Maratse, as he walked along the beach towards the path. The sky was heavy with snow, and the first flakes fell as Sisse tugged the zip all the way to the collar. She stuffed her hands in her pockets and switched sides to avoid the smoke from Maratse's cigarette. They climbed in silence, stopping several times as Maratse took a break. When they reached the graveyard the service was nearly over, and the snow fell heavily on the mourners.

"Let's wait here." Maratse stood to one side of the white picket fence that ran around three sides of the graveyard. The cliff face served as the fourth and final side, a natural barrier protecting the dead from the sea. Maratse stuffed the stub of his cigarette inside the packet and tucked it into his jacket pocket. He blinked in the flash of a reporter's camera, and realised that he probably should have borrowed an overcoat from his neighbour too. The yellow and green police emblem on his jacket was clearly visible on the right breast.

"They are taking our picture," Sisse said, as the two other reporters joined the first in documenting what the papers would probably report as a police presence at the funeral.

"Hmm," Maratse said. He ignored the cameras and watched as Nivi laid a wreath of plastic flowers beside her daughter's grave. Karl and Edvard would arrange the flowers on top of the grave later, but for now, as the snow fell, so did the flowers, as the mourners took turns to place a wreath before saying their last goodbyes and walking down the mountain for the wake. Buuti had arranged it, and agreed with the present occupants of Nivi Winther's childhood home, that they would hold it there. It was to be a small gathering, she had explained to Maratse.

Maratse watched as Nivi put her arm around Tinka's father, pulling him close as he sagged at the side of the grave. He slipped to his knees. Nivi laid one hand on his shoulder and clasped the other over her mouth. Her sobs were quiet, but they filtered through the snowfall blanketing the graveyard.

"Why are they leaving plastic flowers?" Sisse whispered.

"Have you seen real flowers in Greenland?"

"No," she said. "But plastic…"

"Is forever," he said, and watched as Nivi pulled away from her ex-husband, and searched for a way out between the mourners, somewhere she could be alone, just for a moment. She started to walk away from the grave, saw Maratse, and walked straight towards him, growing stronger with each step. She smiled at Sisse as she approached and then looked at Maratse.

"You're a policeman?" she asked.

"I was," he said. "My name is Maratse." He shook her hand, surprised at how cool and firm it was.

"You found my daughter."

"*Iiji*," he said, and nodded at Karl standing close to the grave. "We found her."

"Thank you," she said. "It must have been difficult." Nivi looked at Sisse, and said, "Please excuse us." She hooked her arm through Maratse's and walked with him towards the edge of the mountain, pausing as he slowed. "You're hurt?"

"It's nothing," he said. "I'm recovering from an injury."

Nivi nodded and let go of his arm. Snow brushed her short hair as she looked out at the fjord, glancing once at the mourners as they passed and began to walk down the path. "I grew up here. Perhaps you knew that?"

"*Iiji*," Maratse said. He turned as Martin Winther was guided down the path, and Karl and Edvard began to cover Tinka's coffin. They were alone but for the soft slice of the spades in the dirt.

"Tinka and I used to come up here, when her grandparents were still alive. We climbed this path every day," she said, and pointed to a small knoll to one side. "We would sit there and watch for whales." Nivi caught a tear as it rolled down her cheek and wiped it away. "That's why I wanted to bury her here, so that she can look for whales. Is that silly?"

"*Eeqqi*," Maratse said. "It is a good place."

"You're from the east? Tasiilaq?"

"Ittoqqortoormiit."

"But you chose to move here?"

"For a while."

"Why?"

"A new start."

"I understand," she said. "I need your help, Constable." Nivi looked at Maratse. She took a breath and bit her bottom lip, as if she was making a decision, wondering if it was the right one.

"I'm not a policeman anymore," he said.

"But you still wear the jacket?"

Maratse shrugged. "It is a good jacket."

Nivi tried to smile, and said, "I want you to find out how my daughter died. I know," she said, as Maratse started to speak,

"Sergeant Jensen is working on the case, and the Commissioner himself has assured me they are doing everything they can, but..." Nivi sighed and clenched her fists. She looked out to the sea, licked a stray tear from her lip, and took a deep breath. "I just don't think they have the necessary drive to find the answers."

"Drive? I don't understand."

Nivi tried another smile. "Forgive me, what I meant to say was I'm not sure they are stubborn enough."

"And you think I am?" Maratse frowned.

"Stubborn enough to walk up a mountain when you are clearly in pain," she said with a glance at Maratse's legs.

"I don't know," he said. "I have friends in the Nuuk police department. Sergeant Jensen, for example."

"And I have the greatest respect for Sergeant Jensen, but she will be tied by time and the law."

"I will not do anything against the law," Maratse said.

"Gosh, no, I don't mean that you should. But you could ask questions, in an unofficial capacity. Anything you learn, you could pass on to the police, to Sergeant Jensen."

Maratse shifted on his feet, biting back a flash of pain. "I don't think it is a good idea," he said. "I'm not the right person to help you."

"I think, Constable, that you are exactly that person, and I also think that it is no accident that you are here, in Inussuk, and that it was you who found my daughter."

"I don't know." Maratse shook his head. "I think..."

"Please," Nivi said, and reached out to touch his arm. She pulled back her hand and took a breath. "They examined Tinka in the hospital. The official report says that she died in a boating accident. But what was she doing in a boat, here of all places? I need help, Constable," she said. "Don't decide now. I am leaving tomorrow. We can talk in the morning. I will also pay you," she said, and added, "from my own pocket. Unlike some of my colleagues, I do not believe in dipping into the party war chest when it becomes convenient." She pressed her lips into a tight smile. "If you can help me help the police, and find out how my daughter died, then you will give me the peace of mind I need to move on." She tilted her head and looked Maratse in the eye. "Can you do that?"

"I will think about it," he said.

"Thank you." Nivi squeezed his arm and looked over at Tinka's grave, as Karl and Edvard laid the flowers over the soil and snow. "I heard they buried a baby last Monday, and now they have buried mine. Perhaps they will give each other some comfort." The snow crunched beneath Nivi's boots as she walked towards the path and made her way down the mountainside.

Maratse watched her leave, and cursed himself for being so fond of his jacket. And yet, he wore it for a reason. He wasn't ready to let go of his former life, not just yet. Perhaps he should help Nivi Winther discover what happened to her daughter? Had he not already speculated about the clothes Tinka was wearing when he pulled her out of the water? The name tag intrigued him. But Petra was working the case, and he knew she would keep him informed, no matter how much he pretended not to be interested.

He tapped a cigarette into his hand from the packet in his pocket, lit it and rolled it into the gap between his teeth. He waved at Karl and walked to the graveyard, stopping every other step to draw a cloud of smoke into his lungs, and to allow the pain to settle in his legs. When he reached the grave he offered Karl and Edvard a smoke, lighting their cigarettes before slipping the lighter inside the packet. It had been a small private funeral, and would remain so until the reporters returned to their hotel rooms in Uummannaq and uploaded the images. He could hear the engines of the hotel boat cough and start as they smoked, and soon he would be able to see it, as it sped across the fjord to the town.

"Five," Karl said, as he finished his cigarette.

"What's that?"

"Five graves left." He bent down to extinguish the cigarette butt in the snow, and then slipped it into his jacket pocket. He nodded at the remaining graves.

"And if it is not enough?" Maratse asked. "What then?"

"That depends on the winter," Edvard said and glanced up at the sky.

"Hmm," Maratse said.

Karl and Edvard picked up their shovels and started walking towards the path. They waited for Maratse, but he waved them on, pointing at his legs.

"I'll be there later," he said. He watched them leave until they disappeared from view, and then he looked down at Tinka's grave.

"Your mother wants me to find out what happened to you. What do *you* want?"

Maratse lit another cigarette, taking his time to light it, as if the longer he took, the more time Tinka would have to think it over. The truth was, he knew, that the decision was his, and the dead were dead, forever. He smoked as the skies darkened from graphite to charcoal, and the first real night of winter descended on Inussuk. He realised the path would be obscured, and also that he didn't care.

"I'd have to travel," he said, his voice loud in the cocoon of snow swirling around the graveyard. "And what would Petra think?" He smiled at the thought of seeing her again, and at the realisation that he was speaking more to himself and to a dead girl, than he usually did in the company of others.

He turned at the sound of something padding across the snow. The puppy slowed as it approached the entrance to the graveyard, and Maratse growled a command to stop it before it passed through the gate. Maratse walked away from Tinka's grave, but carried her with him in his thoughts as he followed the puppy down the mountainside, past the store, all the way to Nivi's family home. The lights were on and there were candles burning in the windows. Nivi was alone on the deck as he climbed the steps, one at a time, and turned to shoo the puppy back to the beach.

"Is it yours?" Nivi asked as he joined her on the deck.

"I think it is."

"Soul mates," she said and pointed at the puppy. It rested on the snow, eyes fixed on Maratse. "Have you thought about what I asked you?"

"You said I had until tomorrow."

"I did," Nivi said, "but I think you have made your decision already."

"*Iiji*," he said.

"And?"

"If I help you, I will share everything I find with Sergeant Jensen, before I tell you."

Nivi nodded. "If that's important to you."

"It is."

"Then I accept," she said.

Maratse thought for a second, and then said, "I don't know what to call myself."

"Call yourself?" The candlelight flickered across the wrinkles on Nivi's brow. "I don't understand?"

"I'm not a policeman anymore. Private investigator fits, but I don't like the sound of it," he said, and shrugged, chewing over the title in his mind.

"How about my own private Constable, if that makes you feel easier?"

Maratse nodded. "I suppose it doesn't matter."

"Everything matters, Constable," Nivi said. "Everything *should* matter. Just like my daughter's death should matter." Nivi brushed the snow from the shoulders of her jacket. "Come on, there is food inside, and it's cold out here." She tucked her arm through Maratse's and walked with him to the door.

Maratse heard the telephone ring as he climbed the steps to his house after the wake. He grunted as he kicked off his shoes and walked to the window to pick up the phone.

"Maratse," he said, as he held the receiver to his ear.

"This is Simonsen."

"Hmm."

"Have you forgotten what we talked about on the boat?"

"*Eeqqi.*"

"I don't speak Greenlandic," Simonsen said.

"No, I haven't forgotten."

"Then why did I just get a call from someone telling me about you helping the First Minister? Investigating her daughter's death? Do I have to remind...?"

Maratse ended the call and made his way to the sofa. He slumped onto the cushions, reached for his book on the coffee table, and started to read. Simonsen's veiled threats were forgotten as he concentrated on the small English type in the thick book, distracted in part by the thought of travelling back to Nuuk with the First Minister the following day. He caught a smile as it twitched at the corners of his lips, leaned back and closed his eyes.

Arfininngorneq

SATURDAY

Chapter 14

Petra locked the door of the police Toyota and splashed through the slush to the airport entrance. She held her breath as she passed through the clouds of cigarette smoke from the passengers who were taking a break between flights, or waiting for taxis. Once through the waiting lounge she knocked on the door to the tiny baggage reclaim and arrivals area. The police officer on duty glanced at her through the glass and let her in.

"Here to pick someone up?" she asked.

"Yes. How about you, Atii? Busy?"

Atii Napa grinned and gestured at the empty arrivals area. "What do you think?" She waited for Petra to enter the room, and locked the door behind her. "Actually," she said, "we have a person of interest arriving from Kangerlussuaq later today. I think you know him."

"Who?"

"Mala Toori." Atii raised her eyebrows and waited for Petra to remember the name.

"It's a while since I last heard his name," she said, remembering when she and Maratse searched for a missing girl in a container.

"*Aap*," Atii said. "He has been quiet for a long time, but we had a tip that he may be back in the business of smuggling hash. Not personally, but coordinating it. The narco cops want a word with him."

"And that's why you're here?"

"No, I got dumped with customs duty when Søren called in sick this morning. But picking up Mala makes life a little more interesting. How about you?"

"I'm here to meet David Maratse."

"I heard something about him. He had an accident, and got early retirement."

"Yep, but I have a feeling he is finding it hard to retire." She recalled the message she had received from the Commissioner, something about Nivi Winther hiring Maratse as a private investigator. If it was true, it would make Maratse the first private investigator she knew of in Greenland. Petra's lips twitched at the thought, but her smile faded when she remembered that the Commissioner was less than pleased about Maratse's new role.

Regardless, Petra was excited to see him, and she walked to the window at the sound of the Dash 8 from Ilulissat taxiing to the apron outside arrivals.

"Now you're here," Atii said, reaching out to touch Petra's arm as the ground crew directed the aircraft to a stop.

"Yes?"

"Are you still seeing Gaba?"

"No," Petra said. She looked Atii in the eye. "You don't have to ask permission. It's not like I own him."

"I know. It's just a bit weird, you know?"

"I know." Petra shrugged, as Atii walked over to the arrivals door to receive the passengers. "Good luck," she said, as Atii waved.

Petra's first surprise was seeing Maratse walk towards her without the use of sticks, and the second was his pace as he walked, side-by-side with Nivi Winther. Petra studied the First Minister for signs of grief, she had expected her to be distraught, but it seemed that the tragic conclusion to her daughter's disappearance had boosted her resolve. She looked every inch the right person to lead the country, regardless of what the polls might say. The popular vote still favoured Malik Uutaaq, and Petra didn't know how Nivi Winther was going to change that. It wasn't long before she had her first taste of the minister's new direction and sense of purpose.

"Sergeant Jensen," Nivi said, as she entered arrivals, "you remember Constable Maratse?"

"I do," Petra said, and smiled at Maratse. "Although, I remember him retiring, too."

"He's my Constable now, Sergeant."

Maratse shifted from one foot to the other as the women talked about him. Petra noticed he had removed the police emblem from his jacket, but he still looked every inch a policeman. The thought gave her a warm feeling. Nivi explained the arrangement that had been agreed, that Maratse would be keeping Petra informed of his progress.

The doors to the waiting lounge opened again as Daniel Tukku walked through. Petra caught the look that Daniel shot at Maratse, before he greeted the First Minister and took her bag.

"This is a little weird," Petra said, as she walked with Maratse to the car. "And you seem better. No sticks."

"It still hurts," he said, and got into the passenger side as Petra unlocked it.

Petra climbed in behind the wheel and closed the door. She waited for a second. "The Commissioner wanted me to pick you up. But it's a bit more complicated than that."

"He doesn't want me to get in the way."

"He's worried you might. And we don't know why you are here."

"Nivi wants me to find out how her daughter died."

"But we are doing that."

"I know," Maratse said, and looked at Petra, "but that's why I'm here."

"I'm pleased," Petra said, smiling as she started the engine.

Petra drove out of the parking area and into town, glancing at Maratse, as he looked out of the window. The sun crowned the summit of Sermitsiaq with a golden glow, in stark contrast to the grey slush that stuck to the wheels of the cars on the streets of Nuuk.

Maratse sighed. "Where are you taking me, Piitalaat?"

"Where do you want to go?"

"Nivi said I should talk to Aarni Aviki."

"I interviewed him yesterday," Petra said. She wrinkled her nose at the thought. "It didn't go well, and he didn't say much."

"Perhaps he will say more to me?"

"Because you're a man?"

"Because I'm not the police," Maratse said, and shrugged. "I can try. This is all new to me."

"It's new to Greenland." Petra slowed at a roundabout. "But he seems to have gone into hiding overnight. I have been calling him all morning. Maybe you should talk to Qitu Kalia, the journalist?"

"Why?"

"I think he knows something, but we have no reason to interview him. Perhaps you could, unofficially?"

"I could. And there is Malik Uutaaq."

"No," Petra said. She curled a loose strand of hair around her ear as she drove. "I would stay away from him today."

"Why?"

"The clothes you found on Tinka Winther. You told me they had the name Uutaaq in them. We are going to pick him up after the debate on Sunday."

"Why not today?"

"The Commissioner doesn't want our actions to look politically motivated. If we pick him up today, people might think we are trying to influence the outcome." She looked at Maratse. "A lot of people will be watching. It could decide the election."

"Hmm," Maratse said. He leaned back against the headrest.

Petra laughed. "For someone who doesn't like politics or politicians, you are in the middle of it now."

"I know."

Maratse put his hand in his pocket and pulled out a mobile phone. "Nivi said I had to have one. I should give you the number."

Petra slowed, and then pulled off the road to park outside the offices of the *Sermitsiaq* newspaper. She turned off the engine and pulled on the handbrake, pushing the errant strand of hair behind her ear again as she lifted her head to look at Maratse.

"What's the number?"

"I don't know," he said, and handed her the mobile.

Petra unlocked the mobile and clicked a few buttons before taking out her smartphone and adding Maratse's mobile to her contact list. "I'm adding my number to your contacts, too," she said, returning his mobile to him when she was finished.

"*Qujanaq*," he said, and leaned forwards to peer up at the sign on the building. The outline of Nuuk's most famous mountain rested above its name and the name of the media company. "Qitu Kalia works here?"

"Yes." Petra tapped the steering wheel. "I will wait as long as I can, but the Commissioner made it clear that we are not working the case together. As much as I might like to." Petra smiled.

Maratse opened the door, took a moment to prepare for the flash of pain he knew would come as soon as his feet touched the ground, and then got out of the car. He gritted his teeth and then looked at Petra. "It is good to see you, Piitalaat. Thank you for the ride."

"It's good to see you, too. Where are you staying?"

"Nivi has booked me a room at Hotel Hans Egede."

"Okay," Petra said. "I'll call you."

Petra's smartphone began to ring, and she waited for Maratse to shut the door before answering it. He heard her start the car and turn on the siren before he reached the door of the building. The blue flash of emergency lights flickered in his vision and was gone. Maratse paused, his hand on the door, as he thought about the last time he had driven at speed with the blue lights flashing, and the siren blaring. He pushed the image from his mind and opened the door.

The receptionist directed Maratse to the second floor. He grimaced at the thought, and then started to climb the stairs. Qitu Kalia met him in the corridor by the stairwell, shook his hand, and showed him to his office. Maratse decided that the journalist must be successful to have his own office, and was pleased to be offered a comfortable chair on the other side of Qitu's desk. Maratse started to speak in Greenlandic, only to stop when Qitu raised his hand.

"Danish, please. It is easier to lip read."

"You can't lip read in Greenlandic?"

"I can, but you are from the east coast?"

"*Iiji*," Maratse said.

"It is difficult to understand you."

"Danish then."

"Thank you," Qitu said. He stared at Maratse's lips. "How can I help you?"

"What can you tell me about Tinka Winther?"

"Are you still with the police?"

"No. I am working for Nivi."

"The First Minister?" Qitu made a note on the pad on his desk. "As a private investigator?" he asked, and looked up to study Maratse's lips.

Maratse nodded. "Is there a connection between Aarni Aviki and Tinka Winther?"

"Not that I know of," Qitu said. "What will you do with the answers I give you? Will you give them to Nivi, or the police?"

"Both," Maratse said. "Police first."

"Why should I tell you anything? If there was anything to tell?"

"Because a girl is dead."

Qitu made another note on his pad, and then stood up. "Coffee?" He left the office, returning a few minutes later with two mugs of coffee. He put them on the desk and shut the door. When he sat down, Maratse thought there was something different about the journalist. He thanked Qitu for the coffee and waited.

"I write about a lot of things," Qitu said, "but recently, it is mostly politics."

Maratse sipped at his coffee and wished for a cigarette.

"What do you think about the politics of *Seqinnersoq*? Do you agree with them?"

"I don't like politics," Maratse said.

"But you work for a politician."

Maratse shrugged, and took another sip of coffee. "I am interested in what happened to the girl," he said. "Her mother just happens to be a politician."

"I think you're wrong about that," Qitu said. "I think the two things are closely connected. This election…" He paused to stand up and move his chair closer to Maratse. "This election is corrupt, and I think the issue of language is being used as a diversion."

"You think Malik Uutaaq is hiding something?"

"Yes, but not what you think. I think other people are using the politics of *Seqinnersoq* to hide much more."

"Such as Tinka's death?"

"I don't know," Qitu said, and glanced at the window in the door as someone walked past his office. "In the beginning I was angry at the way Malik Uutaaq and Aarni Aviki used language as a weapon. I had access to Nivi Winther's campaign, and was encouraged to write a piece to expose Malik's double-standards, his hypocrisy, and his lust for young women of mixed blood." Qitu shrugged. "I thought it was the right thing to do, and that I could help change the narrative."

"But you didn't?" Maratse said. "Why?"

"I think I was just being used."

"By who?"

"Daniel Tukku."

"Nivi's assistant?"

"Yes. He is popular among the businesses in Nuuk, and he has a lot of contacts abroad. He has made a lot of promises, promises he can't keep if his party does not win the election."

"It's not his party," Maratse said.

"Not yet. But if Nivi was to stand down, if something happened to make her think about her future with the party. Perhaps something that made other people question if she was fit to lead. A family tragedy, for example. Something traumatic."

"Like the death of her daughter."

"Something like that, yes."

"She has not stepped down."

"Not yet."

Qitu let the thought hang in the air between them. He reached for his coffee, and leaned back in his chair. Maratse bit his lip and moved his legs, fidgeting for a more comfortable position. Qitu watched him.

"The receptionist said you were a policeman, but you have removed your badge, and now you are calling yourself a private investigator."

"You called me that," Maratse said.

"I did. But maybe it doesn't matter what you are called. Maybe you are being used, like me." Qitu finished his coffee and pointed at Maratse's legs. "I think you have been used before."

"Why?"

"Something I heard about you. Something no-one talks about. But there was a car chase here in Nuuk, just before the summer."

"It wasn't me."

"And a fire, at a mine. They said it was an accident."

"I don't know what you are talking about," Maratse said.

"I think you do, but I also think you are loyal," Qitu said. "I like that. I think you are a good Greenlander. You are good for this country."

"Hmm," Maratse said. "Maybe."

"Perhaps we can help each other."

"I thought we already were?"

"Yes, but if you let me write this story, I can help the people of Greenland to make the right choice for the future of Greenland."

"And what is that?"

"The truth. They must vote for the truth."

Maratse shifted position and put his mug on the desk. He stood up, took a moment to find his balance, and then held out his hand. "*Qujanaq*," he said, and shook Qitu's hand. "I think I have enough for now."

"Will you talk to Daniel Tukku?"

"I think I should."

"I think so too," Qitu said. "But please, talk to me again. We can help each other."

Maratse nodded, and walked towards the door. He stopped to answer his mobile, and smiled at the caller's name displayed on the screen.

"Piitalaat," he said.

"David," Petra said.

Something in her voice made Maratse frown. He held the mobile close to his ear and turned his back on the journalist. "What is it?"

Petra took a breath. "We've found Aarni Aviki. I think you need to come and look."

Chapter 15

The taxi driver slowed the black Mercedes, as the policeman in the middle of the road waved for him to stop. The snow in the north had yet to turn into anything more than sleet in Nuuk, and the policeman was wet. As he tipped his cap the rain dribbled off the peak. Maratse paid the taxi driver, got out, and the Mercedes disappeared into the black evening, back the way it had come. Maratse waited a moment for the pain to subside in his legs, and then approached the policeman.

"I can't let you any closer," he said.

"Sergeant Jensen is expecting me," Maratse said. The policeman looked doubtful. Maratse pointed to the two police cars parked in front of a twenty foot container, the headlights of each car illuminated the interior. Maratse could see Petra, pinned between the beams of light, and he pointed at her. "She's just there. You could ask her."

The policeman looked over his shoulder, and nodded. "Wait here." The policeman cut the cone of blue flashing lights from the nearest police car with his body. Maratse studied the blue pearls of rain on the surface of the road, caught in the same flash of emergency, as he wondered what Petra wanted to show him. He started walking as soon as the policeman waved for him to come.

Petra was busy talking to a doctor and a paramedic as they examined the body of a man inside the container. She waved at Maratse to come forward, and then looked up at the body. A voice in Maratse's ear made him turn and he looked up at the face of Gaba Alatak, who was wearing plain clothes.

"Suicide," Gaba said.

"Aarni Aviki?"

"Yep." Gaba brushed his hand through his thick black hair, releasing a shower of water that caught the light. For a moment, Maratse was impressed by the sight of the SRU officer haloed in blue, before Gaba dropped his hand to his side. "I don't think you should be here, Maratse."

"I understand."

"Do you?" Gaba tugged at the sleeve of Maratse's jacket. "You're still in uniform."

"It's a good jacket," Maratse said. He offered Gaba a cigarette, but he declined. Maratse lit one for himself. "You're not in uniform. What are you doing here?"

"The Commissioner called me." Gaba wiped the rain from his face. "Apparently, the Chief of Police in Uummannaq has some concerns."

"Hmm." Maratse took a long drag on his cigarette.

"He thinks you are too involved in the case. He even suggested your involvement was suspicious. That there are too many unanswered questions about you and your past, not to make you a person of interest – someone we should keep an eye on."

"What did the Commissioner say?" Maratse caught a brief smile on Gaba's face.

"He said your past was your own, and that you were now retired from the force." Gaba looked at Maratse. "Of course, that's a little difficult to see."

"*Iji.*"

"The Commissioner also said we were to cooperate with you. So, I can tell you Aarni left a note – a recording. We found a Dictaphone in his jacket pocket." He pointed at the door of the container. "People think you have to hang from something high in order to die, but it's not true. I've found people dead with a tie around their throat, lying on the floor next to their bed. If they had propped themselves up on an elbow they could have survived. Aviki's feet were on the ground, I mean, if he stretched his toes he could have held himself up…" Gaba paused. "Until he got tired, of course."

"You're not sure it was suicide?"

"That's what the doctors are trying to figure out. There's a chair inside. My guess is, if it's not suicide, then someone could have sat in the chair and watched him try to keep himself up, until he couldn't any longer."

"How long has he been dead?"

"Several hours. Of course, if this wasn't suicide, and you consider what he said on the tape, if someone was trying to get him to say something specific, it might have taken a while. There's an echo on the recording. It sounds like it was made inside the container. Out of sight." Gaba stared at Maratse through a cloud of cigarette smoke. "About your past – there's a rumour you were tortured."

"Hmm," Maratse said. He flicked at the filter of his cigarette with his tongue.

"But you don't talk about it?"

"*Eeqqi*," he said, and shook his head.

Gaba sighed. "I can't imagine it. I would probably tell them anything they wanted to hear."

Maratse tossed his cigarette butt onto the road. "The man who tortured me didn't ask any questions. He didn't want a confession." He looked at Gaba, and waited for him to step to one side.

"Fair enough," Gaba said.

"Petra is waving at us," Maratse said, and gestured at the container. "Shall we go over there?"

"You go ahead, I have to get my team ready." Gaba started to walk away.

"For what?"

"To pick up Malik Uutaaq," he said, and raised his eyebrows. "Talk to Petra. She'll fill you in." He paused for a moment. "Don't worry about Simonsen. The Commissioner let slip that you might not be the only one to get early retirement." Gaba shrugged. "Just keep it legal, *Constable*."

Maratse watched Gaba walk to a black SUV parked behind the police Toyotas. He waited until Gaba had driven away before walking between the police cars and into the container. Petra stopped him just inside the door, out of the rain.

The smell of urine was heavy inside the container, and Maratse considered lighting another cigarette. He studied Aarni's inert body as the paramedic checked the chain around Aarni's neck. It was too thick to cut with regular bolt cutters, so Aarni would hang until the firefighters arrived to cut him down. He flinched when Petra touched his arm.

"Are you okay?"

"*Iiji*," Maratse said.

"Do you want to go outside?"

"It's raining. It's better here." Maratse nodded at Aviki. "Gaba said there was a note?"

"Yes," Petra said.

"He said it was interesting."

"And incriminating," she said.

At the sound of sirens blaring down the hill towards them, Petra tapped Maratse's arm and pointed at the nearest police car. They got in and closed the doors as the first fire engine arrived. Petra pulled a Dictaphone from her pocket.

"This is a recording of the message on the Dictaphone we found in Aviki's pocket. They rushed the original back to the station, to transcribe it." She pressed play, and Maratse stared at the recording device in her hands. Aarni Aviki's voice echoed just as Gaba had described it. Petra pressed a button to fast forward the tape, and then turned up the volume. Aarni's voice stuttered into the space between them.

...I already told the police. I never met Tinka Winther.

There was a click, as if the recording had been stopped, and then Aarni's voice continued.

Yes, he did meet with her.

Another click.

Malik Uutaaq.

"That's what I asked him at the station," Petra said, and stopped the recording. "We were told that Aviki can confirm that Malik Uutaaq knew Tinka Winther, and that he was probably the last person to be with her. Maybe the last person to see her alive."

Maratse glanced out of the window, as the fire crew carried a pair of hydraulic cutters from the fire engine into the container.

"Did Daniel Tukku tell you that?"

"What?"

"Was he the one who said Aviki could confirm Uutaaq was with Tinka?"

"Yes," Petra said, as a frown wrinkled her forehead. "Why?"

"The journalist thinks Tukku is trying to frame Uutaaq."

The shudder of a generator and the slow screech of the hydraulic cutters biting through the thick links of chain prevented further conversation until the fire crew were finished, and Aarni Aviki was carried out of the container on a stretcher. The doctor knocked on the window of the police car, and Petra opened it.

"We're taking his body straight to the morgue. We'll do a thorough examination, and then contact you if there's any reason to think we need to do an autopsy. As it is, it looks like a straightforward suicide. But," he said with a nod at the Dictaphone in Petra's hand, "that makes it a little more interesting." The doctor turned at a shout from the paramedic and her driver. "Yes, go, I'll meet you there." He wiped the rain from his face and looked at Petra, as the siren of the ambulance cut through the air.

"You can call the station when you know more," she said, and pulled her smartphone from her pocket. The doctor slapped the door and jogged to his own car. He was already gone by the time Petra was finished with updating the duty officer at the station. She put her smartphone on the dashboard and leaned back in the seat, turned her head to one side and tried to smile at Maratse. "It's been a long day," she said. "Tell me again about Tukku."

"He's made a lot of promises to a lot of people, businesses, countries..."

"Countries?"

Maratse shrugged, and said, "That's what the journalist said."

"So, how does this fit with Tinka?"

"Tukku needs to be in power. He needs to be the one who can make decisions."

"And Malik Uutaaq is too popular, and too powerful," Petra said. She sighed. "I'm beginning to see why you hate politics." She turned as the policeman from the road knocked on the window.

"The fire chief is done. What now?"

"Seal the container for the night. We've documented what we can. The investigative team can continue in the morning."

"And then I can go on my break?"

"Yes," Petra said, cursing the young man as he tipped his cap and a pool of water cascaded onto the window of the police car, splashing Petra's cheeks. He grinned and jogged to the container to shut and padlock the doors.

"So," she said, and started the engine, "I'm cold, wet, and I need food. What about you?" Maratse nodded and Petra reversed into the road, and drove up the hill towards the centre of town. She parked outside a Thai restaurant a few minutes later, and they found an empty booth beyond the buffet tables. Petra ordered for both of them, and then put her notebook on the table. "The Commissioner will want to know what our next move is."

"Our next move?" The muscles in Maratse's face twitched as he stretched his legs into a more comfortable position. "You mean yours?"

"Yes, and *ours*, the two of us. We're working together. That's what Nivi Winther wants, and the Commissioner is playing along with her, for the moment at least. So," Petra said, and smiled, "we're partners."

"Partners." Maratse unzipped the front of his jacket and laughed for a moment. He realised he hadn't laughed for a while, and the fact that he was working again, police work, turned the laugh into a smile.

"You're happy," Petra said.

"I'm working."

The waitress brought two cardboard boxes of food and two large cokes. "In case we have to leave," Petra said when Maratse frowned at the box of noodles and sauce. She peeled back the four sides of the lid, and pushed the disposable chopsticks through the paper wrapping. Maratse picked up a fork.

"Why exactly was Gaba at the container?" he said, and opened the box of food.

"You heard the recording. The Commissioner promised the First Minister that Gaba would be involved in all aspects of the case. Aviki's suicide is a new development."

"If it really was suicide?"

"Yes, I mean if some guy forced Aviki to confess..."

"A man?"

"Maybe," Petra said, and pinched a king prawn between the chopsticks. She dipped it in some sauce and popped it in her mouth. She thought about the Suzuki that Aarni drove away in the day before. "It's one angle. Suicide makes it convenient, but if it was a forced confession that ended in suicide..."

"Or murder."

"Exactly." Petra took a sip of coke. "That's why they are examining the recording."

Maratse frowned. "If it was forced, then the suspect knew that Aarni Aviki had something to say."

"Or," Petra said, "he wanted Aviki to say something, and tortured him to make him say it."

"So, not Uutaaq."

"Obviously."

"So, we're back to Tukku, or some other man?"

"Or woman," Petra said, and then she put down her chopsticks, and smiled.

"What is it, Piitalaat?"

"I was thinking of Gaba. And what *I* thought about doing to him when I found out he was sleeping around."

"And?"

"We're forgetting someone."

"Malik's wife?"

"Exactly," Petra said. She picked up her chopsticks and fished after another king prawn. She skewered it and held it up in front of Maratse. "If you wanted to get back at your husband, if you hated him, what better way than getting him arrested for the murder of his rival's daughter."

"We don't know it's murder yet," Maratse said. He shifted his legs, and looked around the restaurant, nodding at one of the customers as he caught Maratse's eye. He looked at Petra. "Didn't the doctor's report confirm it was a boating accident?"

"An accident? Sure," Petra said. "Except, we both know that it wasn't."

"Hmm," Maratse said.

"Still, Naala Uutaaq, she must want to castrate her husband. That's what I wanted to do to Gaba. And if she could do it publicly…"

"*Iiji*, but would you torture another man to get at Gaba?"

"No," Petra said, the excitement in her voice evaporated. She plucked the prawn from the chopstick and chewed.

Maratse sipped his coke through the straw, thinking about the lengths to which a woman might go to get revenge on her husband, boyfriend, even a girlfriend. He had split up too many drunken fights, women fighting over the same lousy man, and a stabbing, when one woman killed another because she had heard something in town. Gossip, that led to murder. Jealousy was a powerful drug in Greenland, the kind that kept the police busy.

"Still," she said, "we should probably talk to her."

"Malik's wife?"

"Yes," Petra said. She shook her head. "Where did you go?"

"I was thinking," Maratse said. "You said Gaba was going to pick up Malik?"

"Yes, after the debate."

"The debate is tomorrow?"

"Yes." Petra frowned. "What are you thinking?"

"We can't wait to interview Malik, his wife, or Daniel Tukku."

"I know," Petra said. "But the Commissioner doesn't want to create a media storm if he has anyone picked up before the debate, or even right after it. We can't interfere."

"But Aviki's death should be enough for Malik Uutaaq to cancel the debate."

"Because Tinka's wasn't?"

"Obviously not. Nivi Winther is a strong woman." Maratse patted the pocket of his jacket, the one with the packet of cigarettes inside it. He looked at Petra. "Is Malik still popular?"

"Very. Even with the sympathy vote, it will be difficult for Nivi Winther to beat him in the debate." She tapped the ends of her chopsticks on the lid of the box. "Cancelling the debate is risky though, for both sides. It has to be for a good reason."

"Like a death, on both sides."

"Exactly," Petra said, and smiled. "I don't think I've ever heard you talk so much."

"Hmm," he said. "It's good to be working again." Maratse gritted his teeth and stood up; resting his hand on the back of the chair until he felt he was able to walk. "We have to pay and leave," he said.

"Where are we going?" Petra asked, and picked up her box of noodles.

"To Malik Uutaaq's house."

"We're going to talk to his wife?"

Maratse shook his head. "We're going to park outside, and wait."

"Why?"

"Because I think his life is in danger."

Petra's smartphone beeped with a text message as she paid for their meal. She looked at the screen and then handed the phone to Maratse. "It's the journalist. He wants a comment. Someone just sent him an email with a sound file attached."

Chapter 16

Saturday night chaos swirled around Malik Uutaaq, but he didn't notice. He was at home, sat in the armchair by the window, a large glass of gin in one hand, his smartphone in the other. Aarni's debate notes were on a small table to one side. Malik glanced at them once or twice as he dialled his communications chief for the fourth time, or was it the fifth? Malik couldn't remember. Nor could he remember when it was that Pipaluk started shouting, or why Naala had to shout back, something about her daughter acting as if they were rich, and that winter jackets, especially the *Canada Goose* label were not cheap. Malik heard the argument, he heard all the words, but he didn't listen. The debate was tomorrow, and his communications chief, the man he hired to be his shield and to tell him what to say and when to say it, had gone missing. Malik took another gulp of gin. The girl was dead. What did it matter that Pipaluk had lost her winter jacket?

"Malik," Naala said, and Malik realised she was standing in front of him.

"What?"

"Your son is in his room. You need to go and talk to him."

"I'm preparing for the debate. I haven't got time to talk to Sipu."

"No," she said and stabbed her finger towards his chest, "you're getting drunk." She snatched the bottle of gin from beneath his arm and held it up to the light, sloshing what little alcohol was left around the bottom of the bottle.

"Give me that." Malik dropped the smartphone in his lap and reached for the bottle.

"Go and talk to your son."

"You mean *our* son."

"Right now? He's yours," Naala said and marched into the kitchen. She tipped the bottle over the sink and glared at her husband, daring him to say a single word.

Malik drank the last mouthful of gin from his glass and slapped it down on the coffee table as he walked out of the lounge, through the kitchen, and into the hall. He started to climb the stairs, stopping halfway to control his momentum, took a breath and continued onto the landing. Pipaluk looked out of her room and started to complain about her mother.

"Not now, princess," Malik said, as he walked past her room.

"But, dad," she called after him. "It's not fair. I didn't lose my jacket, or the other stuff, I left it hanging on the hook. It was *my* hook, dad. You should call the police or something."

Malik paused outside the door to Sipu's bedroom. He thought about the police, and wondered how he could explain to his daughter why that really wasn't a good idea. He opened the door and instantly wished that he had knocked first.

Sipu's room was dark but for the vivid pink and blue light emanating from the computer screen on his desk. He turned and fumbled for the mouse with one hand, as he tried to cover his crotch with the other. Malik stepped inside the room and quietly closed the door behind him.

"Sipu?"

"I'm sorry, dad," Sipu said. He closed one window on the screen with a click of the mouse, only to reveal another window, and a second and third cascading behind the first. All of them lurid. All of them graphic. Malik walked over to his son's desk, and turned the screen off.

"Pull your pyjamas up," Malik said.

He walked over to Sipu's bed and patted the mattress beside him. Sipu tugged his pyjama bottoms to his waist and crawled onto the bed. Malik curled his arm around his son, as Sipu buried his head in his father's armpit, his body jerking with small sobs.

"I'm not mad at you. You haven't done anything wrong. We just need to talk about it."

Malik felt the room spin around him, and he blinked to focus on the video game posters on the walls. None of them seemed willing to stop moving, so Malik closed his eyes. The room was warm. Malik lowered his head until his chin settled on his chest. He pictured the studio they were preparing for the debate at the cultural centre, the lights, the seats for the live audience, and the position of each of the three cameras. He had visited the studio with Aarni on the day of Tinka Winther's funeral. He had nodded with approval when the studio technicians had explained what they were doing, said *yes* to make-up and *no* to glasses. They showed him how the cordless microphone worked, and he remembered the light touch of the young woman who slipped the clasp of the microphone between his belt and the hem of his jeans. She was pretty. Not his type, but then his *type* seemed to get him into all kinds of trouble. Perhaps it was time to rethink his life?

Malik heard a snore and blinked his eyes open. Sipu had fallen asleep on his chest. He lifted his left hand to look at his watch, but it was too dark to see the hands. He didn't know if he had slept, or if his son's snoring had woken him, or was it the knock at the door. He squinted as a shaft of light from the landing lit Sipu's room as Naala opened the door and crept into the room. She looked at the window, and seemed to relax when she realised the curtains were drawn.

"Malik," she whispered.

"Naala? What is it?"

"Outside," she said. "There's a police car parked outside our house."

"What?" Malik sat up, peeled his son from his chest, and laid him down on the mattress, tugging the duvet over him as he stood up, walked to the window and reached for the curtain.

"Don't," Naala said. "They'll see you."

Malik stepped to one side of the window, and plucked at the edge of the curtain, just enough to see the police Toyota. The streetlights were on, but he couldn't see if anyone was inside the car. He let go of the curtain, and looked at his wife.

"I don't know," he said, but the twist of his guts suggested that he had an idea.

"Are you going to find out?"

"You want me to go and talk to them?"

"Yes," she said. "The police are outside our house, Malik. Yes, I want you to talk to them. What will the neighbours think?"

"Perhaps they are here for one of them?"

"Don't be an idiot," Naala said, and sighed.

They both turned as Pipaluk entered the room. She looked at her mother and then walked over to the window.

"Pipaluk, stop," Naala said.

"I want to see."

"It's nothing, princess," Malik said. "Go back to your room."

"If it's nothing," she said, "why are you whispering?"

"Your brother is asleep."

Pipaluk laughed, and said, "No, he's not, dad." She pointed at Sipu and he pulled the duvet over his head. "Faker," she said, and left the room.

Malik looked at his wife, as Pipaluk shut the door to her room and turned on her stereo. The music was loud enough to be heard, but not quite loud enough for them to tell her to turn it down. Naala beckoned for Malik to come with her, and they went down the stairs, and into the kitchen.

"This is because of you," she said, as Malik shut the kitchen door.

"How is this anything to do with me?"

"Because of *who* you are."

"The party leader of *Seqinnersoq*? Okay, maybe."

"And *what* you do," she said, and folded her arms across her chest.

"Politics?"

"Hah," she snorted, "is that what you call it?"

"Naala," Malik said, and pressed his palm to his forehead, "I don't want to fight anymore."

"No?"

"I'm tired. This last week has been…" He paused. "It's been difficult."

He looked at his wife, watched as the expression on her face softened, and her arms relaxed to her sides. She opened her mouth, as if she wanted to say something, and he wondered if he deserved to hear it, to hear soft words of encouragement, sympathy, and support, from the woman whose love he had betrayed time and time again. And then he saw her lips twitch, and any sympathy he might have received at his remorse was gone.

"You've had a difficult week? Oh, you poor love. How awful it must be to be you."

"Don't, Naala."

"Don't what, you bastard?" Naala jabbed her finger at the living room window, the one that faced out onto the street. "Go out there, and find out what the police are doing outside our house. Do that and I might just let you back in. Otherwise…" She paused to laugh. "Aarni Aviki."

Malik frowned. "What about him?"

"He told me to put up with you. That it was better to be the neglected wife of the First Minister of Greenland, than it was to be a divorced nobody. Can you believe that? He practically said that I should let you screw around, and that everything would be fine because we would have more money. He said that."

"He told me," Malik said, and glanced at the armchair where he had left his smartphone. Malik looked at his wife, and said, "Naala, do you want a divorce?"

The words didn't even surprise him. They just seemed to happen, pouring out together with the energy that was leaving his body, draining him on the eve of the most important day of his political campaign. If it was going to happen, he reasoned, why not make it now. What else could possibly go wrong?

Naala leaned back against the kitchen counter. She stared at her husband, as if he had started speaking a new language, as if he finally wanted to communicate. This second layer of vulnerability within the space of just a few minutes, actually stunned her, and she turned her back on Malik, not wanting to suggest one thing or another. Not yet. She gathered her thoughts, channelled them into words, and said, "Go outside. We'll talk after you've spoken to the police."

Malik waited for her to turn around. When he realised she wasn't going to, he walked out of the kitchen, shut the door quietly behind him, and put on a pair of shoes. He chose a jacket from the rack and left the house. The walk across the street was twice as long as he remembered, and he wondered how much gin he had drunk before Naala tipped the remains of the bottle down the sink. He stopped within half a metre of the police car, wiped a mist of rain from his face, and peered in through the driver's window. Malik waited.

Petra pressed the button in the door to lower the window, and looked at Malik. She nodded and waited for him to speak.

"You look familiar," he said.

"Sergeant Jensen. I'm working on the Tinka Winther case."

"Is that why you're here, outside my house?" He waited as Petra turned to look at the man sitting next to her. Malik took a step closer and peered into the interior. "I don't know you."

"My name is Maratse."

"And you're working the case too?" Malik shook his head. "Two police officers, outside my house, on a Saturday night. Is that really the best use of police resources? I'm sure there are plenty of drunks you could pick up in town."

Petra sighed. "My shift finished an hour ago."

"Really?"

"And I'm not a police officer," Maratse said, and opened the passenger door.

Malik watched him as he took a long time to walk around the front of the car. "Then what are you doing here? Is this some form of harassment?"

"I really wish it was," Petra said. She shot a sharp look at Maratse as he leaned against the side of the car.

"Then one of you had better explain, before I call the Commissioner."

"You don't need to do that, Malik," Maratse said. "I just want to talk."

Petra stifled a laugh, as Malik looked at them both. "My *friend* has recently developed a chatty streak," she said.

"Piitalaat," Maratse said. "Please…"

"No, David," Petra said. She gripped the wheel. "I don't agree with you on this, and," she said, and looked at Malik, "I don't even want to be here."

Malik wiped the rain from his face. He blinked, as he tried to make sense of the conversation. He glanced over his shoulder at his house, almost wishing he was back in the kitchen, arguing with Naala. "What is this? It's like the good cop, bad cop scenario, except neither of you seems to know who is playing who. Why don't I leave you to it? I mean, if you want to figure out your problems, that's fine. I have plenty of my own."

"My friend is angry with me for making her come here tonight," Maratse said.

"I can see that. Why is that my problem?"

"You are a problem, and you have problems." Maratse lit a cigarette, and rolled it into the gap between his teeth. "You are a problem because your politics suggest my friend is not a true Greenlander." Maratse considered switching to Greenlandic, but continued in Danish. "She thinks you are splitting the country, and I agree with her. But that's not why we are here tonight."

"No? Good, because that would be harassment."

"We're here," Petra said, "because my friend is worried about you. He thinks you might do something stupid, or that someone might do something to you."

"Like what? What are we talking about? Why would I do anything stupid?"

"When did you last speak with Aarni Aviki?" Maratse asked.

"Early this morning. Why?"

"He has had a difficult day."

"Has something happened to Aarni?" Malik looked at Petra. "Tell me."

Petra bit her lip, as she thought about what to say. "He committed suicide."

"What?" Malik looked at Maratse. "What did she say?"

"We found his body a few hours ago," Petra said, and glanced at the house. "Is your wife home?"

"Yes," Malik said. He jerked his hands; palms open, and said, "My wife, my kids, everyone's home. Why?"

"That's good," Maratse said. "We're going to stay out here tonight. Perhaps you should get a good night's sleep, prepare for your debate."

"We're sorry about Mr Aviki," Petra said. "Get some rest."

Malik took a step backwards, staring at Maratse and Petra, confused by what they said. Naala met him at the front door, peering around his shoulder at the police car.

"What do they want?"

"They want to make sure I am okay."

"Are they going to stay there all night?"

"Yes." Malik reached out for Naala's hand. "Aarni's dead, Naala."

"What?"

"Suicide. They just told me."

"And that's why they are here?"

"Maybe. I don't know. I think they are protecting me."

"Malik," Naala said, "do you need protection?"

"I don't know."

Sapaat

SUNDAY

Chapter 17

Nivi Winther smiled at her secretary and signed three documents ready to be actioned after the weekend. The secretary paused, hovering at Nivi's desk until the First Minister looked up from her laptop screen. The look on her secretary's face suggested she wanted to express her sympathy for Nivi's loss, the third person to do so this morning, and likely not the last.

"Is everything all right, Bibi?"

"Yes, I just wanted to say..." Bibi paused, clutching the documents to her chest. "I wanted to say how sorry I am, about Tinka."

"It's kind of you to say so," Nivi said.

"If there's anything I can do."

"I'll be sure to ask." Nivi smiled and waited for Bibi to leave the room. She nodded when Bibi asked if she should close the door.

A moment's peace, that's what Nivi wanted most. As the door closed with a click, she leaned back in her chair and closed her eyes. She thought of Tinka's grave, looking out onto the icebergs in Uummannaq fjord. She could almost feel the cold breath of ice on her cheeks, freezing everything in its path, including the tears on her cheeks. Nivi realised she was crying, and opened her eyes. She brushed the tears from her face with her finger, and then swore when she realised her mascara would need fixing, again. It was going to be a long day.

Nivi searched for a distraction, picked her smartphone up from the desk, and called Maratse. She smiled as he answered, in the hope of portraying a positive vibe to hide her moment of sadness. "I just wanted to check-in," she said.

"*Iiji.*"

"Is everything all right? Any news?"

"Nothing yet."

"You're sure?" Nivi looked up as Daniel tapped on the glass in the door. She waved him in. "You sound tired, Constable."

"Everything is all right," Maratse said.

Nivi thanked him, ended the call with a tap of her thumb, and put her phone down. She waved at the chair in front of her desk and waited for Daniel to sit down.

"Constable?" he said. "I thought Sergeant Jensen was handling the case?"

"She is," Nivi said. "I just asked for a little more help."

"Asked? You mean you talked with the Commissioner? Nivi," Daniel said, "that could be seen as abusing police resources. What did the official report say?"

"You know what it said, Daniel."

"An accident." Daniel gestured with his hand. "Tinka's death was an accident. Albeit with a lot of unanswered questions, I understand." He stopped when he noticed Nivi's eyes. "I'm sorry," he said. "You've been crying. That was insensitive of me."

"It's all right, Daniel. I will cry a lot more before I am ready to move on."

"Then, perhaps we should discuss it again."

"It?" Nivi shook her head. "I'm going to the debate. I told you that the first time, the second, and the third. I don't want to talk about it again. That's final."

"Fine. I understand."

"Do you?"

"Of course," Daniel said. "The country needs to see you. They need to feel as though you can lead them, even in times of sorrow. But the funeral was on Friday, Nivi. It's too soon. There's a chance the people will think you are too strong. They might even think you are insensitive."

"If we cancel the debate, Malik Uutaaq wins. You said so."

"We don't have to cancel. There is an alternative."

"Ah, now we come to it." Nivi pushed back her chair and stood up. She walked to the window and leaned against the sill. "You want your moment, don't you, Daniel." She laughed. "And you call me insensitive?"

"It's the right thing to do," he said.

"For you, perhaps. But what about the party? Are you going to debate the politics of language with Malik Uutaaq? And turn the whole evening into a popularity contest. Because if you do, we will lose. Do you understand that?"

"Language is not the only topic for debate."

"It is for Malik Uutaaq."

"I've done a deal with Aarni Aviki. They're willing to debate everything."

"Really?"

"Yes."

"And what did you give away?"

"Nothing."

"I see." Nivi folded her arms. "Then what did you threaten him with?"

Daniel looked away for a moment. "I said I would go to the press."

"With what?" It hit Nivi a second later, and she didn't know if she should be angry or disgusted. "You used Tinka, didn't you?"

"I used what I had." Daniel recoiled in his chair as Nivi took a step towards him.

"I told you I didn't want that article out there." Nivi reached for her phone. "I told you that."

"Who are you calling?"

"The journalist."

"He's deaf, Nivi."

"I'll text him."

"You don't have to. He had nothing to do with it."

"Then tell me what you said to Aviki."

Daniel smoothed his hands on his trousers, steepled his fingers beneath his chin, and looked at Nivi. She tucked the phone into the crook of her arm, and waited.

"I told him we could confirm that Malik was with Tinka at a party before she died."

"And can we? Can we confirm that?"

"Does it matter?"

"It matters, Daniel," Nivi said, her voice rising, "because in just a few hours I will be standing next to a man who might have been the last person to see my daughter alive. He might even…" Nivi started to tremble.

"Yes?"

She lowered her voice, took a breath. "He might even have been responsible for her death somehow. He might even have killed her."

Daniel stood up and put his arm around Nivi's shoulders. He pulled her close, until her head was on his chest. Nivi closed her fist around her phone and leaned into Daniel's body. She trembled, and he held her tight.

"That's why," he whispered, "it should be me doing the debate, Nivi."

"No," she said, her voice muffled by his body.

"Think about it. Rest. Then we'll talk."

Daniel walked Nivi out of her office and down the hall to a lounge with a coffee machine and two long sofas. He guided Nivi onto the sofa furthest from the door, prised the phone from her hand, and placed it on the coffee table. There was a blanket at the far end of the sofa, and he tugged it over her body as she lifted her feet and laid her head on the pillow.

"Don't let me sleep too long," she said, as Daniel walked to the door and turned off the lights.

"I won't," he said, and closed the door.

Nivi let herself drift back to the icebergs in the fjord, as she watched Tinka run along a sandy beach, chasing the spumes of mist from the whales as they surfaced far out in the depths of the fjord. Life was simpler in the north, and harsher. Help, of any kind, was further away. Families had to provide for one another, and rivalry, no matter how strong, and for whatever the reason, had to be overcome, especially now, at the onset of winter.

She woke when Bibi whispered that it was time for her to wake up. Nivi smelled fresh coffee, and wiped her eyes as she sat up and pulled the blanket to one side. She reached for the coffee on the table, and took a bite of the bread and cheese that Bibi had prepared.

"I thought Daniel would wake me," she said.

"He asked me to."

"Where is he?"

"At Katuaq, getting ready for the debate."

Nivi bit back a remark and took another deliberate sip of coffee. She couldn't recall when Daniel had begun to make his play for her position, but she realised she wasn't surprised, just angry that he had chosen to use Tinka as leverage.

"Okay," she said. "Did he leave a message?"

"No," Bibi said, and shook her head. Nivi noticed the twitch of the muscle in the young woman's cheek, but decided not to press her.

"Thank you for the coffee," Nivi said, and stood up. "I'll just freshen up, and then we can walk to Katuaq together."

"Yes, First Minister," Bibi said.

Bibi tidied away the coffee and remains of Nivi's sandwich as Nivi used the bathroom. When Nivi came out, Bibi was dressed for the rain, and had Nivi's jacket over one arm, and her smartphone in her hand.

"I'll need my notes," Nivi said, and took a step towards her office.

"I have them here." Bibi turned to reveal Nivi's bag hanging from her shoulder.

"You've thought of everything."

"Yes," Bibi said, and beamed. "I just want to help."

"And on a Sunday, too. *Qujanaq*."

Nivi put on her jacket, slipped her phone into her pocket, and slung her bag over one shoulder. Bibi walked with her to the door, and they braved a deluge of rain as they hurried across the car park to the entrance of the Katuaq Cultural Centre. They slipped inside and shook the rain from their jackets, invigorated at the blast of fresh air they had just received. Bibi took Nivi's jacket, and said she would wait for her behind the cameras. As she walked away, Nivi caught a glimpse of Maratse sitting at a table in the café by the entrance.

"We're ready for you, First Minister," said a woman from the television studio.

"Just a minute," Nivi said, and walked over to Maratse. "Constable," she said, "it's good to see you." Maratse stood up, and shook Nivi's hand. "You're alone?"

"Sergeant Jensen is inside," he said. "In the audience."

"I see. And you're not coming inside?"

"I don't like politics," he said.

"Constable," she said, and leaned in closer to Maratse. "I want you in the audience. I want you to watch Malik Uutaaq."

"He's no danger to you. And Gaba Alatak is here to provide security."

"I'm not paying you to be my bodyguard, Constable," Nivi said, and checked the irritation in her voice. "I just want you to observe Uutaaq, as part of your investigation."

"I'm not worried about him."

"Well," Nivi said, as the studio assistant called her name, "perhaps you should be."

Nivi strode away from Maratse, and followed the woman from the studio all the way to the temporary make-up room squeezed into a corner of the space behind the stage. Nivi could hear the audience being seated as she sat down and closed her eyes. The light brush of powder on her cheeks tickled, and she focussed on it, calming her nerves and finding a space in her mind within which she could function. Somewhere she had a semblance of control, no matter what forces pulled at her from the outside.

The sense of calm diminished at the sound of a quiet cough to her right. She opened her eyes and saw Daniel standing next to the tall police officer she recognised as the leader of the SRU.

"You forgot to wake me, Daniel," she said.

"I thought it best you get as much rest as possible," he said.

"I bet you did." Nivi looked at Gaba. "Sergeant Alatak. What can I do for you?"

"I want to give you some advance warning, before the debate."

"About what?"

"Excuse me," Daniel said to the make-up assistant, "can you give us some privacy?" The woman nodded, placed her brush on the table, and walked away. Nivi noticed that Daniel was also wearing a light brush of powder on his cheeks. They made eye contact and he retreated a step, nodding at Gaba that he should continue.

"There's been a development in the investigation," Gaba said, "and I am ready to bring Malik Uutaaq down to the station for questioning."

"You're going to arrest him?" Nivi asked.

"I'm going to bring him in," Gaba said.

"That's different?"

"Nivi," Daniel said, "there's something more. The police found Aarni Aviki last night. He committed suicide, and there was a Dictaphone in his pocket."

"What?" Nivi frowned. This was moving too fast.

"The tape confirms that Malik Uutaaq was with your daughter, and that Aarni knew it all along." Daniel paused to swap a look with Gaba. He looked at Nivi. "Maybe now you'll agree that it is best that I do the debate. I mean, it's clear," he said, and placed his hand on her shoulder, "you're in shock. It's understandable. Anyone would be."

"No," Nivi said, "I have to do this. For Tinka." She tried to stand, but Daniel increased the pressure on her shoulder, just enough to push her back down onto the chair.

"Tinka is the reason you shouldn't do this. The police want to question Malik Uutaaq in connection with her murder…"

"I didn't say that," Gaba said.

"I know," Daniel said and let go of Nivi's shoulder. "But still, it's likely he was involved somehow."

"I didn't say that either."

"Excuse me, Sergeant Alatak," Daniel said. "Can you give the First Minister and me a moment?" Daniel waited until Gaba retreated to the shadows beside the stage entrance. "Think about it, Nivi. This is an important event. It could decide the outcome of the election. Can you honestly look at Malik Uutaaq without seeing the face of Tinka's murderer?"

"I…" Nivi started to speak, but Daniel interrupted, his voice a harsh whisper.

"Think about it, carefully. This man slept with Tinka…"

"Daniel stop," Nivi said and lifted her hand, pushing at his face as he leaned closer.

"… he put her in a boat, and he sailed all the way north…"

"Daniel…"

"All the way to Inussuk, so he could kill her right in front of your childhood home."

"You don't know that," she said, her voice trembling, tears glistening on her powdered cheeks. Nivi wiped at them as Gaba walked over. "I'm all right," she said, as he put his hand on Daniel's chest, and pushed him away from her.

"I'll do the debate," Daniel said, as he brushed free of Gaba's grip. "You need to rest, Nivi."

And there it was, her way out. Daniel could stand in for her, and she wouldn't need to be strong for Greenland, or even for Tinka. No one would think any less of her. She had buried her daughter just a matter of hours ago. It was perfectly normal. Understandable. She could walk away, and she almost did.

How far would you go, mum?

Nivi shook a little as she looked up, convinced it was Tinka's voice she had just heard. But, of course, it couldn't be. The question, however, was valid.

"How far would I go?" Nivi whispered. She caught the quizzical look on Daniel's face, and she repeated the question, changing it ever so slightly to say, "How far do you want me to go?"

"I don't understand," he said.

"Don't you?" Nivi almost laughed. She wiped her cheeks with the back of her hand and waved for the make-up assistant to come over. "Malik Uutaaq might be a monster," she said, "but he's innocent until proven guilty. Right now, the only thing he is guilty of doing is causing a rift between the people of this country. I can stop him. For Tinka, and for all the young men and women, mothers and fathers like her, the ones who call Greenland home." Nivi took a long breath and a long look at Daniel. "You're right about one thing, Daniel. I am in shock. But so is the country, and it is time to do something about it."

Nivi sat down and closed her eyes as the assistant applied a new brush of powder to her cheeks. When she opened her eyes again, Daniel was gone. She heard the audience fidget at the arrival of Malik Uutaaq, and she opened her eyes.

"I'm ready," she said.

Chapter 18

From his table in the café Maratse had a good view of the guests as they arrived. He saw Malik Uutaaq and his wife walk through the main entrance. Naala pointed at Maratse, but Malik took her arm and led her into the auditorium. They had been gone less than ten minutes when he heard raised voices coming from the studio, followed by a crash of wood, and what could have been a camera toppling over.

"What's going on?" he said, as Petra darted out of the auditorium.

"It's Uutaaq," Petra said. "He's running away."

Petra grabbed Maratse by the arm and dragged him in the direction of the cloakroom and toilets at the far end of the cultural centre, past the main auditorium. Maratse grunted at the pain, found a rhythm, and picked up speed. The smell of rain on the wind blustered through the emergency exit, as the door swept back and forth across the slight concrete ramp that merged with the gravel and stones of Nuuk's untamed surfaces. Petra stopped, her hand shielding her eyes from the rain as she searched for signs of the pursuit.

"He came this way," she said.

"What happened?" Maratse slowed to a halt beside her. His legs palsied for a moment, before the pain was renewed and he bit down on this tongue and worked hard to control his breathing.

"Malik was on his way to the podium, and then Daniel Tukku came onto the stage, looking pretty pissed-off," Petra said. She stopped when she saw Maratse biting back the pain, but he urged her to continue with a wave of his hand. "From where I was sitting, I saw Daniel shake Malik's hand, and then he leaned in close to say something in Malik's ear. After that, Malik recoiled, ripped his hand free of Daniel's, and ran for the exit."

"And Daniel?"

"He did his best to look bewildered, but I'm sure I saw him hide a smirk behind his hand. Miki, one of Gaba's team, pushed through the crowd from the back of the room, and Gaba was on Malik's heels, from the moment he started to run." Petra took a step closer to Maratse, dipped her head to look at his face, and sighed when he smiled. "How about I get a car?"

"That would be good," he said.

Petra ran back inside as Maratse walked across the rough ground behind the centre to the road. He blinked in the flash of blue lights, as Petra slewed the police Toyota to a stop at the curb. Maratse walked around the front of the car and climbed in. Petra accelerated towards the town centre as Maratse buckled his seatbelt. The radio in the centre of the dashboard chattered with updates and positive sightings. Gaba's voice burst through the static as he gave directions. Malik had just run inside Hotel Hans Egede.

Petra turned on the siren and stomped on the accelerator. Maratse glanced at her face, resisting the temptation to smile at the concentration evident in the way she pressed her lips flat, ignoring the loose strands of wet hair clinging to her forehead and cheeks. Petra swung a hard right onto the road running through the centre of Nuuk. She braked outside the main entrance to the hotel, and rolled the window down.

"Go around, to the rear," Miki shouted from the steps. Maratse noted he had his hand on the grip of his pistol.

Petra acknowledged Miki with a nod, jerked the Toyota into first gear and then braked as a second patrol car shot between the row of taxis parked alongside the pavement. She swore, and then followed the police car through the gap passing beneath the first floor of the hotel.

Maratse reached out and squeezed Petra's arm. "Easy," he said.

"Right." Petra slowed the Toyota to a crawl as they drove past Gaba. He waved them on, and then they heard his voice on the radio, telling all those involved in the search that he was going back inside the hotel.

"He might have doubled back," he said. "Put a car at the end of the road, near the gym."

"That's us," Petra said, as she grabbed the radio and told everyone she was taking that position. Petra roared up the road as the other police car turned and headed back towards the hotel. Petra turned in the gravel parking area of the cross-fit gym and pointed the Toyota back towards the hotel. She switched off the emergency lights and took a breath. A few seconds later she turned the engine off and Maratse looked up as the rain drummed on the roof.

"Why would he run? Where would he go?"

"That's two questions," Maratse said.

"All right, pick one."

"He ran because Daniel told him to."

"Because Gaba was there to pick him up?"

"*Iiji.*"

"And where? Where would he go? Unless he went to the docks, there's no way out of Nuuk. Unless you climb over the mountains."

Maratse sighed at the thought. The pain in his legs had become tolerable when walking, but irregular movement such as running spiralled the pain through his nerves. The thought of climbing mountains was unbearable. He chose to think instead.

"So, he's running because he's guilty?" Petra said, as she peered down the dark street.

"Of what?"

"Sleeping with Tinka Winther."

"Tinka was seventeen. It's not a crime."

"If he forced her."

"We don't know that he did. The only thing that connects Malik with Tinka is his daughter's winter jacket."

"That's enough to begin with." Petra looked at Maratse for a moment, the lights of the radio reflected in her eyes. "I thought you were on my side?"

"I don't understand."

"That man, everything he stands for, is driving a wedge between the people of this country, even between me and my friends, and now you."

"I am still your friend, Piitalaat."

"But you are on his side."

"No," Maratse said. "I just don't think he killed Tinka."

Gaba's voice burst through the speakers of the radio, a little out of breath, but triumphant. Malik was in custody, and on his way back to the station.

"That's it then," Petra said, and started the car. "We'll soon find out."

"Will Gaba do the interview?" Maratse asked.

"Initially, yes."

"Then drop me off at Nivi's office."

"Okay," Petra said. She pulled onto the road and drove at a sedate pace past the hotel, across the main road, past the police station and around the back of the government building. She parked and turned off the engine.

"You're coming with me?" Maratse asked, as he unbuckled his belt and opened the passenger door.

"Yes," she said. "It's been a long night, and another long day. It will feel good to tell her we have taken Malik into custody. It might even help her relax."

Maratse followed Petra to the main doors. They buzzed to be let in, and then waved at a cleaner mopping the floor. He opened the door, and said he was the only one in the building.

"The lights are lit on the second floor," Petra said. "Mind if we go and look?" The cleaner shook his head and Petra led Maratse to the elevator. "It is Sunday," she said, as the doors closed.

They got out on the second floor and walked towards Nivi's office. There was a shadow of movement in the office next to hers, and Maratse recognised Nivi's secretary. She bumped into them as she walked out of the office into the corridor.

"I'm sorry," she said. She looked at their black jackets, and covered her mouth with her hand. "Has something happened?"

"We were just coming to see the First Minister," Petra said. "Is she here?"

Bibi shook her head. She looked at Maratse. "We came here after the commotion in the auditorium. She rested for a short while on the sofa, and then Daniel came over."

"Where did she go then?"

"He took her home."

"Okay," Petra said, as Maratse pulled his mobile out of his pocket. He studied the screen for a second, opened the list of contacts and used the cursor to click Nivi's name. Petra waited as he held the mobile to his ear, but Nivi didn't answer. "I'll try Daniel," she said. Maratse nodded and took Bibi to one side as Petra dialled.

"How was she when Daniel arrived?"

"She was angry. She thinks he said something to Malik Uutaaq."

"And what did he say to that?"

"He said the debate was over, that the police were talking to Malik, and that there was nothing more they could do today. He said something about getting ready for the media on Monday."

"Tomorrow."

"Yes."

Petra slipped her smartphone into her pocket, and shook her

head. "He's not answering either."

"Bibi," Maratse said, "where does Daniel live?"

"In Qinngorput. One of the new apartments."

"Which block?" asked Petra.

"Five."

Petra nodded at Maratse, and they started to walk towards the elevators.

"Is everything all right?" Bibi called after them.

"*Iji*," Maratse said. "Go home. It's been a long day." He waved as they entered the elevator.

"Why Daniel's apartment?" Petra asked, as they walked out of the building and got in the car. "Shouldn't we go to Nivi's house? That's where Bibi said he was taking her." She started the car and began driving towards the new area of Nuuk called Qinngorput.

Maratse stretched his legs and then glanced at the clock on the dashboard. "Faster, Piitalaat."

Petra turned on the emergency lights and the siren. She buckled her belt with one hand. "Back-up?" she said, and reached for the radio.

"*Iji*," Maratse said. He slid his arm into the handle in the door panel, as Petra called for assistance, and accelerated. She weaved the Toyota in and out of the light traffic heading out of the centre, slowed as a bus pulled out, and then gunned the Toyota past the bus and up the hill. Maratse tried calling Nivi a second time, stuffing the mobile back in his pocket when she didn't answer.

"It could be nothing," Petra said, as she braked into the curve of a roundabout, and accelerated out of it. The rain drummed on the roof and splashed from the bonnet onto the windscreen. Petra turned the wipers on full, and concentrated on the road as it dipped past the turning to the airport. The apartment towers of Qinngorput were visible across the black water of the fjord as Petra sped up the hill. She glanced at the rear view mirror, as a flash of blue lights caught her eye.

"Maybe," Maratse said.

"But you don't think so?"

"I think Daniel has worked hard to make sure everything points at Malik Uutaaq."

"If you're right, then he doesn't need to do anymore."

"If I'm right," Maratse said, and looked at Petra, "he's just getting started."

"I'm not sure I follow…" Petra's words caught in her throat, as a black American import clipped the driver's side of the Toyota, forcing them off the road and into a wall of granite through which the road had been cut. Petra gasped as the front end of the Toyota crumpled and the rear wheels lifted on impact. The engine stalled as the back end of the car bounced back onto the road and the black car disappeared down the hill and into the night.

"Piitalaat," Maratse said, as he tried to release the seatbelt clamping him to the passenger seat. He reached out to touch Petra; her head was slumped on her chest, and blood trickled from her nose. The siren of the police car they had called for back-up wailed as it crested the rise of the hill. The Toyota skidded to a stop in the gravel beside them. The policeman in the passenger seat leaped out of the car and ran towards them, as the driver backed up and positioned the police car in the road, lights flashing. The siren stopped as the policeman opened Petra's door.

"Are you hurt?"

"I'm okay," Petra said, the words slurring out of her mouth. "Did you see him?"

"Who?"

"The car that hit us," Maratse said. "A large American car. Black."

"We didn't see it happen. You were just on the other side of the hill." The policeman looked at his partner as he jogged over to Maratse's side of the crumpled Toyota. "Did you see a black import?"

"Yeah, it passed us just as we were coming up the hill."

"Did you happen to see the driver?" Petra asked.

"Not clearly. But it was a male."

"Was there a passenger?" Maratse asked, as the man cut him free of the belt pinning him to the seat.

"Yes. Female, maybe. It was dark," he said, and helped Maratse out of the car.

"Get on the radio, and put out the description of the car," Petra said, as the policeman walked her away from the car and over to the rock wall by the side of the road. "And," she said, as the policeman encouraged her to sit, "we need to find Daniel Tukku and Nivi Winther."

"The First Minister?"

"Yes, the First Minister," Petra said. She nodded as the policeman took a step back and made the call on his radio. She closed her eyes when she heard the static response that his request had been received and broadcasted.

"I need to stand," Maratse said, as the policeman walked him over to where Petra was sitting.

"Sure, go ahead. We'll have an ambulance here any minute."

Petra held up her hand and Maratse took it. She leaned her head back and looked at him. "What were you saying? Something about him just getting started?"

"Daniel?"

"Yes."

"He's the only one to gain from any of this."

"What do you mean?"

"If Malik is revealed to be a hypocrite… because of his affair with Tinka Winther…"

"*Seqinnersoq* loses the popular vote."

"He can't take the risk that Tinka would say it wasn't Malik she was seeing. So he kills her, and frames Malik by dressing Tinka in the jacket…"

"That belongs to Malik's daughter." Maratse squeezed Petra's hand. He let go and bit his lip as he sat down.

"I thought it was better to stand?"

"But I am getting dizzy," he said, and sat down beside Petra.

"Everything changed with Aviki's suicide tape. It was very convenient." Petra looked at Maratse. "You don't think it was suicide, do you?"

"*Eeqqi.*" Maratse shook his head.

"You think Daniel forced him to make the link between Malik and Tinka?"

Maratse nodded. "And it was a mistake. He didn't think it through, but he enjoyed it. Maybe even more than what he did to Tinka. It got the better of him."

"*If* he killed her. We don't know for sure. There's no evidence."

"Which is why we need to find him. He might have discredited Malik, but Nivi could still lead the country."

"And Daniel needs her out of the way, if he is going to have any kind of power."

"*Iiji.*"

Petra wiped a clot from her nose, and then pressed her hand beneath it to stem the flow of more blood. She swore and squirmed her hand into her jacket pocket for a tissue. The rain soaked into the packet as she wrestled one free, pressing the soggy mess of paper against her nose.

"This is hopeless," she said.

A siren wailed up the hill as an ambulance stopped beside the two police cars. The paramedics walked over to assess Petra's injuries, checking Maratse a moment later. Petra called to the policemen.

"I need one of you to call the Commissioner. Ask him to meet us at the hospital."

"Is that necessary? It's Sunday night, Sergeant."

"Didn't you hear what I said about the First Minister?"

"Yes…"

Petra stared at him as the paramedics helped her onto a stretcher. The man nodded, and grabbed his radio.

Chapter 19

Just as Daniel coasted to a stop in the black Dodge RAM, the sodium lamp above the fishing trawler that was idling at the far end of the quay extinguished with a soft thump. He turned off the engine and leaned over the handbrake to tighten the knot of rope binding Nivi Winther's wrists. He winked at her as she followed his every move, her gaze glued to his face. He reached up and tugged at a corner of the duct tape covering her mouth. It was still secure. Daniel leaned back in his seat and tapped a beat on the steering wheel, rising in tempo as a crewman from the trawler walked down the gangplank and onto the quay. The crewman stared through the windscreen, first at Daniel, and then at his passenger. Daniel waved and lowered the driver's window.

"Everything all right?" he asked.

"We're ready to go," the man said. He looked at Nivi and lowered his voice. "Will this come back to us?"

"No," Daniel said, "of course not."

"I'm not so sure."

"I will take care of it," Daniel said. "Just get me to Ilulissat."

The crewman looked at his watch. "The captain says we'll be there before dawn, if we go now."

"Then let's go," Daniel said, and opened the door. He jogged around the front of the big American car, and made a theatrical bow before opening the passenger door. "First Minister," he said and reached over to unbuckle her seatbelt, "your cruise starts now. If you would be so kind as to…"

Nivi kicked Daniel in the knee as he pulled her out of the passenger seat. He buckled and she aimed another kick at his body, but her leg bounced off his side, and she stumbled. Nivi's smartphone skittered onto the quay, as Daniel recovered. He grimaced as he marched past Nivi to pick up her phone. He tossed it over the side, the tiny splash of water barely audible, as he grabbed Nivi by the arm and dragged her up the gangplank and onto the deck of the trawler.

"Hey," the crewman called out from the quay, "what about the car?"

"It's not mine," Daniel said. He opened the door to the wheelhouse, pulled Nivi up the short ladder and thrust her onto the bench. Nivi's coat caught on the corner of the table and he wrenched it free. The captain turned at the commotion and tensed at the sight of Nivi.

"Is that who I think it is?" he said, his voice coarse like the seabed.

"Yes," Daniel said. He slapped at the dirt on his trousers and looked at the captain. "What? Is there a problem?"

"There could be."

"Only if you don't get a move on. Listen," Daniel said, "if you want us off your boat before it gets light. I suggest you get going." He turned at the sound of the crewman drawing the gangplank onboard the trawler. "He has the right idea."

"You never said it would be her."

"That's right, I didn't." Daniel waved his hand at Nivi. "I ask you again. Do we have a problem?"

"No."

"And the money?"

"Now the money makes sense." The captain turned on the trawler's lights and the crewman on the deck looked up at the wheelhouse, shielding his eyes with his hand. The captain opened a window and gave the order to cast off the ropes.

The diesel engines vibrated through the deck as the captain reversed a short distance, before levering the trawler into gear and pulling away from the quay. Daniel pressed his face against the window as they passed two more fishing trawlers and an adventure cruise ship pushing the limits of the Greenland sailing season. He started to relax as the captain pulled away from Nuuk and increased speed. If the weather did not change drastically, as it often did in Greenland, Daniel knew that they would make good time along the coast, and that his own modest powerboat would have no problems sailing north from Ilulissat and around the Uummannaq peninsula. The First Minister didn't know it yet, but he was taking her home, to see her daughter.

Daniel sat down beside Nivi as the captain changed the interior lighting to a red glow, and the crewman entered the wheelhouse.

"Everything's stowed," he said to the captain. He ignored the passengers.

"Good." The captain pointed at the coffee machine. "Make a fresh pot, and then go below. I'll call you when I want to be relieved."

"Right, boss."

Daniel leaned close to Nivi as the crewman prepared the coffee. He whispered in her ear, "You might want to rest. It's been a busy day, and you have another long day ahead of you tomorrow." He kicked off his shoes and stretched his legs beneath the table, propping his feet up on the opposite bench. The trawler rose over a gentle wave as they cleared the mouth of the fjord. Daniel waited for the crewman to go below and then closed his eyes.

Nivi fidgeted beside Daniel, but he did his best to ignore her. He had given her every opportunity to take a step back, to take it easy. But she had chosen to make life difficult. He teased at the thought as he clicked through his actions over the past week. Everything was fitting into place, exactly as he had imagined it would. He had planned every move, every detail, all the way back to the last day of the school term in June, before they broke up for the long summer holiday. Daniel almost smiled at the ease with which he had walked into the school and picked up Pipaluk Uutaaq's winter clothes, carrying them over his arm like any other parent.

The trawler lifted over the crest of another shallow wave. Daniel opened one eye, watched the captain as he casually sipped at his coffee, and then glanced at Nivi, who was wide-eyed, frantic.

"Go to sleep," he said, and closed his eyes.

His masterstroke, he felt, was Aarni Aviki's suicide. It had been difficult to wait until Tinka Winther's body had been found to make the connection between Uutaaq and her death. There had been a time, he recalled, when he had worried that she would never be found. And so, he had to put Aarni Aviki in the spotlight, and a suicide note was the perfect solution, perhaps the only solution.

Of course, the irony was not lost on Daniel Tukku. All this work, all this effort, his *machinations* as he liked to call them, was ultimately going to be for nothing. Any success he might have achieved, any power he might have gained, was lost the moment he abducted Greenland's First Minister. He could sense a feeling of regret. But that regret was easily matched with the feeling of power far sweeter than political leadership, the power over life itself.

He opened his eyes and looked at Nivi, searching for the fear that flickered across her cheeks in tiny muscle twitches. He felt aroused, all of a sudden, even at the tiny blister of red skin tracing the edges of the tape sealing her mouth. An allergic reaction, perhaps. He lowered his gaze to look at her hands, titillating himself at the sight of the blush of irritation where the rope scratched at her wrists. He looked at her eyes last, and was almost lost in the exhilaration that rushed through his body at the sight of pure, naked fear, the terror of not knowing one's fate.

He knew then that he could not sleep. But he would close his eyes, because there, in the darkness, he could replay and rerun his first exploration of true power, when he pinned and penetrated Nivi's daughter in the fear-stoked cabin of his motorboat. And soon, he realised, he would do it all over again, with the mother.

Such thoughts, replayed over and over, entertained Daniel all the way up the coast from Nuuk to Ilulissat, and it was only when the captain shook his arm that he realised they had arrived. Everything was going to plan. He was but minutes away from satisfaction, and he intended to enjoy it. But the gun in the captain's hand confused him, and he was suddenly alert.

"What's this?"

"A handgun," the captain said. "Empty, of course, but," he said, and shrugged, "I just wanted you to see it."

"It's illegal to have a handgun in Greenland," Daniel said, and took the gun when the captain offered it to him.

"Yes," the captain said, with a nod at Nivi, "but then, present circumstances…"

Daniel raised his eyebrows and handed the gun back to the captain. "It's nice."

"It's insurance." The captain slid a pen through the trigger guard and dropped the gun inside a plastic bag.

"Wait," Daniel said. He looked at the captain, and then at the long fillet knife in the crewman's hands, as he climbed up the ladder and into the wheelhouse. "What are you doing?"

"You haven't paid us yet," the captain said. He jerked his thumb over his shoulder in the direction of the Ilulissat marina. The sky was a hazy blue and pink as the sun strained at the limits of its early winter zenith, lighting the snow-clad mountains as it began a slow circle on a low horizon.

"I have the money on my boat. Take me there, and I will pay you. Just as we agreed."

The captain nodded at the crewman and crossed the wheelhouse floor to steer the boat the last hundred metres inside the marina. "Where's your boat?" he asked

"It should be alongside the quay. I paid extra to have it moored close to where you can pull alongside." Daniel stood up and walked to the stand next to the captain. "There," he said, and pointed at a large motorboat with a lighting flash painted on the hull. He glanced at the pistol inside the plastic bag before the captain tucked it into a cupboard to his right.

"If I need to," the captain said, "I can say you forced me to do this, with my own gun."

"An illegal gun," Daniel said.

"Given the scale of things," the captain said with a look at Daniel, "I hardly think that will matter."

"You're probably right."

A sudden pang of fear threatened to spoil everything, but he wouldn't let it. He looked at Nivi, her head trembling, and felt a charge of excitement once again. It threatened to consume him, and he searched again for that fear in his gut, that things might not go to plan, and he found the balance, the focus he needed to execute his plan with a clear mind. And then, he realised, it was time, as the crewman opened the door of the wheelhouse, and lowered fenders on a long rope between his boat and the trawler.

The fresh air roused Nivi, and the captain idled the boat, clicking the gears into neutral.

"Make it quick," he said, as he scanned the docks for signs of activity. He saw only ravens and a single light in the office of the harbour master, partly obscured as it was by a stack of shipping containers.

Daniel gripped Nivi's arm, dragged her onto her feet and pushed her down the ladder. The crewman had a long gaff, hooked around the railings of Daniel's boat, and a ladder hanging over the side of the trawler. Nivi's shoes skittered on the icy deck, and she would have slipped if the crewman had not reached out and caught her with his spare hand. He let go just as quickly, as if she was a disease and he was now infected. Daniel slid his shoes across the deck and forced Nivi down the ladder. He felt the muscles in his arm tremble as he clutched the rope between her wrists and lowered her onto the deck of his boat. He let go and she crashed onto the deck, too dazed to run. Daniel slid down the ladder, grabbed Nivi by the hair, and pulled her to the covered cockpit. He fumbled with the lock of the cabin door, and then thrust Nivi inside as soon as it was open.

"Hey," the crewman called out. "You're forgetting something."

"Just wait," Daniel said. He ducked inside the cabin, and kneeled on Nivi as he pulled a small holdall out of a storage space and carried it onto the deck. The crewman used the hook of the gaff to take the holdall from Daniel's hands and lift it onboard the trawler. Daniel tapped his leg as the crewman unzipped the holdall, nodded at Daniel and gave a thumbs-up to the captain. Daniel had barely acknowledged the crewman before the captain clicked the trawlers engines into reverse and backed away from the dock.

Daniel reached inside the cabin and grabbed an insulated floatation suit and a pair of thick rubber boots. He pulled on his sailing gear, tossed his city shoes inside the cabin, and locked the door. Daniel sat in the captain's chair, primed and started the engine, and let it idle as he untied the ropes and slipped his boat free of the quay. He grinned as his boat bobbed in the wake of the trawler.

The icefjord in Ilulissat might have made the town famous, especially in the fervour of interest in global warming, but Daniel was about to put the town on a very different map, as the starting point of a most wicked and deeply satisfying act of cruelty. His only regret, he realised, was not knowing what he would do after he was finished with Nivi Winther. The twinge of excitement he felt, combined with the flush of adrenaline in his body, reassured him that he didn't really care.

Daniel clicked the motorboat into gear and pointed the nose out of the harbour towards the open sea. The pink glow of the sun was fusing with the blue sky above the gargantuan bergs of the fjord, but Daniel was far too focussed on the thoughts of what he had hidden in the cabin of his boat to worry about the start of a beautiful Arctic day in Greenland. The long winter dark might be another month or two away, but for some people, the darkness had already descended, and the world had turned black as death.

Chapter 20

Maratse had to admit that the Commissioner made an impressive entrance when he strode into the emergency room at Dronning Ingrid's Infirmary, flanked as he was by Gaba and Miki in full SRU kit. After a cursory glance at Maratse and Petra, Lars Andersen asked the hospital staff to leave the room and pointed at Gaba.

"Status on Malik Uutaaq?" he said.

"Confused and confessing," Gaba said, "but unhurt."

"Confessing to what?"

"Sleeping with the First Minister's daughter."

"Any comment on the clothing, the jacket found on Tinka Winther?"

"None. He doesn't know how it got there."

"All right," the Commissioner said, drumming his fingers on his thigh. He glanced at the door, and gestured for Miki to stand next to it. "Second," he said, and pointed at Petra. "Status?"

"On the First Minister?" she asked.

"On you, Sergeant, and," he said, with a nod at Maratse, "on our special Constable, here."

"We're fine."

"Good to go?"

"Yes," Petra said. She looked at Maratse, and he nodded.

The Commissioner gestured for Gaba to step closer, and lowered his voice. "Here's what's happened since Petra and Maratse arrived in the ambulance. Gaba, fill me in if I forget anything."

"Yes, sir."

The Commissioner took a breath, and began. "Since the debate and the apprehending of Malik Uutaaq, we believe that Daniel Tukku has abducted the First Minister. His motive, at this time is unknown, as are his whereabouts, or those of Nivi Winther. However, we believe them to be together. We strongly suspect that they are at sea, most likely in a fishing trawler. How am I doing, Gaba?"

"Just fine, sir," Gaba said. He adjusted the Heckler & Koch MP5 slung around his chest. "I can add that a black Dodge RAM, belonging to Malik Uutaaq, was found on the quay down at the docks. Malik's wife, Naala Uutaaq, confirmed that it was stolen from the parking area at the Katuaq Cultural Centre, sometime during the debate. The panel on the driver's side shows signs of an impact that fits with the description of the collision Petra and Maratse were involved in. The occupants of the car have yet to be identified, but I think we can all agree that there is a high chance it was Tukku and the First Minister."

Maratse longed for a cigarette, but put the thought from his mind, as he thought about what they knew was true, what they supposed was going to happen. It all depended, he realised, on where Tukku was taking the First Minister. An idea began to grow in Maratse's mind, and it made sense if, as he believed, Daniel Tukku had shifted his focus from political power to something more perverse. Petra shot him a quizzical look, but he kept the thought to himself.

"Until we can confirm their location, we have two choices," the Commissioner said, "and I don't like either of them."

"Go on, sir," said Gaba.

"One," he said. "We wait. We put as many eyes on the docks and airports as possible, but I don't have to tell any of you, that it will take time and it will stretch our resources. If Nivi Winther is still in Nuuk, we can do a house-to-house search, and I am ready to do that, but as soon as word gets out that we are searching for her, we risk forcing Daniel to do something stupid. It could get ugly. Waiting, in the hope that this is a hostage situation, may be the smartest thing to do. It just doesn't feel particularly proactive."

"What's the second option, sir?" Petra asked.

"We get a small team aboard the King Air, ready to fly and intercept Daniel, and bring the First Minister home safely."

"My team is ready, sir."

"I know, Gaba," the Commissioner said. "We just don't know where to send them. Unless anyone has any ideas?"

"I think Maratse does," Petra said. "He has been the least distracted by the drama surrounding Malik Uutaaq. I think he might be able to point us in the right direction."

Maratse looked at Petra for a moment, as she mouthed the word *sorry*, and then he turned to the Commissioner. "Inussuk," he said. "He's taking her back to the scene of the crime."

"What crime?"

"The murder of Tinka Winther," Maratse said.

The Commissioner drummed his fingers again as he processed Maratse's hunch. He looked at Gaba. "What do you think?"

"If they sailed through the night?" he said, and shrugged. "Rain won't stop them, and the weather up north is good at the moment. They could get as far as Ilulissat, still further tomorrow, if we let them."

"If we let them?" the Commissioner said. "Explain."

"Stopping a trawler at night, at sea, will be dangerous. Better to get them on land, or in a more controlled environment."

"Such as?"

"If Maratse is right," Gaba said, "then it just might be that he intends to do something drastic in a place that is important to him. If he did kill the girl then it is likely that Inussuk and Uummannaq fjord is exactly where he will be headed. With good weather, good seas, and enough fuel, he can easily get there by the end of tomorrow."

"So," the Commissioner said, "you're saying that Tukku can be in Inussuk by Monday evening."

"Late afternoon at the earliest," Gaba said.

The Commissioner walked to the bed Petra was sitting on, and gestured for her to give him some room. He sat down as she moved and looked at Maratse.

"You think he will take her to Inussuk?"

"*Iiji*," Maratse said. He thought about it for a second, and then nodded.

"Gaba? Can you control that environment?"

"If we get there in good time, put a few boats in the water…" He shrugged. "Our biggest advantage would be surprise. But, sir, if he is going to do something to the First Minister, he could do it at any time. Worst case? We don't even find her body."

The Commissioner looked at Maratse again, gauging what he knew of his past, and wondering at his intuition. Maratse returned the Commissioner's look and rested his hands in his lap. The Commissioner gave Maratse a thin smile and then glanced at the door.

"Miki," he said, "come over here for a minute."

Miki adjusted his MP5 and walked over to stand beside Gaba. The heavy tread of his boots squeaked on the linoleum floor.

"Sir," he said, and waited for the Commissioner to speak.

"Here's the plan," the Commissioner said. "Gaba, split your team in two. I'll keep one half in Nuuk, ready to assist in the house-to-house." Gaba nodded, as the Commissioner continued. "The four of you will fly to Qaarsut." The Commissioner lifted his hand as Gaba started to protest. "I am reinstating Constable Maratse for this one particular operation." He looked at Maratse, and said, "I'll get the paperwork drawn up as soon as we're done here, if, that is, you're willing to go with the team?"

Maratse nodded.

"Good," the Commissioner said. He unbuckled his utility belt and gave it to Maratse. "You can take my gun."

"Sir," Gaba said.

"You've got operational command, Gaba. Don't worry about that. But coordinate with the Uummannaq police, and see if they have a boat available. Have them meet you at the airport in Qaarsut. I'll have the hospital send two medics on the flight, so you have a team of six. Can you work with that?"

"Yes, sir," Gaba said. He turned to Miki and told him to bring the car to the door. When he was gone, Gaba looked at the Commissioner. "I think it is a mistake to bring Maratse in on this."

"It's my decision, Gaba."

"Yes, sir, but," he said with a glance at Maratse, "he is still recovering from whatever it is that happened to him. I need to know I can rely on every member of my team."

"Come on, Gaba," Petra said.

"It's okay," Maratse said. He gritted his teeth and slid off the side of the bed. Maratse picked up the Commissioner's utility belt, and buckled it around his waist. "Gaba is right. I am still recovering, but," he said, and flashed a toothy grin as he patted the belt at his waist, "now I am whole again."

"And ready to go?" the Commissioner said.

"*Iiji*," Maratse said. He nodded at the door, and said, "After you, Gaba."

Maratse bit back a gasp at the sudden flare of pain in his legs, and did his best to match the pace of the SRU leader to the police car. Gaba climbed into the passenger seat, as Petra and Maratse got into the back. Miki shifted the Toyota into first gear and waved at the ambulance to follow. He turned on the emergency lights and the siren and accelerated away from the hospital, cutting through traffic all the way to the airport.

Gaba gave radio commands to the remainder of his team in Nuuk, pausing once or twice to make a note of one detail or another.

Maratse pointed at the number of blue lights flashing at the entrance to the housing areas of Nuuk as the police began their search from one house to the next. The police department, Maratse realised, would be stretched to the limit. The blue lights faded from view as Miki turned onto the road leading to the airport, and accelerated out of the curve in the road at the end of the runway. Petra pointed at the Beechcraft King Air outside the hangar, navigation lights flashing. The gates were open, and Miki drove straight up to the aircraft, with the ambulance a second behind him. The team grabbed their gear from the vehicles, and boarded the plane. Four minutes later and they were in the air and flying north to Qaarsut, the gravel landing strip on the Uummannaq peninsula, just south of the settlement of Inussuk.

Maratse sat next to Petra and dozed as they flew north, waking briefly as Gaba confirmed that a trawler from Nuuk had been seen in Ilulissat a short time ago. Maratse looked out of the window, and realised he had slept for longer than he thought, as the sky brightened with a polar glow of pink and blue. They landed shortly after. Simonsen met them at the airport and drove them down to the hotel boat moored at the jetty, at one end of the beach in Qaarsut.

"You're back," Simonsen said to Maratse, as he gave him a hand onto the boat. "And with a gun?"

"Reinstated," Maratse said. "Temporarily."

"Is there a problem?" Gaba asked.

Simonsen paused for a moment, and then shook his head. He found a seat at the rear of the boat beside the driver.

As soon as everyone was onboard, Miki released the ropes and they pulled away from the jetty. Gaba waited until they were seated, before he started his briefing.

"We're expecting a boat from Ilulissat – large enough to manage a journey like that, so you don't have to worry about spotting anything that looks like a dinghy. It's probably white. As far as we know there are two people onboard, and yes, one of them is likely to be the First Minister."

"So, it's true then?" Simonsen said. "She has been abducted."

"That's what we think, yes." Gaba steadied himself with a hand on a seat as the driver increased power to move away from the wash of an iceberg rolling close to shore. "However, if we get a confirmed sighting somewhere else, then the objective is to get back to the airport as fast as possible." He paused to look at each member of the team, staring at Maratse for a moment, before looking away.

"What if we do see the boat?" asked one of the paramedics.

"We close the distance, as fast as possible," Gaba said, and glanced at the driver of the boat. The man nodded, and Gaba continued. "We'll hail the boat, and we will board it as efficiently as possible. That's Miki and me, if anyone is in doubt. Sergeant Jensen has command on this boat."

Petra identified herself with a wave of her hand. She slapped Maratse lightly on the thigh. "I'm in charge," she whispered.

"On the boat," he said.

"Sure, as soon as he is gone."

"You're going to push him overboard?"

"I might," she said, and grinned.

"When you're done, Sergeant," Gaba said. He looked at Miki, asked if he had forgotten anything, and then looked at his watch. "With the weather conditions as good as they are, we can expect them anytime from early afternoon. So, have some coffee, have a snack, but stay alert." He walked down the centre of the boat between the seats, and stopped beside the driver, describing what he thought would be a good course to sail, sweeping the mouth of the fjord to Inussuk and back again.

Petra stood up to get a coffee. Maratse worked his way to the bow of the boat, and stepped outside onto the small deck. He stood to one side and stuffed his hands inside the pockets of his jacket. The weight of the USP Compact pistol on his hip was familiar, as was the taste of the cigarette he rolled into the gap between his teeth. Petra opened the door and joined him on the deck, pressing a coffee into his hand. They scanned the water as they sipped coffee. Maratse finished his cigarette and flicked the butt into the sea.

"I can see why you like it here," Petra said. "It's beautiful. Peaceful."

"You could visit, when this is over," Maratse said.

"I'd like that."

An iceberg bigger than a shopping mall blocked their view of the mouth of the fjord. Gaba directed the driver around it. The cold air peeled off the iceberg in thick, heavy layers, and the spotters on the deck and the roof shivered in the breath of ice. Petra's hair turned white at the tips, and Maratse felt the familiar tickle in his nose, as the temperature dropped.

From the first dusting of snow at Tinka Winther's funeral, winter had crept down the mountain, from the white peaks of the summit, to the granite walls just above the settlement. The descent of winter could be measured in metres and degrees, but for all its beauty and brightness the winter would be dark, bleak, and cold. Some might call it unforgiving.

Petra was the first to spot the motorboat as it sailed around the tip of the Uummannaq peninsula, unaware that it was the same moment that Nivi had leaped straight into the dark mouth of winter, and was begging for her life.

Ataasinngorneq

MONDAY

Chapter 21

The dark interior of the cabin was a conjuring pit of demons, an evil womb, pulsing on the outside with the rush of water along the hull. Inside it was fetid, with the premonition of death. Nivi could hear the clump of Daniel's boots on deck as he moved around, and, in between, she thought she heard him talk to himself, and sometimes shout. Gone was her shrewd assistant, the devious operator, a force of reckoning on the Greenlandic political stage. Gone was the thirty-something career-driven man, hungry for power, and in his stead was the deviant. She knew that, but she hadn't been prepared for the change, had not seen it grow and consume him. It was as if the devil drove the demon inside. The worlds had been bridged, lines of communication established, serviced with a constant stream of hellish impulse and desire.

Nivi tugged at the tape glued across her mouth. Her skin around the edge of the tape was sore, swollen, an allergic reaction to the glue. An abstract thought reminded her of a similar allergy Tinka had to the tubes of glue they used in schools. And, if she dug farther back into her own childhood, she could trace the same irritation and skin rash when helping her father patch a hole in his boat.

Fibreglass, that was it. She recalled the feel of the fibres, like strands of hair sprayed with a fixing agent, pliable but strong. She had watched her father prepare the formula in the shade cast by his boat. His face, sun-engraved with weather-beaten lines and wrinkles beneath a saggy cloth cap. His hands, rough, the pads of his fingers scored by rope, knife, and hook. The smell of his hands tickled Nivi's nose, as she remembered dark blood in the creases, seal blood, rich and liver-like, fishy. That part of her brain that was detached from her situation was amused that she would find comfort in the memory of her father. What were Tinka's last thoughts, she wondered. Did she think of her father? The man who was supposed to make her feel safe, to protect her?

Nivi shifted her focus to a more immediate concern – breathing. She tugged at a corner of the tape, closed her eyes as she felt her skin around her mouth begin to lift. She tasted blood as the tape tore at her lips, and then it was free, and she gulped the fetid air of the cabin into her lungs. Nivi rolled onto her back, saw the shadow of Daniel's boots through the smoked-glass door, and froze, eyes transfixed to the one part of her captor that she could see, although his demonic face was foremost in her mind.

It appeared then, the face of the demon, as Daniel bent down to peer through the glass door. He stared at Nivi, squinting as he gauged her status, her level of consciousness. And then he saw it, she realised at once, the minute his body stiffened and he stood up. He could see she had removed the tape. Nivi's body reacted with a flood of adrenaline, charging through her veins, pulsing at the tips of her fingers. Her breath changed to short pulses, in and out of her lungs, as Daniel unlocked the door and dropped down into the cabin.

He sat on his haunches, his neck hidden as the thick padding of the suit swelled over his torso. The image of an ape flashed through Nivi's mind, fitting as it was with the primal fear flooding her body. She remembered a wildlife programme on television, primates hunting, branches crashing above the jungle floor, leaves and vines twisting down to the lowest and darkest levels, furthest from the sun. She was on the jungle floor, she realised, where the air was thickest, the odour rankest. She had fallen from the upper levels, she had cascaded. She was prey, to be toyed with, and disposed of. She held her breath, and the hunter spoke.

"You're awake," he said. Daniel removed the fleece hat from his head and stuffed it into the thigh pocket of his overalls. "That's good, because we are close, and I want you to see everything." He licked a bubble of saliva from the corner of his mouth.

"What do you want me to see, Daniel?"

"Ah," he said and wagged his finger, "wonderful things, things that can only be seen with the certain…" He paused to search for the appropriate word. "Stimulus. That's it."

"Daniel, I need to know," Nivi said, her words measured and slow, as she compensated for the rush of chemicals in her body, urging her to flee. She had projected her worst fears onto Malik Uutaaq, in anticipation of the truth that he killed her daughter. Now, faced with the man she believed murdered Tinka, it was almost anticlimactic. She had to know, even if the truth would strip away her last vestige of defence, and she would succumb to the fear. She still had to know.

"Yes," Daniel said, "it was here. She was right here, laying where you are, actually." He swept his hand in the air between them, as if caressing her body.

Tinka's body, Nivi realised, not mine.

"Whatever power Uutaaq might have had over your daughter, I took away when I had her here. I stole it," he said, and reached into another pocket. He pulled out a pair of topaz panties, stretched them between his fingers, and sniffed the length of them. Nivi watched him, and he caught her eye. "These were hers," he said. "Of course, she had already left the nest, a young woman, independent. I bet you never saw these in the wash basket, never hung them on the line." Daniel leaned forwards, and said, "You never knew your daughter like I did, Nivi."

"You're an animal," Nivi whispered.

"I suppose I am," he said, and bunched Tinka's underwear within his fist. "And animals," he said, as he knelt in front of Nivi, "have needs." The punches came at her again and again, until the blood spluttered from her mouth.

The boat spun slowly in the water, and he looked up through the open door as the mountains of the peninsula came into the view, and the witches' hat peak of Qilertinnguit stood tall and proud above Inussuk.

"Look, Nivi," Daniel said and beckoned for her to look out of the door. He grabbed her by the hair when she didn't move, dragging her onto his knee. He pulled her head up, stuck one hand beneath her jaw and lifted her chin. "Do you see that? Do you see the antenna? You can just see the white picket fence. That's the graveyard where your daughter lies. I have brought you home, to bring you together. It's time for you to be reunited."

Nivi tried to turn her head, gasping for breath, and snorting blood from her nose. The top of her left ear creased within the folds of his overalls, but her right ear was unhindered, and free to hear the sound of a motor, and the screech of feedback through a set of speakers, before a voice cut across the surface of the water.

"Daniel Tukku. This is the police."

"No," Daniel whispered. He thrust Nivi to one side, and lifted his head to peer over the lip of the cabin door. He ducked down again, as the voice on the loudspeaker called out his name once more. "No," he shouted.

Nivi watched as Daniel closed and locked the cabin door from the inside. She curled away from him, looped her arms over her knees, stretching the ropes binding her wrists. Daniel stooped to look out of through the glass again, ducking down as a shadow passed the cabin door. He kneeled on the floor and opened a storage panel. It was shaped in a V and Nivi could see lengths of ballast shaped to fit in the bottom of the compartment, flush with the keel. Daniel removed the ballast, heaved it to one side, lips moving as he muttered, and grabbed an axe with a short metal handle. He raised it and struck at the fibreglass at the bottom of the compartment.

"No, Daniel," Nivi shouted. She moved, as he swung the axe again and again, chipping away at the hull of his boat. He stopped at the sound of her voice, turned and swung the axe, catching her on the side of her head with the flat of the adze, a hammer blow that sent her sprawling against the far wall of the cabin. Daniel struck at the hull again as Nivi lifted her hands to her head. Her breath caught in her throat as she felt and heard the shift and crackle of bone beneath the skin just above her ear. Daniel raised the axe again, and again, until the first spray of icy sea water splashed on the front of his overalls.

"Yes," he shouted. "We are going to be all right, Nivi." He turned to glance at her, frowning for a second at the blood pulsing from the side of her head, and then he grinned. "I will take to your daughter."

Daniel looked up at the sound of a motor in the water, looping around his boat. He raised the axe and chopped at the hull until the water plumed through two holes. He jammed the edge of the axe into one of the holes and prised at the tear, twisting the axe in all directions until the hole was bigger, and water swelled into the storage compartment and flooded into the cabin. He stood up as the water reached his knees, and stared at the hole, at once pleased and frightened that he had succeeded, and that his boat was sinking.

Daniel heard the police call his name once more, knelt in the water and lifted the axe, splashing with each swing. Nivi felt the water on her face and tried to move towards the cabin door. Daniel reached out to catch her arm and held on, swinging the axe with the other hand. If he heard the impact of boots on the deck above, it didn't register on his face.

"Nivi," he said, the words trembling as the cold water seeped into his overalls, rising over his knees to submerge his thighs. "Do you know what I called your daughter, just before I pushed her over the side of this boat?"

"No," Nivi whispered. She tried to move out of the water. Daniel pinched her arm in his grip. She looked through the glass door, and stared into the barrel of a submachine gun, as the policeman moved to the left and the right, searching for a clear shot. Daniel lifted the axe again, and lost his balance as the axe plunged through the hull. He let go of Nivi, recovered his balance, and pulled the axe out of the water.

"I called her a Greenlandic bitch," he said, and reached for Nivi. "No, wait," he said, and frowned. "I said she should speak Greenlandic, *bitch*. That's what I said." He pulled Nivi close and she saw the blue tinge to his lips as the cold gripped his body. "I was being Malik," he said. "You understand? Don't you?"

"Yes," Nivi said. She looked up at the tramp of boots on the roof of the cabin. A shadow appeared above the skylight window, and then a masked face, and the barrel of another gun.

"It was an act," Daniel said. "Of course it was." The twitch of muscles in Daniel's face settled and his cheeks smoothed as he exhaled. He stroked the side of Nivi's face. "You're hurt?"

"Yes," she said. "Let me go, Daniel."

"Let you go?"

"Yes."

Daniel rested his hand on the butt of the axe handle. He stroked her face again, and said, "You have your daughter's eyes."

"Let me go," Nivi whispered.

Daniel nodded, and said, "Yes. Why not? I could do it."

"Please."

"I could do it for Tinka," he said, and shrugged, "to make amends."

"Daniel," said a voice from the deck of the boat. "You need to come out now."

Daniel shivered. He reached around Nivi and unlocked the cabin door. He stumbled in the water as he grabbed Nivi by the hair at the back of her head, and said, "Up." He pulled her to her feet and pushed her up the steps to the deck, forcing the masked policeman to take a step back, towards the railings. Daniel held the axe tight in his right hand, shoved Nivi forwards, propelling her into the policeman's chest as he raised the axe and roared.

The policeman let go of the submachine gun attached to his chest, and wrapped his arms around Nivi. The force of Nivi's momentum pushed the policeman over the side of the boat, and he pulled the First Minister with him. The weight of his equipment dragged them below the surface as his partner took aim from the cabin roof, and fired a burst of three bullets into Daniel's back. The axe clattered across the deck as Daniel crashed into the railings, reaching for Nivi as she disappeared within Gaba's grasp into the black sea flecked with ice.

"Gaba," Miki shouted from the cabin roof. He pulled the mask from his face and leaped onto the deck of the boat. He flung his body at the railings, looking up as Maratse tossed his utility belt onto the deck of the hotel boat, threw his jacket to one side, and dived into the water.

Maratse ignored the cold clamp around his chest and grabbed at the clothes on Nivi's back, pulling the First Minister free of Gaba's grip, and propelling her to the surface. He took another stroke downwards as the SRU leader clawed at the equipment on his chest. Maratse grabbed Gaba's vest and kicked. He kicked through the explosion of pain firing through the nerves in his legs, ignored the vice of cold pinching his head, and kicked for the surface. Gaba fumbled with the clasp of his helmet, cut the sling of his weapon with a knife and kicked with Maratse until they breached the surface, grasping each other with stiff fingers as Petra and Miki stretched over the side of the hotel boat, beneath the railings, and hauled them to safety.

Miki peeled the equipment and clothes from his boss, wrapping him in a blanket, as Petra did the same for Maratse. The paramedics triaged their patients, treating them in turn for trauma and exposure. Petra helped Maratse into a chair next to the First Minister. She kissed him on the forehead and made room for Gaba.

Nivi slid her hand out from beneath her blanket to clutch Maratse's fingers. She turned her bandaged head and looked at him. "Thank you, Constable."

"*Iiji*," Maratse said. "You're welcome."

"I'm not going to hold your hand," Gaba said, and nudged Maratse from the other side, "but thank you."

Maratse bit through the pain in his legs and nodded.

Marlunngorneq

TUESDAY

Chapter 22

Maratse woke to the sound of Petra coming down the stairs. He lifted his head as she walked into the living room, stopping in the doorway to wave.

"Did you sleep?" she asked.

"*Iji.*"

"Much pain?"

He nodded and lowered his head, as Petra walked into the kitchen. He listened as she boiled water for coffee, and tutted at the lack of food in the fridge, and the empty cupboards.

"I'm going shopping," she said, putting a mug of coffee on the table next to Maratse. "See if you can get dressed."

Maratse nodded, waiting until she had left before he propped himself up on the sofa and reached for the mug. He grimaced at the pain in his legs, and then shrugged. He had to live with it, he reasoned, but it didn't have to define him, or determine what he did and didn't do with his life. Maratse's temporary reinstatement in the police had expired as soon as the Commissioner was briefed on the status of the operation. Maratse contemplated his second retirement in as many weeks, as he sipped his coffee, and listened to the puppy scratching at the deck outside the house. It tumbled up and down the length of the deck as Petra returned with bacon, eggs, and bread.

"He's so cute," Petra said, pausing for a moment to talk to the puppy. She knocked the snow from her boots, kicking them off and walking through to the lounge.

"He's a she."

"And does she have a name yet?"

"*Eeqqi,*" Maratse said. "I'm working on it."

Maratse dressed, as Petra made breakfast. He looked out of the window as Karl and Edvard walked down to the dock to meet the hotel boat as it bumped against the jetty. Nivi Winther stepped off the boat, together with Simonsen and Danielsen from Uummannaq.

"Is that them?" Petra called from the kitchen.

"*Iji.*"

"And what time is the press conference?"

"In an hour."

"Okay," Petra said, as she put two plates with bacon sandwiches on the table. She beckoned for Maratse to come and eat, waited until he sat down, and then said, "I'm curious as to why she is holding it here, not in Nuuk."

The same thought had kept Maratse awake for the first part of the night, until the painkillers had kicked in. He had given the dark nature of his dreams a name, called it trauma, and set it to one side. Releasing a statement about her daughter's killer beside her grave, he imagined, must be Nivi Winther's way of working through her trauma. Although, he did wonder if she had other plans, a different agenda. She was a strong woman, all the stronger for bouncing back from the death of her daughter, and her own abduction.

"You're far away again," Petra said, when she was finished with her sandwich. She sipped her coffee and watched Maratse eat.

"This is good."

"I know," she said.

They both looked up at the sound of a plane passing overhead to land at the gravel strip in Qaarsut. It coincided with the departure of the hotel boat, and Maratse wondered again if Nivi was planning something.

"Gaba called when I was in the store," Petra said. "He wanted me to say hi."

"Hmm," Maratse said. "How is Miki?"

"He's fine. Filling in forms and being interviewed in Nuuk. It's the first time for him, killing a man, but the union has his back, and there were plenty of witnesses."

"Good." Maratse finished his breakfast. He looked out of the window as Karl, Edvard, and the policemen followed Nivi up the path to the graveyard. "I'll need longer today," he said, "to walk up the mountain."

"Sure," Petra said. "Do you want to go now?"

"*Iiji*," Maratse said, and stood up. He walked to the door, pulled on his jacket, and stuffed his feet into his boots.

The puppy lifted its head as Maratse and Petra walked out of the house. Maratse growled at it, and Petra laughed as the puppy danced back to where it was lying at the end of the deck.

"You have a way with dogs, eh?"

"She's a good dog," Maratse said.

"One that needs a name. You can't call it *she* or *it* for the rest of its life."

"Why not?"

"You just can't," Petra said and walked down the steps. She waited for Maratse on the beach, scuffing the snow to one side to reveal the black sand and shells beneath. They walked towards the path, and started to climb the mountainside.

When they reached the top, Maratse stopped to light a cigarette. He nodded at Nivi as she stood beside the grave of her daughter. Petra tugged his elbow and pointed at the hotel boat on its way back from the airport. The boat was stuffed with passengers.

"So," she said, "any ideas?"

"None," Maratse said, and rolled the cigarette into the gap between his teeth. He smoked for a minute more, snubbed the half-finished cigarette between his finger and thumb, and pushed it back into the packet. He spotted a flash of white fur bounding up the path, and growled at the puppy to stay put. He turned his back on it, and walked with Petra to the entrance to the graveyard. When he looked back at the puppy, it was sitting up straight by the side of the path, its head flicking back and forth between the guests arriving for the funeral. Maratse noticed that most of them carried cameras of various sizes, one of which was a digital video camera.

"The press," he said, and nudged Petra. The photographers moved to one side to take photographs of the last people in the group.

"That's Malik Uutaaq, and his family," Petra said. "What is she planning?"

Malik glanced at Petra and Maratse as he walked past them. He held his wife's hand on one side, and his daughter on the other. Sipu, his son, played with the puppy, until his father stopped and called for him.

Qitu Kalia separated himself from the photographers and journalists to shake Maratse's hand, before rejoining the group that Nivi Winther had assembled in the snow beside five open graves. She stood beside her daughter's grave. The loose sheets of her notes flapped in the wind.

"You're all wondering," she said in Greenlandic, her voice crisp and clear like the air, "why I have you invited you here. The simple answer is, I want my daughter to hear what I have to say." Cameras started to click, and she held up her hand for them to wait. The film crew kept rolling, and Maratse realised she must have asked for that. "Daniel Tukku was my colleague, he was my friend, and he was also the man who murdered my daughter." Nivi paused to wipe a tear from her cheek. "She is safe now, but her death and suffering make me think of all the people suffering in Greenland, even people like Daniel Tukku. He was Greenlandic, just like my Tinka was." Nivi waited for the journalists and photographers to finish taking notes and pictures. "When I visit my daughter, to talk to her about the whales in the fjord, and to imagine the life she might have led, I will also tell her about Greenland and the Greenlandic people. As First Minister of Greenland I have a responsibility to care for all Greenlanders, we all do. But, as First Minister, I failed in my duty to give Daniel the help he needed. I will be reminded of that every time I visit Tinka."

Nivi looked over her shoulder, as if to take strength from the power of the ice in the fjord, to draw on winter's strengths, so that she need not dwell on its hardships. She looked back, and caught Maratse's eye, smiling as she continued with her speech.

"Tinka is safe, but how safe do we feel? How safe are we as a nation, as a people, as Greenlanders?" Nivi beckoned for Malik to come and stand beside her. She embraced him as he walked up to her, and took his hand as he turned to face his family, and the press, and the people of Greenland. "I asked Malik Uutaaq to join me here on this difficult day, because when one has experienced the darkest side of human nature, the darkest side of Greenland, it is important to reach out and embrace all that is good about Greenland, and to go forwards into the dark of winter, with a new heart, a new focus, and a new leadership. Which is why, I am pleased to say, Malik Uutaaq and I have agreed to work together to bring our people together, and to embrace a new Greenland for all Greenlanders." Nivi paused at a renewed frenzy of cameras clicking. "So when you vote in May next year, we can promise you an exciting election, and furthermore, we can promise a stable, political vision, built on trust and common ground embracing the true Greenlandic identity for all Greenlanders."

Maratse felt Petra take his hand, as Nivi repeated her speech in Danish. "Piitalaat," he said, as he felt her tremble. "Are you all right?"

"Yes," she whispered. "I am now."

The press stayed as Nivi rearranged the flowers on her daughter's grave. Maratse didn't know if the camera caught the look in her eye, but he saw a spark of hope between the tears.

Petra held Maratse's hand long after the last journalist had followed Nivi and Malik down the mountain path and back to the hotel boat. He imagined that there would be a question and answer session at the hotel in Uummannaq, and was pleased that the press, politicians and policemen were leaving. He tugged at Petra's hand and they walked over to Tinka Winther's grave. Karl and Edvard joined them.

"Five graves left," Karl said, as he lit a cigarette. Maratse lit his own and Petra stepped to one side to admire the view and avoid the smoke. She walked back to Maratse as Karl and Edvard finished their cigarettes and walked down the path to Inussuk.

"So," she said, "what are you going to do now?"

"Retire," he said, and shrugged.

"You've tried that already."

"*Iiji.*"

"Perhaps you should try a new approach?"

Petra smiled as the puppy bounded into the graveyard and sat at the foot of Tinka's grave.

"You said it was a she?" Petra said.

"It is."

"And she needs a name." Petra nodded at the puppy. "Tinka. How about that?"

Maratse looked at the puppy as it flicked its head between him and Petra. He took a breath and gritted his teeth as he bent down onto his knees. The puppy looked at him, watched him, and then bounded across the snow into his lap when Maratse clicked his tongue.

"A few more, and you've got a team," Petra said.

"Karl's son has more dogs he wants to get rid of," Maratse said, "and a boat he wants to sell."

Petra looked out at the fjord, took a deep breath, and nodded. "So, you've decided then, you're going to be a hunter."

"Hunting and fishing," Maratse said. He curled the puppy's ears between his fingers and thumbs. "Or maybe just sledging."

"I'd like to try that," Petra said.

"Come back in spring. My team will be ready."

"You won't come back to Nuuk?"

Maratse let go of the puppy and looked at Petra. He could feel the puppy's claws on his thighs, and the needle-like points of its milk teeth as it nibbled at his fingers.

"I don't think so."

"You're sure?"

"*Iiji*," he said. "This is where I belong."

THE END

Blood Floe

~ Book 2 in The Greenland Crime series ~

From the Midnight Sun,
from the Winter Night,
tomb-black,
no Word …
We hardly knew
those that were lost

Author's translation from
NORDPOLEN
by
LUDVIG MYLIUS-ERICHSEN (1872-1907)

Fra Midnatssolen,
fra Vinternatten,
den gravkammer-sorte,
intet Bud …
Vi kender jo knapt
dem, der blev borte

Note to the Reader

Blood Floe is the second book in the Greenland Crime Series featuring the main character of Constable David Maratse. While it is not necessary, readers will get more enjoyment out of *Blood Floe* if they read book one in the series: *Seven Graves, One Winter.*

Maratse and other characters such as Petra Jensen and Gaba Alatak have also appeared in short stories set in Greenland. It is not necessary to read these stories before reading Blood Floe. However, each of the short stories does include some information that adds to the character of Constable David Maratse.

If you would like to read even more about Maratse, then you might be interested in The Greenland Trilogy, three thrillers set in Greenland, starting with *The Ice Star*, in which we meet Maratse for the very first time.

The people of Greenland speak Greenlandic – including at least four dialects, Danish, and English. In many aspects of daily life, West Greenlandic and Danish are the working languages. Blood Floe is written in British English with the use of some Greenlandic and Danish words used where appropriate, including:

East Greenlandic / West Greenlandic / English
iiji / aap / yes
eeqqi / naamik / no
qujanaq / qujanaraali / qujanaq / thank you

Just as language defines identity in Greenland, so too does subsistence hunting, i.e. hunting for food, and to make a living from the carving of bone jewellery, and the sewing of skin and fur products, especially for families in the far north.

Hunting is a very important aspect of life in Greenland, and this includes the hunting of whales. This is one of the themes explored in Blood Floe, and, while "we" - myself included - will never truly appreciate how central hunting is to the Greenlanders' way of life, aspects of that life are included in this story as a means of providing depth to the fascinating culture and country that is Greenland.

Chris
May 2018
Denmark

Chapter 1

Even in the unfathomable dark of the long polar winter there is always light – the moon reflecting on the surface of the sea ice, the green and white curtains of Northern Lights twisting across the black night sky, the stars, pinpricks of primordial light scrutinising the tiny villages and settlements clinging limpet-like to the barren west coast of Greenland. The houses add a warm, artificial light, casting yellow squares onto the snow through thick-paned windows, the tiny red lights of the radio mast glowing over the graveyard on the mountain's knee above the settlement of Inussuk, and a cigarette burning a bright orange, a smouldering flame just a few centimetres from the lips of the man wearing a headlamp, drifting the light slowly from left to right, as he searches the snowy black sand beach for the skittish dog that shuns the harness.

Retired police constable David Maratse knew the dark side of all of Greenland. During his active years of service, he had seen more than enough evil deeds that even the blackest winter could not hide. Now, cigarette tucked into the gap between his teeth, he smoothed his bare hands over the webbing harness, pricking his thumb on the knot of waxed thread he had tied at the end of a stubborn line of stitching. The padding of the shoulder straps, as thick as his little finger, had been the trickiest to sew, the size and dimensions hard won as the sea ice thickened and the dog had wriggled and twisted between his knees, biting at the measuring tape each time the end flapped too close to its mouth. Other hunters he knew might have given up on the dog as a lost cause, been less patient, more insistent, but Maratse had time, and he owed the dog a debt of gratitude – the more he chased after it, the less he was bothered by the pain in his legs, the less he thought about the torturous root of it. He stuffed the harness into the cargo pocket of his insulated overalls, and sat on the reindeer skin tied to the battered thwarts of the wooden sledge with a zigzagging sealskin cord. The hollow-haired skin was stiff with cold; he could feel the ridges pressing into his buttocks.

He turned off the headlamp and finished his cigarette in the darkness. The dog would come to him, he reasoned, as it always did when he ignored it. He heard the soft crunch of snow beneath the dog's paws as it padded towards him, felt the smooth wet lick of its tongue on the back of his hand, and the cold of its nose as it pressed its face into the warmth of Maratse's neck. He ran his fingers through the dog's ice-beaded fur, up its chest, past strong shoulders, all the way to the collar around its neck.

"Hello Tinka," he said.

The dog skittered on the snow as Maratse stood up, turned it within his grasp and clamped its body between his knees. Maratse tugged the harness from his pocket, straightened it, and slipped the collar over the dog's neck. He bent the dog's front legs at the elbows and pushed one and then the other through the triangular loops of the harness. He had tied the stiff loop of cord to the end of the harness, and he gripped it now, just above the dog's tail, and let the dog wriggle out from between his legs. He tugged the dog down the snowy beach to the ice foot, and then onto the ice where the team was anchored. Maratse clipped the dog into the team traces with a small karabiner through the cord loop. The dog whined as he turned and walked back towards the beach for the sledge.

"Enough, Tinka."

Maratse took his time with the sledge, fiddling with the sledge bag, hanging it over the uprights at the rear, like a large envelope. He opened the canvas flap of the bag, making a last visual and physical check that he had everything he needed for the journey. The larger items of gear, the canvas tent, the collapsible metal stove, fuel, food, and clothes were tied to the front of the long, broad sledge, leaving just enough space for him to sit, at an angle, between the load and the uprights. The rifle he had bought from the gravedigger, Edvard, was holstered in a canvas bag tied to the sledge like a rifle slung from a cowboy's saddle. Maratse gripped the uprights and started to push the sledge towards the ice.

"Let me help you."

Maratse grunted a hello at Karl as his neighbour crunched through the snow and took one of the uprights and together they pushed the sledge up and over the ice foot.

"How's the dog?"

"Don't ask," said Maratse.

"That's her wriggling the lines into a bird's nest?"

"It is."

Karl laughed. "You're going to have a wonderful trip."

"You could come with me."

"I could," Karl said, as they turned the sledge to within a metre of the team anchored to the ice. He shooed the dogs away from the sledge runners with a clap of his hands as Maratse clipped a large karabiner through the thick rope loops forming a V between the curved tips at the front of the sledge.

"Then why don't you?" Maratse asked, as he walked towards the knot of lines tied through a chain frozen in the ice.

"Buuti is preparing for the meal on Thursday. I have to help."

"Hm."

"Don't forget you are invited." Karl kicked at the gear tied to Maratse's sledge.

"I won't."

"Good." Karl lit a cigarette, offered one to Maratse. "It's a long way to Svartenhuk, even with nine dogs."

"I know." Maratse gripped the bunch of lines in his fist. "Maybe I won't go so far. One, maybe two nights. A short run to the edge of the ice." He straightened his back. "You're worried?"

"*Naamik*," Karl said, "it's just, you're not a policeman anymore."

"I know."

Karl exhaled a cloud of smoke, and said, "You don't have to go looking for trouble."

"I don't." Maratse heaved the lines free of the ice.

"I think you do."

Maratse grunted and tugged the lines to the sledge. Karl moved to the back and gripped the uprights. The ice was smooth underfoot, and he pressed the toes of his boots against a ridge, squirming his foot into a solid stance as Maratse attached the dogs to the sledge.

"*Ah*," Maratse said, and the dogs settled for a moment, all but Tinka. He took a step on the ice and said *Ah*, louder this time, and Tinka lowered her head. Maratse kept an eye on the dogs as he walked to the uprights. He nodded at Karl. "Tell Buuti I won't look for any trouble."

"It was me who said it. She thinks you are a hunter. I know you're still a policeman. Besides, I think trouble finds you."

"I'll be fine." Maratse finished his cigarette, gripped the uprights and nodded as Karl took a step back.

"See you on Thursday," Karl said, as he slapped Maratse on the back.

The lead dog was one of Edvard's old leaders, a small bitch called Spirit. Maratse hoped she would help him train Tinka. Spirit lifted her head, padded forwards to the end of the line, and pulled it tight. Maratse cast a quick glance at the rest of the team and gave the command to pull.

The team tugged at the lines and ran forwards; spread like a fan in front of the sledge, only Tinka was out of formation, until the momentum of the team tugged her into a position on the outside, to the left of the sledge. Maratse jogged behind the sledge, increased speed, and ran to the left, before leaping into the gap between the uprights and the gear. He settled his back against the sledge bag, found a comfortable position for his legs, and tugged the dog whip from where he had tucked it, beneath the cord that tied the tent to the sledge. He uncoiled the pencil-thick sealskin whip and let it run though his fingers into a five-metre line, trailing on the ice behind him. Maratse held the long wooden handle in a loose grip, and then cracked the end on the ice to the left of the dogs, smiling as Spirit pulled the team to the right. He adjusted course with another crack on the right, and then tucked the handle of the whip beneath the cord stretched tight over the reindeer skin. Maratse stretched his legs at an angle so that the heels of his boots tipped over the thwarts to one side. He rested his hands in his lap, clapping soft claps when he felt the team begin to dawdle, or when the scent of a fishing hole and the frozen innards scattered on the surface of the ice turned their heads.

The sunless twilight of mid-morning turned the black sky into a penitent grey. Maratse lowered his head, fumbled for the cigarettes in his chest pocket, and then patted the pocket smooth against the hook and loop closure, smiling at his thoughts

"Piitalaat would say I smoke too much."

He scanned the thick layer of sea ice – an anomaly if one believed the climatologists – and turned his head to explore the shadows of the icebergs locked in place. One berg in particular, massive with three gnarled and twisted towers, would have been right at home in one of Maratse's beloved science fiction novels. He smiled at the thought of setting up camp, lighting the metal stove, and reading by lamplight, as the dogs curled up on the ice by the sledge. Retirement, he realised, held plenty of opportunities, and, despite the pain in his legs, he was still young, a year shy of forty.

The sledge bumped over a fissure in the ice, and Maratse spotted a narrow lead of open water, perhaps a metre wide. He clapped his hands, gave a few encouraging whistles and shouts, and the team picked up speed, dragging the sledge and Tinka onto the firm ice on the other side of the gap, with Spirit taking the lead. Maratse leaned back, proud of his team, content with his surroundings, at one with the environment. They passed the three-towered iceberg, and the shadows diminished as the high-peaked peninsula flattened to a long, thin finger of snow-clad granite stretching into the frozen sea. Maratse could see the smoke of condensing air on the open water, in the distance, at the brittle edge of the sea. He could see something else, too. A thin line pointing straight up, like a mast. He leaned forwards just as the dogs jolted the sledge with a spurt of curiosity to match his own. Maratse didn't chide or encourage the team. He let them run, as his own curiosity grew, and the shape of a broad hull anchored to the ice sharpened with each metre they sledged towards it.

A scent or tang of something had pricked the dogs' noses, and Spirit tugged them forwards. Had Maratse not been equally caught up in the shape on the horizon, he might have noticed that Tinka had shoved her way to run alongside the lead dog, bumping against Spirit's more experienced flank. Maratse shifted position, kneeling, and then standing on the sledge, one steady hand on the upright, as he leaned forwards.

There was a dark stain on the ice in front of the boat, a stripe of something, too thin to make out at this distance, but not altogether unfamiliar. Maratse slowed the team with long, slow commands to stop.

He pulled the whip handle free of the cord and timed his first step onto the ice, ignoring the pain in his legs as he ran to the head of the team and slowed them with casts of the whip, tracing figure eights in the frigid air in front of the dogs. The team stopped, icicles hanging from their muzzles, as Maratse took hold of Spirit and smoothed his hand between the dog's eyes and through the cold fur of its jaw. He spotted a mountaineering axe buried deep in the ice and anchored the team to it before unhitching the sledge and studying the boat in front of him.

It was an aluminium-hulled ice-strengthened expedition yacht, one that Maratse had seen before, on the east coast, a long time ago. He recognised the broad hull, the generous glass cockpit of the bridge, and the name on the side: *Ophelia*.

The yacht was anchored to the ice with two lines, one axe

holding down each line. The bow was embedded in the ice, sealed a few metres along each side of the hull. The sails were furled and stowed, the shrouds caked in rime ice, and the decks heavy with layers of old ice and new snow. It had been there several days, perhaps a week.

He turned away from the yacht and examined the stain on the ice. Two dark stripes of blood led away from the hull. The trail stopped a metre ahead of Maratse's sledge; either the blood was covered with fresh snow, or the wound had been staunched. He looked at the sharp semicircular peaks of Svartenhuk in the distance, and then back to the yacht. The blood was fresher than the ice on the deck. He took a step forwards, catching himself with the memory of Karl's last words. Maratse shook the thought away, and walked the last few metres to the hull. He found a short ladder on the starboard side, shouted a quick greeting in English, and climbed aboard.

There had been a snowfall in the night, and, as he walked on the deck, Maratse stooped to brush snow from a narrow window, shaped like a long, thin teardrop. The interior of the yacht was lit with a weak light. Maratse pressed his nose to the Plexiglas, squinted, and then took a breath as he noticed a body, a man, laying on the floor with a broad-handled knife protruding from his stomach.

Chapter 2

The air in the cabin was heavy with blood and faecal matter, the last physical act of the dying man. Maratse turned his face away from the steps leading from the deck to the cabin. He waited for a second and then descended into the cabin, one hand flat against the bulkhead. He scanned the dimly lit interior of the yacht. Two more crew, a man and a woman, both slim, were slumped at the table, the ends of the woman's long blonde hair playing over the bald head of the man. Another member of the crew, slumped on the floor, looked like she had slipped in the blood. There was blood on her forehead, crusted in her short black hair. Her arms were positioned at uncomfortable angles, as if the fall had surprised her. Maratse took another step inside the cabin, placed his hand on the top of the cabinet that jutted into the room, and then lifted it immediately to stare at the blood glued to his fingers and palm. He peered over the cabinet, tracing a generous spray of blood plastered against the wall. There, on the other side of the cabinet was a fifth crew member, another woman, her feet pressed against the base of a shelf, her neck twisted, her head clamped in the corner by the oven. She had a knife in her throat, smaller than the one in the man's belly.

Maratse lifted a towel from a hook by the sink and wiped the pale palms of his weathered hands, the creases lined with blood. He stuffed the towel in the cargo pocket of his overalls and took a step forwards to peer at the woman laying on the floor, pausing as he lifted his foot; the floor was thick with blood. Maratse turned his attention to the crew slumped at and around the table. He retreated to the cabin steps, sat down, and fished inside his overalls to pull his mobile from an inside pocket.

"I need to talk to Simonsen," he said, when he got through to the Uummannaq police station.

"He's off-duty."

"All right," Maratse continued, "I want to report an incident."

"Your name?"

"David Maratse."

"Maratse? From Inussuk?"

"*Iiji.*"

"This is Danielsen."

"Danielsen, I'm on a yacht at the entrance to Uummannaq fjord.

Two dead, three unconscious."

"Two dead? You're sure?"

Maratse glanced at the man with the knife in his belly, the fibres of his clothes stained black with blood. "I'm sure." He paused at the sound of Danielsen writing notes, the scratch of the nib just audible over the sound of Maratse's own breathing.

"What about the others?"

"Alive, I think."

"You can't check?"

"If I take one more step, I'll contaminate the crime scene."

"I need to know."

"Wait a minute."

Maratse placed his phone on the bottom step and moved towards the crew members at the table, choosing a route with the thinnest layer of blood. He turned the blonde woman's head and elicited a soft snort from her lips. A shiver ran through the man's arm as Maratse slipped his fingers inside his wrist to check for a pulse. The woman slumped on the floor with the head injury had the weakest pulse of them all. Maratse examined her head and took a closer look at the corner of the bench; a few of the woman's black hairs were clamped behind a fleck of wood, sealed with more blood. Maratse moved back to the steps and picked up his mobile.

"Two women and one man, all alive. One woman has a head injury."

"How's the ice?"

"Good along the coast. There's an open lead six kilometres north of Inussuk. You'll have to drive around."

"This is going to take a while. I need you to stay there. Can you do that?"

Maratse looked at the black-haired woman's head. "I can stay, but I need to treat the woman's injury, and check the others. I think they have been drugged."

"Do that. Just don't touch the dead."

Maratse flicked his gaze to the dead man and grunted an acknowledgment before ending the call. He slipped his phone into his pocket and took a moment to study the interior of the cabin. Beyond the blood and the bodies, there was little to suggest there had been a fight. There were empty glasses at one end of the table, brushed to one side by the elbows of the crew. Maratse looked but could not see a bottle of wine, beer, or any trace of the kind of spirits he imagined would be necessary to knock someone out.

Everything else inside the cabin was detailed and ordered. The phrase ship-shape came to Maratse's mind, confirmed by the laminated lists tacked to the walls. All he knew of *Ophelia* was that it was a German boat designed for use in the Polar Regions. There were framed photos screwed to the cabin walls showing *Ophelia* locked in the ice as it wintered over in the Arctic and the Antarctic. The yacht was used to being moored in dark, isolated places.

On first inspection, the only items out of place that Maratse could see were the knives that were no longer on the magnet strip above the hotplates of the oven, but were now implanted in the bodies in front of him.

Unless they had stabbed themselves, Maratse could not see how they had been attacked. There was a curious lack of footprints of any kind in the blood on the cabin floor. He looked from the dead man to the dead woman, judged the distance to be little more than a metre, and then studied the clothes of the three survivors, all clean, apart from the spots of blood on the shoulder of the black-haired woman's fleece shirt. If they hadn't killed themselves, Maratse reasoned, then perhaps there was another crew member hiding somewhere onboard.

Maratse looked behind the steps. The light was off. He saw a panel of switches and tried flicking them up and down. Either they didn't work, or the bulbs had been removed. Maratse glanced at the black-haired woman. Her wound could wait, he reasoned. He pressed his right hand on his hip, forgetting for a moment that he no longer carried a pistol. He took a step towards the door to his right. It was open, a hand's width.

"Hello?"

He waited for a response, took another step.

If someone was hiding inside the cabin, and if they had murdered the two crew members and incapacitated the others, then they would make short work of a single Greenlander in a confined space. Maratse shook the thought from his mind and took another step.

The howl of a dog tricked Maratse's heart into an extra beat. He waited until the other dogs had joined in, and walked to the door. He slapped it open with a flat palm, only to jump back as something black and heavy thumped to the floor of the sleeping quarters.

Maratse peered into the gloom, stared at the shape on the floor, and then jumped again at the sound of a woman's voice.

"It's my bag," she said in English, "a duffel bag. It was on my bunk."

Maratse turned to look at the woman, who had her hand pressed to her head.

"It must have fallen."

"And them?" he said, and pointed past the woman, and into the galley. "Did they fall?"

The woman turned to look in the direction Maratse was pointing. Her hand fell from her head and she screamed. The scream changed pitch as the energy flooded from her body, and Maratse caught her as she lurched back towards the cabin.

"No," he said. "Don't look."

"Henrik," she said, the name pressed through the fingers she clamped over her mouth. She trembled in Maratse's grip as he lowered her to the floor.

"Let me look at your head." Maratse placed his hands either side of the woman's head, and turned her slightly towards the dim cabin lights.

"Is that a knife," she said, "in his stomach?"

"*Iiji.*"

"What?"

"Yes, it is a knife." Maratse let go, and said, "How many of you are onboard?" And, when she didn't answer, he asked, "How many crew?"

The woman turned to look at the man she called Henrik. Maratse stepped over her legs and squatted in front of her, blocking her view. He tilted his head to look in her eyes. They were glassy, pupils wide, unfocussed.

"What have you had to drink?"

"Drink? I don't know," she said.

"How many crew?" Maratse pressed his hand on her shoulder. "How many?"

"Six."

"Six? Total?"

"Yes."

"Stay here," he said, as he stepped over the woman, and walked the two steps to the cabin. There was a torch clipped to the bulkhead between the doors to the sleeping quarters. Maratse unclipped it and turned it on. He shone the beam inside the starboard sleeping area, stepping over the black duffel bag to shine the light into the corner. The beam caught on a reflective strip of a sail visible through the opening, cinched with a toggle and cord. He found more sails stowed in the corner of the second sleeping area, the torchlight reflecting off another patch of reflective tape.

Maratse walked past the woman and shone the torch beam over the other crew members, and then up the short flight of steps and into the galley. He stopped at the outer reach of the blood pooling on the deck. If he jumped he might land on the top step, or tumble down all three of them. Maratse snorted and stepped into the blood. He reached the top step with his second stride, crouched to point the torch beam deeper inside the yacht, towards the stern, and then descended the stairs. The shower was empty, as was the tiny toilet in the on the opposite side of the corridor. He found two more bunks on either side of the corridor, and a storage space in the bow with a crawlspace and hatch, sealing the living area from the compartment used to store more gear. Maratse ducked out of the storage area and walked back to the generous living area. He climbed the steps, placed his foot within his own bloody footprint and crossed the galley to speak to the woman. He paused to look out of the cockpit window, and saw two pairs of lights in the distance, on the ice, beyond his sledge and dog team. He pictured Danielsen at the wheel of the police Toyota, and hoped that Simonsen was in a better mood than the last time they had met at a crime scene. Maratse unclipped a first aid kit from the bulkhead and carried it to the woman.

"Help is on the way," he said, as he crouched beside her. He opened the kit and tore open two alcohol swabs to clean the woman's wound.

"The police?"

"And ambulance."

"I think I know what happened," the woman said. Maratse stopped her with a shake of his head.

"I don't want to know."

"My friend is dead."

"The police are on their way. You can tell them."

"You're not a policeman?"

"*Eeqqi*," he said, and shook his head. "I'm retired."

"But you searched the boat."

"I found the boat."

"You helped."

"I reported it. The police are on their way."

"Why won't you help me?" She wiped her cheeks with the back of her hand.

"I've done all I can do," Maratse said. He stood up at the sound of car motors decelerating, and tyres slipping to a stop on the ice outside. "The police are here now, and the doctor. They will help you."

"You can't just leave," the woman said. She reached for his hand.

Maratse placed the torch on the floor beside the woman, and climbed the stairs onto the deck. He met Danielsen and the Italian doctor on their way inside.

"The chief is waiting for you on the ice," Danielsen said.

Maratse nodded and climbed over the railing and down the short ladder to the ice. He found Simonsen smoking beside his sledge and gear. Maratse's dogs shuffled within their traces, nosing the air, voicing their apprehension with low growls. Maratse shushed them and lit a cigarette of his own.

"Tell me, *Constable*," Simonsen said, as he exhaled a cloud of smoke. "How is it possible that you are always the first at the scene of a crime?"

"This is only my second since we have known each other."

"It's becoming a habit."

"It's a coincidence."

"It's suspicious, is what it is."

Maratse puffed at his cigarette and stuffed his hands inside his pockets. Simonsen squinted at him through another cloud of smoke.

"Do you want my report?"

"Report? You're a civilian."

"You called me *Constable*."

"Because you can't seem to let go. That's going to get you into trouble one of these days." Simonsen nodded at the yacht. "Perhaps it already has?"

Maratse tugged the towel from his cargo pocket, and said, "I put my hand down on a surface. That's where you'll find my prints." He tossed the towel at Simonsen. "There's a set of my boot prints in the blood on the floor of the cockpit, next to the man with the kitchen knife in his stomach. You'll find more prints where I walked to check the rest of the yacht. The woman said there should be six crew members. Two are dead. Two are unconscious, drugged maybe, and there is a woman with a cut on her head. The last member of the crew, the sixth, is missing." Maratse flicked the butt of his cigarette onto the ice and took a step towards his dogs. "That was my *report*. You can call it what you like."

"Where are you going?"

Maratse pointed towards the mountains to the northeast. "Svartenhuk."

"Why?"

"Because that's where I was headed."

"When are you coming back?"

"Thursday. I have been invited to dinner."

"There and back in two days? Less now. You'll never make it."

Maratse reached down and unclipped the dogs from the ice axe. "We'll see," he said, and tugged the line to the sledge.

"You'll answer your phone?"

"Maybe." Maratse turned and watched as Simonsen strode across the ice to the yacht, smoke curling from his lungs, as Danielsen appeared on the deck and shouted for him to hurry. Then he clipped the dogs' traces through the karabiner and gave two soft clicks. Spirit herded the team into position as Maratse ran alongside the sledge. He leaped onboard as Spirit and the team tightened the traces. Tinka ran alongside Spirit, and Maratse wondered if she was as eager to get away from the yacht as he was.

Chapter 3

The man dug his hands into the snow like spades. His fingers splayed inside snow-clad wool mitts, frozen, linking each digit with webs of wool and ice. They were bloody but they did not bleed. They were numb, like the man's mind. And yet, a single thought drove the man onwards, clawing at his conscience as he clawed at the snow. A day earlier, several hours past, he would no sooner have labelled himself a survivor than an explorer. Two equally foreign descriptions for what he actually was – a researcher, and what he actually did – research. Surviving, being a *survivor* was not mentioned in his job description, and he did not recall seeing it as a prerequisite for the *Ophelia Expedition*. He preferred the expedition's subtitle: *The Alfred Wegener Greenland Svartenhuk Expedition*. It confirmed his place on the team, and his position as *the* authority on all things related to Alfred Wegener. Those years of study, endless nights poring over heavy books in German and English, gloving-up to read musty journals from the field in the archives of the Alfred Wegener Institute in Bremerhaven, and removing his glasses to rub his eyes when searching the Institute's online database, that *knowledge* had turned the researcher into a survivor. He *knew* there was a cabin, Wegener's cabin, at the base of the mountain upon which he crawled. The hunters they had approached were unusually reticent to provide details or to even acknowledge the existence of the cabin, but he *knew* it was there, and now he had to find it.

He crawled, bumping his knees on black-lichened rocks poking through the surface, scuffing the toes of his hiking boots, tearing at the elbows of his jacket. He wailed long curses, pressing and spitting the syllables through stubborn bloodless lips. Between curses and on smooth stretches, he prayed, digging deep into his spiritual roots just as he dug deep into the snow, appealing to God, entreating God, and, when the straight-edged shadow of a roof captured his attention, he thanked God, thanked him for every spade of snow he shovelled beneath his body, as he crawled to the cabin door.

The wind, the tail-end of a katabatic downdraught, nipped at the exposed flesh of his cheeks, flung more snow, spindrift, and ice, at his chin, his mouth, his blue lips, as he clawed at the handle of the door to the cabin.

"Please," he said, as the handle proved to be as stubborn as his lips. "Please."

It didn't budge, and the man dragged the stiff cuff of his winter mitts across his eyes to search the cabin for a window. He would smash it if he had to. But the only window was boarded, sealed from the outside, bear-proofing the cabin.

He pressed his head against the blistered flakes of green paint. He would die like this, on his knees, frozen in place like the foetal-cast victims of Pompeii. The cruellest of comparisons. Even in death, of all the thoughts his mind might conjure, it chose one of heat, lava-death, he could almost feel it on his cheeks, almost imagine the brittle patches of exposed lichen bubbling either side of the cabin, consuming him.

"No," he cried, and the survivor in him took over, grasping that one straw of knowledge the man had overlooked. The cabin was designed to confound polar bears. He pushed his hands *up*, and the handle of the door moved as the heavy wooden door creaked. He pulled back and swung with the door until the snow shortened the intended arc and the man, the survivor, was presented with a gap the width of his head.

It was enough.

He rolled onto his side, bit at his lip, and shunted his body through the gap. The wind chased snow up his legs, blasting his face with one last gust of ice needles, and then he was inside. He slumped onto his back and choked, before he realised he was not choking but laughing.

He rolled onto his elbows, blinked at the ice coating his eyelashes, like staring through glue. He recognised the shape of the wood-burning stove, almost chuckled at the absurdity of burning wood in a land without trees, reassuring himself that in winter, the fire is always set. He laughed at the sight of the twists of newspaper and kindling inside the iron belly of the stove.

"There will be matches. A box with one or two matches sticking out, easy to grasp with cold fingers." Dieter forged thoughts that would keep him surviving.

There were three. Three matches sticking out of the box. He tugged his hand from the heavy woollen mitten, the ice beaded into the wool fibres rattled as he dropped it on the black timber floor. He struck the first match and stared at the flame.

He pressed the match to the paper. Too hard. The flame died.

He lit the second match, watched as the flame curled around the paper, blackening the edges. He would have forgotten to add wood from the metal bucket to the fire if the pressing voice in his head hadn't reminded him, *"Light the kindling."*

Every bit of him was pleased, grateful, overwhelmed, and, when the heat from the stove pressed the cold towards the walls, and the flames lit the man's face, the shelves, the two small cots, and the stumpy wooden armchair that had long since sacrificed its legs for heat, he stood up, stumbled to the door, and closed it.

The man crouched in front of the stove, warming his hands as he did a visual inspection of the room, directing his gaze to the shelves for tins of food, the beds for blankets, the bucket for wood, and when that ran out then the cots for kindling. He stood up and plucked a rusty can of ravioli from the shelf, together with a metal can opener. He fiddled with it, and then sat down in front of the fire to warm his hands before working on the tin.

Needles of fire burst through his fingers as his flesh recalled what it was to be made of meat, muscle, sinew and bone, not wood and metal. The fibres were meant to flex, and the pain as they warmed sparked a string of anecdotes from his research. His recollection of those stories had secured him a place on the expedition, regardless of his quirks and social oddities, and now those same stories were coming true, and saving his life, as he opened the can and put it on top of the stove.

Again the voice in his head told him, *"You'll need water."*

He searched for a pan, found one, and filled it with snow from the drift inside the door.

Ice may have been better, but he didn't have ice, and he was not going outside, not now that he was warm. The man crossed his legs in front of the fire, feeding it as the ravioli bubbled and spat in the can on the flat stove top.

He wrapped his mitts around the can, dragged the armchair closer to the stove and listened to the air pop out of the snow inside the pan as he ate, pressing two bent fingers together like a spoon. With his feet flat on the floor, his knees were higher than the arms of the chair, and he smiled at his Lilliputian adventure as he assumed the role of Gulliver of the North. He preferred such thoughts and distractions, as his mind settled, and the voice of the survivor fell back into the shadows.

The dark recess of his mind, black like the polar sky, black like the lichen, black like lava – cooled and inert, but fertile.

A fertile, fervent mind.

The thought made him smile, but still he did not entertain more than a thought. Some things must be suppressed in order to survive.

He had to suppress them.

There were things to do.

He had found the cabin. By luck, perhaps, but he should not disregard his latent knowledge, his studies and education.

He licked his fingers and placed the can on the floor. It took some effort to get out of the chair, then he searched the cabin, beyond the shelves, above the stove, beneath the beds. He kneeled in front a wooden crate turned on its side, its contents seemingly more valuable than the legs of the armchair. He smiled at the slim collection of mildewed magazines with stiff corners, curled and greasy as soap flakes. He flicked through a copy of National Geographic, placed it on the floor, covering it with a tattered Playboy magazine, a Danish western novel – the pages held together by true grit and mould. Then he spotted something else, something that peaked the researcher's interest, flooding his body with warmth, the kind that needs no flame.

"What's this?" he whispered, as if words might damage the leather binding, crack the spine, or even chase the journal at the tips of his fingers into an Arctic mirage, a polar tease.

The leather felt real, pressing into the thick whorls of his skin as he ran a finger down the spine. He tugged the journal out of the crate, teasing the sides from the magazines that gripped it, reluctant to let go. He knew what he had found but suppressed his enthusiasm with the same resolve and detachment that he kept for his other thoughts, the darker ones, hidden in the shadows. He would deal with them when the time came, now he had to be the keen observer and objective appraiser of all things Arctic. This was not the first and only Arctic journal the man had held between his fingers. But if this was Alfred Wegener's missing journal, if this was the one he had been tasked to find, then it might be the last he held for a long time, perhaps forever. He knew it as soon as he opened the journal, the pages crackling at his touch, with a glance at the name, the date, and the location in which the journal was written, Alfred's journal, the missing one, the one that would crown the man's post-doctoral research, and secure a position – any position – at the institute of his choice.

"Anywhere in the world."

The thought reminded him of the satellite phone in his jacket pocket. He had done his job, shelter, warmth from the fire and food to eat, and, soon, he would have something to drink. The man ticked off Maslow's hierarchy of needs – now that the basics had been met he remembered *love*.

He pulled the phone from the deep chest pocket, and the collapsible antenna from the other. He removed the battery, warmed it in his fist, and placed the spare battery on top of the journal, and then moved it to one side. He stared at the journal for a few minutes until he judged the battery to be ready. He carried the antenna to the door, opened it a crack and planted the tiny tripod in the snow. He shut the door and screwed the lead into the satellite phone, inserted the battery, turned the unit on and waited for it to find a signal.

"I found it, Marlene," the man said, when his wife answered his call.

"Dieter?"

"I found it."

"It's late," Marlene said.

Dieter waited as his wife stifled a yawn, and then said, "I found Alfred Wegener's journal."

"You found the cabin?"

"Yes, and the journal."

"That's great, baby, really. You must all be really pleased."

"What's that?"

"All of you must be pleased." Marlene raised her voice, and said, "There's a delay."

"I know."

"… others say?"

"What?"

"Oh, it's getting worse. What do the others say?"

"It's just me. I found it."

"I know you found it. I'm really pleased for you. But what about the others?"

"Others?"

"Oh, baby, I'm too tired for this." Marlene paused. "The others. The team. The crew. What do they think?"

"The crew?"

"Yes."

The man paced within the limits of the wire, and said, "It's just me. I found it."

"Are you alone?"

"Yes."

"Where are the rest of the team?"

"I don't know. I found the cabin."

Marlene sighed, and said, "Maybe it's the connection, but, it sounds like you are alone."

"Yes. I am."

"Where is the yacht?"

"In the ice. No," he said, "at the edge of the ice."

"And the crew? Are they on the yacht? Are they on *Ophelia*?"

"*Ophelia*? Maybe. I don't know."

"Why don't you know, Dieter?"

Dieter stared at the phone. He ran his hand through his hair, turned his head at the crackle and spit of the last piece of wood in the stove, and then looked at the phone again, frowning at the distant, static chatter on the line. He pressed the phone to his ear, and said, "I found it."

"I know you did, baby." The line crackled with static, and Marlene paused. "I'm worried about you, Dieter."

"I'm all right," he said, and then, "I have to go. I love you."

Dieter stabbed the tip of a numb finger on a button and ended the call. He turned the phone off and removed the battery. He shook the snow from the antenna and coiled it beside the spare battery on the floor by the journal. He lined up the parts, cataloguing them in his mind, before adding another piece of wood to the fire, the last, more snow to the water warming in the pan, and then grabbed a blanket from the bed before settling in the armchair with the journal. He tugged a headlamp from his jacket, switched it on, and started to read.

The survivor in him had served many functions. He had helped Dieter find the cabin, helped him survive the cold, and now he would help him to suppress thoughts of the crew, to forget the yacht, for the moment at least. There were other, more important things, for Dieter to consider.

He remembered the briefing at the offices of the Berndt Media

Group, once the final team had been assembled. He recalled the way Aleksander Berndt had stood, one hand in a trouser pocket, as he clicked a laser pointer with the other. Dieter had been fascinated with the man's passion, his fire, and, not least, his fortune.

"This area here," Berndt had said, circling a group of mountains on the map of Uummannaq fjord projected onto the screen, "is where we know Wegener was working, collecting data, before he died on Greenland's inland ice sheet. There should be a cabin. The locals know of it, but have, so far, been reluctant to confirm it. It is my belief," Berndt said, as he faced the team, "that they are tired of expeditions. There have been many of late, and we are just the latest in a long line. But, I also believe that if you find the cabin, establish a base of operations, and conduct a thorough investigation of the area, you will be rewarded."

"With what, exactly? It's a big area. We're going to need a little more information."

"Ah, Katharina," Berndt said, and smiled, "of course, I might have known our captain would be the team sceptic."

"I'm not a sceptic, I'm a geologist. I've seen my fair share of granite. If I'm going to get excited about something, I'd like to know what to look for."

Dieter closed his eyes for a moment, letting the rustle of snow crystals against the wooden shutters, and the teasing of the wind at the corners of the bitumen roof, distract him from the memory of Berndt's briefing. He swapped his memory of the subtle scent of Berndt's expensive cologne for the rich Arctic odour of cold, damp mattresses, mildew, lichen, and earthy roots. He smoothed his fingers over the creased leather cover of the journal and thought about Berndt's reward.

"No-one knows for sure what secret is buried in those mountains," Berndt had said, "Wegener hid it well. The question is *why?*"

Dieter opened his eyes and turned the page. He was about to find out.

Chapter 4

Maratse screwed the last of the spikes into the ice and tightened the shrouds of the tent. He studied the thick clouds of snow hiding the peaks of Svartenhuk and decided that even if he hadn't stumbled across the yacht, the weather would have hidden anything worth hunting in the mountains. The light from his headlamp reflected on the snow caught within its beam as he fed the dogs with dried halibut heads from the sledge, working down the thin dog chain he had anchored to the ice. Once all the dogs had been fed, Maratse crawled inside the tent, tied the canvas door, and assembled the walls, base, door, and hotplate of the collapsible stove. He prised the tubular chimney sheets into one long length and pushed the end through a leather flap in the tent. He lit the stove and arranged his sleeping gear as water boiled in the small kettle Karl had given him. Maratse lay on a cot inside his sleeping bag, with an enamel mug of coffee by his side and a heavy paperback in his hands. He grumbled between the pages, squinting once or twice as he moved the book closer and then further away. After three more pages, he eased himself out of his sleeping bag and rooted through his pack for his glasses. A second cup of coffee later and he had given up reading altogether, as even the most engaging descriptions the science fiction author wrote couldn't compete with the images of the bloody interior of the yacht, and the two dead crew. He stoked the stove with enough fuel for an hour or more, and then turned off the light.

It didn't matter what he might have said to the woman in the yacht, and no matter how many times he told himself he didn't, the truth was that he did care.

"You can't just leave," she had said.

But he did, and yet it gnawed at him, just like the dogs scraping at the skin of the halibut, before they penetrated the cheeks to chew on the frozen white flesh beneath. When he closed his eyes he could see the two dead crew members, slumped in their respective corners of the yacht's living area. The first question that plagued him was not how, but *when* did they die? Were the victims drugged like the crew? How many glasses were on the table? Was it five or six?

Maratse stared at the reflection of the flames from the glass window in the stove door as they licked at the tent walls. Beyond the crackle of the wood in the stove, the swathes of snow cascading down the tent walls, and the dogs fidgeting on the ice, Maratse heard the distant sound of two vehicles retreating into the night, and pictured the police Toyota and the hospital transit van that doubled as an ambulance, racing back to Uummannaq. Another world, his world, one he had left behind.

The small folding cot creaked as he turned on his side and closed his eyes. The dogs settled. Maratse forced himself to think of something else, anything else. He chose the image of police Sergeant Petra *Piitalaat* Jensen, the wayward strands of her long black hair, soft dark cheeks, her smile, her pout, those lips. His final thought was of the thirteen years between them, not particularly remarkable in Greenland, but enough to push any further thoughts from his mind. Maratse felt the frame of his glasses cool against his cheeks, pulled them off, and listened to the snow trickling down the side of the tent.

The next morning he had to dig through the snow to find the ice screws. Everything took that bit longer, as he packed his gear, collapsed the tent, clipped the dogs into their traces, and anchored the team to a fresh bridge of ice he dug with the metal-edged ice staff before breakfast.

It was dark. The sun would not return for another two months.

Maratse secured everything to the sledge, hitched the dogs, and leaped on as Spirit tugged the team towards Inussuk. Their trip interrupted, they were going home. They passed the yacht two hours later. The dogs barely gave it a glance, while Maratse stared, remembering the stripes of blood on the ice outside the yacht. They would be covered with snow now, but the yacht would stay moored to the ice unless a storm and warm winds broke the sea ice into floes, causing the crime scene to drift away. He turned away from the yacht, clapped his hands, and leaned back against the sledge bag. He closed his eyes, felt his breath cool and bead on the light moustache above his lip, and cling to his eyelashes like tiny diamonds on each hair.

The dogs slowed at the open lead in the ice, the black water visible beneath a thin soupy coating of new ice. Not enough to stitch the two plates together, but plenty to fool Tinka as the dog tried to step onto it as Spirit leaped. Maratse clapped, encouraging the dogs with two quick calls, as they pulled the sledge and Tinka onto firmer footing, and the last stretch before home.

Maratse watched as Tinka fell in beside the lead dog, shaking the water from her legs with a strong lope to match the pace of the team.

"Lesson learned," Maratse said, and smiled as he settled on the sledge.

He didn't move again until the team bumped the sledge up and over the ice foot, flatter and easier to navigate at low tide. Maratse slowed the team with soft commands, stepped off the sledge and gripped the uprights, walking behind the team to the anchor points he shared with Karl and Edvard. Their dogs yipped and howled as Maratse sorted his team, marching one dog after another to its chain, throwing it a fish head from the blood and grime-spattered plastic crate hidden inside a wooden chest beside the dogs. Once the sledge was empty, and the dogs fed, Maratse slid the sledge up and onto the box so that the runners would not freeze in a sudden surface melt. It didn't matter quite so much on the beach as it did when the team was anchored on the ice, but Maratse took pleasure in doing things the same way every time. He carried his gear to his house, dumped it on the deck, and opened the door.

The phone started to ring before he had removed his boots. He kicked them off, shook and patted the snow from his overalls, and padded into the living room in his socks. He picked up the receiver on the sixth ring.

"Maratse," he said, and leaned against the windowsill.

"Constable David Maratse?"

Despite the static on the line, Maratse thought the English accent was strange. He waited for a moment, and said, "I'm retired."

"But you are David Maratse?" It was a man's voice, older than Maratse. Not Scandinavian.

"*Iiji.*"

"My name is Aleksander Berndt. *Ophelia* is my boat." He paused, and said, "You are familiar with *Ophelia*?"

"I was onboard, yes."

"That's right, the Chief of Police told me."

"Simonsen."

"Yes."

Maratse unzipped the front of his overalls, and said, "What do you want?"

"Well, I'm sure you can imagine this is a difficult time for the crew, and I feel that I'm very far away. I'm calling from Berlin. It's late here, and I just need to have some things in place, as quickly as possible, to solve this matter."

"What matter?"

"*Ophelia.*"

"Your boat?"

"Expedition yacht, yes. Rather an expensive asset. She is anchored to the ice, as I understand, without a crew. So I need your help."

"I'm not a sailor."

"I appreciate that, but you are a policeman."

"Was."

"That's right, you're retired. But I wonder if you would be interested in earning more money."

"Looking after your boat?"

"No, not quite. I have already arranged to have someone secure the boat in the event of a storm. But even if *Ophelia* is secure, the police will not release it before the case has been resolved, and that's what I want you to help me with."

"To solve the case?" Maratse shifted position. "I'm not interested."

"No? Not even for a substantial payment? I can make it worth your while, Constable."

"I'm retired."

"So you say, but I have an idea that you are not entirely satisfied with that particular arrangement. I understand you were hired earlier this year to help solve another case, one involving a missing girl? You see, Constable, I have done my homework, and I believe you are the very man I need to speed things along, and allow me to get my boat back to Germany, and my crew to their families. You understand, this is a very difficult time for everyone concerned. Greenland is so very far away, so remote, isolated. It would be a comfort for the families to know that the company, and me, are doing everything possible to help with investigation and to speed it along the way to a happy conclusion."

"Happy?"

"Did I say that? I mean successful, of course."

Maratse turned at the sound of someone tramping up the steps to his house. He waved at Karl, nodding as his neighbour kicked the snow from his boots and opened the door.

"You've got company," Berndt said. "Perhaps I could call again, give you some time to make up your mind."

"I don't need more time, Mr Berndt. I cannot help you."

"Because you are retired?"

"Because I won't interfere with a police investigation."

"I didn't ask you to interfere, I asked you to investigate."

"It's the same thing, the minute I get involved."

Berndt sighed, and said, "I think you are making a mistake, Constable."

"Perhaps."

"But more than that, I think we both know that it will be difficult for you *not* to get involved. Hell, you are already involved; it was you who discovered *Ophelia* and the fate of her crew. Are you not in the least bit curious as to what happened? Don't you want to see the killer brought to justice? Is that why you retired? Because you stopped caring?"

"Goodbye, Mr Berndt."

"Wait…"

Maratse ended the call and looked at Karl. "I need a smoke," he said, and walked towards the door.

"I thought you were trying to quit?"

"I still am."

He pulled on his boots and followed Karl onto the deck. Snow squeaked like brittle rubber as they walked to the railing and lit a cigarette each. Maratse brushed at the snow on his wool sweater and zipped his overalls to just below his neck.

"How was your trip?" Karl asked.

"I think you know."

"We saw the police car and the ambulance from the window," he said, and pointed with the cigarette between his fingers. "We saw them come back too. You know Sammu? The local reporter?"

"*Iiji.*"

"He said someone was murdered on a yacht." Karl studied Maratse's face as he smoked. "He said you were the one who called the police."

"He's right, and so were you."

"How?"

"You said trouble seems to find me. It did."

"Again."

"*Iiji.*" Maratse finished his cigarette. "When are we eating?"

"Buuti says to come when you are ready. She told the Danes to come at dinnertime."

Maratse laughed. "I bet that confused them."

"*Aap*," Karl said. "I told them to come at six."

"That was nice of you."

"I know." Karl squashed his cigarette against the metal lid of the rubbish bin attached to the railings. He dropped the butt inside. "See you later."

Maratse nodded and watched him leave.

The Danes – Sisse, her daughter, Nanna, and partner, Klara – lived in the house beside Maratse. The women were artists, working with natural materials washed up on the beach, or, in winter, discarded from ravens, foxes, and hunters. When Maratse arrived at Karl and Buuti's house, the Danes were already seated at the table, and Nanna was playing with a dog whip Karl had made for her with a short length of wood and a long piece of string. Sisse called out for Nanna to be careful as she swished the whip back and forth in front of Maratse as he walked into the lounge. Buuti hugged him and guided him to a seat next to Sisse.

"We watched you leave yesterday," Sisse said, curling her arm around her daughter as she bustled past with an imaginary team of dogs. She kissed Nanna on the head, prised the whip from her hand, and said something about playing again later, once they had eaten. Sisse turned back to Maratse. "Was that Tinka leading the team?"

"Spirit," Maratse said. "Tinka has to learn."

"But she is learning," said Klara, "from Spirit?"

"It's the best way."

"Nanna likes Tinka, don't you," Sisse said, and stroked Nanna's long blonde hair as she fidgeted on her seat.

"She smells of fish," Nanna said.

"Nanna likes to kiss the dogs," said Klara.

"Oh, she shouldn't do that," Buuti said, as she placed a heavy pot in the centre of the table. Maratse caught the smell of seal meat wrapped in bacon, a wonderful combination of meat from the sea and the store. "Sledge dogs are not pets. They are working dogs. You should teach her to throw stones at the dogs instead, to keep them away, stop them coming too close."

"Stones?" Klara said.

"She's right." Maratse nodded. He reached down to pick up Nanna's whip and studied it in the light. Nanna watched him as he turned it within his fingers. "If you stay away from the dogs, I'll teach you to use the whip."

"How about that, Nanna?" Sisse said. "Would you like that?"

Nanna nodded with a sharp dip of her chin. "Yes," she said.

"Yes, what?"

"Thank you."

Maratse put the whip on the floor, nodded when Karl offered them all a beer, and smiled as Buuti heaped a generous amount of meat and potatoes onto his plate. He let the Danes lead the conversation around the dinner table, as they always did at mealtimes. It was as if they didn't know how to enjoy their food without adding words to it. Maratse ate. He sipped at his beer, smiled at Nanna, and raised his eyebrows, *yes*, when Buuti offered him a second helping.

The seal meat settled in his stomach, and Maratse felt the beer relax him, to the point where he began to nod in the heat of the living room. Karl kicked him under the table, and Maratse lifted his head as he heard Sisse say his name.

"What's that?" he said.

"I said what are you going to do?"

"About what?"

"The yacht. We were just talking about it, and Karl said you had a call from the owner. He said he wants your help."

"*Iiji.*"

"So what will you do?"

Maratse turned the beer bottle within his fingers and shrugged. "I don't know," he said.

Chapter 5

Simonsen leaned against the door of the room designated as Uummannaq hospital's morgue. He tucked his hands inside the pockets of his police jacket and watched as the doctor examined the dead body of the Danish man from the yacht. A nurse followed the doctor around the shallow metal basin, nodding and making notes as the doctor spoke into the microphone hanging from a cord around her neck. The doctor, Elena Bianchi, was Italian, but had a better grasp of Greenlandic than Simonsen ever would, and a more than passable Danish, although her pronunciation of some of the odd Danish vowels made him smile. He twitched when she caught his eye, chiding himself at being caught watching her and not what she was doing.

"You realise we will need ice," she said, "for the bodies."

"I'll call the fish factory," Simonsen said.

"Of course, if you keep bringing me dead bodies, I might put in for a cold storage." Elena wiped her nose with her wrist. She gestured at the room, and said, "Although, I wouldn't know where to put it."

Simonsen stepped into the room and peered at the stomach wound. Cleaned of blood, it looked insignificant, hardly worthy of the moniker: *cause of death, knife wound to the stomach*. But he knew the wound had been deep, he had the knife in an evidence bag at the station.

"What about the woman?" Simonsen glanced over his shoulder and into the corridor behind him. He could just see the toes of the second body they had recovered from the yacht.

"When I'm done with him," Elena said. She tapped the nurse on the arm and said something in Greenlandic. Simonsen moved to one side as the nurse walked past him. He waited until the sound of her clogs, plastic heels tapping along the corridor, diminished, and then closed the door.

"There's not a lot I can do about the bodies, Elena," he said. "These two were imported."

"They are people, Torben; you make them sound like cars, or washing machines."

Simonsen scoffed, and said, "It would be easier if they were."

Elena caught his eye, and then flicked her gaze back to the dead man. "You don't mean that."

"I don't?"

"No. You care about these people."

"I care about the people of Uummannaq. I'm just concerned that we seem to be getting more than our fair share of imported crime."

"You're worried about your statistics?"

"I'm worried about Aqqa. We're only two. We need more officers."

"Then ask for them."

"It's not that simple." Simonsen sighed. "I could always retire."

"You're too young."

"I'll be fifty-nine in September."

Elena looked up. "A year older than me."

"Maratse retired at thirty-nine."

"He was invalided off the force. You know that. You of all people know he didn't choose to retire."

"But nobody talks about it."

Simonsen stepped back as Elena moved around the table to take a closer look at the dead man's ear. She took a swab and worked it inside the cavity, before holding it up to the light. She turned the swab in her fingers and clicked the microphone to record her observation of a pale green residue.

"What about Maratse's legs?" Simonsen asked. "I heard he came for a check-up recently."

"He was here at the beginning of November."

"And?"

Elena dropped the swab onto a paper dish. She peeled the gloves from her hands and dropped them into a yellow biological waste bin for incineration.

"That's confidential," she said, and moved to open the door.

Simonsen stepped to one side. "But is he getting better?"

"Yes," she said, and walked into the corridor. "Help me switch these two."

"I thought he was," Simonsen said, as he pushed the metal gurney that Elena guided through the door. She covered the man with a thick paper sheet, and then helped Simonsen roll the woman's body inside the makeshift morgue.

"The man died from his wound, but there's something odd inside his ear," Elena said. She clicked the brakes of the gurney with a quick jab of the toes of her clogs, and moved directly to peer inside the woman's ear. She tugged on another pair of gloves, found a swab, took a sample, and held it up to the light. "Nothing," she said.

"Nothing what?"

"I wondered," she said, as she inspected the dead woman's other ear, "if they had something similar in their ears."

"Like what?"

"Hamlet," she said, and waited for Simonsen to react. "Poison in the ear?"

"I prefer war movies."

"It's not a movie, it's a play. Set in Denmark?"

"I know what Hamlet is."

"Who," Elena said. "*Who* he is."

Simonsen lifted his hands, palms up, an apology. "Okay," he said, "tell me."

"The man showed no signs of struggling. Almost as if the knife was pushed into his stomach while he was sleeping."

"The rest of the crew were unconscious – drugged."

"Yes," Elena said, "Ketamine. It's also used to treat tinnitus by dripping it into the ear. We might not have a freezer for dead bodies, but our lab technician is a gift. She came in as soon as I called, took a blood sample, and identified Ketamine within an hour. I'm trying to convince her to extend her contract." She pointed at the swab. "I'll ask her to check if that is Ketamine too."

"What about her?" Simonsen pointed at the dead woman on the gurney.

"Cause of death – knife in the throat – but she has cuts here…" Elena lifted the woman's forearm and pointed at her wrist and the base of her palm. "And here." She lowered the woman's left arm and splayed the fingers of her right hand. "She fought. She wasn't drugged."

"The other member of the crew – the German woman," Simonsen said, and paused to check his notes, "Nele Schneider – said the dead woman was having an affair with…" He flicked to another page. "Henrik Nielsen. The dead guy in the corridor." Simonsen tapped his ear, and said, "You don't just squirt something in someone's ear. You have to be pretty close." He paused. "Intimate. Kissing, maybe?"

"He would notice," Elena said. "But, in a passionate embrace? She could distract him." Elena held up her hands, and said, "I had better stop while I'm ahead. Just listen to me. It's not right for me to speculate. It's your case, Chief."

"And I rather wish it wasn't." Simonsen tucked his notebook inside his pocket, and jabbed a finger in the air above the ragged wound in the woman's neck. "So, she was murdered?"

"Yes."

"When can I talk to the crew?"

"They are under observation right now. The captain and the man are still a little groggy, but you can talk to Nele Schneider."

"Aqqa is outside the door," Simonsen said. "I'll have him move her to one of the offices upstairs, if that's all right with you?"

"It's fine. Take the office next to mine. It's empty." She sighed, "Another vacancy I'm trying to fill. If I can get a doctor for the month of December, I might be able to have a few days off over Christmas."

"When did you last have a holiday?"

"April."

Simonsen nodded at the dead body. "Thanks for your help." He turned to leave.

"You'll remember the ice?"

"I'll have Anton at the factory send someone over."

"Today?"

"As soon as they can," Simonsen said. He smiled and left the room.

The soft clap of clogs caught Simonsen's attention, and he thanked the nurse as they passed in the corridor. He tried to remember her name as he walked to the lift. Danielsen would know, he seemed to know all the young Greenlandic and Danish nurses who worked at the hospital. Simonsen found his young constable busy with his smartphone as he leaned against the wall between the two rooms where the crew of the *Ophelia* were being treated and observed.

"Busy?" Simonsen said. He stopped and adjusted his belt.

"Two of them are sleeping. The woman is pretending to. That's what the nurse said."

"Well, I want to talk to her. Bring her upstairs to the office next to Elena's."

"You don't want to talk to her here?"

"I don't want anyone listening in."

"Okay." Danielsen paused, and said, "What about Maratse?"

"What about him?"

"Do you want to talk to him?"

"Why? Do you think he did it?"

"*Naamik*, definitely not."

"Then why would I want to talk to him?"

Danielsen shrugged. "He's all right, Chief. He's one of us."

"He *was* one of us."

"You're always a policeman," Danielsen said.

"Tell that to Maratse." Simonsen turned to leave.

"Why don't you like him? Is it because of that Sirius woman?"

Simonsen took a breath and turned. He took a step closer to Danielsen, and said, "She cold-cocked us with a pistol downstairs. You do remember?"

"*Aap*," Danielsen said, and lowered his voice. "I won't forget that."

"Neither will I."

"But what has that got to do with Maratse?"

"He *helped* her, Danielsen. She was being held for the murder of her partner, and he helped her escape."

"We don't really know what happened."

"You're right," Simonsen said, and nodded. "We don't. But until we do, I don't trust him."

Danielsen tucked his phone into his pocket, and looked Simonsen in the eye. "Well, with respect, Chief, I do. And I hope you will too, one day."

"We'll see," Simonsen said. "Bring the girl upstairs."

The cleaners were using the lift when Simonsen pressed the button. He took the stairs instead. Thoughts of Maratse needled him as he climbed to the first floor of the hospital. He turned left, and walked through the waiting room, glancing at the tank of fish without breaking his stride. Tropical fish in Greenland. Each time he saw the tank, he entertained the idea of releasing the fish into the sea. If it wasn't for the pleasure it gave the kids when they came for an appointment, he would have done it already.

Simonsen opened the door to the spare office, sat down and placed his notebook on the desk. He closed his eyes for a moment, until he heard the squeak of Danielsen's rubber soles, and the flap of hospital slippers in the corridor. He stood up as Danielsen showed the young German woman into the room, and gestured for her to sit. Danielsen leaned against the wall at the back of the room beside a poster used to check patients' eyesight.

"How are you feeling?"

Nele glanced at Danielsen and then smoothed the hospital gown over her knees and zipped her fleece jacket to her neck. "It's cold," she said.

"I thought you'd be used to that?"

"It's warmer on *Ophelia*."

"But you have been outside. You skied with the rest of the crew to Svartenhuk, didn't you?"

Nele nodded.

"All of the crew?"

"The captain stayed onboard *Ophelia*."

"So," Simonsen said, and checked his notes, "five of you skied across the sea ice, and hiked into the mountains?"

"Yes."

"But only four of you came back?"

"Dieter…"

"Dieter?"

"Our Wegener expert, Dieter Müller." Simonsen waited as a frown wrinkled Nele's brow. "We were having an affair. We argued on the mountain. He said he wanted to stay. I thought he did."

Simonsen made a note. "What do you mean?"

"Isn't it obvious?" Nele fidgeted in her seat. She held her arm across her chest and pinched her bottom lip between her finger and thumb, biting her nail between sentences. "He came back. Later," she said, "when he came back, later, he must have killed Henrik and Antje. He must have."

"How do you know he came back at all?"

"Who else could have killed them?"

"Why would he?"

"Because Henrik was sleeping with Antje."

"The dead woman."

"Yes."

"Because…" Nele bit her thumbnail. A thin line of blood flooded beneath the nail, swelling onto the skin beneath. "Because Dieter was jealous."

Simonsen glanced at Danielsen. He looked at Nele, checked his notes, and then said, "I thought you were having an affair with Dieter?"

"I was."

"And did you know about Dieter and Antje?"

"Yes," she whispered.

"But you didn't kill them?"

"No," she said, and lifted her chin.

Simonsen frowned and made a note. A rumble of bubbles from the air unit in the fish tank drifted into the office, and Nele flicked her head towards the door.

"It's just the fish," Danielsen said. "It always does that."

Simonsen's chair creaked as he leaned back and studied the woman sitting on the opposite side of the desk. She started to bite her nail again, and, together with the fidgeting, she fitted the textbook description of nervous, traumatised, victim. Except for her eyes. Simonsen scribbled a word in his notebook: *predatory*. Nele Schneider had the look of a predator.

"You were unconscious when David Maratse found you."

"We were drugged."

"How?"

Nele shrugged, and said, "The water? He must have spiked the drinks before we left the yacht."

"Who?"

"Dieter."

"But you said the captain was alone on the yacht."

"Yes." Nele lowered her hand to her lap, her shoulders sagged, and she twisted to look over her shoulder at Danielsen. Her mouth opened, and, Simonsen noted, her eyes softened. "It was the captain," she said, "*she* drugged us."

Simonsen said nothing. He put his pen on the desk beside his notebook, and folded his arms.

"You don't think so?" Nele said. "I wouldn't have thought it, if you hadn't suggested it."

"I didn't suggest anything," Simonsen said.

"But it makes sense, doesn't it?" Nele reached forwards and placed her hand on the edge of her desk, steadying herself, as her soft eyes lost their predatory sheen, and she tumbled onto the floor. Danielsen ran across the room to help her as Simonsen stood up.

"Back to her room, Chief?" he said, in Danish.

"Yes."

Simonsen watched as Danielsen helped the young German woman out of the office. He picked up his notebook and pen and followed them to the lift. Danielsen helped Nele with an arm around her slim waist. He nodded at Simonsen through the glass doors of the elevator, and sank from Simonsen's view.

Something about those eyes teased at Simonsen's mind as he processed the evidence, considered the angles, and wondered just how plausible it was that four of a six person crew were sexually involved, with more than one partner. Of course, they didn't need to have sex to become jealous, and jealousy – a Greenlandic trait – thrived in isolated communities, and what could be more isolated than the cramped confines of an expedition yacht?

Simonsen walked back to the waiting lounge. He sat down on the red-cushioned sofa. Designed to appeal to kids, he dwarfed it, with his knees on the same level as his chin. It was quiet. The bubbling rumble of the air filter, a soothing antidote to the jumbled thoughts he tried to corral. He tapped the corner of his notebook against his knee, and studied the fish. They wouldn't last very long in Arctic waters, and neither had *Ophelia*'s crew. There was more to this. Perhaps the mystery residue on Elena's swab would provide more answers, that and an interview with the captain of the yacht. He wiped his hand across the stubble on his chin, thought about retirement, and thought once more of Maratse, pitching his tent somewhere on the ice. Perhaps it was time to discard what he didn't know, and accept the idea of having a retired police constable in the area.

He allowed himself a few seconds of contemplation as he chewed on the idea that Maratse was somehow involved with the murders, and then tossed it out, recognising it for what it was – just another malicious thought. There was currently enough malice in Uummannaq without Simonsen contributing to it.

The arms of the children's sofa crumpled beneath his weight as Simonsen pushed himself onto his feet. He took a last glance at the fish tank, and walked out of the waiting room.

Chapter 6

The sun does not rise in December, but, for the hunters of Uummannaq, every day with good ice was a gift not to be wasted. Maratse sat on the deck of his house and watched three large teams sledge past the settlement of Inussuk, as he smoked and drank his first coffee of the morning. The full moon lit the ice, the three teams, and the sledge carrying a fishing boat to the edge of the ice. It wouldn't be the last team to pass Inussuk, narwhal had been spotted south of Upernavik in the north, heading south. Small narwhal tusks could be sold for at least one thousand Danish kroner, but it was the meat the Greenlanders valued above all else, that and the *mattak* – the skin. Maratse swallowed at the thought of a spicy curry with soft squares of narwhal *mattak*, or a rich stew with large chunks of dark narwhal meat; the preferred meat dish for Christmas together with tiny Greenland potatoes from the south. Maratse pictured Buuti badgering Karl to sledge to the open sea in anticipation of the arrival of the whales. Of course, Berndt's yacht was going to provide a delicious topic of conversation for the hunters camped at the edge of the ice, while they searched for thin spumes of mist from the pods of narwhal. Simonsen was going to have his hands full protecting the crime scene.

Karl staggered down the steps from his house with an armful of gear clutched to his chest and a thermos flask tucked under his chin. He grinned at Maratse as he crunched through the snow to his sledge. Maratse waved and watched as Edvard helped Karl with his gear and dogs. After half an hour, and a second cup of coffee, Karl climbed the steps and joined Maratse on his deck.

"You could come with us," he said, and lit a cigarette.

"I might come later."

"Have you decided what to do about the yacht?"

"Not yet." Maratse flicked the dregs of his coffee onto the snow. "I thought I would go to Uummannaq, talk to Simonsen, and see if he needs me to write a statement."

Karl nodded. "You can take my snowmobile. Buuti has the keys."

"Thanks, but I think I'll take the team."

"Sure." Karl finished his cigarette and shook hands with Maratse. "See you in a few days."

"Good hunting." Maratse waited until Karl and Edvard hooked the teams to their sledges and watched as the dogs pulled them up and over the ice foot. It really was a good year for ice, despite global warming. Everybody was happy, the settlements were connected, and the wind was light, the temperature a steady minus twenty degrees. The conditions were perfect.

Maratse kicked the snow from his boots and went inside his house. He left his boots at the door and dug deep in the pocket of his overalls to find his mobile. He wrinkled his nose at the battery icon flashing at the top of the screen, searched for Petra's number, and called her on the landline.

"Hello, Piitalaat," he said, as she answered.

"David."

Maratse pictured her smile, and waited as she berated him for not calling for over a week. "I've been busy," he said, "training the dogs."

"Have you caught any fish?"

"*Eeqqi.*"

"Have you even put out a long line?"

"*Eeqqi.*"

"I thought that was the plan. To fish and hunt."

"I have been training the dogs."

"So you say, to fish and hunt." Petra laughed. "You're still struggling to adjust."

"You laughed."

"I'm sorry. I know it's hard."

"*Iiji.*" Maratse paused for a moment, and then said, "You heard about the yacht?"

"The double murder? Yes. They are sending two police officers from Ilulissat, and a detective from Nuuk."

"I called it in."

"You were the one who found it? The report said it was a hunter from Uummannaq area."

"Simonsen must have left my name out."

"He really doesn't like you, does he?"

"I suppose not."

Maratse fiddled with the lead connecting the handset to the receiver. Petra waited, and then said, "David, why did you call?"

"To talk to you."

"That's nice, I'm glad, but that's not all, is it?"

"The owner of the yacht called from Germany. He wants me to help speed up the investigation."

"That sounds familiar."

"It was different with Nivi, she was the First Minister."

"She still is."

"I know."

"But you don't want to get involved?"

"I'm trying not to."

Maratse waited as Petra thought for a moment. He listened as she breathed and pictured her biting her bottom lip, or curling a loose strand of hair around her ear. When she spoke again, he could hear the change of tone in her voice, she had made a decision.

"Hunting isn't working out for you," she said. "You miss police work too much. It's not your fault you were given early retirement, David, but you can't change that. I think this is what you have to do, I mean, if people are going to pay you to help solve crimes, to assist the police, then I think you should do it."

"You do?"

"Yes."

"Hm." Maratse said, "I'll think about it. Thank you, Piitalaat."

"Promise me one thing."

"*Iji?*"

"If you have to go to Germany, take me with you."

"I don't speak German."

"Exactly, but I do. You'll need a translator." Petra giggled and ended the call.

Maratse boiled the kettle and filled a thermos with fresh coffee. He changed clothes, tugged on his overalls, and pulled on his boots. He could feel the stiffness in his legs as he carried the thermos to his sledge. Sisse waved to him from the deck of her house.

"Are you going to the join the hunt?"

Maratse shook his head, and said, "I'm going to Uummannaq." He nodded at his sledge. "Do you want to come?"

"Really?"

"*Iji.*"

"I'll check if Klara will look after Nanna.

"She can come too."

"Oh, she'll love that, thank you." Sisse opened the door, then paused to knock the snow from her boots. "We'll be five minutes," she said, and disappeared inside the house. Maratse walked on, pulled the sledge down off the wooden box, and pushed it a short distance away from his dogs.

Nanna was the first to come out of the house. She bounded down the steps with her toy whip in one hand and a tiny backpack in the other. She raced across the snow to where Maratse sat on his sledge. She jerked the whip back and forth in front of her, giggling as the knot at the end of the string slapped against Maratse's boots.

"Like this," he said, and took the whip from Nanna's hand. He showed her how to swish with her wrists, rather than snap with her arms. The string whip arced in front of him. "Now you." Maratse crouched behind Nanna and guided her hand. She giggled, swishing the whip in small arcs as her mother arrived and helped her put her arms through the backpack.

"We must do what David says, Nanna. All right?"

Nanna nodded and coiled the whip, as Maratse pushed the sledge towards his dogs.

"You remember what I said, Nanna?"

"Yes."

"Stay away from the dogs unless I'm with you."

"Even Tinka?"

"*Iiji*," he said, "even Tinka."

Sisse wrapped her arms around Nanna, pulled her hat up for a second and kissed the top of her head. They watched as Maratse harnessed seven males and Tinka, and attached them to the sledge. He nodded for Sisse and Nanna to sit at the back, where they could lean against the sledge bag. Maratse held the uprights, growling as the dogs fidgeted at the end of the traces.

"This is Tinka's first test as a lead dog," he said, with a glance at Nanna.

"Okay," she said, as Sisse clamped her arms around her daughter.

"Ready?"

"Yes."

Maratse gave the command to go and leaped onto the front of the sledge, he tugged the whip out from under the cords stretched tight across the reindeer skin, and guided the team with commands and snaps of the whip to the left and right. Tinka hesitated at the ice foot, the tide was in, and Maratse leaped off the sledge to help push them up and over the ridge of ice and onto the frozen surface of the sea. As soon as they were clear of the ice foot, Tinka settled into her position at the head of the team. Maratse had given her the longest of the ganglines, and she raced across the ice, a dog's length ahead of the males. Maratse grinned at Sisse and Nanna, tucked the handle of the whip under his thigh, and rested his palms in his lap. The moon was a creamy yellow in a deep polar blue sky, and the only sound beyond the shush and grate of the runners, was the soft panting of the dogs and the creak of the sledge as it flexed within its bindings.

"What do you think, Nanna?" Sisse said, as she teased the hair from Nanna's brow and smoothed it under the lip of her hat.

"I like it."

Three sledges with large dog teams of more than fifteen dogs each raced past, heading towards the mouth of the fjord, and the open sea. Nanna waved at all of them as Maratse snapped the whip on the ice to help Tinka focus and to avoid a collision.

"Do sledges ever crash?" Sisse asked, as the last team raced past them and they sledged across the fjord to the icy coastline of the island of Uummannaq.

"*Iiji*," Maratse said. "I know of a *qallunaaq*, an Englishman, who crashed when a larger team enveloped his." Maratse slapped his palms together like crocodile jaws. "The hunter had to cut the lines to free the sledges. Just out there," he said, and pointed into the distance as he guided Tinka into the frozen harbour of Uummannaq, with a snap of the whip on the ice to her right. They sledged between the fishing trawlers and boats locked in the ice until Maratse slowed the team with soft commands and they approached a ramp of ice leading up to the road. A taxi waited for them to pass before driving down onto the ice.

"It's so busy," Sisse said, as Maratse secured his team to a metal loop sticking out of a rock between the fishing crates, pallets, and wooden boxes marking the winter storage areas for the hunters and fishermen. The dogs tethered here were in the older and younger brackets of the teams. More dogs were tethered to the ice, but the fastest dogs were racing for the sea, and Uummannaq bustled with the purchase of last-minute supplies. The majority of men and women that Maratse saw held a mobile to their ear, and the radios in the private cars and taxis were tuned to the local channel.

Nanna took a step closer to Tinka, only to be stopped by Maratse as he placed a gentle hand on her shoulder.

"What did we say, Nanna?"

"That I should stay away from the dogs."

"That's right."

"Even Tinka?" she asked, and looked up at Maratse.

"*Iiji*," he said, and pointed at the sledge. "Can you coil my whip?"

"Yes," she said, and ran to the sledge.

Nanna stumbled and fell over a clump of ice just as a snowmobile roared up the ice ramp and swerved to avoid her. The driver, a grizzled Dane with a bloody bandage wrapped around his hand, braked and yelled at Nanna. Maratse walked over to him.

"Hey," he said, "you're scaring the girl."

"She got in my way."

"You should have looked." Maratse waved his hand at the dogs and the people walking on the street. "You should be more careful."

The man let the snowmobile idle as he pulled the goggles from his face. He let them hang around his neck as he stared at Maratse; the whites of his eyes were red, flecked with venom.

"Do I know you?" the Dane said.

"My name is Maratse."

"The Constable from Inussuk? Hah. I've heard of you." He beckoned Maratse closer with a bloody finger. "The Chief doesn't like you much, eh?"

Maratse wrinkled his nose in the wake of the man's breath, and said, "That's not your concern." He looked at the man's hand. "What happened to you?"

"Enthusiastic butchery," he said, and sneered. "Some of us have to work for a living."

"You're a hunter?"

"I hunt lots of things."

"David," Sisse called out, waving as he turned. She nodded at Nanna whose face was buried in her mother's jacket. "Perhaps we can go to the store?"

"I have to go," Maratse said. "What's your name?"

The man revved the engine and grinned. "That's for you to find out, *Constable*." He let go of the brake and spat before accelerating along the road to the right, past the café in the direction of the hospital. Maratse watched him all the way to the door, where the man parked and disappeared inside the hospital.

"He wasn't very nice," Sisse said, as she peeled Nanna from her body.

Maratse nodded. He looked at Nanna and forced a smile. "Shall we say hello to Tinka?"

"I thought you said I wasn't allowed?"

"When you're with me, you can," Maratse said, as he walked across to his team, and unclipped Tinka from the gangline. He held the dog by the harness and walked her over to Nanna. "Tinka is still young," he said, as Nanna stroked the fur around Tinka's ears. "The problem is," Maratse said to Sisse, "that children have the same height as the dogs. They look the dogs straight in the eye, and they don't back down. Sledge dogs are not pets; they're the closest thing to the wolf. They spend their life jockeying for position in the pack. They sometimes interpret a child's actions as a challenge, and when dogs are challenged, they either submit…"

"Or they fight," said Sisse. She nodded in the direction of the hospital, and said, "Not unlike men."

"Maybe," he said, and grinned.

Tinka strained within Maratse's grasp, and he pulled her back, as Nanna withdrew her hand, and Sisse helped her with her mittens. Maratse walked Tinka back to the team and clipped the line into the loop at the back of the harness.

"I think we'll go shopping," Sisse said. "Perhaps we can meet in the café before going home?"

Maratse nodded. "I'll be at the hospital."

"Why? Are you going to find that horrible man?"

"No, I'm going to talk to the police." He pointed at the blue Toyota as it parked in front of the hospital.

"Does that mean you are going to take the job?"

"We'll see," he said, and waved as he walked along the road, crushing the stiff snowy tracks of the snowmobile beneath the soles of his boots.

Chapter 7

Constable Aqqa Danielsen stopped Maratse with a flat palm against his chest the moment he walked through the main entrance of Uummannaq hospital. He turned Maratse around and guided him back outside. Maratse lit a cigarette as Danielsen tugged a thin fleece hat from his pocket and smoothed it onto his head.

"Simonsen will kill you if he sees you in there," Danielsen said, as he took a cigarette from the packet in Maratse's hand.

"I doubt that."

"I don't." Danielsen took a long drag on the cigarette. "You weren't in the car with him. When we drove back from the yacht, I had to remind him we had people in the back. He ranted all the way to the hospital."

"Then what happened?"

"*Naamik*," Danielsen said and raised his hands. "Forget it. I can't tell you anything."

"You just told me that Simonsen was ranting all the way home."

"About you. I can't tell you anything about the investigation." He frowned at Maratse. "You're not working this case, are you? Privately?"

Maratse wrinkled his nose, *no*.

"Okay," Danielsen said. "One thing I can tell you is that one of the crew is missing, unaccounted for."

"There were patches of blood on the ice. Perhaps they were his?"

"How do you know it was a male?"

"A guess."

Danielsen squinted at Maratse though a cloud of smoke. He flicked the butt of his cigarette into the snow. "A male, mid-thirties, some kind of Alfred Wegener expert."

"Wegener?"

"Dead polar explorer. A German."

"The one who visited Svartenhuk?"

"*Aap.*"

"There's a cabin up there," Maratse said. "Why are you laughing?"

"It's the cabin they wanted to find."

"They?"

"The crew. They said no-one would tell them where it was. Who told you?"

"Karl."

Danielsen smiled. "He would know."

"So, they sailed here to find a cabin in Svartenhuk." Maratse finished his cigarette. "People don't kill each other because of a cabin. What were they really looking for?"

"They won't say. Simonsen has interviewed all of them, but no-one is talking."

"They were drugged, weren't they?"

"*Aap.*"

"By the missing man?"

Danielsen scuffed at the snow with the heel of his boot, and Maratse waited.

"Dieter Müller. That's his name. It's the only thing they do agree on."

"You need to find him."

"We're waiting for backup; they're sending a detective and couple of extra officers up from Nuuk. They're arriving on the flight to Qaarsut around lunchtime. We'll pick them up and drive to Svartenhuk."

"And the yacht?"

"We'll drop the detective off there, pick him up on the way back."

"But if the crew are at the station…"

"Being interviewed again by Simonsen."

"What are you doing here?"

Danielsen nodded at the window of the room closest to the nurses' office, three metres from where they stood. He pointed at a man sitting on the hospital bed. "Do you know who that is?"

Maratse recognised him as the man with the bloody hand on the snowmobile who he met earlier. "I just met him. I don't know his name."

"That's Axel Stein. He frightens the nurses, scares the children. He moved to Greenland before I was born. Drank his way through a job as a carpenter, beat more than one wife, and had his kids taken from him by the council, twice."

"The same kids?"

"Two lots. Two girls and one boy." Danielsen adjusted his belt. "He lives alone in a hunter's cabin with nothing but a bad smell and a bad temper. He hasn't hit anyone since he stopped drinking, but he hasn't been nice to anyone either. Never, as far as I can recall. He comes into town once a month for supplies, and to draw some cash from the bank. Most of the year, no-one sees him, and they forget how nasty he can be. He reminds them every chance he gets. I think he does it so he can keep living in the cabin. No-one will go there as long as he lives there."

"But he hasn't done anything criminal, recently?"

"Nothing on record since he beat his last wife, and that was fifteen years ago, maybe more."

"But he has a temper?"

"Wicked, according to Simonsen." Danielsen held out his hand and Maratse shook it. "I like you, Maratse. No matter what Simonsen says, you're all right. You helped in the search for Nivi Winther, and you pulled one of our own out of the water. You might not be a cop anymore, but you haven't stopped acting like one."

"That's what gets me into trouble."

"*Aap*," Danielsen said, and laughed. He nodded at the window. "I have to go. Stay out of Simonsen's way, and you'll be fine."

"What did I do wrong?" Maratse asked, as Danielsen reached the entrance.

"He thinks you were working with Fenna Brongaard, when she came through here. He thinks there are too many secrets in your past."

"And what do you think?"

"I try not to," Danielsen said. He smiled, and Maratse wondered if his smile was the real reason the nurses liked to have him around. "Look after yourself."

Maratse waited until Danielsen was inside the hospital. He looked through the window as the young police constable entered the examination room, saw the way the nurse touched his arm, and then watched as Danielsen gripped the front of his belt and weathered a string of abuses from her patient. He could hear the curses out on the street. Axel Stein, it seemed, was working on his reputation. The thought occurred to Maratse that the cut on the old man's arm could have come from a knife, either by accident or during a scuffle. He shook the thought from his mind, finding it difficult to imagine a reclusive Danish hunter travelling across the ice to rendezvous with a yacht and guide them into the mountains.

Of course, *that* actually did make sense.

Maratse tilted his head to one side and watched as Axel stood up and faced off with the young constable. To his credit, Danielsen didn't back down, and Maratse nodded. He was all right. He made up for his boss.

Maratse walked from the hospital to the café, ordered a coffee and a plate of twice-fried chips that had the consistency of greasy cardboard. They were just about edible with a generous sprinkling of salt. He had finished eating when Sisse walked in with Nanna. The little girl had a track of tears on each cheek and a stubborn twist to her lips.

"I'm sorry," Sisse said, "but do you think we could just go home? If you want to stay, I can maybe find a taxi. I heard they drive across the ice."

"We can go home," Maratse said.

"Thank you." Sisse frowned. "But you haven't bought anything."

"There's nothing I need. The shop in Inussuk has more than enough for me."

"No treats? Chocolate? Beer?"

"Buuti spoils me with her cooking," Maratse said, as he followed Sisse and Nanna out of the café, "and I smoke too much. They have run out of cigarettes in Inussuk and if I buy more in town I'll only smoke them." Maratse shrugged and pointed in the direction of the sledge. "That way."

"Are you trying to quit?"

"Maybe."

"That doesn't sound very convincing," Sisse said. She helped Nanna onto the sledge, and then sat down behind her. Maratse unhooked the dogs from the loop in the rock, attached them to the sledge, and led the team down the ice ramp. He jumped on when the dogs were on the sea ice and Tinka tugged the team into motion.

"I'm not convinced, but a friend thinks I should quit."

"The policewoman? Petra."

"*Iji.*"

"She's very nice. Very pretty." Maratse glanced at Sisse. "Don't look at me like that. Klara and I are very happy together. Besides, Petra is only interested in men. That's easy to see."

Maratse pulled up his collar and shrank inside his overalls.

"Am I making you uncomfortable?"

"Hm," he said, and adjusted the hat on his head.

Sisse laughed. "I'm sorry, David. I let my mouth run away with my thoughts. I think your friend is very nice, and I like the way she looks at you."

"She's twenty-six."

"So?"

"I'm thirteen years older than she is."

"Why should that matter?"

"Hm."

Sisse leaned forwards to squeeze Maratse's shoulder. "You're not very good at this, are you?"

"*Eeqqi.*"

"Don't worry," she said, and let go. "You'll get better. We women like to think we are mysterious, but we're still human, most of the time." Sisse laughed and kissed Nanna on the top of her hat. "What about you? Are you happy again?" Nanna curled to one side and hid her face inside the crook of her mother's arm. "She wanted a doll, and I said she had too many already, and now she is pouting."

Maratse looked at Nanna, tried to catch her eye, but she buried her face even deeper beneath her mother's arm. He looked up at the sound of a plane landing in Qaarsut, the icy landing strip south of Inussuk. It would be gone by the time they had passed the remote airport, but the helicopters would be shuttling all day between the mainland to the island. He remembered what Danielsen had said about backup arriving from down south, and replayed the conversation in his mind as Tinka led the team home. He chose not to tell Sisse anything more about Axel Stein, but thoughts of the man, and what he was capable of, nagged at Maratse until it was time to leap off the sledge and guide the team up the beach to the rest of the dogs. Nanna ran across the snow and up the stairs to her house. As soon as the dogs were tethered, watered, and fed, Sisse hugged Maratse.

"Thank you, David. It was very generous of you."

"Will she be all right?" Maratse said, as Nanna curled her tiny mittened hands around the handle and slammed the door.

"She'll be fine. It's my own fault. I've dragged her halfway around the world to satisfy my passion for art and nature. At some point, before she starts school, we'll settle somewhere, find a routine."

"Is that what you want?"

"Hell no," Sisse said, and laughed. "But, it will be good for her."

Maratse smiled as Sisse waved and followed her daughter's footsteps to the house. It was only when she had gone inside that he noticed the lights of his own house were lit, and a slim shadow passed the window.

Maratse coiled the whip and tucked it inside the wooden box with the rest of his sledging gear. He pulled the thermos flask from the sledge bag and poured a cold cup of coffee into the lid. He sipped at it as he stared at the shadow passing back and forth across the window. Maratse dumped the coffee onto the snow, lifted the sledge onto the box, and carried the thermos under his arm to his house. He paused at the top of the stairs, banged the snow from his boots, and opened the door.

The smell of perfumed soap pricked at his cold nose, as Maratse took off his boots, and shrugged out of his overalls. He left his thermos by the door and walked into the living room. The shadows had been cast by a young woman, her red hair twisted into a wet knot at the top of her head, with damp strands plastered to her pale and freckled shoulders. Maratse stared at her, as she danced around his living room, his towel knotted above her breasts; it barely covered her thighs. She hummed as she danced, and Maratse noticed the tiny buds pressed inside her ears, and the white cord leading to the iPhone in her left hand, the cord whipped up and down as she danced.

Maratse coughed, and the woman danced. He raised his voice, shouted hello, and waited as she stopped, opened her eyes, and pulled the buds from her ears. Maratse could hear the beat pumping out of the buds until the woman dialled down the volume with a swipe of her thumb.

"You're out of water," she said in English. "I think I drained the tank."

Maratse stared at her.

"Hello?" she said, and waved her hand in front of his face. "Did you hear what I said?"

"About the water?"

"Yes, about the water. Honestly, daddy said you were smart."

"Your *daddy*?"

"My father, yes."

"And who is he?"

"Aleksander Berndt. He owns *Ophelia*."

"Is he here?"

"No," she said, and snorted, "obviously."

Maratse tapped his top pocket and walked to the door. He heard the woman say something. He ignored her. Maratse found his cigarettes in the pocket of his overalls, tugged on his boots and walked onto the deck.

He smoked as he wrestled with his thoughts. He flicked the cigarette into the snow, and lit a new one, turning his head as the woman appeared at the door. He half expected her to walk onto the deck in her towel, but her practical and slightly worn outdoor gear surprised and impressed him, fitting her like a glove. The way she wore her clothes suggested the cuts, tears, and repairs, were all her own. She plucked the cigarette from Maratse's mouth and held out her hand.

"My name is Therese," she said, and took a long drag on Maratse's cigarette.

"Therese Berndt?"

She shook her head. "Kleinschmidt. My family – my *ancestors* – probably spawned a whole bunch of Greenlanders. Mostly up north."

"Upernavik?"

"Right," she said, and blew smoke in Maratse's face. "But you're from the east."

"*Iji.*"

"See," she said, and held out Maratse's cigarette. He took it from her fingers. "I know these things. I've seen a lot of Greenland, and I studied you and your people. I have a PhD in Arctic Anthropology."

Maratse let the cigarette burn in his fingers as he listened, she took it back and leaned against the railing, making a show of studying him.

"Your skin is darker than most of the Greenlanders I have met. You're a little shorter than the average male, and," she said, and pointed the tip of the cigarette at Maratse, "your moustache is wispier than the men in Nuuk. No," she said, as she pressed her fingers to the hairs above his top lip, "you should keep it. It gives you that oriental look. Makes you look hot."

Maratse felt the colour rise to his cheeks, and he wondered if that was sweat beading on his brow.

"Why are you here?" he asked. His tongue was dry, and he had a sudden urge to get drunk on Edvard's home-brewed spirits.

Therese frowned. "I really thought you would be smarter than this." She stubbed the cigarette on the wooden railing and dropped it onto the deck. "Daddy hired you, and he sent me to boss you about." Therese ran the tip of her tongue around her teeth.

"What?"

"I'm kidding," she said. "I'm here to give you instructions, to help you investigate."

"But I haven't agreed to anything."

"Oh," she said, and took Maratse's arm, "I wouldn't worry about that. Come on inside, and I'll tell you what you need to know. We've got a busy day ahead of us tomorrow."

Chapter 8

Alfred Wegener was a genius. With each turn of the mildew-tinged thick pages of the journal, Dieter knew he had struck gold. What he had found was academic collateral, a currency that could change his fortunes and move Marlene and him from the slums of Berlin, to a more upmarket location, with, perhaps, room for a baby. These thoughts occupied Dieter as he read the journal in the breath-fogged light from his headlamp. He curled the tattered blankets around his shoulders, blew on the tips of his fingers, and drank lukewarm water straight from the pan. He had already sacrificed the book crate for heat, and, if he looked through the smoky glass window of the stove door, he would see the iron nails glowing bright between the flames.

Dieter pored over Wegener's field notes, nodding at the descriptions of the lichen, tapping the page when Wegener's itinerary fit with what he knew to be true. There was just one thing that eluded Dieter, something that made him read and reread the journal, tracing Wegener's words with the frost-nipped tips of his fingers. The late polar researcher seemed to have invented some kind of code, something about archaeology. But Wegener was a meteorologist, climatologist, and geologist by default, and Dieter could not recall an archaeologist being present on this particular expedition

"Unless I missed something," he said, his breath like dry ice, obscuring the pages of the journal in his lap.

Dieter put the book down and assembled the satellite phone. Once the antenna was set up, and the battery warmed and installed, Dieter punched in his home number. He stifled a yawn, ignored the fact that he couldn't remember having slept, and waited for Marlene to answer.

"Dieter?" she said. "I've been trying to call you. Why didn't you answer the phone?"

"I turned it off to save power," he said, and picked up the journal. "Marlene, I need you to find my notes. They should be in a box, by the side of my desk."

"We need to talk, Dieter. There was something posted online…"

"This is important."

"So is this." She paused. "A man came to the house. He asked all kinds of questions. He wanted to know if you had contacted me."

Dieter rested the journal in his lap and rubbed his face with his hand. He blinked sleep from his eyes – or perhaps it was ice crusting his eyelashes, his own breath sticking to the hairs on his skin.

"Marlene…"

"No," she said, "you have to listen. You are in the newspapers, even *Die Welt*. It says you are missing…"

"I'm not."

"…and that two of the crew are dead." Marlene stopped for a breath. "They were murdered, Dieter. Stabbed to death."

Dieter sighed. "Marlene, there is a box by my desk."

"Are you even listening to me? Stop talking about the box. I don't care about the box, and neither should you. They are looking for you. They want to find you, to question you."

"Who?"

"The police, the authorities. They have sent more police from the south of Greenland."

"To find me?"

"Yes."

Dieter let the phone drift from his ear. He almost dropped it. He turned the pages of the journal, found the first entry about something buried in the mountains. He pressed the phone to his ear, and said, "They know, Marlene."

"What do they know?"

"The secret. That's what they are looking for, not me."

"Secret? You're not making any sense."

"It's all right, my love…"

"No, it's not. Nothing is all right. This is not okay. You have to leave that cabin, go down to the ice and give yourself in to the police."

"But then they will find out the truth. I can't let that happen. It's my secret now."

"Dieter," Marlene said, her voice shook, and she bit back a sob. "You're not well. I see it now, just like the man said."

"What man?"

"The one I told you about. His name was Stefan. He said he was from Berndt Media. He looked like a soldier. He said he had some difficult news to tell me, that it was shocking. He asked if I wanted to call someone, or if there was someone he could call, to be with me."

"Why?"

"Because he said you were ill, that you were struggling, that the dark had affected you, that it had triggered a depression. He said the crew confirmed it, and that you had done… things. Terrible things."

"I left the yacht."

"How?"

"I had to get away, Marlene."

"When?"

"I didn't go back. I stayed on the mountain, after our first search."

"But when, Dieter? The man said you killed those people. That you were crazy, obsessed with finding something…"

"I did find something. It is wonderful, Marlene. It can change our lives."

"Our lives will never be the same again," she said. "That's what the man said. That's why he took your box of notes."

"What?"

"Your notes. He took all of them. He said it might help, if they could find evidence of your obsession, some kind of mental health problem, they might be able to help you."

"You gave him my notes?" Dieter's breath condensed in the cold glare of the lamp in gusts.

"I had to. Don't you see? I want to help you, Dieter. I want you to come home. I love you."

"My notes."

Dieter put the phone down on the floor and stood up. He twisted around the cabin, placing his hand on imaginary boxes, shuffling from one cot to the other, crouching to look beneath them, as if the wooden cot was his desk, the cabin his office, and the soft green glow of the Northern Lights were the streetlights on Admiralstraße, Berlin.

He heard Marlene's voice pleading from the satellite phone's tiny speaker. He whirled on it, and shouted, "Where are my notes, Marlene?"

She didn't answer. He kicked at the phone, ripping the cord for the antenna out of the unit. Marlene's soft cries slid into the corner of the cabin as the screen blinked with the symbol warning that the battery was low, drained like Marlene.

Dieter stopped in the middle of the cabin. With a short leap to either side, forwards or backwards, he could have touched the outer walls, slipped his nails behind the newspaper pasted to the old wood.

Instead he clawed at his face, his blunt grimy nails drawing red lines on his cold, stiff cheeks, but no blood, it was too cold to bleed.

The satellite phone died with a single beep, and the screen went blank, and then black, like the night, as the clouds obscured the polar moon and the wind dropped to a reverent whisper.

Dieter gathered the journal into his hands, bound it with the sealskin thongs around the cover, tucked it into the inside pocket of his jacket and tugged the zip to a close. He collected the different parts of the satellite phone, hid the spare battery in the pocket closest to his body, coiled the antenna lead, and collapsed the tripod into one jacket pocket, the phone into another. Dieter looked at his mitts, studied the jagged holes and tears in the ragg wool weave. He zipped his jacket, pulled his fleece hat over his ears, and shaped his hood like a funnel to hide his face.

He crouched in front of the stove and waited for the fire to die.

As the flames flickered and the fiery nails began to cool, Dieter dug into the shadows, and glanced at the drift of snow spread, fan-shaped, inside the door. The still polar night enticed him out of the cabin, and he shut the door, smiling as he lifted the polar bear handle. The snow crunched beneath his boots, as he traced his route a few steps away from the cabin, turning his whole head, up, down, all around, staring through the funnel of his hood with his tunnel vision.

Was it really such a good idea to leave the shelter of the cabin?

"They are coming for me," was Dieter's answer, a new-found strength and determination, driving him on. Stronger than the will to survive, Dieter was driven to succeed, to discover Wegener's secret.

The lighter layers of windblown snow dusted the trail in Dieter's wake as he lifted his heels, picking his way down the glacial valley towards the sea ice. If they were looking for him, as Marlene suggested, Dieter convinced himself he knew why.

"They might have taken my notes," he said, his voice muffled, his warm breath tickling his nose, "but they don't know how to read them. They don't know what they are looking for."

Dieter pictured his bunk onboard *Ophelia*, and his duffel bag stowed beneath it. He thought about the thumb drive hidden between the bottom of the canvas bag and the stiff layer that gave the duffel bag its shape. His smile was hidden by the hood, but the astute observer might notice a lighter gait, a renewed purpose in his stride.

Conflicting thoughts countered his enthusiasm, thoughts that included the police, they could be armed. He was a wanted man. The police thought he was a murderer.

He shook the thoughts away. *"It won't be a problem."*

Only when he drew close to the ice at the foot of the mountain, where the sea lifted its frozen edges to the rhythm of the tide, did Dieter stop to pause, to think again. He stared in the direction he knew *Ophelia* was anchored to the ice; he himself had dug one of the two ice axes into the frozen sea.

Dieter unzipped the funnel hood, pressed his head into the cool air and cinched the hood into a high collar. He took a step onto the ice foot, slid over its smooth edges, and stumbled onto the sea ice. He started walking, fascinated at the smooth, wide, empty path ahead of him, interspersed as it was with the occasional iceberg. He sought out the familiar bergs they had used as waypoints from the yacht to the mountains, found them, altered course, and concentrated on walking at an efficient speed through the night, his second night without sleep.

"I can't sleep. Not yet," Dieter said, his breath curling over the collar of his jacket. Ice began to bead on the zip, and above his own lip, clinging to the hairs on his cheek bones, and making his eyelashes tacky. He blinked and walked on.

The wind had blown the snow into shallow eskers, like an old three-dimensional map fashioned from layers and plates of cardboard. The going was straight, firm, and smooth, but not without danger. Dieter mustered the strength to walk over the black ice, reminding himself that it was thick enough to drive a car on, forcing himself not to look, not to second guess. He hoped the narrow lead ahead had not widened, and was relieved to find it had shifted, the two edges of the ice had moved closer. Dieter leaped over the gap and walked on.

At one point he thought of polar bears, only to forget all about them when he spotted the lights and activity around *Ophelia* still a kilometre, maybe more, from where he stopped and stared. It was as if the carnival had arrived, disgorging the carnies, performers, and animals onto the ice, into tents pitched alongside boats instead of trucks, dogs instead of lions. Someone had turned on *Ophelia*'s lights, and her mast was lit like a sparse Christmas tree, a single red and green navigation lamp, lost in the black polar night.

There were noises too, and Dieter realised that only the hungriest of bears would approach the whale carnival, with its Arctic revellers – howling dogs and high-spirited men. Even the heavens crackled, with the occasional shooting star arcing across the night sky beneath a curtain of green and white.

The carnival lights were celestial, the shadows of tent, boat, dog, and man, thin and angular with only the occasional beam of a snowmobile or even a car capable of catching Dieter in its glare as he approached. He noticed that the Greenlanders were laser-focused on the ice bobbing sea. Only the dogs looked towards the mountains, relegated as they were to dormant modes of transport, as the men whooped, pointed, jabbered into mobile phones, and hurried to slide the flotilla of fibreglass skiffs and dinghies from the ice into the sea. Harpoons were raised, rifles loaded and slung, outboard motors dipped, and boats boarded. In the space of just ten minutes, Dieter and the dogs were alone on the ice, as the hunters chased thin spumes of mist far out to sea.

If he had binoculars, and if he knew where to look, if a Greenlander had stood by his side, placed a hand on his shoulder, and turned Dieter in the right direction, he might have seen pearl tusks and grey rubber flanks between the growlers of ice in the black sea. He might have seen the narwhal. But Dieter's eyes were drawn to another jewel, another prize, and he slipped between the tents, stepped over the anchor lines, and climbed the ladder onto the deck of *Ophelia*.

Dieter opened the door to the cockpit and climbed down the short flight of steps. He flicked a switch and the cockpit lights blazed through the glass, bright squares lined with thick icy frames. The blood-soaked floor of the galley gave Dieter a start, and he steadied himself with a hand on the panel to his right.

It was clear where the victims had died, and *how* they had died – it was bloody. He shrugged and let the survivor in him guide him past the blood and deeper inside the yacht. He opened the door to the cabin on the right, found his duffel bag in the middle of the floor, as if it had fallen from his bunk. He unzipped it, slipped his hand around and between the clothes he had folded inside, and pressed his fingers into the space where he had hidden his thumb drive.

Dieter frowned, sat on his heels, and drew the duffel onto his thighs. He plunged his hand inside the bag again, and a third time. Then he switched on the light, emptied his clothes onto the deck, and ripped the bottom layer out of the bag. When everything was spread before him, and he had patted and unfolded every piece of clothing, checked inside every sock, Dieter threw the duffel bag against the sail bag in the pointed bow end of the cabin, tore off his hat, and gripped his head in his hands.

The dogs mistook Dieter's roar for a howl and joined in.

Chapter 9

Maratse heard the telephone ring three times before he understood what it was. He blinked, rubbed his eyes, and rolled over in his bed just as he heard Therese pick up the phone and answer the call. She answered in German, and, when she continued, he decided the call must be for her. He rolled onto his side and tugged the pillow over his head. He didn't hear Therese when she called to him, nor did he hear her run up the stairs in her bare feet. It was her perfume that pricked at his consciousness and forced him onto his elbows to stare at her. When she came into focus, he looked away.

"There's a woman on the phone. She wants to speak to you," Therese said.

"Hm."

"I told her she could call back, but she said she would wait."

"Okay," Maratse said, and rubbed his eyes, blinking in the glare of the light from the landing.

"You've got balls, Maratse," Therese said. "I only spoke to her for two minutes, and, if I were you, I wouldn't let her wait longer than it takes you to run downstairs." Therese giggled as Maratse pulled back the covers and slid out of bed. He stumbled on his way to the stairs, but only when he reached the top step did he feel it was safe to open his eyes.

"I'm not naked, Constable," Therese called, as he climbed down the stairs.

"Might as well be," he said, his mouth dry with sleep.

Maratse bit through the standard morning pain in his legs, before his muscles warmed up. He reached for the phone and pressed the receiver to his ear.

"Maratse," he said, and pressed his free hand against the windowsill as his legs trembled.

"Your girlfriend told me you were sleeping," Petra said.

Maratse waited for her to laugh, but when no laugh came, he felt compelled to answer straight away.

"She arrived yesterday, when I was out."

"And who is she?"

"The boat owner's daughter, I think."

"You don't know?"

"They have different surnames." Maratse looked up as Therese walked into the living room. Even the skin on her flat stomach had freckles. He looked away, caught his breath, and focussed on the pain in his legs – a necessary distraction.

"So you accepted the job."

"Not yet."

"I don't understand, David. There's a German woman living in your house?"

"Staying in my house…"

"Fine, let's call it that."

"What do you want, Piitalaat?"

"What do I want?" Petra caught her breath, and Maratse pictured her biting her lip. "How about you call me Petra from now on?"

"Hey…"

"In fact, let's just say, as far as you're concerned, my name is *Sergeant* Jensen."

"Don't be like that, Piitalaat. I didn't invite her here."

Therese carried two mugs of coffee into the living room and placed one on the windowsill. She leaned close to Maratse and whispered into the handset that his coffee was ready, and then giggled as she walked to the sofa. Maratse stared at her as she unzipped her sleeping bag and pulled it over her bare legs. He pulled his eyes away from the flesh-coloured sports bra pinching her breasts and pressed his forehead against the cool glass of the window.

"She's leaving soon," he said, and wondered if Therese could speak Danish. When Petra didn't answer Maratse tried a different tack. "Sisse told me to say 'hi'."

"I'm sure she did." Petra sighed. "Listen, let's talk later."

"We can talk now."

"No," she said, "we really can't." Petra ended the call, and Maratse put the phone down. When he turned around to look at Therese she was smiling.

"She's a handful," she said, in English. The sleeping bag slipped as she bent her leg and tucked her knee against her chest.

"Her name is Piitalaat."

"Greenlandic?"

"*Iiji.*"

"But you spoke Danish."

"Piitalaat doesn't speak Greenlandic."

"Funny, her German is pretty good."

Maratse tugged his t-shirt over the waistband of his underwear, picked up his mug, and slumped in the chair opposite Therese.

"You said your name was Kleinschmidt."

"That's right."

"Not Berndt?"

"It's not important." Therese curled long freckled fingers around the mug and rested it on her knee. She stared at Maratse until he coughed and looked away. "You're wondering why I'm really here, aren't you?"

"*Iiji.*"

"I was in Ilulissat when daddy got news of what happened on *Ophelia*. He put me on the first plane to Qaarsut to come and take care of her."

"*Ophelia?*"

"Yes."

"You sail?"

"I have my Yachtmaster Ocean certificate. What about you?"

"Small fishing boats."

"Daddy always said it's not the vessel it's the water. I respect anyone who sails in these waters."

Maratse relaxed as the topic shifted to more familiar territory. If it wasn't for Therese's long legs and minimal sleeping wear, he might have enjoyed the conversation.

"Tell me what you want," he said, and sipped his coffee.

"I need to get *Ophelia* into a safe harbour, and I need the ship's log."

"Doesn't the captain have that?"

"No," Therese said. "She was unconscious when they took her off the boat. That's all I know."

Maratse nodded. "I found her like that."

"I know." Therese placed her empty mug on the table between them. She wrapped the sleeping bag around her waist and Maratse decided he could relax just a little bit more. "I need you to take me to *Ophelia*. Today."

"We would need permission from the police."

"Daddy's working on that. He says they might be willing to let me sail it back to Ilulissat."

"Not without an escort," Maratse said. He wrinkled his brow as Therese tilted her head and smiled.

"That will be one of your jobs."

"I haven't said yes."

"No? That's strange when you consider that your bank account has an extra five thousand Euro in it." Maratse frowned, and Therese said, "Our branch in Berlin confirmed the transfer this morning, while you were sleeping, before your girlfriend called."

"I didn't agree to that."

"I wouldn't worry; we tend to jump over that part. It's much easier to get someone to do what you want when the money is already in place. You'll get another three thousand once you have completed the other tasks daddy wants you to do."

Maratse sighed. "What other tasks?"

"I'll let you know," Therese stood up, let the sleeping bag fall to the floor and tucked her thumbs into the panty elastic around her waist. "I'm going to get changed now. I suggest you do the same. We're going to be gone all day, longer if we get permission to sail." Therese plucked the elastic from her waist and let it snap against her skin. "Well?"

Maratse put his mug on the table and stood up. He heard the smooth slip of Therese's underwear on her skin as he climbed the stairs to his room. Things were moving just a little too quickly, and of their own accord. A helpless feeling wormed its way into his mind, and he gripped the thin duvet in his fist. Police work often had an element of helplessness attached to it, but this feeling was different, it had an edge, Maratse recognised it for what it was, he felt used.

He let his thoughts simmer as he dressed, tugging on Karl's hand-me-down thermals that Buuti had brought over the day the sun disappeared for the winter. When he was ready, and had enough layers for a day on the ice, he opened the wardrobe and pulled his police jacket off the hanger. He ran his fingers over the dark square of material and loose threads where the police shield had once been attached, and pulled it on, amazed once again at how good it made him feel to wear it. He felt almost whole, stronger, empowered, and ready to steer this private investigation into something more agreeable.

Therese was right about one thing, he realised, it was easier to say yes to something when the decision had already been made. He might be in Berndt's debt, but Therese was in his country, and Greenland had its own rules, its own climate, and its own culture.

Strengthened by the weight of the jacket on his shoulders, the pain in Maratse's legs didn't bother him as climbed down the stairs. Therese packed a small backpack in the living room as he pulled on his overalls, and tied the arms around his waist. Maratse pulled on his boots and opened the door.

"Where are you going?" Therese asked.

"To get the keys."

"Keys?"

"For the snowmobile. My dogs are staying here."

Maratse shut the door as Therese started to speak. He was halfway down the steps when the police Toyota bumped over the ice foot and drove onto the beach. Danielsen waved him over as Simonsen got out from behind the wheel, leaned against the side of the car, and lit a cigarette. The engine rumbled as Maratse crunched through the snow and accepted a cigarette from Simonsen.

"A peace offering," he said, as Maratse leaned in to the flame from the lighter cupped in Simonsen's hands. Simonsen tucked the lighter in his pocket. "There's a woman in your house, Constable. Who is she?"

"Berndt's daughter." Maratse blew a cloud of smoke over his shoulder as Therese stepped onto the deck. He nodded at her as she lit a cigarette of her own, curled the hood of her jacket over her fiery-red hair, and watched them.

"Berndt called us this morning. He wants permission to sail his yacht to a safe harbour."

"She said the same."

"Did she also say he wants you on the boat with her?"

"*Iiji.*"

Simonsen glanced at Danielsen. "You see, it's this kind of thing that makes it difficult for me to like you, Maratse."

"I haven't done anything wrong."

"No, you haven't, but you always seem to be in the thick of it." Simonsen turned his head at the sound of the radio crackling inside the car. Danielsen reached inside to answer it. "I haven't made a decision yet. I need to wait for the investigative team to finish up." He paused as Danielsen spoke rapidly in Greenlandic. "What is it?" Danielsen held up one finger and looked away. Simonsen looked at Maratse. "What is he saying?"

Maratse translated, "Something has happened onboard the

yacht."

"I sent two policemen and a detective out there early this morning."

"Someone's been hurt." Maratse flicked his cigarette onto the snow as Danielsen leaned inside the car, clicked the radio into place, and then leaned over the bonnet to speak to Simonsen.

"The detective has been stabbed."

"Onboard the yacht?"

"*Aap.*" Danielsen held up his hand, as Simonsen reached for the door handle. "There's more."

"Go on."

"The assailant took the police car. He's driven off, deeper into the fjord."

Simonsen opened the door and climbed in behind the wheel. "Get in," he said to Maratse. He shifted into first gear as Danielsen climbed into the passenger seat, and Maratse opened the door behind Simonsen. He was half inside the vehicle when the door opposite him opened and Therese climbed in.

"This is not a taxi," Simonsen said. "Get out."

"That's my boat, Chief," Therese said, and shut the door. "I'm coming with you."

"This is police business. You're a civilian."

"So is he," she said, nodding at Maratse.

Maratse closed his door, as Simonsen cursed and accelerated off the beach, slipping the Toyota into four-wheel-drive to negotiate the ice foot.

"Don't," Maratse said, as Therese reached for the seatbelt and began to stretch it across her chest. "We might need to get out quickly." She nodded and let it slip back against the seat.

Simonsen accelerated through the gears, steering wide of the icy coastline, and following the peninsula to drive around the open lead of black water. Maratse noted the softer patches of ice as Simonsen raced across the frozen surface of the sea towards the hunters' camp in the distance. The moon lit the ice with a searchlight-white beam as the police emergency lights flashed blue against the bergs, and the winter dark was charged with colour.

Therese punched Maratse on the arm, her teeth flashing, her eyes green and bright, as Danielsen chattered on the radio, and Simonsen concentrated on the road ahead. Maratse wondered if Therese would be smiling if she knew the road was just twenty centimetres thick, perhaps less. He decided she probably would, shook his head and laughed, her excitement was infectious.

Maratse stopped laughing when he heard Danielsen ask the policeman to repeat what he had just said.

"What is it?" Simonsen said, as he downshifted to slow the Toyota. Maratse could see the dogs stirring as they approached the yacht.

"It's the detective. He was first onboard. That's when he was attacked."

"All right." Simonsen glanced at Danielsen. "There's more?"

"*Aap.*"

"Spit it out."

"The assailant took the detective's gun."

"He's armed?"

Danielsen nodded as Simonsen slowed to a stop beside the yacht.

Simonsen turned in his seat and nodded at Therese. "Out," he said. "No discussion. You said it was your boat, I want you to get on it and stay on it."

Therese opened the door, and stepped onto the ice. She looked at Maratse, and said, "What about him?"

"He's coming with me." Simonsen nodded at Maratse, and then held out his hand to Danielsen. "Give me your sidearm."

Danielsen hesitated, and glanced at Maratse.

"I know what you are going to say, Aqqa, but I need you here." He looked up as one of the policemen from Ilulissat jogged over to the Toyota. "Get the ambulance out here, and keep an eye on the German girl. Quickly."

Danielsen tugged his pistol from his holster, leaned between the seats, and pressed it into Maratse's hand. "I want it back," he said, and opened the passenger door. He slapped his hand on the policeman's shoulder and told him to get into the car. Simonsen shifted into first and accelerated into a tight turn as Therese joined Danielsen on the ice.

"Which way?" Simonsen said, as the policeman closed the passenger door.

"Northeast, past that pointy berg."

"How long ago?"

"Forty minutes."

Simonsen gritted his teeth, and then nodded at Maratse in the back. "Introduce yourselves."

"Inuk Taorana," said the policeman. "From Ilulissat."

"We've met," Maratse said, "a few years ago."

"Really?"

"You came to Ittoqqortoormiit onboard *Sisak II*."

"Yeah, I remember. Maratse?"

"*Iiji.*"

"Okay, enough introductions," Simonsen said. He pointed at a dark stationary shape between two icebergs. "Get ready, because that's my patrol car."

Maratse sat on the edge of the seat and peered through the windscreen as Simonsen slowed the Toyota to a crawl. Clumps of ice frozen into the surface crunched beneath the Toyota's tyres. Simonsen stopped the vehicle and turned off the emergency lights.

"Inuk," he said, "I want you to go to the right. Maratse?"

"*Iiji?*"

"Go left of the bergs. I'm going to drive straight up to the car."

Maratse opened the door and stepped onto the ice. He stepped away from the car, gripped the pistol in both hands, and nodded once at Inuk as Simonsen pulled away. The engine rumbled, but beyond that, all was still, dark, and cold, as the moon retreated behind a thick cloud and it started to snow.

Chapter 10

Petra woke early on Sunday morning. The winter sun had yet to rise, and the Northern Lights blazed in the pre-dawn sky. She made coffee and stood at the window of her new apartment in Qinngorput and looked out over the bay towards the centre of Nuuk. The building cranes stood proud of the cityscape, lit in such a way that the stars might have fallen like snow to rest on the long metal arms, illuminating and approving Nuuk's steady climb to fame and fortune, a modern jewel in the Danish Crown waiting to be prised free of its colonial masters.

A flash of blue light caught Petra's attention. She tracked the police car's emergency lights from the harbour until they were lost, hidden, gone, as the weekend night shift wrapped up, and the day shift slipped out of their houses leaving families, loved ones, friends and pets to sleep on. Petra finished her coffee, turned her back on the Nuuk nightscape, and slipped under the covers of her bed. She picked up her smartphone and considered calling Maratse, and then slapped the phone, screen down, on the duvet as she remembered the woman, the German floozy, currently embedded in Maratse's tiny house in Inussuk.

"Embedded." Petra said the word aloud, and then swore. "So long as she hasn't *bedded* Maratse, I might still forgive him." She blew a strand of hair from her mouth as she wondered why it was so important. What would it matter if he did sleep with her? The heavy curtains absorbed her words, and Petra, alone in the dark, slipped another half metre beneath her duvet.

After a while she rolled over, picked up her phone and checked her social media. She saw that one of her colleagues had shared a link to a *Sermitsiaq* article about the murders in Uummannaq. Petra clicked on it, read the name of the journalist: Kitu Qalia, and then slid her finger down the screen as she read. According to a quote from the Chief of Police in Uummannaq, none of the crew had been charged yet, nor was there sufficient evidence to pursue the case. The next paragraph made Petra sit up, as Simonsen was further quoted to say that one member of the crew was still unaccounted for, and that they were keen to find him, and talk to him.

"Greenland's first manhunt," Petra said, and smiled.

There had been plenty of chases in Greenland that she knew of, and many more that were too old to interest her, and they were all affected by the weather. She knew that Maratse had once chased a murderer into the mountains around Ittoqqortoormiit. A Danish writer had tagged along, and published an article in an American magazine. Few people in Greenland had read it, and Petra wondered how much of it had been true. Knowing Maratse as she did, it wouldn't surprise her if all of it was true, but he rarely spoke of it. She smiled at the thought of another manhunt on Maratse's doorstep, and couldn't resist imagining him pursuing the killer across the ice and into the mountains.

She slapped the phone down on the mattress, and sighed at the sound of her own voice, muffled as it was beneath the duvet. "Get it together, *Piitalaat*."

Petra gave up trying to sleep and threw the duvet further down the bed. She dressed in her workout clothes, prepared a bag, and then pulled on her salopettes and jacket, bracing herself for a moment before leaving her apartment, climbing down the stairs, and stepping out into the snow, swirling and drifting between the apartment blocks overlooking the bay. She found the keys to the car she was looking after for her Danish friends on vacation, cleared the windscreen, and then drove to the gym. Petra parked alongside the other insomniacs, and punched her code into the door.

The musky smell of sweat pricked at her nostrils as she peeled off her outer clothes in the changing rooms before stepping into the gym. Petra didn't recognise the Dane lifting weights in the corner, but guessed he might be on a temporary contract, with access to the gym a perk of the job. She knew the other man running on the treadmill far too well.

Petra pressed her water bottle into the holder of the machine next to Gaba Alatak, stretched, and then stepped onto the treadmill to programme her preferred distance and speed. Gaba tugged the ear bud out of his left ear as Petra began to run.

"You're up early," he said. The gym lights reflected in the sheen of sweat blistering his bare torso.

"Couldn't sleep." Petra allowed herself a single glance at her ex-lover's pectoral muscles and then concentrated on finding her running rhythm.

"I was at a meeting on Friday," Gaba said. "Your name came up."

"What meeting?"

"It was very interesting." Gaba grinned as Petra did a double step to lengthen her stride.

"You ape," she said. "Are you going to tell me about it or not?"

"Not if you keep insulting me."

Petra picked up her water bottle and squeezed a mouthful into Gaba's face.

"Speak," she said.

"I tell you what, Sergeant," Gaba said, as he wiped the water from his face, "if you stop calling me names, and play nice, I'll let you buy me brunch at Katuaq when we're done here."

"Brunch? It's still too early for breakfast."

"You don't know how far I'm running."

Gaba pulled the remote from the holder next to his water bottle and turned on the television mounted on the wall in front of them. He flicked to the Teletext channel. Even in the technological wake of modernisation, some things never changed. KNR's Teletext channel had, somehow, been overlooked, but not forgotten. The news cycled in Greenlandic and Danish with one or two slow moving pages for each story.

Petra read the Danish news as she ran. She was just about to give in and invite Gaba to brunch when breaking news of the Uummannaq manhunt flicked onto the screen. She glanced at Gaba as she read about a policeman being stabbed with a knife, the suspect now considered armed and dangerous. Petra had to give the Teletext reporters credit; with a very limited amount of available text they had set the scene for a drama that would grip the nation. Even in the areas where Internet was either unavailable or unaffordable, nearly every household had access to a television and the Teletext channel. She imagined Maratse following the story as it developed, and then remembered that his was one of the few households without a television. She decided to call him as soon as the sun was up in Nuuk.

"Have you heard anything about this?" Petra asked Gaba.

"Nothing. This is news to me."

"Do you think they will send you in?"

"The SRU? Maybe. That's up to Simonsen."

Petra read the same news item each time it cycled through the channel until her own running programme neared a close and she slowed before stretching and hitting the showers. Gaba continued running.

"How long?" she asked.

"Just another five kilometres," he said, "maybe eight."

"I'll wait, and buy you brunch."

Gaba grinned, and said, "I thought you might."

"You're still an ape." Petra turned off her running machine, grabbed her water bottle and let Gaba run in peace.

She was dressed in her salopettes, the straps and bib hanging loose at her sides, with her jacket over one arm when Gaba walked out of the changing rooms. He nodded at his car and said he would meet her there. Petra wiped more snow from the windscreen and then drove to the Katuaq Cultural Centre. Gaba parked his SUV next to her Volkswagen, and followed her inside. They found a table and hung their jackets over the backs of the chairs, but as Gaba picked up his plate for the buffet brunch, Petra outlined the rules.

"Rules? For brunch?"

"Yes," she said."

"Like what?"

"This is not a date."

"Sergeant…"

"I used to be Petra, remember?"

"Yes."

"Then, we can agree, this is not a date."

"We agree."

"Second," she said, and pinched her middle finger.

"Are you giving me the finger?"

"I will, if you don't agree to rule two."

"All right. What is it?"

"You'll tell me everything."

"Everything I *can* tell you, yes."

"Fine," she said, and waved at the buffet tables, "you can eat."

Petra watched as Gaba weaved his way between the tables. She had to admit that the leader of Greenland's Special Response Unit took care of his body. She pushed the memories of that same body aside, pulled her smartphone from her pocket and called Maratse. She pressed the phone to her ear and waited for him to pick up.

"Piitalaat," he said, his voice a whisper with static from the wind making it hard to hear what he said.

"I can hardly hear you."

"I can't talk. Not now."

"Are you all right?"

"I'll call you," Maratse said, and ended the call.

Gaba put a plate of pancakes, sausage, and egg between his cutlery and picked up one of two empty coffee mugs. "Everything all right?" he asked.

"I just called David."

"Maratse?"

"Yes." Petra looked up. "I think he was on the ice. He said he couldn't talk." She frowned and said, "You don't think he's involved in the manhunt, do you?"

"I think our friend, the *Constable*, is always involved. One way or the other." Gaba tapped the table. "Don't worry about him. Get something to eat." He waited as she bit at her lip. "Petra?" he said. "Breakfast?"

"Okay," she said.

Petra slipped her phone into her pocket, picked up her plate, and walked to the buffet. Gaba filled both mugs of coffee while she filled her plate. She smiled as she returned to the table – he had even remembered the juice.

"So," she said, as she pushed the thought of Maratse out of her mind, "what was this meeting about?"

"The one where they talked about you?"

"Yes," she said, and slapped the back of Gaba's hand with her fork.

"Sergeant?"

"I'll behave as soon as you stop teasing me."

"Deal," he said. Gaba took a sip of coffee, followed by a forkful of pancake. He grinned when Petra started tapping the table with the bottom of her knife. "Sergeant Jensen, you have been placed on a very short list of suitable applicants for a new policing initiative."

Petra made a face. "I don't want to babysit any more politicians, or visiting VIPs, show them around Nuuk, or…" She stopped when Gaba picked leaned back in his seat. She studied his face. "It's not that, is it?"

"*Naamik.*"

"What is it then?" Petra put her knife down. She reached for her coffee, but barely tickled the handle with her fingers before Gaba started to speak, and she forgot about breakfast.

"It's like an Arctic task force, in fact, they might even call it that: *ATF*. Although," he said, and frowned, "I'm sure the Americans have something called that already."

"They have a lot of things." Petra smoothed a pile of crumbs from the tablecloth onto the floor. "Tell me."

Gaba leaned forwards. "Multidisciplinary, with officers from each and every Arctic nation. Yes," he said, as Petra opened her mouth, "even Russia."

"And they want me?"

"Your name is on the list."

"How long is the list?"

"Ah, Sergeant, that would be telling."

Petra thumped her glass on the table, spilling juice, and rattling the cutlery. She turned and apologized to the people eating at the tables nearby. "Are you on the list?"

"I'm not," Gaba said. "You look surprised?"

"Maybe I am," Petra said. She shook her head. "They'll want a Dane. Greenland is still Danish."

"No," Gaba said, "they want you."

Petra brushed long strands of her hair behind her ears and then cut a generous square of pancake. Her hair slipped loose again as she turned the pancake around the plate, idly chasing the maple syrup as her cheeks dimpled in a smile.

"You're a talented officer, Petra," Gaba said. "You speak three languages. You're single, no ties, and…"

"And?" Petra said.

"You're pretty good in bed too." Gaba ducked as Petra lifted the pancake on her fork. "Lower your weapon, Sergeant," he said. "I was joking, I didn't tell them that."

"But you told them the other things?"

"Yes," he said, and pushed back his chair. "And, if you're wondering, the Commissioner told me to tell you. He thought I might see you over the weekend." Gaba picked up his mug. "I'm getting a refill."

As Gaba moved away from the table to join the line of people waiting for fresh coffee, a Dane showed an American to the table beside Petra.

Petra took small bites of her breakfast as she thought about what Gaba had said. The thought might have lingered had it not been for the conversation between the two new arrivals. While Petra sipped at her juice she heard the American mention mining in Uummannaq fjord.

"What's the current status of the operation?" the Dane asked.

"Precarious," the American said, "and damned difficult to trace. There's a rumour of mining rights for the Svartenhuk area – legal documents, mind you, signed and stamped with official approval from the Danish and Greenlandic governments."

"And where are these documents? Who has them?"

"Arbroath Mining Co."

"They took over the mine in Marmoralik, Uummannaq?"

"Because of the extended rights," the American said, "I'm sure of it. Of course, these murders will slow things down."

Petra risked a glance and a smile when the American caught her eye. He said hello in English, and Petra answered with the little Greenlandic she knew. The American nodded and continued with his conversation. Petra turned back to her food, but continued to listen.

"So what has this got to do with the murders on some rich German's yacht?" the Dane asked.

"That depends on the purpose of his expedition. Berndt gave a statement to *Die Welt* when the story broke. He said the expedition had an environmental focus – something about microplastics…"

"Just following the current trend, eh?"

"Exactly, but he did let slip that his expedition team were also interested in exploring Svartenhuk to find the cabin built by Alfred Wegener."

"They want to find the cabin?"

"Perhaps," the American said, and lowered his voice. Petra stopped chewing. "But maybe they are looking for something else."

"Like what?"

"A journal, perhaps."

"Wegener's journal?"

"Yes." The American reached for his plate, and pushed back his chair. "You know what's in the journal?" He gave the table a theatrical rap with his knuckle. "Only Wegener's expedition notes, including a detailed geological survey and analysis of the Svartenhuk mountain range."

"Thorium?" the Dane whispered. "That's incredible."

"Who knows?" The American stood up. "Arbroath Mining is a

very small company, just waiting for someone to buy them out."

"But if Svartenhuk has Thorium…"

"Yep," the American said. "Wegener's journal is quite the item of interest all of a sudden."

"I'll say," the Dane said. He stood up and walked with the American to the buffet table as Gaba sat down with a fresh mug of coffee.

"You've barely touched your food," he said. "Too excited to eat?"

"Something like that," Petra said. She turned and looked at the American as he took a selection of food from the buffet. The metal lid of pan with scrambled eggs clanged as he put it down. "Do you know who that is?" Petra asked. "The American?"

"No," said Gaba, "but the Dane next to him works for GEUS. You know? The Geological Survey of Denmark and Greenland."

"Yes, I know what GEUS is."

"Anyway, he's new. Arrived last month. Why?"

"I don't know, but maybe I just found the motive for murder in Uummannaq."

Chapter 11

The winter was unseasonable. The thought pricked at Dieter's mind with every metre he drove on the sea ice in the stolen police patrol vehicle. It was the thought of driving on ice, not the act, which made him slow to a stop. He lowered his hands from the wheel and stared at the knife protruding from his stomach. Somehow, in the scuffle below decks, when the policeman had surprised him, Dieter had fallen, and the knife that had been in his hand was now in his stomach. His blood soaked through his thermal layers of clothing and into his waxed jacket, the cotton kind that needed to be waxed to be waterproof. The jacket was old, uncared for and now, without its protective wax, it was dark, saturated with his own blood.

He turned off the engine, and pushed his head back until he could feel the headrest pressing through his fleece hat. Dieter stared through the windscreen as snow swirled within the beam of the Toyota's headlights. He switched off the lights, and closed his eyes. He could still see the snow, floating in his vision, white flecks on a dark background, black like the sea, the death water beneath the ice.

The policeman had told him to stop, several times. Stop, Dieter mused, is the same word in a lot of the Anglo Saxon languages, but rarely had he heard it spoken in so many different ways as he did inside the yacht. The policeman had commanded him to stop, ordered him, pleaded with him, and then begged him when Dieter's knife was pressing against the man's windpipe. But when Dieter had slipped, and the knife had burst through the lining of his own stomach, the policeman's tone had changed, softened, he had told him to stop as if there really wasn't an alternative, suggesting that if he didn't stop fighting and resisting, the knife in his stomach would cause more damage, it would not stop, and neither would the flow of blood.

It didn't.

Dieter didn't know if it was going to stop.

He gritted his teeth and fumbled the battery and the satellite phone out of the different pockets in his jacket as the air inside the Toyota cooled. Each time he moved the knife snagged on his jacket. Dieter fought back the nausea and grimaced through the pain as he assembled the satellite phone, turned it on, pointed the aerial towards the window, and dialled Marlene's number. His breath escaped his lungs in ragged bursts of frost, the choke of an ice dragon. Marlene answered on the third ring and Dieter's breath settled on the screen, as tears crackled into desiccated orbs in the corners of his eyes.

"Hi," he said.

"Dieter."

"Yes."

"You sound so far away."

"I am."

"I know, but more than that."

"I think I'm dying, Marlene."

"No," she said. "Don't you say that. It's not fair. That's not fair, Dieter."

"It's so peaceful here." Dieter turned his head. He looked at the iceberg on his left, brushed the knuckles of his left hand against the glass. He sighed as his breath froze upon the glass in a fractured steam of crystals, each breath adding another layer to the first. The steam obscured his view and he felt the stretch of cold skin as he wrinkled his brow and concentrated. Someone was saying something to him. "Marlene," he said.

"I need you to come home, Dieter. I need you home with me."

"So far."

"No, Dieter. It's not. You have to move. You have to stay warm."

Dieter dipped his chin and stared through his breath at the knife in his stomach. "Can't," he said.

"You can. Dieter," Marlene shouted. "You have to live."

Dieter felt something slide down his ear. Smooth, cold at the edges. His hand dropped to his side, and the satellite phone slipped between the handbrake and the seat.

"Marlene." Dieter tried to lift his hand. It slid it off his lap and he let it dangle beside the seat cushion. He moved the tips of his fingers, tried to grasp the phone's stubby aerial. He wondered at the blue hue of the Northern Lights. "It's usually green," he said. "Flowing. Doesn't flash."

He didn't hear the command to get out of the car, didn't react at the sudden flash of white light that pinned him to the seat. Dieter closed his eyes, touched the tip of the phone. His head lolled to one side when the door opened, and there were voices, voices he could barely hear. Not German.

"We'll have to pack it," said Inuk. "We're not pulling it out here."

"*Iiji*," Maratse said. He opened the boot of the Toyota and pulled out the first aid kit. Maratse tore the paper wrappings and passed the bandages to Inuk. Simonsen opened the passenger door, shining the powerful beam of his torch around the interior of the Toyota as Inuk and Maratse dressed Dieter's wound.

"There's no gun," said Simonsen. "What about his pockets?"

"Nothing," said Inuk.

"Wait." Simonsen reached over the handbrake and slipped his hand under the driver's seat. He pulled out the satellite phone, pressed it to his ear, and then placed it on the dashboard. "Dead battery," he said.

"We need to move him now," Inuk said.

"I'll bring the car."

The beam of Simonsen's torch lit the ice as he jogged to the police car. He backed up, stopped, and opened the boot. Simonsen fiddled with the cross-hatched guard and the backseat. When he had lowered it, Maratse and Inuk lifted Dieter out of one police car and into the other. Dieter groaned as they slid him across the carpeted interior. Maratse climbed in after him, cupped his hands under Dieter's knees, bending them as Inuk closed the door.

"I'll let the hospital know you are coming," Simonsen said, leaning through the driver's door. Then he stepped back to allow Inuk to climb behind the wheel. "I'll go back to the yacht." He slapped Inuk on the arm. "Keep me updated."

Inuk nodded, waited until Simonsen closed the door, and then shifted into first. Maratse searched for a comfortable position as Inuk accelerated across the ice towards Uummannaq.

"You sure he hasn't got a gun somewhere?"

Maratse checked Dieter's body, and said, "*Eeqqi*. No gun."

"Okay," Inuk said. "It's been a while since I drove on the ice so…"

Maratse was about to say something, but the sudden tilt of the front end of the Toyota thrust his body against the back of the driver's seat. The Toyota bobbed once, and then started to sink. Black water pooled at Inuk's feet, ballooning under the mat beneath the pedals.

"Shit," Inuk said. "Shit, shit, shit…"

"Inuk," Maratse said, as he worked back towards the rear door. "This way. Crawl over the seat." Maratse grabbed Inuk's arm and tugged him as the young policeman crawled between the seats. Black water swelled over the leading edge of the bonnet.

"Open the door," Inuk said.

Maratse fumbled with the handle. It moved like a hinge with no spring. The door did not open.

"It's child-locked."

The headlights of the second police car lit the boot with a triangle of white light, cut with Simonsen's black shadow as he raced to the back door of the Toyota and yanked it open.

"Out," he yelled, coughing in the Toyota's exhaust fumes as he gripped Maratse by the shoulder. Once Maratse was on the ice, Simonsen reached in and grabbed Inuk as he clambered over the bumper. The three of them dragged Dieter out of the boot and onto the ice as the Toyota dipped and the engine started to stutter. They ignored Dieter's groans and dragged him into the light of the headlights. The Toyota righted itself as the back wheels broke through the ice and the front end lifted. It bobbed in a square of black water. They watched as the sea rushed in through the open door at the rear and the fumes were stifled as the Toyota sank.

"Shit," Inuk said.

Maratse pointed at the ice, and said, "I'll walk in front. Check it's safe."

Simonsen nodded. "Let's get him on the back seat."

Inuk opened the rear passenger door, and then helped the others lift Dieter onto the back seat. They laid him flat and shut the door.

"I'll drive," Simonsen said. He waited until Inuk was in the passenger seat, lit a cigarette and gave it to Maratse. "For the nerves," he said, and grinned.

Maratse raised his eyebrows, stuck the cigarette in the gap between his teeth, and picked a route around the thin ice. Simonsen climbed behind the steering wheel and shifted into first gear. He turned off the lights when Maratse turned and made a cutting movement with his hand across his throat.

Simonsen rolled down the window, and shouted, "Better with the emergency lights?"

"*Eeqqi*," Maratse said. "I can see better now." He walked on, the cigarette clamped in his mouth as he guided Simonsen to the left and right with his hands.

Ophelia's navigation lights were visible in the distance when Maratse waved Simonsen to a stop and walked to the passenger side of the vehicle.

"We've reached the older ice. We should be fine all the way back to the yacht."

"All right," Simonsen said. "Get in. I'll call Danielsen."

Inuk started to apologise as soon as Maratse closed the passenger door.

"No apologies needed," Simonsen said, once Danielsen was briefed. "It's paperwork and time, that's all. It could have been me who drove through the ice." He shifted into third gear. "This is my jurisdiction. I'm responsible. I'm just pleased we're all alive." He glanced in the rear-view mirror and caught Maratse's eye. "Even you, *Constable*."

Maratse nodded.

"There is just one thing," Simonsen said, as they approached the yacht.

"What's that?" Inuk asked.

"You owe me a car."

Simonsen stopped a short while later, as Danielsen climbed down the ladder onto the ice and jogged across to the car. "Everyone okay?" he asked.

"We're okay," Simonsen said. "A bit shook up."

Danielsen nodded at Inuk. "The ambulance will be here in a few minutes," he said, and pointed at a pair of headlights jerking across the ice towards them.

Maratse reached around Simonsen and handed Danielsen his pistol. "Thanks for the loan."

Danielsen nodded, and holstered the pistol. He pointed at the yacht. "The detective is okay. We found his gun in the cabin. It had slipped under the bed."

"And we found the knife," Simonsen said with a glance at Dieter on the back seat.

"What about Therese?" Maratse asked.

"She's been a little weird, emptying drawers onto the floor, going through all the lockers and crew kit bags. I had to stop her three times. I told her she was polluting the crime scene. She told me it was her boat. We went back and forth like that for a bit, and then I locked her in the bathroom." Maratse laughed as Simonsen ordered Danielsen to let her out. "You really want me to let her out?"

"Yes," Simonsen said. He took a long breath, and looked over his shoulder. "Stop laughing, *Constable*."

"*Iiji*," Maratse said, and opened the door. The ambulance pulled up alongside the police car. Inuk and Maratse helped the hospital orderly and nurse carry Dieter to the back of the ambulance, securing the stretcher between the wheel arches. Just before he turned away from the patient Maratse noticed something square pushing out of one of the cargo pockets of Dieter's trousers. He unzipped the pocket and pulled out a small leather-bound diary. It was fastened with a thin sealskin cord. Maratse slipped it into his pocket as he crawled out of the ambulance.

"I could go with him," he said, as he walked across the ice to Simonsen.

"Inuk will go with him," Simonsen said. "He needs to be in police custody. We have plenty of questions for him, as soon as he is able to answer them. Besides," he said, and smiled, "I need you to deal with the crazy German girl."

"On the yacht?"

"I'll send Danielsen back to get you, once we get everyone back to Uummannaq."

"That's okay," Maratse said. He looked at the teams of dogs tethered to the ice. "I'll borrow Karl's dogs."

"You're sure?" Simonsen said.

"Karl won't need them for another day. They'll butcher the whales they catch here, on the ice. I'll take Therese back to Inussuk, bring the dogs back tomorrow."

They turned their heads at a shout from the yacht. Maratse grinned as Danielsen took a step back from Therese as she climbed from the deck onto the ice.

"Maratse," she shouted, as she approached the police car. "We need to go."

"*Iiji*," he said, and gestured at the closest team of dogs. He waved at Danielsen as the young police constable got into the passenger seat. Inuk's colleague from Ilulissat helped the detective into the rear of the police car, and, a few moments later, Simonsen pulled away, following the ambulance along the trusted ice route to Uummannaq.

"There goes our ride," Therese said. She slapped her hands

against her thighs, and said, "Wonderful. Now how do we get back?"

Maratse coiled a dog whip into his hand, and said, "You're sure you don't want to stay on the yacht?"

"It's not there."

"What isn't?"

"The digital log. Katharina Fischer, the captain, made a back-up of the ship's log each night, and saved it to a thumb drive. They couldn't always establish a link with the satellite, so she didn't send the last few updates. Her laptop is missing too." Therese jabbed a finger at the rear lights of the vehicles. "I should have gone with them. I bet one of the crew has it."

"The laptop?"

"Yes, or the thumb drive. I really need to talk to them."

"What would the log tell you?"

"The basics, coordinates, position. That kind of thing." Therese took a step closer to Maratse. She tilted her head, and said, "What happened out there? Why did you only come back in one vehicle? What about the man, Dieter?"

"Is that his name?"

"Yes."

Maratse pulled Karl's sledge off the wooden box and onto the ice. He explained what had happened, and pointed at the vehicles disappearing into the polar night. "There was no room for us. I said we would go home by dog sledge."

"Great," she said. "The slow way home."

"Are you in a hurry?"

"Yes, actually."

Maratse turned his back on her and Therese snorted. She pointed at the dogs.

"Fine, which ones do we take?"

"You can handle dogs?"

"Sure." She took a step towards the team. "Which ones?"

"That one." Maratse pointed at a large, black male, with two cream spots of fur above its eyes. "And those three." He watched as Therese marched towards the dogs, clamped them one at a time between her knees, unclipped them, and brought them to Maratse.

Ten dogs later, and Maratse nodded that he had enough. Therese sat at the rear of the sledge, and Maratse gave the order for the dogs to run. The sledge creaked across the ice, bumped over the ridged tyre tracks, and settled onto the smoother, thinner ice close to the shore. Instead of sledging around the open leads of water, Maratse used the whip to guide the team to the narrowest part, encouraging the dogs over the crack in the ice with clicks of his tongue and short, repetitive commands. He let the whip trail behind the sledge after the lead, and tucked the handle beneath a length of cord. The edge of the journal dug into Maratse's thigh as he stretched his legs.

"Tell me about Dieter," Therese said. "Do you think he is the killer?"

"Maybe?" Maratse said. "I don't know. But now all the crew are accounted for, maybe you can sail the boat back to Germany?"

"I still need that log."

Maratse reached for the cigarettes in his pocket, and then let his hand slip to his lap. The journal in his pocket weighed heavier on his mind than the need for a cigarette. The thought occurred to him that he was withholding evidence, but something suggested it was the right thing to do. He thought about that as the dogs increased speed, encouraged by the scent of home.

Chapter 12

Petra parked outside the police station, shrugged her backpack over her shoulders and locked the car. The snow crunched beneath her boots as she walked across the car park. She stopped to wave as the police Commissioner Lars Andersen pulled up alongside her. He wound down his window and beckoned for her to come over.

"Good morning, sir," she said.

"Sergeant," he said, and nodded at the passenger seat. "Get in."

Petra walked around the front of the car, kicked the snow from her boots and then opened the door. "Where are we going?" she asked as she sat down on the passenger seat.

"I have decided to buy you breakfast." The Commissioner reversed into an empty spot and pulled out of the car park. He stopped to make a quick phone call to his assistant. "Have someone clear Sergeant Jensen's schedule too," he said, and ended the call.

"You officially have my interest now, sir." Petra buckled her seatbelt and dumped her backpack in the foot well.

"You mean I don't always?" The Commissioner attempted a glare, before his face relaxed and he laughed. "Relax, Sergeant, that was a joke."

"I knew that," Petra said. They stopped at a T junction and Petra waved to a group of young Greenlanders crossing the road.

"Actually," the Commissioner said, "I talked to Simonsen in Uummannaq early this morning. One of their cars went through the ice last night."

"What? I didn't hear about that. Was anyone hurt?"

"Everyone is fine. One young constable from Ilulissat is a bit shook up, but everyone got out in time." The Commissioner put the car in gear and pulled out into a space in the stream of early morning traffic. "Maratse was in the car."

"What?"

"It's okay, Petra, he is fine."

"What was he doing in the car?"

"It seems that Simonsen deputised him, if you can believe that." The Commissioner chuckled. "It must be my fault. I was the first to bring Maratse out of retirement. Remind me never to do that again."

"That was an extreme situation, sir."

"So was this, apparently. Maratse got caught up in the search for the missing crew member."

"I did read about that."

"Dieter Müller is his name. He is now in custody. To be more precise, he is in hospital with a constable outside the door."

"They caught him?"

"He had a knife in his belly." The Commissioner drove to the harbour and along the quay. He parked beside the steps leading to the deck of a United States Coast Guard Legend-class cutter. Petra read the name stencilled on the bow: *Logan*. The Commissioner pointed at the bow of the ship. "This is where we are having breakfast, but, before we go onboard, I need us both to be clear, once again, that we don't talk about Maratse."

"Sir?"

"There's a lot of fallout still surrounding the activities of the ex-Sirius Konstabel Fenna Brongaard. She seems to have a hard time doing anything quietly. You'll find that the Americans are just as interested in her as the Canadians, the Chinese..." He sighed. "Everybody, really. I think they would all like an intimate chat with our favourite, and retired Constable Maratse, and I'm doing everything I can to keep his whereabouts and availability as vague and unconfirmed as possible."

"Thank you, sir."

"Of course, if he could just stay out of trouble, for a year or more, it would make things a lot easier. You understand?"

"More than you know," Petra said.

"Right, now about this meeting."

"Yes?"

"Did Gaba talk to you?"

"He did."

"Good. He might not always show it, but he thinks very highly of you, Petra, as do I."

"Thank you, sir."

"Don't thank me before you know what you are getting into. Now, before we go onboard, I want you to be aware of something." Petra waited as the Commissioner checked a text message on his mobile. He tapped a quick reply and slipped the phone back into his pocket. "They're ready for us."

"You were saying something, sir. Before the text."

"Right, there is an American onboard, a civilian, and I honestly don't know what his role is, or why he is here, but I want you to be on your guard, and not just because of Maratse."

"Sir, Gaba said I was being recommended for a joint task force covering the Arctic. He talked about police, not spies."

"When it comes down to issues of sovereignty and borders," the Commissioner said, "the differences between the two tend to get a little blurred. I have a feeling this particular American is interested in the *Ophelia*."

"The yacht in Uummannaq?"

"Exactly. Which is why I'm putting you on the case. You're going to liaise with Simonsen, but you will report directly to me. Understood?"

"Yes, sir." Petra slipped her hand around the door handle. "It's an American ship, sir, how will I know which American is the one to be wary of."

"I have confidence in you," the Commissioner said, "but as a general rule of thumb, I would suggest being wary of them all."

"All Americans?"

"It couldn't hurt." The Commissioner laughed, as he opened the door. "I was joking, Sergeant."

"That's two bad jokes in one day, sir."

"I'm doing well, aren't I?"

Petra got out and closed her door. She followed the Commissioner up the steps leading to the deck of the *Logan*. They handed in their sidearms to a security detail waiting for them at the top of the stairs, signed a form, and took turns to be searched before being escorted inside the ship. Petra worked hard to dampen her excitement, to control it, but the smile she wore was as stubborn as Maratse. She thought about him as she followed the Coast Guard officer to the wardroom below decks. She couldn't quite imagine how Maratse had become involved in the manhunt, and she was having difficulty believing that it was Simonsen who suggested it. Petra decided Simonsen must have been under a lot of pressure, but stopped thinking about it when the officer in front of her stopped outside a door and knocked. She took a breath, smoothed the front of her jacket, and straightened her back.

"See," the Commissioner whispered with a nod at their escort, "you're already infected."

"What?" Petra frowned, and then studied the ramrod position of attention the officer held before the door was opened and they were invited inside.

The wardroom was cramped but well-equipped. One of the bulkheads doubled as a flat screen, displaying the desktop of a Windows computer. There were two printers and a shelf of laptops fixed at the opposite end of the room, together with a coffee machine, and what looked like an old photocopier and a fax.

"Sergeant Jensen?" said the man who opened the door. He shook her hand, and said, "My name is Inspector Etienne Gagnon. I'm with the Royal Canadian Mounted Police." He gestured at the table filling the room and introduced, "Evelyn Odell with the Alaska State Troopers, Vitaly Kuznetsov from the Russian Militsiya." Petra waved hello, as Gagnon continued by pointing at a tall man in a wool sweater standing to one side of the screen. "This is Hákon Sigurdsson from the Icelandic State Police. The task force is still in the early stages of development. We're waiting on confirmation of the representatives from Finland, Norway, Sweden, and Denmark."

"Denmark?" Petra asked.

The Commissioner coughed as he sat down. "We're lucky enough to have two representatives on the task force." He unzipped his jacket and accepted the offer of a coffee from the Icelander. Petra sat down beside him.

"The *Logan*," Gagnon said, as Sigurdsson placed a tray of mugs on the table, "will function as the mobile base of operations. The idea is that each country will take turns providing the task force with a ship, and a helicopter. The US has the first watch."

"Okay," Petra said. She sipped her coffee and tried not to stare too hard at the different members of the team. This wasn't how she had imagined her Monday was going to start.

Sigurdsson walked around the table and pulled out the chair opposite Petra. She noted that all of the team members were in good physical shape, all under thirty. Odell shared the same long black hair and coffee-coloured skin as Petra, and she wondered if she was a Native Alaskan. She wondered too who would lead the task force.

"If you're wondering who the boss is," Gagnon said, with a smirk, "it's a bit of an inside joke."

"I don't understand," Petra said.

"He means you don't have one, yet," the Commissioner said. "Nor do you have a name."

"Polarpol has my vote."

Petra turned just as a new face entered the room. He looked American, and, when he stopped to shake her hand, she realised she had seen him before.

"You speak English," the man said.

"Yes," Petra said.

The man let go of her hand, and said, "You must be a quick learner, as I don't recall you could yesterday."

Petra felt a sudden heat in her cheeks. She glanced at the Commissioner, and then looked up at the man. "I apologise."

"Don't do that," he said. "But don't imagine you fooled me either." He placed his gnarled hands on the back of the chair beside Petra, and looked at each of the team members in the room. "How about you guys take a break? Take a ride into Nuuk, I can recommend the Katuaq café," he said, with a glance at Petra.

"We were just getting started," Gagnon said.

"I'm sure you were, Inspector. Now, take a break."

The man waited until the room had emptied but for Petra and the Commissioner. The Icelander paused to say something in Danish to Petra, but the American ushered him out of the room with a firm hand on his arm. He closed and locked the door once the Icelander stepped into the corridor.

"Didn't Iceland used to be a Danish colony?" he said, as he poured himself a mug of coffee.

"They became independent shortly after World War Two," the Commissioner said.

"So they can speak Danish?"

"Yes."

"As do the Greenlanders?"

"We do," Petra said.

"So this *Polarpol*," the man said, "could just as easily be called *DanPol*, seeing as the Swedes and the Norwegians speak a similar language." He took a sip of coffee, and then smiled. "I'm joking," he said.

"Save me," Petra whispered. The Commissioner kicked her leg and she hid her smile behind her mug.

"Sergeant Jensen," the man said, "my name is Samuel Johnson. For the purpose of this briefing you will assume that I'm with the United States Geological Survey. You can call me Sam."

Petra said nothing.

"Furthermore, you will not repeat anything said inside this room to anybody, unless the Commissioner or I tell you to do so. Do you understand?"

"Yes," she said.

"Good." Sam reached for the remote in the centre of the table and used it to control the mouse on the screen. He clicked to open a folder. "Do you have any questions about your briefing?"

"What briefing, sir?"

"I told you everything you needed to know over brunch, yesterday. Unless, you believe that was purely coincidental?"

Petra looked at the Commissioner. He shrugged and turned his attention to the screen as Sam opened a PDF document with a photo of a man stapled to the top right corner.

"Let's assume you remember everything I said," Sam said. He pointed at the photo of the bearded man in the document. "Do you know who that is?"

Petra pointed at the text below the photo. "It says his name is Berndt, but I have never seen or heard of him before today."

"Berndt is a person of interest to us," Sam said, "as is his so-called daughter: Therese Kleinschmidt." Sam clicked on a second document. "She is currently in Uummannaq. It seems the Berndts have hired a local to help them. I believe you both know this man." Sam clicked a new document onto the screen. Petra bit her lower lip as she looked at a recent picture of Maratse. "Tell me, Sergeant Jensen, just how well do you know David Maratse?"

"I have worked with him."

"More than that?" Sam asked. "Any personal entanglements you think I should be aware of?"

"No," Petra said. "None."

"You said Maratse had been hired to help Berndt," the Commissioner said. "With what, exactly?"

"As I told the Sergeant yesterday, it is our belief that Berndt is looking for evidence to prove that the Svartenhuk area is rich in Thorium. If it is correct, then that would make this particular range a very wealthy piece of real estate, especially for the company who owns the rights to mine in that area."

"Arbroath Mining," said Petra.

"I'm impressed, Sergeant, you *were* listening after all."

"What proof do they need?" she asked.

"This is the fun bit," Sam said. "Do you like treasure hunts?" He moved the cursor to a new folder and clicked another document onto the screen. "This is Alfred Wegener," he said, "a renowned polar researcher, who, as you probably know, died in Greenland, on the inland ice sheet, in November 1930. He was German, which, if you will allow me to digress," Sam clicked on a fifth document, "makes your secondment to the Arctic Task Force, quite interesting all of a sudden. Do you agree, Sergeant?"

Petra gripped her mug in both hands as she stared at a file with her photo, name, and a brief service record.

"It's all right, Sergeant. Denmark and the United States are allies, friends, if you will, and friends share information." He circled her name with the cursor, and said, "Piitalaat? Is that Greenlandic?"

"Yes," she said.

"But no-one calls you that, do they?"

Petra looked at Sam, caught the glint in his eyes, as he stared back at her.

"It's a lovely name, although I'm sure I didn't pronounce it properly. Anyway," Sam clicked back to the Wegener document. "Berndt believes that Wegener presented a misleading report of the mining potential for Svartenhuk. And we believe he wants to find the clue that will lead him to the treasure."

"And what is that?" the Commissioner asked.

"Wegener's missing journal," Sam said.

"Forgive me," the Commissioner frowned, as he tapped a finger on the table, "I did not have the benefit of Sergeant Jensen's briefing. Why would Wegener deliberately write a misleading report?"

"Who knows? Perhaps he fell in love with the area."

"And what will Berndt do with the journal?"

"Destroy it," Petra said.

"What?"

"Good girl," Sam said.

Petra pointed at the screen, and said, "If the journal is destroyed, no-one can prove the existence of minerals in that area without another expedition."

"So," the Commissioner said, "the Danish Technology University can send a bunch of students up there next summer."

"They won't do that," Sam said. "Tell him why, Sergeant."

Petra understood that she was being tested. She folded her hands on the table in front of her, and said, "If Svartenhuk is as rich as Berndt believes it is, he will want to keep the information a secret so he can buy the mining company that has the rights, for very little money."

"But he can't stop the Danish or Greenlandic government from carrying out a survey next summer," the Commissioner said.

"No," Petra said, "but he can use the media to make it very difficult for the government, any government, to commission the survey."

"How?"

"By appealing to the people of the world to think of the families of those murdered in Svartenhuk, and by making it very difficult for a survey team to explore the area without being labelled as insensitive. He would suggest they wait at least another year."

"By which time he will have convinced his board to buy the struggling company sitting on the Svartenhuk mining rights." Sam closed the open documents with a click of the remote, and tuned the screen off. "Well done, Sergeant."

"Yes," the Commissioner said, "very good, but answer me this, Sergeant, are you saying the murders were planned for that purpose?"

"I don't know, it just came to me, sir. But if you are asking me if people are prepared to kill for the secrets in Svartenhuk, I think they already have."

Chapter 13

Maratse clumped down the stairs, glancing at Therese asleep on the sofa, one long freckled leg curled over the sleeping bag, as he walked to the kitchen. He decided on fresh coffee, and held a jug beneath the tap. The water limped up the pipes and the electric pump juddered with little or no resistance.

"I told you, I emptied the tank," Therese called from the living room. She appeared at the kitchen door in her pants and bra, forcing Maratse to look away.

"I'll get more water," he said, and brushed past her.

Therese stopped him with her arm. Her skin seemed to glow and Maratse could feel the heat from her body through his t-shirt as she pressed in close to him. "What did you find when you searched Dieter?"

"Nothing."

"I'm not so sure," Therese said. She shifted position and brushed her hand across the wispy black hairs of Maratse's oriental beard. "I told you I liked this style, didn't I?"

"*Iiji.*"

"Then why don't we find out how much? What do you say?"

Maratse took Therese's hand and peeled it from his cheek. He looked into her green eyes, spared a glance at the blush of freckles across her cheeks, her nose, her lips, and said, "I didn't find anything." Maratse let go of Therese's hand and walked into the living room.

"Where are you going?"

"To fill the tank with water." He pulled on his overalls, boots, and hat, and stepped outside.

Inussuk had a water tank with a pump in a small insulated wooden building behind the store. It was blue, just like all the utility buildings in Greenland. Hospitals were yellow, stores and schools painted a dark red, police houses were green. Maratse collected two twenty litre plastic jerry cans from beneath the deck of his house, and carried them to the water tank. His boots slid over the finger-thick rime of spillage ice on the metal grate beneath the tap. Maratse unscrewed the cap of the jerry can, lined up the mouth with the spigot, and pushed the button to pump the water; he repositioned the can, and waited for it to fill. Buuti surprised him with a pinch to his waist.

"You're up early," he said, as he switched cans, and capped the first one.

"Karl has caught a whale," she said. The light of the water station danced in her eyes, and she pressed a set of keys into Maratse's hand. "He wants you to bring the snow scooter."

"*Iiji.*"

"But not the woman," Buuti said. "He thinks she is a journalist."

"He's probably right," Maratse said, and tucked the keys into his pocket. "Her father owns a media company."

"I'm not ashamed," Buuti said.

"Of what?"

"Hunting whales. But they don't understand, do they?"

Maratse screwed the cap onto the second jerry can and straightened his back.

"Europeans?"

"Non-Arctic people."

"I think there is a big distance between them and their meat." He shrugged, and said, "I'll fill the tank and then go and get Karl."

"*Qujanaq,*" Buuti said. "We have narwhal for Christmas." Buuti smiled, wriggled her shoulders within her jacket and walked back to her house.

Maratse picked up the cans of water, grunted with the strain, and then carried them inside the house and to fill the tank. Therese was in the bathroom, and he called out that he was leaving.

"I'll be back in a few hours," he said.

He waited for a reply, and, when none came, he pulled on a few extra layers and left the house. Maratse tugged a thick fleece neckie from his overalls, and slipped it over his head. He pulled on the gauntlets tucked beneath the seat of the snowmobile, checked the tank, and started the engine, grinning at the sudden roar of power. Maratse considered himself a traditional hunter. As long as there was ice, he would never give up his dogs. But the warning signs were clear, and, despite the welcome cold snap and the lack of wind that allowed the sea ice to cover the fjord, he knew it was far from the norm. The days of the sledge dog were disappearing, even north of Uummannaq. Perhaps in ten years, maybe fifteen, the number of dogs in Uummannaq would be reduced to a handful, kept for show, or for the dwindling stream of tourists failing to come further north than Ilulissat. Maratse didn't know exactly how he felt about that, he tried not to feel, to think; mostly he just wanted to live.

He let the engine idle for a moment, tugged one of the gauntlets off his hand, pulled out his mobile, and dialled Petra's number.

"Piitalaat," he said, when she answered.

"You didn't call."

"When?"

"After the car went through the ice. Why didn't you call?"

"I didn't think."

"*I* would have called," she said, "but I heard it from the Commissioner. He said Simonsen took you on the search, and that's why you were in the car."

"*Iiji.*"

"David," Petra said. Maratse heard her take a breath. "If we are going to be friends…"

"We *are* friends, Piitalaat."

"If we are going to be more than that, one day, I really need to know about things like this."

The snow crunched beneath his boots as he paced around the snowmobile. "I'm sorry," he said. "But I'm calling now."

"And I'm pleased. Pleased you are calling, and that you are all right. I'm sorry too," she said. "It's been quite a morning. I want to tell you about it."

"I'm here."

"I know, and I'll tell you, when I see you."

"I don't know when that will be," Maratse said. "I have to help Karl, and…"

"I know," Petra said. "I'm flying to Qaarsut today. I'll see you this afternoon." She paused, and said, "The Commissioner wants me to interview the crew of the *Ophelia*. I'm liaising with him, and…"

"And?"

"Some other people. I'll tell you when I see you."

"This afternoon?"

"Yes."

"I'll pick you up."

"I'd like that."

Maratse ended the call, slipped the mobile into his pocket, and pulled on the gauntlet. He ignored the discomfort in his leg as he lifted it over the seat and made himself comfortable on the snowmobile. He clicked it into gear and throttled up and over the drift of snow before racing past the dogs, slowing to negotiate the ice foot, and then accelerating onto the sea ice. Karl looked after his snowmobile, and Maratse increased speed to a steady seventy kilometres an hour. On a straight stretch of smooth ice he pushed it over one hundred, the wind biting at his cheeks, the bubbles and bumps of ice rattling through the skids and vibrating into his body. Even traditionalists are allowed to have a little fun, he thought. Maratse patted one hand against his chest pocket, and then gave up the idea of smoking as the left skid jarred on a stubborn clump of ice, and Maratse was forced to steer with both hands, wrangling the metal beast onto an even course. He throttled down to eighty and concentrated on the ice ahead. The moon reflected on the new layer of snow that had covered the ice in patches through the night, and the deep *deep* blue of the polar sky pushed at the fringes of the black night and suggested that a new day was dawning, although the sun would not rise for another two months.

The smell of blood and intestines steamed in the distance, as Maratse approached the edge of the ice. A single floe, covered in blood, had broken free of the edge, with one hunter securing it with the tip of his ice staff while another worked on the carcass of a narwhal. Maratse had seen blood floes before, thick plates of ice where hunters had butchered a whale. In the winter they would steam until the heat had long since left the carcass, the hunters motoring home in bloody fibreglass skiffs with a bounty of food for the winter. Maratse understood Buuti's concern, and imagined the uproar the western media would have at the sight of so much blood, the sprawl of intestines with a heavy tang of hot cabbage, and the positioning of toothed heads cut flat to stand on the ice as the men worked. This was not an industry, it was a livelihood, meat for the family, the tooth sold whole or carved into earrings and tupilaq – small figures polished to a smooth creamy finish – so much richer and ornate than those carved in reindeer bone. Tourists were not allowed to buy products made of narwhal, but there were plenty of Danes looking for a souvenir. As long as they lived in Greenland for six months or longer, they were free to take such rich treasures home.

Maratse found Karl and Edvard wrapping huge steaks of dark red meat in plastic tarpaulins. The dogs jerked back and forth, to the very limits of their tethers, intoxicated by the smell. Karl grinned at

Maratse as he cut the snowmobile's engine. He beckoned to him and pulled back a corner of the tarpaulin under which Maratse saw a stack of thick grey-mottled skin and blubber. Karl took the knife in his bloody hand and carved a finger-thin length of whale skin – *mattak* – and pressed it into Maratse's hands. Maratse reached deep into a pocket and pulled out a small knife, grinning as he clamped the *mattak* between his teeth and cut a chunk free. He wiped a smear of spit and fat from his lips and nodded at Karl.

"Good," he said, and grinned.

"Six whales," Karl said, and pointed at the men working on the ice. "And there is another pod on the way." He pointed at a man standing alone at the edge of the ice. "The game officer says we can take another three. That's nine for Uummannaq. Not enough," he said, with a shake of his head.

"Buuti is pleased," Maratse said.

"I know," Karl said. He wiped a bloody hand across his brow. "I must work, or I'll get cold." He nodded at the overalls, rolled down and tied around his waist by the sleeves.

"Here," Edvard said, as he stood up. He pressed the wooden handle of a thick blade into Maratse's hand. "I just sharpened it," he said, and tapped the blade with a bloody fingernail. It wasn't the first time it had been sharpened that night, nor was it the first time it had been used. The blade was narrower than the hilt of the handle, curving in a smooth arc to the point. Both sides of the blade were scratched from use, the grains of the handle filled with blood. Edvard pointed at the carcass he was working on and Maratse kneeled beside him and got to work.

The trick, he knew, was to cut a handle in the thick whale skin, and then carve a square around it, teasing, cutting, and pulling the skin from the meat until a square of skin and blubber was released roughly the size of school atlas, thicker than a fist. Maratse stopped to shrug out of the top half of his overalls, tied the sleeves around his waist, and continued. Edvard smoked as he cut, and Karl's blade was not idle. They were finished with the whale an hour later.

"You go back," Edvard said to Karl. "I'll stay and help my brother-in-law."

"Okay," Karl said. He slapped Maratse on the back, and they wrapped the meat in another tarpaulin, securing it to the sledge with lengths of cord tied around the wooden thwarts and pulled in a zigzag across the bloody prize. Karl whistled, and said, "I can taste Buuti's narwhal stew already. And," he said, patting the stack of *mattak*, "she promised to fry the *mattak* and marinate it with onions, vinegar and…"

"And?"

"Something else. Something delicious."

"Aramat?" Maratse said, with a thought to the classic spice mix in every Greenlander's kitchen."

"*Naamik*," Karl said, with a wrinkled brow. He waved his hand. "That's for fin whale or *sildepiske*. This," he said, and patted the tarpaulin, "is narwhal."

Maratse laughed. He climbed onto the snowmobile and shunted it into position in front of the sledge with gentle twists of the throttle. Karl attached the sledge to a thick loop of rope at the back of the snowmobile, and climbed onto the seat behind Maratse. He clapped the retired policeman on the back, and Maratse shifted into gear, driving around the dog teams on the ice before opening up the throttle and racing towards Inussuk. Karl lit two cigarettes, and pushed one between Maratse's lips. The smoke drifted across their bloody brows, tickled the clogged pores of their blood-stained fingers, and blew across the bounty of meat and *mattak* on the sledge.

"I heard about the police car," Karl shouted in Maratse's ear.

"*Iiji.*"

"You were inside it."

Maratse nodded.

"But you are all right?"

"I am."

"What about the man? He stabbed a policeman."

"Maybe," Maratse said. "Piitalaat is coming to interview him."

"She's coming today?"

"*Iiji.*"

"That's nice. She must come to dinner. Perhaps she has never tried narwhal?"

"Do you think there is enough?" Maratse chuckled a cloud of smoke from his lungs.

"There is never enough," Karl said. He leaned back in his seat, finished his cigarette, and flicked the butt onto the ice.

High tide had pushed the ice foot into a thick slippery wall that took some time to negotiate. Karl guided the sledge from the back, leaning into the uprights as Maratse tried to pull the sledge up and over the ice. After twenty minutes, and under the silent gaze of a small crowd, Karl unhitched the snowmobile and Maratse parked it on the sea ice. They fetched a team of dogs and pulled the sledge up and over the ice foot, all the way to Karl's house. A group of six small children, Nanna among them, raced after the sledge. The dogs whirled with the smell of fresh meat, and Karl found a bucket of entrails to reward them once Maratse had secured them at the ends of their chains. It was only when the meat was in Karl and Edvard's freezers that Maratse realised the lights were not on in his house, and Therese was nowhere to be seen.

"A taxi came from Qaarsut," Buuti said, as she handed Maratse a square slab of *mattak*.

"Qaarsut?"

"*Aap.*"

"Not Uummannaq?"

"*Naamik*. I think she is leaving."

"Leaving?"

Maratse pressed the *mattak* under his arm as he ran up the stairs and into his house. He left the whale skin on the mat and clumped up the stairs, ignoring the bloody ice cascading from the soles of his boots. He threw back the sheets on his bed, and tossed the pillow onto the floor. The journal was gone.

The thunder of the four rotors of the de Havilland Dash 7 shook the house as it descended for a short landing on the icy strip in Qaarsut. Maratse raced down the stairs, out of the house, and along the beach to the snowmobile.

"What's the rush?" Karl yelled, but Maratse ignored him.

The engine started at the first turn of the key, and Maratse felt the snowmobile leap across the ice as he accelerated. He pushed the machine from seventy, past ninety, felt his arms start to shake as the snowmobile shuddered around one hundred and thirty kilometres an hour. Maratse squinted through the cold air pricking his cheeks into solid cubes of flesh. He saw the lead of open water, another one, about ten seconds after he should have decreased speed to turn to avoid it. Instead, committed, Maratse increased speed, gritted his teeth, and held his breath as the skids skimmed across the first metre of the open lead, crashing into and biting at the brittle edge half a metre further away. Maratse felt the rear of the snowmobile dip into the water, felt the splash of icy water as it sprayed across his overalls, and then felt nothing more than relief as the snowmobile found purchase on the other side of the lead, and the leading edge of the tracks spun and gripped the ice, propelling Maratse forwards, and out of the sea. Maratse slowed for a second to study the ice ahead, steered around the thicker patches of snow that would warm and degrade the ice below, choosing instead to race along a path of black ice. That route, more cracks, and a few open leads, took him deeper into the fjord, away from the runway. The first passengers would have disembarked by now, he realised, Petra among them. But it wasn't Petra he was racing to meet. Maratse knew that he had maybe twenty minutes before the Dash 7 took off again, together with Therese Kleinschmidt and Alfred Wegener's lost journal, the one worth killing for.

Chapter 14

The Dash 7 was still parked outside the airport building when Maratse bumped the snowmobile up and over the ice foot beside the dock in Qaarsut. He swerved to avoid a string of loose sledge dog puppies and then powered up the road. When he braked to a stop outside the door, the fumes from the exhaust caught up with him creating a halo of smoke that followed him through the door and into the waiting lounge. A small girl screamed at the sight of Maratse, blood streaking his hands and face, and a sharp glint in his eye. A young woman enveloped the girl in her arms as Maratse took another step and glared at the passengers preparing to board the Dash.

"That's quite an entrance," Petra said, as she pushed back her chair and shouldered her pack.

"What?" Maratse twitched as she placed her hand on his arm.

"What's wrong?"

"Have you seen her?"

"Seen who?" Petra said, as Maratse stalked between the tables. "David, I just got here. Who are you looking for?"

"Therese Kleinschmidt," he said, and then again, louder, for the benefit of the passengers, personnel, and visitors.

"You're scaring people," Petra said, and slipped her hand down Maratse's arm to take his hand. "And why are you covered in blood?"

"Narwhal," he said, as he pulled free of her grasp. Maratse opened the door to the toilets, and banged on each locked door, shouting Therese's name.

"Okay," Petra said, and dumped her pack on the floor. "That's enough. She gripped Maratse's elbow and steered him behind the check-in desk and into the small office behind it. She shut the door, pushed him into a chair, and tucked her hands onto her hips. "You're lucky I'm in uniform," she said. "Now talk."

"Therese, the German…"

"Yes?"

"She took something from me, something I took from the man on the ice."

"The one who killed the two crew members?"

"Maybe. Dieter. He had a journal, and I took it from him."

"A journal?" Petra gripped the back of an office chair and pulled it in front of Maratse. She sat down. "Alfred Wegener's journal?"

"Maybe." Maratse shrugged. "It was old and written in German. I couldn't read it," he said, and looked at Petra.

"And you thought Therese was leaving on the plane?"

"It made sense." He glanced at the door.

"She's not here." Petra ran her fingers through her hair, tugging at her pony tail as she thought.

Maratse tapped his bloody nails on his knees, looked at Petra, and said, "It's good to see you, Piitalaat."

She laughed. "It is good to see you too, although, the way you barged through the door, it was pretty wild."

"*Iiji*," he said. Maratse's cheeks twitched and he ran a bloody hand over his wispy beard.

"Do you know what's in the journal?"

"*Eeqqi*."

"I have an idea, and, if it had been stolen from me, I might have reacted just like you." Petra reached out to touch Maratse's knee. "Why did you take it? Why not give it to Simonsen?"

Maratse shrugged, and said, "I just took it."

"A policeman wouldn't do that."

"I'm retired," he said, and grinned. "But, I thought it might be important, and I thought you could read it." He glanced at the door. "What do we do now?"

"If she's not here, where else would she go? The yacht?"

Maratse shook his head. "I came from there." He lifted his hands to show her the blood-streaked palms. "They were working on the whales on the ice. I didn't see her."

"She must have gone to Uummannaq. Maybe she's trying to talk to the crew."

"She said something about the ship's log, and how she couldn't find it."

"Then one of the crew must have it." Petra stood up. "She's in Uummannaq. Without a doubt."

"Then we can find her." Maratse pushed back his chair. Petra bent over to kiss him on the cheek as he stood up.

"It *is* good to see you," she said, "but now we need to get going."

"You're not dressed for the snowmobile."

"Give me a minute, and I will be." Petra left Maratse alone in the office. He watched her leave, and then loitered at the door.

In truth, he had surprised himself when he took the journal. He had no need for it, but somehow it had seemed important. It was clear it meant a great deal to Dieter, it was the only thing he had on him when they found him. He would ask Petra to ask him, as soon as they got to Uummannaq.

"You're looking for a European woman with red hair?" One of the airport staff said, as she walked into the office.

"*Iiji.*"

"She was here, and then she borrowed a snowmobile."

"*Qujanaq,*" Maratse said, and waited for Petra.

She appeared a few minutes later wearing thick ski salopettes the colour of blushed mango. She zipped the sides beneath her black police jacket and nodded that she was ready. She tucked her arms inside the backpack, sat on the snowmobile and then circled her hands around Maratse's waist as he climbed into the driver's position.

Petra spoke in his ear as he started the engine. "No cigarette?"

"I'm trying to quit," he said, and reversed away from the airport building, before clicking the snowmobile into first gear and driving down the hill to the ice. The skids bumped over the ice foot, and Maratse accelerated towards the white peaks of the heart-shaped mountain that gave Uummannaq island and the town its name.

They cruised alongside the tracks carved by the taxis, police cars, and the ambulance that had driven between Uummannaq and the mainland, once the ice had been declared safe to drive on. Petra rested her head on Maratse's shoulder, content to observe the winter landscape, so very different from a few months earlier, when the sea was exposed, along with the evil that drove some men to seek power, and to be consumed by it. She spared a thought for Tinka, the daughter of Greenland's First Minister, and the circumstances of her last case in the area.

"You're quiet," Maratse said, as he slowed at the mouth of the harbour.

"Just thinking."

Maratse drove up the ramp to the right of the boats and a dog team tethered on the ice beside a bloody sledge. He drove down the road to the hospital, and parked outside. He turned off the engine as Petra climbed off the snowmobile and adjusted the straps on her back.

"Does Simonsen know you are here?"

"He knows I'm on my way," she said. "He said I should call him from the hospital."

"He'll meet you here?"

"Yes."

Maratse nodded. "Then I'll try and find Therese." He climbed onto the snowmobile. It stuttered into life after three turns of the key. "Needs more fuel," he said when Petra frowned. "Dieter is bound to be in the hospital still. You stay here and speak to him and I'll ask Danielsen to take me to the other members of the crew – the survivors. They are not behind bars, but they have not been allowed to leave. Danielsen will tell me where they are."

"I'll need to talk to them too."

"*Iiji*," Maratse said, "but Dieter first."

"Why?"

"Because I don't know if he'll live. He had a knife in his belly when I found him." Maratse backed the snowmobile until he was positioned right beside Petra. "Talk to him first."

Maratse waited for Petra to go inside and then pulled out of the hospital parking area, and drove up the hill, past the blue offices of Nukissiorfiit, the power company, and further up the hill to the police station on the right. Danielsen grinned when he saw Maratse's hands.

"Narwhal?"

"*Iiji.*"

"Christmas is saved, eh?" Danielsen stood up. "What do you need?"

"Petra is here. She's going to meet Simonsen at the hospital."

"He's on his way, and then maybe I get the car for an hour or so."

"It must be difficult with only one car."

"That's not the worst; my CDs were in the one that sank." Danielsen lifted the flap of the counter and nodded for Maratse to follow him. "You want to talk to the crew?"

"I'm probably not allowed."

"You can be a guest. It's allowed. But why do you want to talk to them."

"You remember the German girl?" Maratse waited as Danielsen said something about Therese's looks and temperament. He raised his eyebrows in agreement, and said, "She left my house earlier, and I think she came here."

"Of course," Danielsen said, "she must think the crew has what she wants."

"How do you know?"

"I watched her pull the yacht apart, remember?"

"She also has a journal, the one they were looking for."

"Wegener's journal? How does she have that?"

"Because I took it from Dieter," Maratse said. He shrugged at the look Danielsen gave him, and said, "When I searched him for a weapon."

"And you think she has it?"

"*Iiji*, and Petra says it is important."

Danielsen took his jacket off the rack by the door and pulled it on, adjusting the waistband to free the grip of the pistol on his hip. He noticed when Maratse glanced at it. "*Naamik*, you can't have it." Maratse opened the door and gestured for Danielsen to get on the back of the snowmobile. The engine spluttered into life. Maratse turned in the parking area and pulled out onto the road.

"Where are the crew staying?"

"In the old Youth Hostel. The council bought it from the hotel owner. We put them there."

Maratse nodded and drove up the hill, turned left and accelerated past the fire station, passing the old police house on the rocks above the road, and then along the upper road through the village. He reduced speed when a group of children ran across the road to the store. Maratse slowed into the next bend and then accelerated to the hostel.

Danielsen tapped him on the shoulder and pointed at a woman getting onto a snowmobile parked under the hostel's staircase. "The hair," he said, and waited for Maratse to react to the shock of red hair flowing out from beneath the woman's helmet and across the shoulders of her jacket. Even in the dark of early afternoon, there was no mistaking Therese. She turned as she started the engine, her head fixed in their direction as she recognised Maratse. Therese flipped the visor into position, revved the engine, and gripped the handlebars as the snowmobile lurched forwards.

"On or off?" Maratse shouted.

"I'm staying on," Danielsen said. "Go get her."

Maratse twisted the throttle and thundered down the hill, past the hostel on the right. Therese's snowmobile slipped on a swathe of ice outside a water station. She recovered, and sped up a hill cut into the mountain with steep rock walls on both sides. Maratse slid across the same patch of ice, and followed her.

"We're high above the sea here," Danielsen said, as Maratse braked into a hard left as Therese raced between two dog teams, snow pluming from the track churning beneath her seat. "But if she gets to the end of the road, there's a narrow path that zigzags between the rocks." Danielsen pointed. "There," he said. "She must know about it."

"She's been here before."

"She must have been." Danielsen tapped Maratse's shoulder.

"What."

"It's steep."

"Okay."

They heard the change in engine tone as Therese braked to navigate the sharp turns to the left, and the sharper turns to the right, as she snaked the snowmobile between the rocks and down to the sea ice below. Maratse followed, invigorated by the chase, as eager and reckless to catch Therese as she was to escape. He accelerated when she bumped the snowmobile off the island and onto the ice.

"Go," Danielsen shouted, as Maratse throttled up, and twisted the skids with two quick jerks onto the ice to follow the path Therese carved through the fresh snow that had fallen in the night. The red rear light of Therese's snowmobile, almost as vivid as her hair, glowed like the eye of the devil as she topped one hundred kilometres per hour, pushing the snowmobile towards one hundred and fifty.

Maratse felt the bite of the air on his ears, his cheeks, the tip of his nose. He pushed on, chasing the eye of the devil. He felt Danielsen shift his grip, clutching him tighter around his waist.

"Hold on," Maratse said.

He accelerated.

Maratse knew the location of the leads he was forced to work around close to the mainland, and he also knew the current ran strongest closer to the island. Therese, he noticed, favoured the perceived safety of the island and hugged the coastline, whereas Maratse drifted away from the island, and further out. The advantage Therese gained by gunning the snowmobile along the island, would, he gambled, be lost once she encountered bad ice, and had to slow down.

"There," Danielsen said, and pointed. "She's slowing."

Maratse grinned, as he turned in a wide arc towards Therese, but as she slowed to negotiate thinner ice, the engine started to splutter, and they lost speed.

"Fuel?" Danielsen said, as he released his grip around Maratse's waist.

"*Iiji.*"

The engine coughed to a stop, thrusting them into a quiet bubble of sound defined by the grating of the skids on the ice as the snowmobile slid to a halt. Maratse reached for the packet of cigarettes in his pocket and offered one to Danielsen. They smoked in silence as they watched Therese pick her way across the ice, away from the poorer surface eroded by the current beneath.

"She's going to get away," Danielsen said. "But where will she go?"

Maratse said nothing. He knew where she was going.

Therese stopped and let the engine idle. There was just thirty metres between them. It might has well have been three hundred. She unclipped the strap of the helmet and lifted it from her head. Therese placed the helmet in front of her, ruffled her hair with gloved fingers, and then stopped to wave at the two men.

"She's playing with us."

"*Iiji.*"

Maratse pictured the flush of red in her cheeks as her skin cooled. He saw her freckles – so many – her red hair, those green eyes. He felt a flush of heat when he remembered seeing her for the first time wearing nothing more than his dirty bath towel that barely reached her thighs. She was a beauty, he knew that, but there was a beast driving her, and he knew too, that he would have to be smarter if he was going to catch her. And he would need more fuel.

"The Navy," he said, as Therese pulled the helmet onto her head, adjusted her position, and revved the engine.

"What's that?"

"Maybe the Navy can catch her."

Maratse rolled the cigarette between his teeth and placed a warm palm against his cheek. He dipped his head at Therese as she waved. He heard the click of gears and then she was gone, accelerating into the polar night.

"She is going to *Ophelia*," Maratse said.

"The yacht?"

"That's how she is getting out of Greenland."

Danielsen tugged his phone out of his pocket, and said, "She must be crazy to sail alone in winter."

"*Iiji.*" Maratse said as Danielsen called Simonsen. He listened as the young constable briefed the Uummannaq Chief of Police, and watched as the tail light of Therese's snowmobile blinked with each bump in the ice.

Danielsen finished the call, and said, "Simonsen says he'll call Ilulissat, see if they can intercept her. She's sailing away with our crime scene."

Maratse remembered what he had read about *Ophelia*, what the boat was capable of. He recalled the pictures of *Ophelia* locked in the ice in Arctic and Antarctic waters. Given what the boat was designed to do, all it needed was a capable and adventurous skipper. From what he knew of Therese Kleinschmidt, the Greenlandic police, even the Danish Navy, would be hard-pressed to catch her.

"Simonsen is sending someone to pick us up. He wants us both at the hospital. The German guy, Dieter, has started talking."

Chapter 15

Dieter tried to blink his eyes open. He was in a bed, a real one, not a broken cot in a hunter's cabin. The fabric he could feel with his fingertips was cotton, not wool stiff with mould. It was sore when he moved. He kept trying to open his eyes, turning his head in the direction of the sounds – a scrape of a chair leg perhaps, maybe even voices. He sensed there were people waiting for him to open them, and the minute he did so, he would have to answer some hard questions.

"I need to open my eyes," Dieter said, his words morphine-slurred.

The woman's face was as unexpected as it was angelic, lit as it was in the soft light of the bedside lamp. She smiled at him, and Dieter squinted at her. She spoke his language, and he blinked again to focus.

"Take your time," she said. "There's plenty of time."

"Who are you?"

"My name is Sergeant Petra Jensen," she said. "I'm with the Greenland Police."

"Am I under arrest?"

Dieter rubbed his eyes with his fingers, and focussed on the policewoman sitting beside his bed.

"You're not under arrest, not yet, but I do need to ask you some questions."

"Who's that?" Dieter asked, and looked at the man leaning against the wall.

"He's the Chief of Police here in Uummannaq. His name is Simonsen."

"Have we met?"

Simonsen nodded, and said, "I pulled you out of a sinking car."

Dieter concentrated on the man's words, which were not quite as clear as the woman's German, not as practised. But the image of the car sinking through the ice seemed familiar.

He heard the shush of black water sluicing into the car, pushing at the mats and the carpet hiding the wiring, the metal shell, the bolts and welded joints. He heard the shouts of the policeman, the rising panic in the man's voice, and he felt the press of another man as he crawled over Dieter's body to tug at the door. There was a sense of urgency about the man, but Dieter remembered him being calm, and it was a similar feeling that flooded through his own body, dampening the pain from the knife sticking out of his stomach, a liquid darkness washing through his body as the police car sank beneath the ice.

"I remember," Dieter said.

"That's good," Petra said. "Now, if we work back from there. What else do you remember?"

Dieter sniffed at the strange smell he imagined was coming from the wound in his stomach. He looked from the Police Chief to the Sergeant, and then reached for the glass of water by his bed. Petra helped him take a sip. He licked at the flakes of skin on his lips and then spoke.

"I stole a police car. I was trying to get away."

"From who?"

"Not who, *what*. I wanted to get away from the yacht, from *Ophelia*."

"What were you doing on the yacht?"

"I was trying to find something." Dieter glanced at Simonsen, and said, "The policeman, the one in plain clothes, he caught me going through my bags in the cabin. I was hiding in the cabin, that's when I heard him come in."

"And what did you do?"

"I wanted to get out. I felt trapped, so I grabbed a knife, the kind we wear on our belts when on deck. I think I cut him when I slashed at him, and then we fell – we slipped, I think… on blood." Dieter paused as Petra made a note with a pencil in her notepad. He waited for her to look up. "We fell, and the knife went into my stomach."

"But you kept going?"

"Yes, I had to get away from the yacht."

"Why?"

"Because I couldn't let them have it."

"Have what?"

"The journal. Wegener's journal."

Dieter waited as Petra said something to Simonsen. It had been a long time since he had spoken Danish, but he understood the woods for *book* and *stolen* and something about a man called Maratse.

"Sergeant," Dieter said, "where is the journal?"

"Why don't you tell us why it is so important?"

"You don't have it?" Dieter tried to sit up, but the pain in his stomach forced him to lie down again.

"We know where it is."

Dieter closed his eyes, and said, "The journal is a record of Alfred Wegener's explorations of Svartenhuk. It includes his findings, and information about the samples he took, and where."

"What samples?"

"Thorium."

Dieter opened his eyes at the sound of Petra's pencil scratching the surface of the paper in her pad. He waited for her to stop.

"You said you didn't want *them* to have the journal. Who is *them* and why shouldn't they have it?"

The light in the room brightened as a nurse opened the door. Dieter watched as Petra waved her away. The door closed, and he relaxed into the dim light cast by the lamp at his bedside. It reminded him of the flames licking at the thick glass window in the door of the cabin stove.

"I was hired for the expedition as an expert on Alfred Wegener," Dieter said.

"Are you?"

"Yes. I have worked at several institutions. Berndt found me through a contact of his at the Alfred Wegener Institution at Bremerhaven."

"And Berndt is?"

"Aleksander Berndt is the CEO of the Berndt Media Group. He is also the owner of *Ophelia*. It is his step-daughter who runs *Ophelia Expeditions*."

"Therese Kleinschmidt?" asked Simonsen.

"Yes, exactly."

Dieter continued. "I was flattered to be asked to join the expedition, and excited. The chance to find and recover one of Alfred Wegener's lost journals was too good to miss."

"So you said yes?"

"At once, at the first meeting."

"And the journal you found was the one you had hoped to find?"

"Yes." Dieter took another sip of water as Petra made a note. "It was a bit of a disappointment, really. The journal was exactly where we thought it would be."

"In the cabin?"

Dieter nodded. "We asked local hunters many times if they knew of the cabin, and, if they did, if they had seen a journal, but they said nothing. I was worried they might have burned the journal to start a fire."

"But they didn't."

"A Danish hunter – I think he was called Axel – told the captain he knew where the cabin was. She paid him for the information, and she was going to pay him to take us there, but I don't know what happened after that."

"What do you mean?"

"I mean that we prepared to leave the boat – five of us. The captain would stay behind. But the hunter did not show. At least, not before we left. I don't know if he came later." Dieter gritted his teeth as a wave of pain flashed through his body.

"This was when you skied across the sea ice to the mountains?"

"To Svartenhuk, yes."

"Did you find the cabin?"

"Not at first. We were caught out in a wind blowing down the mountain. There was a lot of snow. The team wanted to go back. Nele was the guide, but Henrik was leading the team. He said we should turn around."

"And did you?"

"Not me. I knew we were close, and if they had listened to me, we would have found the cabin together."

"So you stayed on the mountain?"

"Yes."

"And found the cabin?"

"Just. It was difficult."

"But no-one can prove you were in the cabin," Simonsen said.

"I found the journal. That is proof."

"But no-one saw you."

Petra frowned at Simonsen, but the Chief of Police held up his hand, waited for Dieter to answer.

"I called my wife, on the satellite phone."

"From the cabin?"

"Yes."

Petra asked for the telephone number and Dieter gave it to her. "Remember the country code," he said, "forty-nine."

Petra tapped the pencil on the page. "So the team returned to *Ophelia*, and you found the cabin, found the journal, and then went back to the yacht."

"Yes."

"But when you went onboard…"

"It was empty. Everyone was gone. Just lots of dogs on the ice. And then the policemen came."

"Dogs?"

"Hunters' dogs," Simonsen said. "The narwhal came down from Upernavik."

Petra nodded. "But you didn't think it was strange that the yacht was empty? I thought they were supposed to wait for you."

"I didn't think about it," Dieter said.

"Because you wanted to find something," Petra said, as she flipped through her notes.

"Yes, a thumb drive."

"Like a USB?"

"Yes."

"What was on it?"

"A backup of my notes. I scanned them into my computer before leaving Berlin."

"And they are important?"

"Most important, especially now."

"Why?"

"Because a man came to my house, and took the notes from Marlene." Dieter glanced at Simonsen. "She told me when we talked on the satellite phone. She said the man needed the notes to help find me, and to help me."

"With what?"

"This," Dieter said, with a wave of his hand. He grimaced, and pushed his head back onto the pillow. When he spoke again it was barely more than a whisper. Dieter caught the faint trace of Petra's perfume as she leaned over him to hear what he said. "When I was invited to join the expedition I was given a list of the other members, and a brief contact sheet with details about their career and education. When I searched for the same people online, I found different photos, but the same names. The dates and degrees were correct, but some of the specialist areas were slightly off."

"In what way?"

"Geology instead of geography. Marine science not meteorology."

"Why does it matter?"

"When you read Wegener's journal, it matters."

"Tell me."

Dieter looked into the Sergeant's eyes, and said, "Wegener found thorium in the mountains, a lot of it, but it was never reported, when he lost his journal it was forgotten, and when he died, the secret was buried with him."

"And a geologist?" Petra asked.

"Would be far more interested in minerals than a geographer."

"Marine scientists…"

"They look down at the seabed, meteorologists look up."

"What did you think they were going to do with the journal?" Simonsen asked, as she took a step closer to Dieter's hospital bed.

"After being scanned, it would be preserved, papers would be written, and I could move Marlene into a nice house on the outskirts of the city, perhaps even to Bremerhaven."

"You could advance your career?"

"Yes, Sergeant, a find like this is priceless."

"You would get paid more?"

"Maybe, that's not important. But I could have my pick of jobs. Maybe even teach abroad."

Dieter closed his eyes. He heard his name being called, twice. He blinked and focussed on the police sergeant standing by his bed.

"Dieter," she said, "two people were murdered onboard *Ophelia*. Henrik Nielsen and Antje Jung."

"Murdered?"

"Yes. You remember the blood?"

"Yes," he said, and lifted his head. "I was focussed on the thumb drive. I needed to prove my theory."

"Which is?"

"Berndt didn't want the journal, he wanted Wegener's secret."

"But Berndt picked the team."

"Yes."

"So he knew about the fake references?"

"Maybe he didn't," Simonsen said. He placed his hand on the rail at the foot of the bed, and said, "Nele Schneider says you and she were having an affair. Is that correct?"

"What?"

"She also said that the two deceased, Nielsen and Jung, were romantically involved."

"I don't remember," Dieter said.

"Don't, or can't?"

"Chief," Petra said.

"I have a wife in Berlin," Dieter said. "Marlene and I are very happy together. We want to have children."

"Were you having an affair?"

Dieter looked at Petra. He shifted position, wincing at the pain in his stomach. "*Ophelia* can be quite cramped, intimate," he said. "We sailed from Germany. It took a long time. We all got to know each other, some more than others." Dieter took Petra's hand, and said, "I have been unfaithful, just one time, on *Ophelia*."

"With Nele Schneider?"

Dieter shook his head.

"Who?"

"The captain. Katharina Fischer. Just one night, when we were in Ilulissat, before we sailed to the edge of the ice."

The door opened and Dieter let go of Petra's hand. The nurse entered the room with a bedpan, a thermometer and a sleeve to check his blood pressure. She waved the police officers out of the room, and pressed the thermometer into Dieter's ear.

Dieter watched her as she worked, listed to the click and clack of her pen as she recorded his temperature on the chart hanging from his bed, and then pressed the pen into the metal coil holding it in place in the breast pocket of her uniform. He could see the police sergeant watching him from the corridor. He tried to smile, but the nurse blocked his view as she took his blood pressure, pumping the sleeve around his arm until it was tight, almost uncomfortable. Another click of the pen, and then she asked him something in English, he knew it was important, but not as urgent as his confession to the policewoman. He needed to tell her that he loved Marlene. He needed to tell Marlene, but the nurse was insistent. She placed the bedpan by the side of his bed, and then rolled back the sheets to look at the bandage plastered to his abdomen. He smelled it then, as she peeled back the plaster and released a whiff of decay, bacteria, something hot and active in his wound. Dieter started to sweat. The room dimmed, and he heard the clap of the nurse's feet as she walked to the door and called out something in Greenlandic. A doctor arrived at Dieter's bedside. It was time for Dieter to dig in and focus on recovering from his wound.

"For Marlene," he whispered, and closed his eyes.

Chapter 16

Petra tugged the collar of her police jacket around her neck and walked outside. She found Simonsen smoking beside the police Toyota. He flicked the butt of his cigarette onto the ground and scuffed it into a patch of ice with the toe of his boot. Petra stuffed her hands into her jacket pockets and waited for Simonsen to speak. The burr of a snowmobile across the hard-packed snow covering the road distracted her, and she caught the eye of the driver, a grizzled Dane with what looked like a permanent sneer scarred into his top lip. Petra held his gaze until the man turned his head and accelerated up the road towards the ramp leading down to the sea ice.

"About time," Simonsen said. "He's been in town far too long."

"Who is he?"

"Axel Stein."

"The *Axel* Dieter mentioned?"

"Yep."

"Then why are we not interviewing him?"

"Danielsen spoke to Axel when he was in hospital. He cut his own arm with a knife."

"A knife?" Petra took a step towards the car as Axel weaved between the dogs and the fishing boats locked in the sea ice.

"Forget it, Sergeant. Axel isn't the killer."

"He has an alibi?"

"He told Danielsen that he was approached by one of the crew – he couldn't remember which one. They called his mobile and he talked to them for about three minutes before hanging up. His phone log shows the call, from a German mobile."

"And there's nothing strange about that?"

"The strange thing is that he had a mobile at all. Axel has taken a hunter's cabin and called it his own. He has a history of alcohol and abuse. Children are frightened of him, especially when their parents tell stories about the *Stein Monster*. It suits Axel just fine. He'll die in that cabin."

"What makes you so sure he didn't kill the crew?"

"Axel is an evil man, there's no doubt, but he's also a coward. He wouldn't fight a man. Besides, this is too sophisticated for him."

"In what way?"

"The way the crew were drugged. Axel couldn't figure that out.

He's more of a blunt-force-trauma than anything fancy. Although," Simonsen said, with a glance at the shadow of Axel Stein disappearing across the ice, "I didn't expect him to stay so long in town. I'll have Danielsen look into it." Simonsen nudged Petra's arm and pointed at a taxi bumping across the ice, up the ramp, and along the road to the hospital. "Here he is now."

The taxi driver waved as Danielsen and Maratse opened the doors and stepped out of the car. Maratse took a can of fuel from the car boot, and gave the driver a few hundred kroner. The smile on Maratse's face tugged at his cheeks as he walked over to join Petra and Simonsen. He put the jerry can on the ground by his feet as Danielsen leaned against the side of the police car.

"Our brave knights," Simonsen said, with a quick glance at Danielsen.

"We screwed up, Chief," he said.

"You did. Now how about you make up for it and go inside the hospital. You can warm up while you wait outside the German's door."

Danielsen looked at his watch, and said, "My shift's nearly over."

"I know, I'll send one of the assistants to relieve you."

Danielsen nodded, winked at Petra, and then walked inside the hospital.

Simonsen waited until the door closed with a thump, and then said, "You ran out of fuel?"

"*Iji.*"

"Well, she shouldn't get far. The Navy has the *Ejnar Mikkelsen* just south of Ilulissat. They'll find her." Simonsen nodded at the car, and said, "Get in."

"Where are we going?" Maratse asked.

"To talk to the crew," Petra said. She climbed into the passenger seat as Maratse put the fuel can in the boot and got in behind Simonsen. Petra caught Maratse's eye in the rear-view mirror, and, even in the dark, she was almost certain she saw him blush.

Simonsen backed out of the parking spot, and drove to the hostel where the crew were staying. The moon ducked behind a cloud, and the polar afternoon did its best to pretend it was later than one thought.

There was a crowd outside the youth hostel, a flash of bright blue-tinged beams from smartphones, and a dark patch of something on the snow. One of the crowd ran to the driver's side of the car as Simonsen wound down the window.

"What's going on?"

"Someone is dead."

"Slow down, Angut," Simonsen said, as the man chattered through a description of what happened. Petra got out of the car, and Maratse followed.

The crowd peeled to both sides as Petra approached. She stopped to look at the blood staining the packed snow on the road, stepped around it, and knelt beside the body on the ground. She pressed her fingers to the man's throat, pulled out her mobile, and called the hospital.

"What did you see?" she asked. When a young woman began to answer in Greenlandic, Petra turned to Maratse for help.

"He fell from the balcony," Maratse translated, pausing as the woman continued. "There was some shouting in the house, women's voices, and then he came out onto the balcony. He might have been pushed. She can't remember, but they did film the fall." Maratse took the phone from the woman's hand and showed it to Petra. The video – barely six seconds long – caught the man halfway into his fall and the sound of the wet crack of his head on the road.

"The fall killed him," Petra said, and looked up at the balcony. "She thinks he might have been pushed?"

"Maybe. She's not sure."

Petra turned at the metallic clap of Simonsen's door. His boots crunched through a shallow drift of snow as he joined them beside the body.

"There's a video," Maratse said, as he turned the screen towards Simonsen.

The Chief of Police nodded, looked at the young Greenlander, and said, "I'll need a copy."

"*Aap*," she said, as Maratse returned her phone.

"You really are a crime magnet," Simonsen whispered to Maratse. He nodded at the balcony surrounding the first floor of the hostel. "Go with Sergeant Jensen." Simonsen caught Petra's eye, and said, "You do the talking, Sergeant."

"Yes, sir."

Each step on the way up to the first floor was caked with a layer of snow-turned-ice. Petra slipped on the deck of the balcony, caught the railing, and looked over the side to the body below.

"He could have just slipped?" she said. Petra waited for Maratse to join her and then knocked on the door.

Petra knocked another three times before a young woman opened the door, her eyes widened as she recognised Maratse.

"It's you," she said in English, "the hunter on the yacht."

Petra glanced at Maratse, and then pushed gently at the door. "Can we come in?"

"Yes."

Maratse banged the snow from his boots and followed Petra inside the hostel. There were four rooms spaced evenly around a central living area. Petra touched Maratse's elbow and nodded at two empty bottles of wine on the kitchen counter. They followed the woman into the lounge area where another woman, was sprawled on the sofa.

"Katharina," said the young German, shaking the woman gently. "It's the police."

Katharina took a long breath and turned on the sofa, clutching the cushioned arm with thin fingers as if it was a railing on the *Ophelia*, as if they were crashing through waves, and their guests were obstacles to be avoided. She leaned back and pointed at Maratse. "Who is he?"

"His name is Maratse, and I'm Sergeant Jensen. When did you start drinking?"

Katharina sighed, and said, "Early. What else is there to do?"

"Is it just the two of you?"

"No," said the young woman. "Our friend, Abraham – he just went to the bathroom."

"And what is your name?"

"Nele Schneider."

"I'm sorry to tell you this, but your friend is dead," Petra said. "He fell from the balcony."

"What?" Nele started towards the door, but Maratse stepped in front of her.

"We need you to answer some questions," Petra said, as Maratse helped Nele onto the sofa.

"More questions?" Katharina said. "All we do is answer questions."

"Your friend just died. I'm sure you want to help us find out how, and why?"

"Not without a lawyer," Katharina said. She took Nele's hand. "Don't say anything."

Petra unzipped her jacket and pulled her notebook from the cargo pocket in her trousers. She sat down on a chair opposite the two women. Maratse retreated to the kitchen to wait.

"You're the captain of the *Ophelia*," Petra said, and looked at Katharina. "Surely you can answer that."

The woman shrugged, and said, "Yes."

"And you're one of the crew?"

"Yes," Nele said, "I'm the mountaineer." She fidgeted on the sofa and glanced at the door.

"The mountaineer?"

"The one with the climbing and skiing skills. That's why I'm on the expedition." Nele started to stand up. "I want to see him."

"A few more questions, first," Petra said. She heard the captain whisper something in German, and Petra made a note, something about *too many deaths.*

"Abraham is our friend," Nele said. "We really must see him."

"His body will be taken to the hospital. I'll arrange for you to see him soon, until then, I need to know when he was last with you?"

"Twenty minutes, maybe," Nele said. She looked at the captain, and said, "You remember?"

"Not without a lawyer."

Petra switched to Danish and asked Maratse to fetch Simonsen. She looked at her watch, turned back to the captain, and said, "The time is seventeen minutes past five, and I'm arresting you on suspicion of being party to the death of Abraham Baumann."

"You can't prove anything," Katharina said, as Petra removed a pair of handcuffs from her belt.

"Not without a lawyer, apparently." She tugged the woman to her feet, pulled her hands behind her back, and snapped the metal bracelets around her wrists. She pointed at the sofa and ordered the younger woman to sit and wait as she walked the captain to the door. Simonsen met her on the balcony and Petra let him take her down the stairs.

"Refusing to cooperate?" Simonsen said.

"Yes," Petra said. "She wants a lawyer."

"That'll take some time." He caught the woman as she slipped.

"Careful now, I can't have two dead bodies in one night; the doctor will never forgive me."

Petra waited until Simonsen opened the rear passenger door of the police car, and helped the woman onto the seat. He waved just before driving off in the direction of the police station. Petra closed the door to the hostel and joined Maratse at the railing of the balcony.

"He's letting you stick around," she said, with a nod towards the police car.

"I think he feels guilty."

"For being mean to you?"

"For nearly drowning me."

"That's right," Petra said. "You need to tell me more about that sometime."

"I'm okay, Piitalaat."

"I'm glad," she said, and curled her hand around his arm. Petra leaned her head against Maratse's shoulder for a second, and then pulled free. She nodded at the door. "Are you coming?"

"*Iiji.*"

Nele hadn't moved from the sofa. Her legs were tucked beneath her bottom. She had wrapped a blanket over her knees. Petra sat down opposite her, while Maratse stayed in the kitchen. The young woman looked at him for a moment, and then turned her attention to Petra.

"I'm happy to answer any questions," she said.

"That's good." Petra opened her notebook.

"But not about Abraham. I don't know how he fell. I just remember him going outside. That's all."

"Was he drunk?"

"Yes."

"And you didn't hear anything?"

"No," Nele said. She looked at the floor. "We were shouting. We didn't hear anything."

"We?"

"The captain and me."

"What were you shouting about?"

Nele lifted her head, slowly, as if she was pulling against something that was wrapped around her neck. When her eyes were level with Petra's, she said, "It was about Therese. She was here earlier. She took something from the captain."

Petra heard Maratse fidget in the kitchen. She lifted her pencil from the page of her notepad. "What did she take?"

"A thumb drive. You know, a mini hard drive?"

"I know what it is," Petra said, "but why is it important?"

"The ship's log," Maratse said, as he walked out of the kitchen to stand beside Petra.

Nele shook her head. "That's not important. It was something else. I'm not sure, but I think it was files of some kind. Documents."

"Did the thumb drive belong to the captain?"

"No."

"Who then?"

"I think it was Dieter's."

Petra reached over the arm of the chair and tapped Maratse's leg. He found a chair in the kitchen and carried it into the living room area. The woman watched him as he sat down beside Petra.

"I have one more question," Petra said.

"Okay." Nele shifted position, and then smoothed the blanket over her legs. The sofa sighed as she moved.

"Were you having an affair with Dieter?"

Nele flicked her head towards Maratse, and then pressed the tip of her nail against her lip. "No," she said, her eyes locked on Maratse's.

"You told Simonsen that you were."

"I was covering for the captain." Nele gripped the arm of the sofa and looked at Petra.

"Okay, Nele. Just stay there."

Petra closed her notebook and nodded for Maratse to join her in the kitchen. She filled the kettle with water and switched it on. She leaned on the counter and watched the girl from the kitchen as the kettle boiled. When the water started to bubble and spit, she switched to Danish and spoke quietly to Maratse.

"The thumb drive is Dieter's. He said his notes include scans of documents that prove the crew of the *Ophelia* are not who they claim to be."

Maratse leaned against the counter, crossed his arms across his chest, and said, "Therese has the journal and the USB drive. What will she do with them?"

Petra shrugged. "Destroy them. Toss them overboard. Dieter

said that somebody collected a box of notes from his house, that the USB was a backup. He scanned the documents."

Maratse turned his back on Nele. He leaned close to Petra's ear. "You know I'm not good with computers, but I do know that he had to scan something onto the computer before copying it to a USB."

"And if they didn't take the computer…"

"There will be a copy on the hard drive." Maratse grinned, and said, "I like it when you smile, Piitalaat."

"I like it when you talk about computers."

"Because it makes me sound smarter than I am?"

Flecks of light from the kitchen danced in Petra's eyes. "No," she said, and hid her mouth with her hand. "But I like the serious pinch of skin you have, right there." Petra pressed her finger into the centre of Maratse's forehead.

The lid of the kettle flapped as the water boiled. Petra brushed past Maratse and found clean mugs in the cupboard. She made coffee with instant granules from a jar on the counter. Maratse picked up two mugs, and took a step towards the living room area.

"Wait," Petra whispered.

"*Iiji?*"

"How do you feel about going to Berlin?"

Maratse wrinkled his nose.

"Oh, come on, it will be fun."

"Why, Piitalaat?"

"Because it might be the only way to prove who has done what in this case." She paused. "You want to find the murderer, don't you?"

"I'm retired," he said, and shrugged.

"Not from where I'm standing."

Chapter 17

Therese had never seen a blood floe, neither was she prepared for the thick stench of intestines that washed over the fleece tube around her neck, soaking into the soft fibres like oil. The skids at the front of the snowmobile rattled over globs of frozen blood as Therese slowed on her approach to the *Ophelia*. She turned off the engine, and the last rumble of the motor was lost in the vast black sky and even blacker sea beyond the ice. Therese slid the visor up and over the front of the helmet and clawed at the straps. If she thought she could escape the bloody, heady smell of dead whale, she was mistaken. She dumped the helmet on the ice, gagged her way to the ladder, and climbed onto the deck of her father's yacht.

"Stepfather," she said, as she looked down upon the bloody ice, and wondered what he would think of it. He would say *quotas* when she cried *butchery*, say *subsistence* to counter her *slaughter*, but either way he would be impressed, it was hard not to be.

Another thing that impressed Therese was the fact that *Ophelia* was untouched. Apart from traces of the police, she could see no sign that anyone else other than the expedition crew had been onboard. Therese opened the hatch and climbed down into the cockpit. She caught the same smell of blood, but the lack of bloody organs and the cool temperature presented her palate with a more tempered smell, something she intended to clean up as soon as she was underway. Therese checked the generator, switched on the battery, and started *Ophelia*'s engine. The lights flickered as the big, sturdy, diesel engine fired and sent the first rumbles of irritation through the hull.

"I know, baby," Therese said. "Soon."

Therese climbed on deck, checked the lines and shrouds, thumped the ice from the decks with the stubborn handle of a broom, and kicked the jagged clumps over the side. The ice was so thick it reminded her of toffee, hammered into assorted pieces to be boxed, sold, and sucked until the edges smoothed and the caramel slid down one's throat. If she tried hard enough Therese could almost imagine the smell of warm toffee, could almost ignore the smell of whale intestines.

When she was done with the deck, and the lines were free of rime ice, Therese bashed the railings with a heavy rubber mallet, flicking her gaze once in a while to the sea ice, searching for headlights.

"If they use dogs, I won't even hear them," she said, her words misting in the light from *Ophelia*'s deck lights. "I have to get going."

Therese worked her way around the deck, secured the mallet and the broom, and then climbed back onto the ice to free *Ophelia* from her wintry berth. The ice axes were buried deep and she decided to leave them. Therese returned to the deck, and released the yacht with a few swift saws of her knife through the stiff rope wound through the cleats. She knew *Ophelia* was well-equipped and tossed the ends of the rope onto the ice. Therese moved quickly across the deck, rolled the ladder into place and slipped the safety wires across the gap to complete the rail running around the deck.

She stopped for a second to listen to the sound of the engine, freeing her ears from her fleece hat, tilting and twisting her head for anomalies. It all sounded good, exactly as she had left it.

Therese dropped down through the hatch, wrinkled her nose and adjusted the thermostat as the temperature in the cabin rose. She didn't have time to clean, not yet, but neither did she want the *Ophelia*'s interior to compete with the cloying cabbage smell of the ice. She jogged down to the forward cabins, tucked the journal and thumb drive into a small locker next to the toilet, and pulled her personal kit out of stowage below the starboard bunk. Therese pulled off her outdoor gear, added a second mid-layer of thermals, before pulling on her insulated sailing suit. She checked the pockets for extra gloves, hats, and fleece tubes, before securing the trouser cuffs over her boots and zipping the suit to her neck. She twisted her fiery hair beneath a thick fleece hat on her way through the cockpit and onto the deck. The moon flickered between grey clouds pregnant with snow as she pulled on a thin pair of gloves, before stabbing the GPS unit into life and plotting her waypoints. A quick glance at the ice suggested she had plenty of time, and she relaxed.

The course to Ilulissat was familiar. Therese couldn't remember just how many times she had sailed it this past year, but the shifting bergs and the merciless winds and waves that toyed with craft of all sizes on the west coast of Greenland, made waypoints more like guidelines. She would have to be vigilant, again, and be patient, *again*, as the journey would take longer than expected.

It always did.

Therese finished plotting her course, checked the fuel levels, wind levels, pressure levels, and battery levels on screen, punching them with the stubby tips of her gloved fingers, before taking a last look on the port and starboard side of the deck. The ice brushing against the front half of *Ophelia*, from the tip of the bow and another two metres towards the stern, was white, opaque in the glare of her head torch. She returned to the starboard wheel, clicked into reverse gear and throttled *Ophelia* into the black sea.

Once free of the ice, Therese turned the thirty-six metre-long expedition yacht in a slow arc until the bow was aligned with the first of the waypoints glowing green on the screen in front of her. Therese decided to run on diesel until she was free of the rocky tip of the Uummannaq peninsula, where she might find some favourable winds and save on fuel. The course set, and the autopilot engaged, Therese ducked into the cockpit, grabbed a handful of chocolate bars from the kitchen, the satellite phone from the wall mount, and then killed the cockpit lights on her way back onto deck. She switched off the navigation and running lights as soon as she was back at the wheel.

Therese's green eyes reflected the GPS glare, and she blinked once, before dimming the screen. She unwrapped and stuffed a chocolate bar into her mouth, chewing as she pulled on a second pair of gloves and tightened the draw cord of her hood around her neck. Therese clipped a safety line from the belt at her waist into a D hook behind the wheel, sat down on the chair and switched on the satellite phone. She was still chewing when her stepfather answered her call.

"I've got it, daddy," she said.

"The thumb drive?"

"Yes." Therese giggled and waited for her father to react.

"You're laughing?"

"Yes."

"You've got the journal too, haven't you?"

"I have."

Therese smiled at the sound of Aleksander Berndt thumping the desk in his Berlin office.

"But you haven't read it?"

"Not yet, daddy, I've been busy."

"And the crew?"

"I gave the captain her instructions. The police should have plenty to occupy them for the time being."

"And Dieter?"

"I never saw him. But he is in hospital."

"He'll recover?"

"That's what I heard." Therese waited for her stepfather to finish swearing. "It doesn't matter, daddy, just print the next article anyway, like we planned."

"I suppose you're right."

"I'll be in Ilulissat before midnight, Greenland time, but I have to keep sailing."

"Just long enough to read the journal. You haven't done anything illegal, Therese, don't do anything stupid. All I need is proof, and then you can throw the journal overboard."

"You don't even want to see it? It's a little piece of history."

"The past is only important when shaping the future. Once we own the future, we can rewrite the past. Remember that."

"I will." Therese paused to tap the screen as it dimmed more than she liked. "I have to go, daddy. Sailor stuff – you know?"

"I know. I want you to take care, and I want you to call me every two hours – earlier if you find the proof in the journal."

"I have to sail. I'm not sure how much I'll be able to read."

"Try."

"Okay," Therese said. A lick of chill wind caught a twist of her hair as she shook her head.

"I can hear you tutting, Therese."

"I'm not."

"It doesn't matter. As long as you realise how important this is."

"I wonder," she said, as another slug of wind, stronger than the last, flapped her hood from her forehead, "would you push Andrea as hard if she could sail."

"That's not fair, Therese. You are both my daughters."

"But only one of us is blood," she whispered.

"Therese?"

"I have to go," she said. "Wind's picking up."

"Call me in two hours."

Therese stabbed the button to end the call, and zipped the phone into her pocket. The light of the moon leaked through a cheesecloth-thin cloud. The filtered glow caught something glinting in the black water some twenty metres in front of *Ophelia*. Therese unclipped her safety line, and snapped it onto the wire running along the starboard railing. She bent her knees to compensate for the shallow bumps of incoming waves, the first to tease *Ophelia* since she was released from the ice. When she reached the bow, Therese held onto the railings and squinted into the polar night. The cloud dispersed and the moon lit the pearl-white, cream and ivory tusks of the narwhal as they pierced the surface of the sea. Therese held her breath and watched as the pod of whales swam away from the shore and further out to sea. They must have escaped the hunt, she realised, or slipped past the northerly settlements in the troughs of deep waves, when the moon was hidden, and the snow needled at unprotected eyes.

She wiped at soft needles thumping against her cheeks, catching several in her eyes, blinking, the snow thawed against her eyeballs. The sea was in league with the earth – reluctant to give up its bounty, she thought, or was it Wegener's ghost, making one more attempt to claim his journal and bury the secrets of Svartenhuk at sea?

Therese searched the water ahead. She tried and failed to find the narwhal again. She turned and walked back to the wheel, clipped into the safety lug behind her, and formed the wire-frame hood into a visor to protect her face. The thought of a prolonged battle with the elements, encouraged Therese to unclip her safety line, and to duck down into the cockpit. She spent a few minutes boiling water for coffee and draining her bladder before returning to the wheel. She stuffed the flask into a rubber-lined fibreglass tube welded into the deck, pulled on Gore-Tex sailing gauntlets, and squirmed her feet on the deck. She flipped the seat into a high saddle and leaned against it. Therese took the wheel, and let it jerk through her hands with small autopilot adjustments.

"I'm ready," she said, taunting the wind.

There were bergs on the black horizon, black shadowy behemoths, mostly ranged like teeth along the shore. Therese wasn't worried about them, but a chop of thunder began to bother her, and she flicked her head from side to side trying to locate it.

A beam of light, stronger and lower than the moon, cut through the snow swirling above the sea, and Therese realised she had discovered the source of the anonymous thump, in the shape of a Danish Navy Lynx helicopter, most likely from the deck of one of the Thetis-class ships like *HDMS Vædderen* or the smaller Knud Rasmussen-class *HDMS Ejnar Mikkelsen*.

"They've obviously got nothing better to do, eh?" she said.

Ophelia responded with a tug of the wheel. Therese dimmed the screen to the lowest setting, lifted her finger in anticipation of turning the autopilot off, and grinned.

"Now we're sailing." She bit at the snow, licking it from her lips as she grinned. "This is what it's all about."

A childhood memory of stealing her stepsister's favourite t-shirt – the blue one with the rainbow-streaked pony stencilled on the front – and splashing down the muddy lane to the stables, flickered into Therese's mind. She pushed it to one side, and listened for the helicopter, looked for the cone of light from its searchlight, and then remembered once again being chased by her stepfather, the groom, and the stable manager.

She remembered being hunted.

It didn't occur to her at the time, that it was an awful lot of men chasing her for something as silly as a t-shirt. But it didn't seem silly when she heard them cough, wheeze, and swear from running.

Therese had been light on her feet then, quick to climb trees, higher than she should. She hid in the branches of her favourite oak, stayed there until just before the dawn, creeping back to the house with a tattered t-shirt, and twists of moss braided in her hair. Daddy had beaten her the next morning, pulled the t-shirt from her body and thrust her into the shower. Her mother had protested, but he had said something about her leaving if she didn't like it.

"This is my house," Therese whispered, remembering her father's words. "My rules."

She was twelve then, her stepsister was fourteen. It was too bad both their mothers had died. There was nothing Therese could do about that. Her own father was too busy, too successful to show any interest in her, much less in her mother. So when Therese realised that Aleksander Berndt cared enough to punish her, she decided he might just care enough to love her, to be proud of her, and to treat her like a daughter.

"And that's what he did, with a little help from me," she said, at the sound of the helicopter drilling another circle in the sky, sweeping the black sea with radar, night vision goggles, and *Mark 1* eyeballs. "Now it's time to make daddy proud."

Therese tapped the screen and switched off the autopilot. The wheel twitched in her grasp, as *Ophelia* trembled with the anticipation of being released, let off the hook, just as Therese hoped.

The Lynx thundered into another circular sweep. Therese squinted into the distance, caught the pinpricks of light which could have been the navigational lights of the *Ejnar Mikkelsen* or its big brother.

"It doesn't matter," she said. "This is my house. My rules."

Therese turned *Ophelia* into the wind, stifling a grin as the bow bit into the first obsidian wave, crashing through the crest as Therese throttled up the side of the next wave, and the next, set after set, as she drove *Ophelia* deeper into the Arctic waters of the Davis Strait.

"My house," she said. "My rules."

Residents of Nuuk see the sun in winter. The days are short, but the sun makes an appearance, however brief. For Greenlanders living further north, in Inussuk, Uummannaq and in Qaanaaq – the most northerly village pretending to be a town – the sun does not shine for two to four months each winter. These northerly residents, Danes and Europeans among them especially, are easy to spot on winter flights from Kangerlussuaq to Copenhagen. When the Airbus 330-200 rises above the clouds, Nuuk residents tend to shield their eyes or turn away from the sun, while those from the north stare right at it, even though they shouldn't. Some, like Maratse, might acknowledge the sun with a mental dip of the head, a nod to a long-lost friend. It's been a while, they might say, and then turn away, fiddle with the foil-packed pretzels, or wonder if there is less leg room than the last time they flew on the Denmark flight. Others stare that bit longer, until the sun hurts their eyes, just as its absence hurts their soul. I'm struggling, they might say, won't you come back?

The sun comes back every year, rising at the same place, at the same time, unless the glacier has melted a little more since the previous year. Then the sun might return a day early, gone again if you missed it. The sun is visible in Uummannaq roughly fifteen minutes more each day after its first appearance mid-January. In Qaanaaq the sun will shine thirty minutes longer than yesterday, from the day of its return around the eighteenth day of February. Once it has reached its summer height by the end of March, it won't set again before September. In Ittoqqortoormiit, on Maratse's east coast, the hunters, the fishermen, and their families share the same light and darkness as their west coast neighbours in Inussuk, only the mountains are different.

Maratse recognised a few of the passengers from his home town, and looked at them as he did the sun, just like intimate strangers.

"You're quiet," Petra said.

"I don't like planes."

"You don't like flying?" She took Maratse's packet of pretzels and opened them, splitting the packet down the middle as a hunter might gut a seal, exposing the innards.

"Just planes, the insides of them."

"You're just bored," Petra said, and ate a pretzel.

"*Iiji.*"

"Then why don't you read?"

"I need a new book." Maratse caught Petra's eye as she reached for the last pretzel. She lunged for it, giggling as the pretzel crumbled beneath her fingers.

"I like pretzels," she said.

"I can see that." Maratse wiped the crumbs into the foil packet, and pushed it inside his empty coffee cup, the wrapper crackled as it expanded within the circumference of the cup. Maratse wiped his hands, and said, "Tell me what the Commissioner said."

"We're to meet with Hannah Mayer, a contact of his in the German Bundespolizei."

"I can't even say that."

"That's why the Commissioner sent me. He said you were 'on your own dime', or something like that."

"Berndt's money," Maratse said, "he made a deposit into my account."

"Right." Petra waited as the flight attendant removed their empty cups. "Simonsen is going to visit Axel Stein. He'll probably send Danielsen."

"*Iiji.*"

"And the German captain, Katharina, will remain in custody until the deaths have been cleared up, all of them. As captain of the *Ophelia* she is responsible for her crew."

"And Nele?"

"I'm not sure. The German embassy has been putting pressure on the First Minister, Nivi Winther, and she is pressurising the Commissioner. He is stalling them by sending me to Berlin, but, as for Nele Schneider, I think she is being sent home, something about being traumatized and needing therapy from a German trauma psychologist, someone who speaks her own language."

"So, free to go?"

"I suppose so."

Maratse tapped his fingers on the tray table.

"You don't think she's innocent?"

"I don't think Dieter did it."

"And yet, he's the most likely suspect."

"Because he has no alibi."

"Because he was the only one not dead or drugged, and he

attacked a police officer." Petra shrugged. "That's the circumstantial evidence. I didn't say he did it. But he has some interesting theories."

"The fake CVs?"

"And who knows what else. The CVs alone should be cause enough to dig deeper into who these people are. And what they were looking for."

"And Therese?"

"Apparently she slipped past the *Ejnar Mikkelsen*, but they are chasing her, and the *Knud Rasmussen* is heading for Cape Farewell to cut her off." Petra looked up at the clatter of the service trolley. "Once that part of the story breaks in the news, Greenland will gain a lot of exposure."

"And?"

"And that's exactly what Berndt wants." Petra leaned back as the flight attendant placed a tray on the table in front of her. She swapped Maratse's dessert for her salad.

"I like dessert," he said.

"But you don't eat enough vegetables." Petra slapped at the back of Maratse's hand as he tried to recover the plastic tub of chocolate mousse. He gave up, as Petra rearranged the items on her tray table, pushing the desserts further away from Maratse.

"You didn't finish," he said. "What does Berndt want?"

"He wants Uummannaq in focus so that he can apply emotional pressure to keep people away from Svartenhuk." Petra paused, and said, "Out of respect."

"For the dead?"

Petra nodded. She brushed a length of hair behind her ear, and prised the thick foil lid from the lasagne dish, stopping to blow on the tips of her fingers.

"You think he staged the murders?"

"No," Petra said, "but I think he intends to use them. It's convenient, otherwise he would have thought of something else."

"To keep people away from Svartenhuk?"

"To stop them digging around in the mountains." Petra folded the lid to one side, and opened the plastic bag of cutlery. "It's a shame you didn't read the journal."

"I can't read German."

"I know, but if you could, if there had been time, you might be the one who could prove what Wegener found in Svartenhuk."

Maratse thought about the snowmobile chase across the ice and Therese's long red hair as she pulled off her helmet to stare at him. He had been reluctant to get involved, and then he had been used.

"Next time, I won't get involved."

"With what?"

"An investigation. Of any kind."

"You'll just retire?"

"*Iiji*," he said, "again."

"What if next time, the case is personal?"

"There won't be a next time." Maratse peeled back the lid of his lasagne.

"But if something happened to someone you care deeply for?" Petra turned her head, strands of jet black hair drifted over her cheek. She pulled them to one side with the tips of her nails, searching for Maratse's eyes with a deep brown gaze.

"I'll go fishing," he said, and plucked his dessert from Petra's tray. He waved his prize in front of her, and said, "You never know what I might catch."

"Fair enough, *Constable*," Petra said, and leaned back in her seat. "But I don't think you can retire, not even if you tried."

Petra dozed after the meal, her head resting on Maratse's shoulder, her hand curled around his arm. He thought about what she said, about people he cared about – deeply. Yes, he realised, if anything happened to Petra, to Karl, Buuti, the people of Inussuk, even the temporary residents, he would not go fishing. He would hunt, instead, and he would find them, help them, solve the case, but not for money, he would do it because it was the right thing to do. He looked at Petra, and realised he would also do it out of love. He tugged a length of hair from the corner of Petra's mouth and brushed her cheek. She twitched and smiled at the light touch of his creased and calloused hands, squeezed his arm, and repositioned her head. She didn't wake before they landed in Copenhagen.

It was Petra who took over once they arrived in Denmark, leading Maratse through customs, vouching for him when she showed her police identity card, and collected her pistol.

"You're flying on to Berlin?" said the customs officer.

"Yes."

"Then you may as well leave that with me," he said, and nodded at the USP Compact pistol Petra was about to holster.

"I can do that?"

"It's the only thing you *can* do," he said. "It would be different if you were driving, or had official papers."

"We are meeting a German officer."

"Not good enough."

"Then I'll leave it with you."

Petra placed her pistol onto the desk and signed her weapon over to customs. She smiled at the officer, and then whisked Maratse through the crowds to the departure gate, shaking her head as he stopped and started while she weaved a line in and around the passengers.

"You're hopeless at this," she said, when she stopped to let him catch up for the fourth, maybe the fifth time. Petra laughed, as Maratse stopped to wait for another family, and then an older woman, and her daughter.

"There are fifty-eight people in Inussuk."

"And?"

"*Fifty-eight*, Piitalaat," Maratse said, as he hurried through a gap to stand next to Petra.

She took his hand. "Ready?"

"Holding hands?"

"It's that or we miss our flight," she said.

"I'm not ready for Berlin," he said.

"I can see that. But," Petra said, and tugged at Maratse's hand, "let's worry about that once we're on the flight."

Petra pulled Maratse through the crowd, all the way to the gate, letting go of his hand only when she thought he could keep up. Once they were boarded, buckled into their seats, and airborne, Petra stole the bag of peanuts from his tray.

"Airport tax," she said. The corners of her eyes twitched as she opened the peanuts, nibbling at them, one at a time, between smiles.

"Who are we meeting?" Maratse said, stirring sugar into his coffee.

"I told you earlier."

"I forgot."

"Hannah Mayer. I think the Commissioner worked with her in Nicaragua. Some kind of special task force. A bit like Polarpol."

"What's that?"

"Something I have been invited to be a part of."

"Like Europol?"

"Yes, I think so." Petra frowned. "The first meeting never really came to anything. There was this American, supposedly with the United States Geological Survey, although he admitted all of that was really only a cover."

"And he is with *Polarpol?*"

"I don't think so, but he had enough influence to end the meeting and pick my brains about the *Ophelia* case. This could come down as a simple case of murder for minerals."

"There's nothing simple about this case," Maratse said, and grabbed the peanuts from Petra's hand. The packet was empty.

Hannah Mayer called Petra's name as they walked through customs. She shook their hands, and then said, "Shall we speak English?"

"*Iiji,*" Maratse said.

"That means, *yes,*" Petra said, and tapped Maratse's arm. "Behave."

"You must be tired after the flight."

"Not yet," Petra said.

"All right then, that's good, because I want to take you to see Marlene Müller." Hannah gestured towards the exit, pulling her car keys from her pocket as she began to walk. "I spoke to her this morning. She is quite shaken, but very keen to meet you both, especially you, David. She heard that you pulled her husband out of a car that was sinking through the ice. Is that right?"

"I helped," Maratse said.

"It's true," Petra said, "but there are also lots of questions, still unanswered, regarding Dieter's whereabouts, and his involvement in the murders."

Hannah paused at the door to pull up the collar of her jacket. Maratse shivered as they stepped out of the airport and into the damp cold of Berlin. Hannah smiled at him as she held the door.

"The murders of the *Ophelia* crew? Yes, I understand," Hannah said, as they approached a black Mercedes Benz. "Lars briefed me over the phone." She clicked the fob on her keyring. "This is us."

Maratse buckled up as Hannah pulled out of her parking spot and accelerated into the late afternoon Berlin traffic. She switched on the GPS unit, clicked on a preset button, and used the radio mounted to the dash to check-in with her department as the map of their route loaded onto the screen. Maratse watched their progress from the backseat.

"Albertstraße, the street where Marlene lives, is not the nicest of areas, but it's not a slum. We'll be there shortly." She glanced in the rear-view mirror. "Shall I turn up the heat?"

"Please," Maratse said.

Hannah smiled. "I thought it was cold in Greenland?"

"Not like this."

"It's the damp," Petra said. "Although David thinks Nuuk is cold too."

"It is," Maratse said. He zipped his jacket and stuffed his hands in his pockets.

"Is that a police jacket?" Hannah said. "It looks like Petra's."

"*Iiji*."

"You used to be a policeman?"

"David is retired," Petra said. She turned in her seat to catch his eye, continuing when he nodded. "He was the first on the scene. The first to find the yacht."

"And you were also with Dieter in the car?"

"Yes," Petra said. "He was involved in the search for Dieter Müller."

"Is that what they call retirement in Greenland?" Hannah caught Maratse's eye in the mirror.

"I'm working on it."

Petra laughed. "He really is."

"Okay," Hannah said, as she slowed for traffic. "We're nearly there. Tell me what we're looking for."

"Dieter received some information in the mail, CVs to be specific, for the crew of the *Ophelia*. He left the originals at his apartment, together with his notes, but scanned the documents onto a thumb drive."

"Which was stolen?"

"So he says."

"And you want the originals?"

"No, we want to see if he has a copy on his computer. We understand the originals were taken, together with his notes by a man supposedly working for Aleksander Berndt."

Hannah nodded as she turned onto Albertstraße and looked for a place to park.

"You might be too late. When I called Marlene she told me that when the man took Dieter's notes he took the computer as well. She gave him everything, so we can't even accuse Berndt of stealing. Apparently, the man told her he needed to access to everything to be able to help Dieter. Dieter's face has been all over the newspapers, Berndt's included." Hannah paused to park the car. She turned off the engine, and said, "Marlene is pretty keyed-up. I think her doctor wanted to prescribe Valium, but she refused. She just wants Dieter home. She is going to ask you when that might happen."

Hannah opened the door and waited on the street for Petra and Maratse to join her. She pointed at the door on the other side of the street; it was tagged with graffiti, as were the shutters protecting the windows of the local shops. Hannah's car was the newest and brightest car in a long line of rusting European cars, sporting bruised panels and bald tyres. She led them to the door and stopped, one finger extended to push the button to Marlene's apartment.

"What is it?" Petra asked.

Hannah nodded in the direction of a black Sprinter van, perhaps only a year older than her Mercedes. "It's probably nothing." She pushed the button, and opened the door as Marlene buzzed them into the building.

Chapter 19

Heat leaked out of the windows of Marlene Müller's apartment, but it was still the first time Maratse had felt warm since arriving in Germany. She showed them to the living room, excused the mess and disappeared into the tiny kitchen to make tea. Maratse understood little of what was said in the beginning, but, as Petra started to translate, he noticed that Marlene would pause after everything she said. That and the way she looked at him suggested it was important for her that he could follow the conversation. Maratse sipped his tea, and nodded for her to continue.

"She's worried, naturally," Petra whispered. "And the guy Berndt sent to pick up the notes and the computer – she doesn't trust him."

"She has no reason to," Hannah said, "not after Berndt released a statement to the press with a detailed description of Dieter's battle with depression."

"He made him a *Sündenbock*," Marlene said.

"A scapegoat," Petra said.

"*Ja, das ist korrekt.*"

Tea from Marlene's mug splashed onto the table as she put it down. She hadn't touched it, Maratse noticed. He watched her get up and walk to the bedroom, when she returned she had a plastic shopping bag in her hand. She placed it on the table. Hannah leaned over and opened it.

"An external hard drive," she said, and folded the sides of the bag to reveal a small hard drive with a USB cable attached.

"A backup," Petra said, once Marlene had finished speaking. Petra asked something in German, Marlene answered, and Maratse waited for Petra to confirm that everything was on the hard drive, including the scans of the documents he received in the mail. "We can use this," Petra said.

"*Iiji.*"

"When will Dieter come home?"

"That's difficult, Marlene," Hannah said. "We're working on it. One, he has to be fit to travel, and two, he has to be allowed to travel." She paused as Petra translated for Maratse. "There are still lots of unanswered questions."

Maratse placed his mug on the table and leaned back in the sofa. He found a tear in the cushions and resisted the urge to pick at it.

The condition of the sofa, the tired wallpaper on the walls, and the faint smell of damp surprised him. He had seen worse conditions in Greenland, but, in comparison, there was not a great deal of difference. He allowed himself to feel some of Marlene's despair, shelving his professional objectiveness for a moment. He was, after all, retired. A change in tempo, and Petra's light tap on his knee suggested that they were leaving. Maratse stood up and thanked Marlene for the tea.

"You're welcome," she said, her accent abrasive, like the tears stinging her cheeks.

Maratse waited for Petra to pick up the plastic bag, and then followed Hannah out of the apartment and down the stairs. He heard the squeal of tyres as Hannah opened the door to the street.

The first pop of bullets surprised them, the impact louder than the act of firing. Maratse wondered for a second if the shooter was using a silencer screwed onto the barrel of his weapon, but then Petra pulled him down the steps and Hannah returned fire, loosing two rounds, and then a third into the side of a dark Sprinter van, the same one she had spotted earlier.

The side door rumbled open to reveal a man holding onto a length of rope looped into the roof with one hand, and a Heckler & Koch MP5 with the other. Hannah shot him twice in the chest as he pulled the trigger. The submachine gun spit an arc of bullets in a burst that chipped stone from the steps, chunks of masonry from the walls, and shattered the window of the downstairs apartment. Maratse shoved Petra over a low wall and into a sunken garden, a metre below street level. He stumbled down the steps as Petra disappeared from view and a second man leaped out of the van. The driver emptied the magazine of his Beretta at Hannah, forcing her behind two parked cars as Maratse tumbled onto the pavement.

"David," Petra shouted, as the passenger of the van hit Maratse on the back of the head and dragged him inside. The driver accelerated down the street and the last man dived inside the van. Hannah fired at the retreating vehicle as the man pulled the dead shooter inside and slammed the door shut.

Maratse pressed his hand against the back of his head, his hair matted and tacky beneath his fingers. He squinted in the gloom of the van, saw his assailant fumble the MP5 from the dead man's grip, change magazines, and turn to point the submachine gun at Maratse.

He held up his hands, slipped to one side as the van squealed around a corner, and then settled onto his knees. The man holding the MP5 nodded, and banged on the tiny window between the cargo area and the cab, shouting something that made the driver slow down.

"Don't do anything stupid," the man said in English.

"Okay," Maratse said.

They stared at each other for another ten minutes before the driver slowed to a stop, and the man with the gun opened the door. He snapped his fingers for Maratse to follow him. Once out of the van, Maratse blinked at in the harsh glare of the streetlights, as they walked past large rubbish bins, stacks of flat pizza boxes, and crates of empty bottles. The man reached out and grabbed Maratse by the arm, pulling him through an open door and into a kitchen as the driver closed the van and drove away.

The kitchen was bright compared to the mood lighting of the restaurant. He bumped into the back of a chair as the man led him around the empty tables. Maratse glanced at the windows, but could see nothing of the street, the blinds were drawn. His head hurt when he turned at the sound of a chair being dragged out from beneath a table. The man pushed Maratse into it, tugged thin plastic strips from his pocket and tied Maratse's wrists, lower arms, and ankles to the chair legs and arms. He looped another strip through Maratse's belt, and tied him to the back of the chair. Maratse watched as the man checked the ties, pulled the sling of the MP5 over his head, and slid the weapon onto the red and white-checked tablecloth of a table against the wall. He pulled a second weapon, a pistol, from his pocket and tucked it into the waistband at the front of his jeans. The man rested against the table in front of Maratse and lit a cigarette.

Maratse felt his body begin to charge itself in anticipation of the next stage in what he felt was an all too familiar situation. If he closed his eyes he would see the Chinaman, metal paddles in hand, standing in front of him in the cabin of a remote mining camp, deep in the fjord north of Nuuk. He might even hear him complain at the unreliable generator, spluttering to keep up with the demands of torture. But Maratse would not close his eyes. Even so, the American voice, when he heard it, surprised him.

"Constable David Maratse," the American said, as he walked around Maratse and stood next to the man with the gun. "Retired."

"*Iiji.*"

"You look resigned to that chair, and your record – the little that is available – suggests that if I told you my name, you might fear the worst, knowing that I would have to make sure you couldn't repeat it."

Maratse dug deep, and was surprised for a second time by his response. "You could give me a false name."

"And tell you it was false? To what end?"

"To give me hope."

The American snorted, pulled the gun from the other man's waistband, and said, "Stefan, get us a drink." He tapped the barrel of the Beretta against the surface of the table and studied Maratse. "You're funny, Constable. Not as pretty as your friend, but funny."

"My friend?"

"Sergeant Jensen," said the American. "Who should be here," he said, with a look at Stefan as he returned with a bottle of whisky and shot glasses gripped between his fingers. "Three glasses, Stefan? You really think you have cause for celebration?"

Stefan put the glasses on the table. He shrugged as he uncorked the whisky. "They had a German cop with them. She returned fire."

"Of course she did." The American took a glass of whisky from Stefan's hand. "That's what she's trained to do."

"All the same," Stefan said, and downed a shot of whisky, "that's why he's alone."

"All right," the American said. He took a slug of whisky and then slapped the Beretta into Stefan's palm. "I guess we just have to do this the hard way." He pointed at the third glass of whisky. "That's for you, Constable, when we're done. Just to keep you amiable."

The American pulled a mobile from his pocket and dragged the table so that Maratse's knees were beneath the surface. He placed the mobile in the middle. Stefan took off his jacket and rolled up his sleeves. Maratse stared at the snake tattoos twisting from the man's wrists to his elbow. Stefan winked at him.

"In German, if you please," the American said, and pointed at the mobile. Stefan picked it up and dialled a number, as the American laid a heavy hand on Maratse's shoulder. "You probably know how this works. Your friend has something I want, and I have you."

"You want the hard drive?"

"Amongst other things." He smiled, and raised a hand for Stefan to wait a second. "Can I be candid with you, Constable?"

Maratse nodded.

"I'm surprised to say this, but I find our friend incredibly attractive. You agree, of course?"

Maratse said nothing, but the bitter taste in his mouth must have tightened the skin around his eyes, because the American laughed, and slapped him on the shoulder.

"You see," he said, "Already we have something in common. A love of dark, attractive women." He spun his finger and Stefan pressed the dial button and placed the mobile on the table.

When a female voice answered, Stefan said, "Hannah Mayer?"

"Ja?"

Stefan spoke in German as he looked at Maratse, but Hannah answered in English.

"I need proof that you have David Maratse, that he is well."

The American slapped the back of Maratse's head, and said, "You're on."

"Hannah, this is Maratse."

"Are you all right?"

"I'm tied up in…"

A second blow from the American fused the words behind Maratse's bloody lips. The chair tipped to one side, and the American helped it crash to the floor with a toe beneath one leg as Stefan grabbed the phone from the table.

"I'm going to text you with an address. Bring the hard drive in one hour," Stefan said. "Send the Eskimo." He swiped the screen to end the call.

"One hour?" the American said. "That's cutting it a little fine."

Stefan shrugged. "It's up to your asset now."

"Sure."

The American knelt down beside Maratse. He held out his hand, and Stefan pressed the glass of whisky into it. The American poured the whisky onto Maratse's face, dribbling it into his eyes. Maratse blinked and tried to turn away.

"This is a waste," the American said, and gripped Maratse by the hair. "But I heard Greenlanders like their drink."

"Some Greenlanders," Maratse said, and licked whisky and blood from his lips.

"Only some?" The American tossed the glass at Stefan, and said, "Help me get him up."

The plastic straps dug into Maratse's skin as the two men pulled the chair onto its legs. He let his head roll back and then forwards, wiping the blood from his chin on the collar of his jacket.

"Your friend," the American said, "thinks my name is Johnson, so that's the name you can use. How about that, Constable?"

"It's a false name?"

"It's one of many. Why?"

Maratse spat a clot of blood from his mouth, and said, "Just wondering if I'm going to live."

Johnson folded his arms and looked at Maratse. "You're a curious one," he said. "This really isn't your first time, is it?"

"This is better than my first time."

"Ha," Johnson said, and pulled up a chair beside Maratse. He sat down, and said, "Do tell."

"There's nothing to tell."

"Because it's confidential?" Johnson gestured for Stefan to give him the bottle of whisky. "But you're among friends, Constable." He uncorked the whisky and mashed the glass lip of the bottle into Maratse's mouth. "Now," he said, and tipped the bottle, "either your teeth rotted out or were pulled out, which is it?"

Maratse spluttered on the whisky. He turned his head, but Stefan walked behind him, clamped bony hands around his ears and jaw, and tipped his head backwards. Maratse squinted in the light above, coughed and choked on the whisky.

"Come on, Constable. This isn't even about you. Just give us a few details from your life, and explain to me why that pretty young Petra finds you so attractive – a retired Constable with bad teeth and a wispy beard. Hell, Stefan," he said, "I might even be in with a chance here. I mean I'm only ten years or so older than the Constable, and he's practically twice her age." He laughed, and then removed the bottle as Maratse spluttered to talk. "What's that?"

"Thirteen."

"Your lucky number?" Johnson winked at Stefan.

"Thirteen years older."

"Ah," Johnson said, "I get it. You've done the math. And you know what that means don't you, Stefan?"

"What does it mean?"

Johnson lifted the bottle to the light, sloshing the contents in front of Maratse's eyes; there was half a bottle left.

"It means the Constable here is interested. He might even shave that ridiculous beard if the young Petra with those dark almond eyes, chocolate skin, and silky black hair, popped the question, or, you know, just grabbed him one night. I mean, if that's not worth a drink, I don't know what is."

Johnson pressed the bottle to Maratse's lips as Stefan held his head. Maratse tried to concentrate, to listen to the tiny voice reassuring him that most of the whisky was dribbling down his chin, onto his clothes, but the whisky burned, prevented him from breathing, and Maratse realised once again what he already knew to be true, torture wasn't about information, it was never about information, it was all about power. The American knew that, and Maratse had the idea that this wasn't his first time either.

Maratse coughed, ratcheting air into his body as Stefan let go of his head, and he spluttered whisky from his lungs. Johnson tossed the bottle onto the floor and it rolled beneath a table.

"Waste of a good bourbon," he said, and gripped Maratse's chin between thick fingers. "What do you think, Constable? Had enough?"

Chapter 20

Petra slammed her palm against the interior panel as the driver swung the heavy assault vehicle around the roundabout and accelerated away from the *Siegessaule*. Hannah tugged at the straps on Petra's vest while a member of the German GSG 9 group stuffed ceramic plates into the back of the vest. He lifted a ballistic helmet from the seat and tried to press it onto Petra's head.

"If I wear that, they will think I'm one of you," she said, and waved him away.

"You might get shot," he said.

"I *will* get shot if I'm wearing that thing."

Hannah nodded for the man to step away and guided Petra into a spare seat.

Petra took a breath of adrenalin-stoked air, glanced at the men and women of the Bundespolizei's counter terrorism unit, and forced a smile for Hannah. "I'm okay," she said.

"I know." Hannah smiled. "Greenlanders are tough, eh?"

"I wouldn't know," Petra said. "I guess so."

"This one is," Hannah said. She slapped Petra on the thigh and dug into a satchel on the seat beside her. Hannah handed Petra a thin sheath of papers. "The CVs," she said. "We printed them off the hard drive.

Petra flicked through the documents, as Hannah sat down beside her.

"Do you know what you are looking for?"

"Not yet."

Petra lurched into the shoulder of the policeman checking his gear beside her. He smiled and said something about a rookie driver. Petra nodded, braced herself for another turn, and then looked up when Hannah called her name.

"Call for you," she said, pressing her phone into Petra's hand. "It's Lars."

"Commissioner," Petra said, as she held the phone to her ear.

"This is the official *talk*, Sergeant."

"Yes, sir."

"I need to hear you say you volunteered for this."

"I did."

"Say it."

"I volunteered, sir."

"All right. Now I need to know why?"

"They have Maratse." She waited as the Commissioner sighed.

"I understand," he said. "What I don't understand, is what this has to do with the case? I sent you to Germany to find answers, not stir up a storm. You've been gone less than twenty-four hours. What's going on?"

"They want the hard drive. I think they are trying to erase all the evidence."

"What evidence?"

"The real identities of the *Ophelia* crew. Once we know who they really are, we'll be able to confirm what they were really doing in Svartenhuk, and why people had to die for it."

"Who's they?"

"I don't know, but we are heading to the offices of the Berndt Media Group. I think we can assume that he is involved."

"He hasn't been picked up by the police?"

"They are looking for him, Sir." Petra looked at Hannah. She nodded. "What about Berndt's daughter?" Petra bounced off the shoulder of the man on her left as they drove over a set of asphalt speed bumps.

"Now that's a topic I haven't talked about at all today."

"Sir?"

"I think the First Minister, the German Ambassador, and the Danish Foreign Minister have my number on speed dial, but then I have the General Major for Arctic Command's number, and he is just as tired of me as I am of them."

"Where is Therese?"

"She is approaching Cape Farewell with full sails. The Commander can't decide if she is talented or suicidal. He suspects both. She's riding with the storm, and the size of the waves is making it impossible for the crew from either the *Ejnar Mikkelsen* or the *Knud Rasmussen* to board her. The helicopters are grounded."

"So she's getting away?"

"She'll either get away or die trying, that seems to be the general opinion. That's some journal you found."

"Yes, sir."

"Personally, I don't know how much it has to do with the journal. The way she sails, well, I believe the devil drives." The

Commissioner paused to take an incoming call, when he came back he asked to speak to Hannah. Petra handed her the phone and tucked the documents into her vest.

"Yes," Hannah said. "I'll look after her." Hannah smiled. "Yes. I agree."

Petra frowned as Hannah slipped her phone into her pocket.

"What was that last bit about?"

"He's very fond of you, thinks you are a very competent police officer. I agreed."

"Thank you."

"Don't thank me, Sergeant," Hannah said, as the driver slowed and turned off the siren. "I'm about to send you into the lion's den."

"We don't know that."

"Oh, I think we do." The vehicle stopped and Hannah waited for the team to get out before standing up. "It's not every day we have a shoot out on the streets of Berlin. Make no mistake; we don't know what's inside that building, which is why I requested GSG 9, and not just the regular police. These guys are the best."

"That sounded like a pep talk," Petra said, as she followed Hannah out of the vehicle and onto the street.

"It was." Hannah led Petra to an officer standing beside the second van. Petra could only see his eyes. His height, his gear, and the weapon slung across his chest reminded her of Gaba. When she looked at the team members, she realised they all did.

"Great," she whispered, "I'm channelling my ex-boyfriend."

"What's that?" Hannah asked.

"Nothing. I'm ready."

"Okay." Hannah introduced Petra to the GSG 9 leader and took a step back.

"You're Sergeant Jensen?"

"Yes."

"Right, here's what you need to know."

Petra listened as the leader of the counter terrorism team described the layout of the building, the location of the office on the second floor, and a detailed description of the lobby and reception, the position of the elevators, and the stairwells.

Petra nodded when he asked if she understood.

"Good," he said. "Do you have the package?"

Petra tapped the front pocket of her vest.

"And the wire? Your mic?" he turned to the officer on his right. The man tapped his headphones and gave him the thumbs-up. "Okay." He took a step back. "This is the back-brief. Tell me what the plan is."

Petra glanced at Hannah. "I go inside, take the elevator to the second floor, meet with the contact, ask for the location of Constable David Maratse, and give them the hard drive. No negotiations. I won't try to bargain. I'll repeat the address," she said, and pressed her fingers to the microphone hidden beneath her collar, "then I leave the hard drive on the floor, and go back to the elevator."

"Good," the man said. He stepped behind Petra, held her by the shoulders and turned her to look at the position of the sniper teams in the opposite buildings. He tilted her head to see the teams scrambling into position on the roof, and then dipped her head to see the GSG 9 men taking position behind cars, and ballistic shields. "We are deliberately overt," he said, and let go of Petra. "We want the kidnappers to see us *before* you go in. If they've done this before, they will give you the address once they are clear of the building, but then we've got the GPS tracker hidden inside the casing of the hard drive. Hopefully, the sight of so many heavily armed, steely-eyed professional marksmen will put them off doing anything stupid." The man tugged at the balaclava hiding his mouth. "I'm smiling, Sergeant."

"Okay."

"We've got your back."

"I know."

"Now, will you put on a helmet?"

"No," she said, and took a breath. "I'm ready."

Hannah thanked the GSG 9 leader, curled her arm around Petra's, and guided her to a gap in the police cordon, nodding at the officers as they passed. She stopped three metres beyond the police line.

"He didn't tell you about the teams already inside the building."

"Inside?"

"In the basement, working their way up."

"They only had an hour."

Hannah shrugged, and said, "They're good. They've got your back, now it's up to you to go in there and make the exchange."

Petra looked up at the large glass windows. The lights were

dimmed.

"Do you think he's in there?"

"David? No, I don't think so."

"Neither do I."

"The truth is, we have no idea what to expect. You probably won't even recognise the person inside. Hell, it could even be a drone, remotely piloted from one of these buildings," she said, and waved a finger at the offices overlooking the Berndt Media Group building. "Maybe there's a pouch on the drone, and..."

"Hannah," Petra said.

"Yes, sorry," she said. "I was getting carried away. But, hey, now you have plenty to think about."

"I liked the other pep talk better," Petra said, and made a sound that could almost have been interpreted as a laugh. She gripped Hannah's hand for a second, nodded once, and let go. Petra walked across the street, stepped up onto the pavement, and continued walking to the door.

As soon as she entered the elevator, Petra realised Hannah had been wrong about the contact person being a stranger; she recognised Nele Schneider the moment the young German woman pressed the barrel of a gun into her cheek.

"Going up?" Nele asked, as she pressed the button for the sixth floor, and then ripped Petra's microphone from her throat. She tossed it into the lobby as the elevator doors hushed to a close.

Nele pushed Petra against the wall of the elevator, shifted the barrel of the gun to Petra's forehead, and then opened the Velcro pouch at the front of her vest. She tucked the hard drive into the cargo pocket of her trousers and took a step back.

"This is where it gets complicated," she said.

"It doesn't have to, Nele."

"Nele? That's right, that's my name." She shrugged. "Sometimes I forget. It's not easy playing the victim all the time. It's far more fun to get physical, if you know what I mean?"

"I'm not sure I do." Petra worked on her breathing, felt her chest press against the inside of the vest, wondered if it would help to loosen the straps, and then decided that it wouldn't.

Not one bit.

Nele glanced at the elevator's progress, grabbed Petra by the hair, and pressed the gun to the side of her head. When the elevator doors opened, Nele kicked Petra's legs, dropping the Sergeant to her knees, and then ducked behind her. She made Petra shuffle into the corridor, turning her like a shield with a twist of her hair, first to the left, then right. Satisfied, Nele told Petra to get up, and then shoved her forwards, through the open office, and into a more luxurious workspace with a door, and a large side window facing the street. The rear wall of the office separated the Berndt building with the adjoining offices of an insurance company. Nele flicked off the lights and pushed Petra into the corner.

"Snipers," she said. "I know their game."

"Who are you?" Petra asked, as Nele relaxed her grip on her hair.

"That's not important."

"Where's Maratse?"

Nele laughed, and said, "That's even less important."

"You have what you want. You can at least tell me where he is."

"He's safe," Nele said, "for the moment."

Petra crumpled to her knees as Nele let go. She watched as the young German woman opened a black backpack tucked beneath a desk. She pulled out a remote with two large safety switches. Nele grinned and mouthed the word *boom* at Petra.

So this is how it feels, Petra thought, as she imagined Maratse being tortured by the Chinaman. This is how it feels when someone holds your life in their hands, and has every intention of ending it. Total control, total power.

"You're thinking too much," Nele said. "Stop it. It bothers me."

"Why?"

"Because I'm working on getting out of here. Your friends are good," she said, with a nod to the street. "I should know, I trained with them once or twice."

"You're a soldier?"

Nele laughed. "I might have been, if he hadn't found me."

"Who?"

"You'll see," she said, with a nod to the whiteboard covering the adjoining wall. Petra watched as Nele crawled to the wall, tugged a set of wires from behind the whiteboard, and attached them to the remote in her hand. She crawled back to Petra, and then toppled a desk in front of them.

"You're going to blow us up?"

"I'm going to blow *that* up," she said, and pointed at the wall.

"That's our way out."

"You're taking me with you?"

"Sure," Nele said, "I need insurance." She furrowed her brow and said, "Of course, premiums are high, and I can't promise to keep up the payments. Do you understand?"

"You'll shoot me."

"Shoot you? Hell no, Eskimo, I'll *kill* you."

Petra ignored the pressure in her bladder, and took a chance. "Like you killed the crew of the *Ophelia*?" Nele whipped her head around and stared at Petra. "You stabbed them to death, didn't you?"

"You can't prove that."

"I don't need to, if you tell me." It was Petra's turn to shrug. "You're going to kill me, you said so."

"I did," Nele frowned. "But why do I get the feeling you are playing me?"

"Because I want you to save Maratse. I don't care about me."

"The old guy with the funny beard?"

"Yes," Petra said. She felt the corners of her mouth twitch, and she amazed herself with a smile. "He means a lot to me."

"There's a shortage of men in Greenland?"

"Not exactly?"

"Then why?"

"You wouldn't understand. I love him."

Nele stared at her, and then turned the remote in her hand. Petra continued.

"You didn't love Henrik."

"What?"

"You wouldn't have stabbed him if you did."

"Henrik had to go."

"Because he found out about Arbroath Mining?" Petra waited as Nele shuffled closer. When Nele was close enough that Petra could smell the sweat beneath her shirt, she said, "But you didn't need to kill Antje, unless…"

"Unless what?" Nele said, her top lip twisted, a cruel slant.

"You did love Henrik. That's it, isn't it?"

"I was told someone had to die. That was my role on the expedition. Not ski guide or mountaineer. That's what I was hired for, but my job was to kill. To make a mess."

"Who hired you? Berndt?"

"You won't get that from me."

"But Antje?"

"Henrik tried to stop me. He woke up too soon." Nele shook her head. "I only put half the drug in my drink. I think he took that one. I had to put more in his ear, couldn't cope with his screams."

Petra heard something click outside the door. She kept talking.

"What about Dieter?"

"Hah, fall guy, the patsy. Idiot." Nele laughed. "He made it easy. Wouldn't go back to the yacht. Something about not trusting himself around the captain."

"So you left him on the mountain?"

"Hardly. We were on the path to that cabin the Greenlanders like to keep so secret, like it's a shrine. He said he knew where it was. All I had to do was push him to disobey orders, turn him against Henrik."

"So you could kill them and pin the murder on Dieter?"

"It was a good plan. Guilty lover, confused with exposure. He was supposed to die on the mountain."

"But he didn't."

"No," Nele said, as she clicked the remote.

The blast from the shape charge behind the whiteboard filled the room with a cloud of grey plaster, as the whiteboard shattered the window opposite the wall, and revealed a hole into the adjoining office. Nele scrambled over the desk, and disappeared through the cloud. Petra scrabbled on the floor, shuffling bits of debris through her fingers as she picked herself up, and staggered after Nele.

The second explosion was louder and brighter than the first, but without the physical shock of the blast. Petra tumbled to her knees as the GSG 9 team crashed through the office, green lasers lancing through the plaster cloud as they moved through over the rubble, the stocks of their submachine guns pressed to their shoulders, the barrels and lasers sweeping left and right in sync with their eyes.

One man knelt beside Petra as the rest of the team moved forwards. He wiped dust from her eyes with rough brushes of his thumb, turned her head to check her ears for blood, to see if her eardrums had been perforated in the explosion, and told her to stay put. He pressed his fingers to the microphone around his throat and then gagged as Nele crawled out from beneath a desk, and slid a knife into the base of the man's skull. He toppled forwards on top of

Petra, as Nele tugged the pistol from her waistband and aimed it at the rearguard of the GSG 9 team. She loosed off two shots before she was shot in the back, by team two moving in from the rear.

Nele slumped to her knees, and took another two bullets in her back before collapsing at Petra's feet. Petra crawled free of the GSG 9 man pinning her to the ground, and twisted Nele onto her back.

"Where is Maratse?" she shouted, as Nele started to gag on the blood in her mouth. Nele's head lolled back to her neck, and Petra caught it. "Where is he?"

"You already know," Nele said, as her body slumped to the ground.

Two men from the GSG 9 team worked on the body of their fallen team member, as the other men cleared the room. The first team returned, declared the area clear, and then clumped around the men working on the man with Nele's knife in his head.

Petra searched Nele's pockets, and tucked the hard drive into her vest before one of the team pulled her to her feet. He took her through the hole in the wall, and found a chair for her in the middle of the open office.

"Stay here," he said, "Mayer is on her way up."

Petra waited for him to hurry back to the medics, and then slipped out of the office. She took the stairs, stumbling all the way to the ground floor. Petra pushed through the fire door, and staggered down the street, holding her ears as the fire alarm drilled into her head.

She hailed a taxi, cursed it as the driver took one look at her, and drove on. The same happened with the second, but the third taxi stopped. Petra opened the passenger door, and pulled the documents from inside her vest.

"Where to?"

Petra laid the documents on her bloody lap. She found three with the same address in the references section, whispered a quick thanks to such sloppy attention to detail, and told the driver where to go.

Chapter 21

The plastic strip securing Maratse's ankle to the chair leg snapped just before midnight. His foot twitched and knocked one of the empty bottles of whisky. It rolled under the table and rattled against another, the sound of glass knocking against glass woke him, and he tried hard to open his eyes. Johnson pressed two fingers under Maratse's chin and lifted it, prising one eye open with the fingers of his other hand.

"To be fair," Johnson said, "I thought Greenlanders had a weakness for alcohol, something in their genes that means they can't handle their drink." He let go of Maratse's chin, sucking air through his teeth with a whooshing sound as Maratse's head snapped to his chest. "But this one did okay. Although he's gonna have a hell of a hangover in the morning." Johnson turned to Stefan, and said, "She should have been here by now. She should have called."

Stefan waved the iPhone. "Nothing. Not even a text."

"All right," Johnson said. "Phase two. Go and get Berndt." He looked at his watch. "If we can get this sorted before office hours tomorrow, I can fly back to the States, be home with the wife for Thanksgiving."

Stefan stopped at the door. "You want me to bring anything to eat?"

"You do know we are in a restaurant?"

Stefan shrugged. "I don't like Italian."

"Whatever." Johnson waved his hand. "Just bring me Berndt, and soon."

Johnson waited until Stefan had left, and then picked up the empty whisky bottles, lining them up on the table in front of Maratse, until he had a row of three. He picked up a spoon and tapped the side of one of the bottles until Maratse lifted his head and squinted at him.

"There you are, Constable. I'm bored. Entertain me."

Maratse had the vague sensation of drool dribbling from the corner of his mouth. Another sensation, a pressure in his bladder, made him realise he needed to piss, but he couldn't recall if he had already, or just needed to. He tried to focus on Johnson as he placed a fourth bottle of whisky on the table.

"Don't worry," he said, "you spilled most of that one."

"Why?" Maratse said, the word longer and more complicated

than he remembered.

"We don't always need a reason, do we? Why do anything?" Johnson dragged a chair across the floor, placed it beside Maratse, and sat down. "We're driven," he said, and patted Maratse's arm. "Some are more driven than others, I'll grant you that, but we are each, in our own way driven to do things. If you ask me, greed drives most people. A want for more. I see it every day. They might *want* different things such as power, a new car, a bigger house, but greed drives them. I'll admit to being a little power hungry at times, but I wouldn't say that drives me, not completely." He stopped, leaned closer to Maratse, encouraging him with small, slow waves of his hand. "You can do it. That's it."

"What then?" Maratse said.

"Well it's not lust, not all the time, but sex is certainly something that drives me. I mean, you must be having sex up there in Greenland, eh? Not much else to do in that crab-fart of a settlement in the winter. No," Johnson said, "I think I'm driven more out of curiosity. For example," he said, and leaned forwards, "take this particular job, chasing a forgotten journal half-way around the world, just to find out if an area is viable for mining, you know? I found that curious. My curiosity was aroused."

Johnson clicked his fingers in front of Maratse's face, sighed, pushed back his chair, and walked into the kitchen. When he came back, he emptied a jug of cold water over Maratse's head.

"I find that stimulating conversations work best when both parties are awake, Constable. Now," he said, as Maratse spluttered at the water dribbling over his lips, "as I was saying." Johnson put the jug on the table. "This job was about solving a problem. As you know, the Greenland government, in their wisdom, put a stop to geological surveys in areas within one hundred kilometres of towns, villages, and settlements. They were a bit more accommodating with what you call 'living places' with one or two inhabitants too stubborn to die, but Svartenhuk was out of bounds. Unless – and this is where I pride myself on being more than a little ingenious – a survey had already been carried out, prior to the new law in 2013."

"Wegener," Maratse said.

"Exactly. Well done, Constable, I'm so pleased you are keeping up."

"My pleasure." Maratse moved his lips into what he thought was a smile.

"Ah, yes," Johnson said. "One thing at a time, I think." He tapped the table, and said, "I heard a rumour that an old acquaintance was speculating in a Scottish mining company. Arbroath Mining is the name. My friend knows nothing about mining, but he does know the energy business. Nuclear energy to be precise. Tell me, Constable, have you heard of Thorium? No?" Johnson reached over to the next table and tugged a napkin from beneath the cutlery and wiped Maratse's chin. He tossed the napkin into Maratse's lap. "Thorium is a radioactive mineral, and can be used to produce nuclear energy, more or less on a par with uranium. My friend discovered two things of interest concerning Arbroath Mining Company." Johnson held up a finger. "One, they were struggling. And two." Another finger. "When Arbroath bought the rights to the old marble mine in Uummannaq, they also bought the rights that included the mountains of Svartenhuk. Now, Arbroath might be struggling, but they had a solid business plan – invest everything in proving the viability of their concern, and then get bought out by a bigger company. Bigger companies tend to keep an eye on the likes of Arbroath, but it is a risky strategy, as they are just as likely to be forgotten."

"Not by you."

"Again, Constable, I must praise you for keeping track. Remarkable, really," Johnson said, with a nod to the row of empty bottles on the table. "My curiosity was peaked. I looked into Arbroath, Greenland, even Wegener, and I discovered a riddle, that might, if it were solved, prove very profitable to the people I represent." Johnson laughed. "Is that a look of surprise? I can't tell, but let's assume that it is. I'm not personally capable of fronting this operation, although I'm flattered you might think so. No, I'm just good at pointing the right people in the right direction, at the right time, and then adding a few elements of my own to spice things up."

"Like Nele Schneider?" Petra said, as she opened the door to the kitchen. "I let myself in," she said, and raised the pistol in her hand.

"Sergeant Jensen," Johnson said, and clapped. "Good girl. I can see why they picked you for the task force." He gestured at Maratse. "Your friend and I were having a chat over a few drinks, although the Constable did most of the drinking. He's got quite a thirst."

"Are you all right, David?"

"*Iiji.*"

Petra pointed the gun at Johnson, and said, "Untie him."

"What happens if I say no?"

Petra pulled the trigger and clipped Johnson's shoulder with a bullet from Nele's gun. The American swore, checked his shoulder, and lifted his hand to show Petra a stripe of blood across his fingers. "That, Sergeant, was not smart."

"Untie him."

"Fine." Johnson pulled a buck knife from his boot, opened the blade, and locked it in place, cutting the ties, one by one. "I must say, you look a little rough, Sergeant. How is Nele?"

"Dead," Petra said, and waved the gun. "Keep going."

"That's unfortunate. She was quite useful."

"She said she was ordered to make a mess, something newsworthy. Did you tell her to do that?"

"Anything to do with the news is Berndt's business, literally. I told her to kill Henrik Baumann because he was an activist. Greenpeace, or some other organisation with more balls than money. I thought he might destroy the journal before we had made use of it." Johnson cut the ties around Maratse's hands. "There's another one through his belt," he said, and offered the knife to Petra. "Why don't you cut that one?"

Petra took a step forwards, only to stop as something hard was pressed into the back of her neck.

"If I pull the trigger," Stefan said, "I will kill you, and your friend. Now, lower the gun, and take a seat on that chair over there. Stop," he said, as Petra started walking. "Put your gun on that table, and *then* walk over to the chair." Stefan waited for Petra to sit down, and then picked up the gun, stuffing it into his waistband as he beckoned for Berndt to come in.

"I hope you have good news, Aleksander," Johnson said.

"Berndt has a call scheduled with his crazy daughter for one o'clock," Stefan said, and nodded for Berndt to place his phone on the table between Johnson and Maratse. "That's in seven minutes."

"Seven whole minutes, eh?" Johnson looked at Petra. "I might have managed that in my youth, but I have to admit that it takes a little longer these days. Perhaps later, darling, what do you say to that?"

"*Eeqqi,*" Maratse said.

"What did he say?" Johnson said, and leaned closer to Maratse.

"It means *no*." Maratse lunged for Johnson's throat. His fingers caught around the American's shirt as he stepped back, tearing a flap of cotton and ripping a few buttons before Stefan smacked Maratse on the back of the head with the butt of his pistol.

"You see this?" Johnson said to Berndt, pushing at Maratse's head with his knuckles. "This is what you hired."

"Maratse?"

"The one and only. Pathetic, eh?"

"Leave him alone," Petra shouted.

"Sit down, sweetheart, don't exert yourself, it looks like you've had quite a night already." Johnson waved at Stefan to lower his gun. "Unless you've got something to trade?"

"I have Dieter's hard drive," she said.

"Here?"

"Close."

"Of course," Johnson said. "But now I have to do more than get your boyfriend drunk to make you hand it over." He gripped the knife in his hand. Petra held her breath as he held the knife to Maratse's chin.

"Wait," Berndt said, as his phone rang. He swiped the screen, and turned the phone on the speaker setting, dialling up the volume as Johnson lowered the knife.

"Daddy?"

Maratse recognised Therese Kleinschmidt's voice, but the shriek of wind in the background, and the crash of what sounded like waves, made it difficult to hear her.

"Therese, where are you?"

"I'm not going to make it. I'm sorry."

"What are you saying?" Berndt cast a wild glance at Johnson at the sound of something heavy cracking in the background.

"The mast?" Johnson said, with a shrug.

"Therese?"

"I'm sorry, daddy."

Petra sat up as Johnson walked to the table and spun the phone towards him with his finger.

"Do you have the journal?" Johnson waited a beat. "Therese? The journal?"

"I always loved you, daddy, like you were my own father."

Berndt pushed Johnson away from the phone and placed his hands either side of it. He leaned over the table, and said, "You should have been my daughter. You were the bravest..."

"Oh please," Johnson said. He pushed Berndt to one side, and shouted at the phone. "Kleinschmidt. Do you have the damn journal? Have you read it?"

"Yes," Therese said, her voice barely audible above the waves crashing over *Ophelia*'s stricken hull.

"Have it or read it?"

"Read it."

"Finally," Johnson said. He tapped the tip of the knife on the table. "Tell me about Thorium. Is that Wegener's secret? Is that what he found in the mountains?" Johnson placed his palms on the table and pressed his face towards the phone. "Come on, Therese. Daddy is waiting."

Johnson frowned, recoiling at a violent crash of static through the speaker, and the sound of something groaning, tipping, as if *Ophelia* was rolling into the massive jaws of Greenland's dark seas.

"You're not my daddy," Therese said, and nothing more. The line went dead.

Johnson lifted the knife in his fist, raised it above his head, and curled it down in an arc towards the iPhone, just as Berndt collapsed onto his knees, and the windows of the restaurant imploded with a bang, and the flash and flare of magnesium.

The first GSG 9 officer to crash through the blinds and glass of the window put two bullets through Stefan's chest, and a third through his forehead. Two more officers slammed Johnson into the floor. One of them knelt on the American's chest, while his partner cinched plastic ties around his wrists. A fourth man covered Berndt while the fifth and sixth members of the team secured Maratse and Petra, dragging them out of the restaurant to the ambulances parked behind the police cordon at the end of the street. Hannah took Petra's hand and helped her into the ambulance.

"You're all right?"

"Yes."

Hannah moved to one side as the paramedics lowered Maratse onto a stretcher. He smiled at her, and said, "Don't mind the smell; I've had a bit to drink."

Petra waited for the medic to finish strapping Maratse to the stretcher, and then leaned over to brush a tear from his cheek with a dusty finger.

"Funny guy," she said, and smiled.

"Piitalaat."

"Yes?"

"I'm ready to go home."

"Yes. Let's do that." Petra waited as Maratse turned his head to one side and coughed; when he looked back he whispered her name. "What?"

"Don't eat my peanuts."

"Right," Petra said, as Hannah tapped her on the shoulder.

"You took a big risk," she said, "running away like that."

"I didn't run away." Petra opened the front of her vest and pulled out the hard drive. "I knew you would find me."

"The GPS tracker could have been damaged in the blast."

Petra shrugged. "It wasn't." She turned at the sound of Johnson's voice as the GSG 9 team marched him towards the police car parked behind the assault vehicle. Berndt followed, flanked by two more GSG 9 men. "What happens to them?"

"Berndt's easy. With the evidence on the hard drive, and the testimony of the captain of the *Ophelia*, we can charge him with obstruction of justice at the very least, possibly conspiracy to…" Hannah paused at the sound of a vehicle braking hard outside the police cordon. She glanced at Petra, and took a step towards the car at the sound of two doors opening, shouts from police officers in German, and a loud male voice with an American accent.

"Who the hell's in charge here?"

"I am," Hannah said, as she took a step towards the tall man flashing a badge at her colleagues. Petra followed a step behind her.

"Your name?"

"Hannah Mayer."

"And you're in charge?"

"Yes. Who are you?"

"Who I am is above your pay grade. Now, here's what you are going to do." The man pulled out his phone and dialled a number. He held up a finger as Hannah started to speak. "Yes, sir, here she is now." He gave the phone to Hannah.

Petra watched as the man pulled Johnson away from the GSG 9 team holding him, and waited for Hannah to finish talking on his phone. Johnson caught Petra's eye and took a step towards her, nodding for her to join him.

"You see what's happening here, don't you, Sergeant?" Johnson said.

"I see you're still cuffed," she said, with a glance at the plastic ties around his wrists.

"An oversight."

"Really?"

"Of course," he said, "but in the meantime, now that we have a moment, and your boyfriend is otherwise engaged, how about you ask me the question."

Petra looked over her shoulder at Maratse. She caught his eye and smiled.

"Hurry now, Sergeant."

Petra lifted her chin and looked Johnson in the eye. "You're CIA."

"Am I?"

"Nele was working for you. She said so."

"She didn't say my name."

"She didn't need to."

"So ask the question, *Piitalaat*." Johnson grinned. "I'm a quick study."

"Why?"

"You're gonna go with *why*?"

"Yes."

Johnson glanced at Hannah, frowning at the curl of her lips. "I'll tell you why," he said, and looked at Petra. "Because oil is running out, and Greenland has no viable oil. But what you do have is two handfuls of people on a frozen rock in the middle of the Atlantic, with no connecting roads, and a national desire for independence. You want to be free of Denmark, and I can make that happen."

"One mine at a time?"

"Why not?"

"I'll tell you why not," Petra said, and took a step closer to Johnson. "Because while you win the hearts of one handful with your promise of money, you'll be poisoning the minds of the other by dumping waste from the mines into the water. We've been down that road already. People like you promise jobs for Greenlanders, and then claim we don't have the qualifications. You promise the government huge payouts once your overheads have been met, but neglect to tell them it will take thirty years or more for a tiny percentage of the profits. It's been done before."

"And it will be done again, Sergeant. Don't you want to know why?"

"Because we're a bunch of ignorant and uncultured Eskimos?"

"I was going to say *natives*, but I'll go with Eskimos. Anyway," Johnson said, as he held out his wrists, "I think I'll be going now. This conversation is getting boring."

Petra took a step back as the American in the suit pulled a pair of metal handcuffs from his belt and slapped them around Johnson's wrists.

"What the hell?"

"Sam Johnson?"

"Yes?"

"I have been authorised to detain you for questioning in regard to matters concerning espionage, conspiracy, and," the man paused, "insider trading. It seems you own a mining company Mr Johnson, and they appear to have gone bust."

"I don't own a mining company."

"We'll let the lawyers deal with the specifics, but, as of today, you do. The Greenlandic part, anyway."

"What the hell?" Johnson looked at his watch. "It's past midnight, for God's sake. I told them not to sign if they didn't hear from me by the end of the day."

Petra leaned forwards, and said, "We're four hours behind in Greenland. How's that for ignorant?"

Petra smiled all the way to the ambulance, climbed up the steps and sat down on the seat beside Maratse. She took his hand and kissed him on the cheek as the paramedic adjusted the saline drip and the driver closed the doors.

"We're going home," she said.

Chapter 22

The Commissioner called it extended leave and the police union agreed, provided that Petra receive the proper psychological support following an extensive debrief. It should have happened in Greenland, but, given her German language skills, a generous licence was applied and the union accepted the assistance of the Bundespolizei, with a representative from the Danish police sitting in on the different meetings. The debrief took three days, and Maratse met Petra at the same café at the foot of the television tower in *Alexanderplatz* at the same time each day. Petra translated the articles in *Die Welt* and *Berliner Zeitung* while Maratse fiddled with the tubes of sugar, watched the crowds and looked at Petra. He lost interest in the story once Petra confirmed that Dieter was fit to fly, and he and the captain of the *Ophelia* were being escorted out of Greenland in the custody of the German Bundespolizei, after negotiations at the political level. Petra read about Berndt and a shadowy figure referred to as an American. She started to read the articles mentioning the two Greenlanders involved in the police operations in the city, only to stop, and look up when Maratse placed his finger on the paper.

"Don't bother with that one," he said, "I know what happened in the restaurant."

"I'm sorry."

"Don't be." He tapped an article next to the account of the storming of the restaurant. "Read that one."

Petra frowned, and said, "It's about a political scandal. Unrelated."

"Read it anyway,"

"You're sure?"

"*Iiji.*"

Petra started to read, curling her hair behind her ear, and tracing her finger beneath the words in the article. She tapped the page each time a particular word challenged her, as she searched for the Danish translation of more specific terms. When she had to pause for a fourth time, she stopped, her gaze focussed on the paper, and said, "I know what you're doing." She bit at the smile quivering on her bottom lip.

"I'm listening."

"Okay," she said, and looked up. "What's it about?"

"I'm not listening to the words, Piitalaat."

"I know."

Petra pressed her hand on top of Maratse's, brushing her fingers across the tiny fishing scars, the nicks and cuts in his nails.

"I don't know what this is," she said.

"Neither do I."

"Maybe it's the trauma, shared experiences, something." Petra looked up. "But I feel safe with you. I can be myself."

"Thirteen years, Piitalaat."

"I don't care about that," she said, and squeezed his hand. "You hear about it all the time."

"Famous people, maybe."

"Not just famous people. We both know lots of couples in Greenland, with a bigger age gap than ours."

Maratse smiled, and said, "The man is usually better looking."

"You worry about that?" Petra let go of Maratse's hand, and placed it over her mouth, suppressing a giggle. Her eyes danced, the red and green Christmas lights flickering in her deep brown irises. Petra's shoulders twitched, and she said, "Really?"

"Maybe," he said. "Sometimes."

Petra wiped a tear from her eye, folded the newspapers onto the table, and stood up. "Come on," she said, and held out her hand.

The Berlin Christmas markets were crowded, and Maratse let Petra lead him by the hand between the stalls, through the maze of ornaments, past seasonal aromas – candied and curried spices. They ate *currywurst* from paper trays with wooden forks, shared a beer, and spent their last night in Berlin in the same hotel room, his arm curled around her slim, warm body, her hair tickling his nose.

"I still don't know," Petra whispered.

"Neither do I."

It took a day to fly from Berlin to Copenhagen, to Kangerlussuaq, to Ilulissat, to Qaarsut. Karl met them outside the airport and they got a lift down to the ice in the yellow and red-striped airport Land Cruiser. He fiddled with the sledge as Petra changed into her salopettes, zipped her jacket to just below her chin, and tugged a thick fleece hat over her long black hair.

"We're taking the dogs," Karl said. "You can't get three on a snowmobile."

"Any peanuts?" Maratse asked, with a look at Petra.

"What?"

"Don't mind him," Petra said. "He just doesn't understand the rules of flying."

"There are rules?" Karl said.

"Yes. Petra gets the peanuts," she said.

Karl looked at them and shook his head. "Come on. Let's go home."

The open leads of black water had stretched since they had last travelled across the ice, and Karl swung the team away from the coast before curving in a long arc to the beach of Inussuk. Petra leaned into Maratse's arms as the frost coated the tips of her hair in brittle white sleeves. Maratse relaxed as Karl drove the team with soft claps of his hands, and the occasional snap of the whip on the ice.

Buuti met them on the ice, together with Edvard and his wife, Nukannguaq. Maratse smiled as the two women enveloped Petra with soft shrieks and warm hugs, tugging her away to the house as the men unsnapped the dogs from the team, secured them to the ice and fed them. Maratse shook Edvard's hand, frowning as the women shrieked again on the deck of Buuti's house.

"It's Nukannguaq," Edvard said. "She's pregnant."

"Congratulations," Maratse said, and slapped Edvard on the back.

"We're pleased," he said, and nodded at Karl. "What about you?"

"Me?"

"You and Petra?"

Karl crunched through the snow and shook his head. "Don't ask, Edvard. It has something to do with peanuts."

"Peanuts?"

"Come on," Karl said, and pointed at the house. "Let's eat."

The houses of Inussuk glittered with paper stars. They filled the windows, hanging from electrical cords, lit with soft bulbs. The lights were turned on the first night of advent, and would stay lit until Christmas was past, and the sun had turned, creeping towards the horizon. There were two stars hanging in the windows of Maratse's house, and he thanked Karl as they clumped up the stairs after the women.

"Thank Buuti," he said.

The windows steamed as they ate into the night, laughing at stories shared around the table, tales of the hunt, the condition of the ice. Maratse caught Petra's eye at the end of the table, watched as she teased at a strand of hair hanging over her cheek, smiling as Nukannguaq filled Petra's glass with more wine. They didn't talk, just looked, until the meal was over, the stories had been repeated twice, maybe three times, and it was time to leave.

"I'll sleep on the sofa," Maratse said, as they hung their jackets in the hall.

"No," Petra whispered. She took his hand, bit at her bottom lip and then led him upstairs.

Maratse found a note beside the bed in the morning. He squinted as he read it, curling his head on the pillow, breathing in the last of Petra's perfume, before he slipped out of bed, and clumped down the stairs. He ignored the familiar ache in his legs, made coffee, and smiled at the thought of Petra sledging into Uummannaq with Karl to do some shopping. She would stay for Christmas, the note said.

Maratse sipped his coffee by the window, his face lit in the soft glow of the paper star. He tugged at his t-shirt, and waved at Buuti as she climbed the steps to his house, kicked the snow from her boots, and opened the door.

"Hi," Maratse said. "Coffee?"

"*Naamik*," Buuti said. She waited by the door.

"You're not coming in?"

She shook her head. "Karl called."

"*Iiji?*"

"He said your mobile is off."

Maratse nodded. "Battery needs charging. What is it?"

"He's ready to leave Uummannaq, but he can't find Petra. She's not answering her mobile."

"It's here," Maratse said, and pointed at the two phones charging on the windowsill.

"Okay, but Karl needs to come back. He told his sister to look out for Petra."

"I can pick her up."

"Sure." Buuti nodded. She turned to leave, and then stopped. "We're happy for you, David."

"*Qujanaq.*" Maratse smiled as Buuti shut the door.

He tapped the screens of the phones in the windowsill, and then walked to the kitchen. Maratse boiled more water, made fresh coffee, opened the fridge only to shake his head and close it again. Karl had fed his dogs while he was away, but the cupboards were bare. If Petra had her phone, he realised, he could ask her to buy some food – potatoes, before the store ran out.

Maratse closed the fridge as the landline rang. Coffee dribbled out of the machine and spat on the hotplate warming the glass, as Maratse walked around the sofa to answer the phone. He picked it up, smiling at Petra's scent locked into his t-shirt.

"Maratse?"

"*Iiji.*"

"It's Aqqa Danielsen. Simonsen needs you to come into town."

"Why?"

Danielsen waited a beat, and then said, "I can't really say. It's best you come."

"What's going on, Aqqa?"

"It's Sergeant Jensen…"

"*Iiji?*"

"We think she's been taken."

THE END

We Shall Be Monsters

~ Book 3 in *The Greenland Crime* series ~

It is true, we shall be monsters, cut off from all the world; but on that account we shall be more attached to one another.

— *Mary Wollstonecraft Shelley (1816-1822)*

from Frankenstein; or, The Modern Prometheus

Note to the Reader

We Shall Be Monsters continues the story of retired Police Constable David Maratse. This is the third book in the Greenland Crime series following *Seven Graves, One Winter* (book 1) and *Blood Floe* (book 2). While the story in *We Shall Be Monsters* is resolved, some of the themes explored will continue in book four. While each book deals with a separate story, the characters continue to develop and I intend to explore each character arc over the course of several books. The series is connected, and the reader will enjoy *We Shall Be Monsters* far more if they have read books one and two.

As usual, I blame Maratse.

The people of Greenland speak Greenlandic – including at least four dialects, Danish, and English. In many aspects of daily life, West Greenlandic and Danish are the working languages. *We Shall Be Monsters* is written in British English with the use of some Greenlandic and Danish words used where appropriate, including:

East Greenlandic / West Greenlandic / English
iiji / aap / yes
eeqqi / naamik / no
qujanaq / qujanaq / thank you
Imaqa / maybe

Ataasinngorneq

MONDAY

Chapter 1

There are ridges and knots on the sea ice, like nodes plugged into the dark sea below the hard surface. These crystal webs of primitive communication, blisters of information, create patterns to be read, deciphered; a provocation of fractured threads of ice snaking through Uummannaq fjord, bordered by mountains, cut off by storms, remote, inhospitable for some, a refuge for others.

The taxi's wheels bumped over the ice before settling into another line of communication, the ice road snaking from the village of Uummannaq to the settlement of Saattut to the north and east. The tyres rumbled with the bumps, vibrating through the tired chassis and into the seats. The driver and the Chief of Police sitting next to him smoked cigarettes; thin trails of grey tugged from the smouldering tips, sifted through the harsh black gap at the top of the window. Retired Police Constable David Maratse sat in the back seat, eyes closed, and all but invisible but for the tapping of his fingers on his thigh to the rhythm of the bumps on the ice. The moon lit the fjord all the way to the sharp granite edges and peaks of the mountains, where pockets of darkness waited to spill onto the ice in the wake of a cloud and the moon's passing. The taxi's lights paled in comparison. When the Chief pointed, the driver bumped the taxi out of the grooves and drifted towards the corner of Salliaruseq – the big island. Here, the current ate into the ice and the driver slowed, parking beside the dark blue police Toyota. Constable Aqqa Danielsen waved as he stepped out of the Toyota and onto the ice.

Simonsen, Uummannaq's Chief of Police, glanced over his shoulder. "We're here," he said.

Maratse opened his eyes, stared past the Chief, through the cracked windscreen, and looked at a shape on the ice, flat and inert, naked and pale beneath the moon. The skin on the back of the body glittered.

"That's not Petra," he said.

"No it's not."

"You said you had found her."

"I did. But this is the first stop."

Simonsen got out of the car and flicked the butt of his cigarette onto the ice. Maratse followed him, fingers still by his side. The thin wind that shivered through Simonsen had no effect on Maratse. He acknowledged Constable Danielsen with a tiny nod as he walked to the body on the ice.

"I found him," the taxi driver said, as he stood beside Maratse.

"Who is it?"

"Salik Erngsen," Simonsen said. "Seventeen years old. He's Anton's boy."

"Anton?" Maratse asked, as he crouched beside Salik's body.

"He manages the fish factory."

"I want to see Petra." Maratse stood up.

"Please," Simonsen said. "Just give me a minute. Tell me what you see."

Maratse scratched his rough fingers on the stiff cloth of his police jacket. He tapped his fingers twice before stuffing his hands into his pockets and looking at Salik. The boy's eyes were frozen open, pocked with spots of frost. There was blood frozen in his nostrils, at the corner of his mouth, and in a deep gash running the length of his left forearm. Maratse leaned over the body and found another cut on the right, dark red, frozen. He frowned as the taxi driver walked past the beam of the headlights, and then he examined the glittering skin on the boy's back. He walked around the body as Simonsen nodded for Danielsen and the taxi driver to step to one side, out of the light. The glitter between streaks of frozen blood on Salik's back was not ice but hooks; barbed fishing hooks used on long lines, baited and snaked on the sea bed to catch halibut. Maratse counted more than thirty, before he leaned closer and pressed the tip of his finger to the end of one of the hooks. He traced a thin length of cotton, frozen taut from the end of the hook to the blood on Salik's back. Each hook had a different coloured thread, blue here, green there, pink, red, orange and purple.

"The colours of the rainbow," Simonsen said. "Do you see the wrists? The blue marks?"

"He was tied?"

"It looks like it."

Maratse looked at Salik's ankles and found more blue marks, a chafing of the skin. He stood up and looked at Simonsen as he lit a cigarette.

"I've looked," Maratse said. "Now, take me to Petra."

"But what do you think?"

"I'm retired."

"I'm asking for your opinion," Simonsen said. "Christ, it's an olive branch for God's sake."

"You're stalling." Maratse walked to the police car. He pointed at Danielsen. "Where is she?"

"Maratse," Simonsen shouted. "I've got a dead boy on the ice with a back full of hooks. I want your opinion."

"Why?"

"Because," he said, his voice softer. "Because you were tortured once."

"This isn't torture," Maratse said. "It's punishment." He flicked his finger at Danielsen. "Take me to Petra."

Danielsen looked at Simonsen, waited for the Chief's nod, and then walked to the police car. Maratse got into the passenger seat and looked straight ahead, past the glittering back of Salik's body, caught in the Toyota's headlights as Danielsen drove around it. The police Constable bumped the Toyota into the parallel grooves of the road to Saattut and drove around the corner of the island. The eastern side of the island was in shadow, the ice black, and the current stronger. Danielsen stopped after half a kilometre.

"We have to walk from here," he said and opened the driver's door.

The air was denser, colder, the bite sharper. Maratse's legs were stiff as he stepped onto the ice, his body heavy and reluctant. He saw a dark hole in the ice and Danielsen led him to it. The hole was rectangular with lengths of wood frozen into the sides. A wooden stand with a drum of fishing line was frozen into the ice on one side of the hole. The line was taut, and Maratse knew there would be a sheet of metal with rocks tied beneath it, down at the bottom of the fjord. He thought of the metal drifting with the current, pulling the line straight as it sank, spreading the halibut hooks. He shook his head free of the image, free of the hooks, and looked to where Danielsen was pointing.

"These are her clothes," he said.

Maratse walked around the fishing hole and peeled the stiff layers of Sergeant Petra Jensen's clothes from the ice. He recognised Petra's blushed mango ski salopettes, ran his fingers across the dark stains of blood spotting the insulated bib. Danielsen tugged at the collar of one of Petra's boots, kicking the heel free of the ice before collecting the pair of boots in his arms. There was a full set of Petra's clothes, including her underwear. Maratse closed his eyes, felt the tug of ice beading around his eyelashes, catching and sticking as he blinked a tear onto his cheek. He remembered the smell of Petra's hair, the warmth of her creamy brown skin, her thin fingers, and her smile. Danielsen carried her clothes to the police car and placed them in a plastic fishing crate in the boot.

"We took pictures," he said, as Maratse handed him the salopettes. "Of everything. Simonsen said I should collect her clothes as soon as you had seen it – the fishing hole."

Maratse picked at the wispy hairs of his light beard; he wouldn't cry, to cry was to accept, to give up. He walked back to the hole in the ice, crouched on one side, and looked more closely at the wooden drum. There were two handles. He stood up and grasped one in each hand. The drum creaked and thumped with uneven spins as he wound the fishing line in, dragging it from the surface of Uummannaq fjord.

"We've done that," Danielsen said. "There was nothing, so we let the fisherman put the line in again."

Maratse ignored him. The drum thumped and the metal squealed in the brackets as he turned the wheel. The crate laying on one side of the hole was covered in fish blood. Danielsen kicked the crate free of the ice and dragged it to over to Maratse. He tugged a pair of thick gloves from his pocket, and opened the multi-tool on his belt. When Maratse reeled in the first fish Danielsen grabbed it, freed the hook from the lip of the fish with the pliers at the end of the tool and dumped the halibut into the crate. With each fish he brought up Maratse got slower until the crate was full. Danielsen had stacked more fish to one side of the crate. The halibut flopped on the ice, suffocating as the oxygen froze inside their lungs. The metal plate thudded against the wooden spar frozen into the side of the hole. Maratse grabbed it with his bare hands, gripped the line with rocks beneath it, and dragged it onto the ice. He shook the seawater from his hands and stuffed them into his jacket pockets. Danielsen closed the multi-tool and slipped it into the pouch on his belt.

"There's something else," he said, and pulled a sheet of paper from his pocket.

Maratse recognised the handwriting, but the words seemed foreign, without meaning.

"You found this here?"

"That's a copy," Danielsen said. "We found the original in a plastic bag nailed to the side of the fishing wheel. It's her handwriting, isn't it?"

"*Iiji.*"

"And you know what it is?"

Maratse shook his head.

"It's a suicide note."

Maratse folded the paper and slipped it inside his jacket.

"That's evidence."

"It's a copy," Maratse said. He turned towards the corner of Salliaruseq; the taxi lights were just visible in the distance.

"We're calling it a suicide," Danielsen said. "There's nothing to suggest that the two are related; the death of the boy and this…"

"Simonsen thinks so."

"What makes you say that?"

"Why did he show me the boy before you brought me here?"

"I don't know."

"You called me, Aqqa. You told me she'd been taken."

"That's what we thought."

"Then it's not suicide."

"But the note," Danielsen said and pointed at Maratse's pocket. "It's the Sergeant's handwriting."

"Hm."

"I have to call the fisherman," Danielsen said. "This is the second time he needs to collect his catch."

Maratse ignored Danielsen and walked back to the fishing hole. He imagined the fisherman digging the hole with the thick metal blade of his *tuk*, chipping the ice and scattering it across the surface. There was half a plastic bleach bottle screwed into a length of wood hanging from the crossbar beneath the fishing reel. Maratse used it to scoop ice from the hole, peering into the dark sea below. He was no stranger to suicide, but it was rare to find a note, and he could not recall anyone killing themselves by crawling into the sea. Pills and bullets, yes. Hanging and jumping, but never crawling through a fishing hole. Drowning was usually by accident rather than design. Most Greenlanders couldn't or didn't swim, at least the ones he knew. He'd never asked Petra, but whether she could or she couldn't, no-one swam in the sea in winter.

"This is something else," he said, his breath misting into his wispy beard.

He looked over his shoulder and thought about Salik. Maratse tossed the bleach scoop onto the ice, looking up as Danielsen slipped across the ice towards him.

"Simonsen wants us to go back," he said. "If you're ready?"

"*Iji.*"

"I'm sorry, Maratse. I liked Petra. We all did."

Maratse nodded and walked beside Danielsen to the car.

"She has no family," Danielsen said. "You were the closest one to her. What do you want to do?"

"You say she's dead?"

"*Aap.*"

"Then we bury her," Maratse said. "We'll bury her clothes. In Inussuk."

Pingasunngorneq

WEDNESDAY

Chapter 2

The soft bulb shone through the paper Christmas star in the window, blushing Nivi Winther's cheeks with a red glow. She slipped her mobile into the top drawer of her desk as yet another message of condolence beeped onto the screen. A third message escaped the drawer as Nivi closed it, just as Bibi, her assistant, entered the First Minister's office.

"It's alright, Bibi. I'll look at them later." Nivi gestured at the table. "Just put the coffee there."

"He's waiting in the conference room," Bibi said.

"Then ask him to come in."

Nivi poured two cups of coffee, adding cream to hers as Malik Uutaaq knocked on her door and entered her office.

"Hello Nivi," he said, as he placed his coat over the back of the chair.

"You don't want to hang it up?" She pointed at the coat rack behind the door.

He shrugged, fingering the back of the chair as he waited.

"I don't want this to be awkward, Malik. Please. Sit down." She caught his eye at the sound of a muffled beep seeping out of her desk. "I've been getting them all morning. Friends, family and colleagues who don't think I should have come to work today."

"It is very soon," Malik said. "After what happened."

"Daniel is dead. Tinka is dead too," Nivi said with a slight shake of her head. "I can't bring her back."

"I'm sorry."

"It's okay," she said and sat down. "You knew her; she wouldn't want me to be sad all my life."

"I hardly knew her," Malik said.

"Oh, I wouldn't say that. In some ways you knew her better than I did." Nivi caught her breath for a moment. "I'm sorry. That was uncalled for."

"It's okay."

"It's just hard, you know. Of the two of us, you were the last one to see her."

Malik placed his hands flat on the table. He was quiet as he looked at Nivi, watching her, waiting.

"If it makes you uncomfortable..."

"No," she said. "Stay. There's something I want to discuss."

Malik let out a soft sigh as Nivi straightened her back and tapped her finger on two folders laid out on the table. She waited as he added sugar to his coffee, folding her arms as he took his first sip.

"Like I said at Tinka's funeral, I'm excited about us working together. I would rather work with you than against you. So," she said, and opened the folder, "I have a suggestion, a position I would like you to consider."

"I'm the leader of *Seqinnersoq*. I don't work for you."

"I know that."

"I can't be a part of your government and at the same time lead the opposition."

"A coalition of sorts, we need to be bipartisan, and show strength and unity to bring our people together. To do that we need to be active, to show that what I said in Inussuk was not just empty words. You understand?"

"*Aap.*"

"Good. Then I want you to consider a ministerial post, in my government, not in my party."

"That's unusual."

"It will make people stop and think, that's for sure. And I can't think of a better way to start Christmas than by demonstrating just how serious we are about bridging the gap and serving the people."

"What's the position?"

"Cultural Minister," Nivi said.

"Not fishing and hunting?"

"Do you fish and hunt?"

"A little, sometimes."

"But the people know you for your position on language and identity. Not fishing. Besides, fishing and hunting is taken care of, for the moment at least."

"For the moment. It's a bit of a swing door, or so it seems."

"It's true, it is a demanding post." She sighed. "This is different. I believe with your support, we can appeal to the diversity of the Greenlandic people and," she paused and caught Malik's eye, "tone down the language issue."

"We did agree to that," he said.

"Thank you." Nivi smiled as she slid the folder across the table. "This sets out the way I see the post working. It's a draft for now, we're tweaking some of the language, updating it, but I wanted you to see it first. Why don't you read it through, and I'll see if Bibi can find us some lunch."

Nivi walked out of her office, slowing as soon as she was in the corridor, and out of Malik's sight. Bibi found her there, leaning against the wall, eyes closed, hands shaking.

"Nivi?" she whispered.

"I'm alright, Bibi." Nivi took three slow breaths and opened her eyes. "It's difficult. You understand?"

"Do you want to go home? I can call a taxi."

"No. I have to stay. Please find us some lunch."

Nivi waited until Bibi was gone before returning to her office. Malik had finished his coffee. He poured another as she sat down.

"What do you think?" she asked.

"I'm not the right man for this."

She knew it, of course. For all his rhetoric, his passion for claiming Greenland for Greenlanders, placing so much emphasis on the Greenlandic language, it was all a sham. The reason he never engaged in any other topic, such as housing or employment, topics that really mattered, was that Malik Uutaaq was a poster boy, and nothing more.

But I need him, she thought.

"Are there no other positions?"

"Forgive me, Malik. I'm not sure I understand."

"Let's be honest for a moment, Nivi. You have never rated me highly as a politician, even less as a man." He held his hand up as Nivi started to speak. "It's true that Aarni Aviki was the brains behind *Seqinnersoq*. He ran a good campaign."

"He was a thorn in my side."

"*Aap*," Malik said and smiled. "That's what I paid him for. He would have been perfect for this post."

"You are perfect for this post."

"But I'm not comfortable with it."

"What part?" Nivi asked.

"I think you know."

"Tell me anyway."

Malik leaned over the folder, pushed the top papers aside, and pressed his finger beside the first paragraph on the third page.

"Embracing diversity," he read. "You want me to speak publicly about homosexuality in Greenland?"

"Among other things, yes."

"I can't do that."

"The Danish Prime Minister has embraced the gay culture. He has spoken out about hate crimes. Their Minister of Justice is gay."

"Then give him the post. I won't do it."

"You won't work for me?"

"I won't speak out for gay rights. I can't."

"Why not?"

"I'm a *man*, Nivi."

Nivi scoffed. "I'm aware of that."

"I mean I am a *real* man. I like women."

"A little too much, perhaps," Nivi said. She clenched her fists. "I'm sorry. Say what you want to say."

"If I publicly support diversity in all its forms, I will be laughed at. What will my friends say? My political career will be over."

"Your political career was over the minute Aarni Aviki died. I'm giving you a second chance."

"Only because you need me." Malik brushed the papers to one side. "This tastes like revenge. You're punishing me for sleeping with your daughter."

Malik turned at a knock at the door. Bibi entered the office and the break in their discussion gave Nivi the pause she needed to bury the words she had intended to say, and choose a more diplomatic path. She waited for Bibi to place the sandwiches on the table, nodding her thanks as she left.

"I thought," Nivi said, "that because of Aarni Aviki..."

"You thought because he was gay, that I supported gay rights?"

"Yes."

"Aarni's private life was no concern of mine. We worked well together. He did his job."

"Then I really don't understand."

"Because you're not a man. Because you're more Danish than Greenlandic."

"What's that supposed to mean?"

"It means that just because something is culturally acceptable in Denmark, it doesn't mean it is here. Greenland is its own country, its own people; it has its own culture."

"A diverse culture that includes minority groups, Malik, not just hunters and fishermen. It's people like you who encourage the outside world to think we still live in igloos and turf huts."

"Because that's what sells, Nivi," Malik said, as he stood up. "I'm not as stupid as you think." He pointed at the sea and the snow-lined mountains on the other side of Nuuk fjord. "We've got no oil, and we can't mine without help from other countries. But what we do have is tourism. That's something we can sell. So, forgive me if I want the world to think we are a simple people, living in the Stone Age. The point is we can sell that. That's our future. It's what we can control. You know, in Britain they think of Greenland as *exotic*. A faraway place, off the map. I don't want to disappoint them. I want them to come here and satisfy their curiosity, to send them back home with tall tales so we can fill another cruise ship with ignorant tourists, so we can play the ignorant native and make some money, Nivi. It's all we've got."

"That's what you think?"

"It is."

"And you think presenting a diverse culture will spoil that?"

"I do. It will burst the bubble."

Nivi sat down. She gathered the papers into the folder and leaned back in her chair. She knew the meeting would be difficult, but no-one could have prepared her for this. She thought she knew Malik Uutaaq. She thought she understood his agenda, that it was all about power, but now she realised she underestimated him. His passion surprised her. It was something she could use, something the people needed, something Greenland needed.

"Malik, please sit down."

"I'd prefer to stand." He looked at his watch. "I should be going, anyway."

"Then before you go, tell me, why can't we do both? Why can't we embrace our culture, in all its diversity, *and* play the role of the exotic Greenlander and give the tourists what they want?"

"Because it doesn't work like that."

"You think the tourists read our newspapers?"

"Some might."

"And you think what they read will stop them visiting our country? That's a pretty simplistic view, Malik."

"I'm a simple man, with simple views, Nivi. You knew that."

"My daughter liked you."

Malik sat down and topped up his coffee. He fiddled with the sugar, cursed when he spilled it, the grains scattering over the table.

"She was a little drunk, Nivi. I may have taken advantage of that." Malik looked Nivi in the eye. "I *did* take advantage of that."

"I know."

"And you can still look at me?"

"I would be lying if I said it was easy, Malik. But I need you. The people of Greenland respect you, and even though it hurts me to say that, it's true. You can reach them in ways I can't. They think I'm too close to Denmark."

"You are."

"In some respects. But I'm right about this, you are the right man for this post, and I'll help you. If you bring the people together."

"I need some time."

"I want to make an announcement before Christmas."

"That's ten days."

The phone on Nivi's desk rang, and she lifted her finger, gesturing for Malik to wait as she answered it. He watched her, saw her cheeks pale as she pressed the receiver to her ear.

"What is it, Nivi?"

"That was Lars Andersen, the Police Commissioner."

"*Aap?*"

"You remember Sergeant Petra Jensen? They found her clothes beside a hole in the ice a few days ago, with a suicide note. She's dead, and she's going to be buried in Inussuk, right next to Tinka."

Chapter 3

Qitu Kalia stood in front of *Katuaq*, Nuuk's Cultural Centre, and kicked the snow from his shoes. He plucked his hearing aids from the inside pocket of his jacket and pressed one into each ear. The waitress behind the counter of the café smiled as she recognised him and tapped her ear.

"Are they new?"

"*Aap*," he said.

"And we can speak Greenlandic now?"

"I can *hear* Greenlandic now. It makes it easier to lip read."

Qitu frowned as the waitress whispered, gesturing for him to lean over the counter.

"Latte is Italian," she said, smiling as she prepared his usual order.

Qitu felt his cheeks blush. He paid and pointed to a seat by the window, tugging his *MacBook Air* from his satchel as he sat down. He remembered a recent visit to the new Gymnasium building, when he was writing a piece about the academic reform plaguing lecturers and confusing students. The examination hall had glowed with white apples, as the majority of students made the most of VAT-free computers bought in Denmark. Although, there was a fine line between aesthetically pleasing and robust in Greenland and the latter cost less in the long run. Qitu smiled as he felt the tap of the waitress's shoes along the floor.

"*Qujanaq*," he said, as she put his latte beside his computer.

Qitu opened his email and checked the time of his meeting. A quick look at the clock on the screen confirmed he was early, so he opened the rough draft of his latest assignment.

The door opened and a young woman scuffed her way into the café. Qitu lifted his head at the prick of cold air on his skin and watched as the woman drifted past the counter to a seat a few tables away from him. He had seen her before; he recognised the black whalebone studs in her ears, her lips, and her nose. The two large studs in the skin below her bottom lip caught his eye, tusk-like they jutted out above her chin. The rest of her outfit was black, which made her pink hair all the more shocking. She caught Qitu's eye and he quickly dipped his head, allowing the glare of the screen to consume him.

She was still staring when he looked up a second later, and again when another guest entered the café. Qitu knew the man by name and waved him over.

"It's good to see you, Qitu," the man said.

"You too, Palu."

Palu Didriksen glanced at the woman with pink hair and then pulled out a chair.

"I'm glad we could meet. I thought you would be busy in the run up to Christmas."

Qitu studied Palu's lips, and then nodded.

"I have been busy. You heard about Nivi Winther's daughter?"

"I was in Denmark and Germany, but yes, I heard. Shocking."

"It was very sad."

"But it has shaken up the politicians, eh?"

"*Aap.*"

"Weren't you working on a piece about Malik Uutaaq? What happened to that?"

"I stopped. It didn't seem right. Daniel Tukku commissioned it."

"He was the one who killed the girl?"

"And kidnapped the First Minister."

"I understand." Palu leaned over the table and gestured for Qitu to close his computer. "Did you hear anything about what happened in Berlin?"

"Rumours about Greenlandic police involved in a shoot-out. Nothing was confirmed."

Palu nodded. "It was all covered up. Quite well, actually."

Qitu remembered trying to get a comment from the Police Commissioner in Nuuk, but had been unsuccessful. The deadline for the Nivi Winther piece had forced him to drop the investigation and concentrate on something much closer to home. But he did remember hearing something about Sergeant Petra Jensen and David Maratse – the busiest retired police Constable he knew. The thought made Qitu smile.

"I was invited to Berlin to meet with Aleksander Berndt. He used to be the CEO of the Berndt Media Group, but has since been replaced," Palu continued.

"Why?"

"That was part of the cover-up. Berndt was involved in the shoot-out in Berlin. So, we never met. But, I got a call on the morning I was leaving, and I met with the new CEO's assistant."

"What about?"

"That's what I'm coming to."

Qitu tilted his head to one side to look past his friend. The young woman with the tusks was still watching him. She hadn't ordered anything and the waitress avoided her table.

"You're not listening, Qitu."

"Sorry," Qitu said. He fiddled with his hearing aids, and focused on Palu's lips.

"Berndt wanted to invest in Greenland, but when it was revealed he was more interested in exploiting Greenland than helping it, the new CEO stepped up and made me another offer."

"I thought you met with his assistant?"

"I did, and he said that instead of investing, the Berndt Media Group would make a donation, to support a new company, with no strings attached, no agenda, and only two conditions."

"And they are?"

"That the company is a media company, digital first, print later, and that they investigate stories that affect the people of Greenland, independently of government or business." Palu leaned back in his chair and grinned. He stabbed his chest with his thumb. "You're looking at the new CEO of NMG."

"What?"

"Nuuk Media Group." Palu waved his hands. "I know, not very original, but that's not important. The thing is I have the money and the office space. I even have a story. All I need is an investigative reporter to write for me."

"You want me to work for you?"

"I'll pay you twice what *Sermitsiaq* is paying."

"I don't know."

"You're thinking about your future? This *is* your future. I've got enough funding for three years. I think the CEO was embarrassed by the whole Berndt affair. He wants to make up for it."

"And what's the story?"

Palu jerked his head backwards, flicking his eyes to one side.

"The girl," he whispered when Qitu frowned.

"The one with the..."

"Pink hair and tusks, yes." He held two crooked fingers in front of his chin.

Qitu looked at the girl, caught a glimpse of her fingers as they shrank inside the long sleeves of her hoodie, and then focused on her face. She wore no make-up that he could see and she was familiar. He had seen her before, but struggled to remember where. Then it came to him, when he was researching the Malik Uutaaq story in *Mutten*, she had been working behind the bar on Nuuk's main street. He remembered the pink hair, although the tusks were new.

"What's her name?" he asked.

"Tertu," Palu said. "I'll call her over."

When she stood Qitu was surprised at how tall she was. He looked at her heels and saw the flat soles of her boots; they left wet prints on the tiled floor. The rubber squeaked as she sat down.

"I know you," she said. "You're the journalist. You wrote about Tinka."

"Did you know her?"

"No."

Qitu studied her face; saw the lighter complexion, the colour of skin that resulted in the death of Tinka Winther. Tertu spoke in Danish, and he wondered how much Greenlandic she knew.

"I choose to speak Danish," she said. "It's quicker."

"But your mother?"

"Is Danish. I speak Greenlandic when I don't want her to understand. English when I don't want my dad to understand." She stared at Qitu and whispered; the tusks above her chin moved more than her lips.

"What did you say?"

"I said in your case I'll whisper."

"I told you we could trust him, Tertu," Palu said.

"I don't trust anyone."

"Why?" Qitu asked.

He had other questions that started with *why*. Why the tusks? Why the black clothes? Why the attitude? Why did she hide her hands? And why did her cheeks tic, just below her eyes, when she saw him looking at her cuffs?

Tertu glanced at Palu.

"I can't tell him."

"We agreed, Tertu."

"He could be police."

"He's not."

Qitu caught himself staring. There was something fascinating about her, beneath the surface. The journalist in him was curious; perhaps even enough to quit his steady job and to work for Palu and the Nuuk Media Group. They would need a new name, something to match the story he imagined, hoped even, that the girl was reluctant to tell.

"You want to know if you can trust me?" Qitu asked. "How about this?"

He rolled back his sleeve and held his arm beneath the bulb of the lamp hanging above the table. He circled three round blemishes in the soft crook of his arm.

"I was in Copenhagen when I was younger, sleeping rough for a while. I missed my home. I did this," he said, and tapped his arm, "to forget." Qitu rolled down his sleeve and nodded at Tertu's fingers. "Most young people cut their inner arms, or thighs, when they want to forget. Is that why you're hiding your hands?"

Tertu teased two fingers out of her sleeve and pulled back the cuff to reveal one hand. The skin between her knuckles was striped with two black bands joined with diagonal lines. Qitu smiled as he recognised the traditional stick and poke tattoos of the Inuit. Tertu rolled back both her cuffs to reveal more bands above the middle knuckle. She had bands wrapped around her wrists too.

"Greenlandic?" he asked.

"Aleut. When I was fifteen I went to the Inuit Games in Alaska. I did some there, more at home."

"I like them."

"Show him," Palu said.

Tertu turned her hands and held her palms upwards, tilting them towards the light. There were more bands between the knuckles on the inside of her fingers. Unlike the bands on the front, these were different colours. Ink from the bands bled into the skin, as if the tattooist was not a professional, a *scratcher* in a hurry. The bands were linked with jabs of ink, large and small, splintered as if the bone needle was fractured. Tertu's skin was blistered with assorted welts of raised skin; her little fingers were curled as if the nerves had been pinned.

"Two more," she said, and pricked her thumbnail against the empty spaces between the joints of the second and third fingers of both hands.

"Two more what?"

"Until I am free."

"I don't understand," Qitu said.

Tertu slipped her hands inside her cuffs and nodded for Palu to speak.

"Each tattoo is a mark. Just like the loyalty cards they give out in the cafés in Denmark."

"*Aap?*"

"When the card is full, you get a free coffee. Here," Palu said with a nod towards Tertu's hands, "when her hands are full, she is free."

"Free from what?"

Palu gestured for Qitu to come closer.

"You know how society looks at homosexuality in Greenland?"

"We have Gay Pride in Nuuk…"

"And Sisimiut and a few other towns, but in the small villages and settlements, it is taboo. Young people have needs and others are exploiting them. Tertu is *qaleralik*."

"Halibut?"

"She's treated like a flat fish, a bottom feeder. The lowest of the low. The marks on her fingers are made with paint and fish hooks. When a man or woman wants sex with someone of the same sex, they go fishing. Tertu's bills are paid – just enough to keep her afloat, but not enough to let her swim, not until her debt is paid, and her fingers are full. I paid for her to come to Nuuk. To get her away from the settlement she lives in."

"And she's gay?" Qitu looked at Tertu.

"Yes."

"I still don't understand."

Tertu held up her hand and pointed at the two empty spaces.

"I have two times left."

"And then you are free?"

"Free?" she laughed. "When my fingers are full he will kill me."

"Who will?"

"The man I want you to investigate," Palu said. "This is big, Qitu. There is a man controlling this underground world of sex. He finds vulnerable people and promises to protect them. He says the marks are bands of loyalty, but Tertu has never met anyone with all their fingers banded."

"He kills them?"

"Maybe," Tertu said. "Or maybe the client kills them."

"Client?"

"The ones paying for sex."

"But you said you would be free, Tertu. Death isn't freedom."

"No," she said, "just preferable. He can't hurt you when you're dead."

"And you escaped."

"I don't want to die."

Tertu held Qitu's gaze for a moment before looking away.

"Qitu," Palu said. "This is the kind of story NMG needs to investigate. The kind that can change lives. Will you take the job?"

Qitu caught Tertu's eye and nodded.

Chapter 4

Gaba Alatak rolled back the duvet and swung his legs over the side of the bed. The woman beside him turned onto her side. He ignored her, walked to the bathroom and took a long shower, rinsing the woman's scent off his body. He let the towel drop to the floor and shaved, clipped an errant hair from his nostril, and rubbed a light oil into his scalp. *Bald is strong*, he thought. So very different from the thick hair that made him look half his age. He would let it grow when he was older, somewhere past middle age. Gaba picked up the towel and hung it over the rack, grabbing his phone from the kitchen counter as he made coffee. It was still dark. He checked his messages in front of the window looking out over old Nuuk as the coffee machine spluttered behind him.

"Miki," he said, when his partner answered his phone. "Training at nine. Get everyone."

"What about Atii?"

"I'll pick her up," Gaba said and glanced at the door to the bedroom.

He took a fresh mug of coffee into the bedroom, climbed onto the bed and wafted it beneath Constable Atii Napa's nose.

"Time to get up," he said.

"Too early."

Gaba put the mug down on the bedside table, crawled off the bed and whipped the duvet off Atii's body.

"What are you doing?" she said, clawing at the duvet, but Gaba pulled it out of her reach.

"Come on. You'll be late."

"For what?"

"SRU training. You've got five minutes."

Gaba dressed, fixed two plates of toast, and waited for Atii to pad out of the bedroom and into the shower. He banged on the door a minute later.

"Two minutes, and we're leaving."

"You're a bastard, Gaba Alatak."

"What's that?" Gaba said, as he opened the door.

"I said, you're a bastard, *Sergeant* Alatak."

"Of course I am. Now get ready. We leave in one minute."

Gaba turned off the coffee machine and grabbed his car keys. He took the stairs, kicked at the stone someone had propped the security door open with, and walked to his car. The Northern Lights drifted across the December sky as Gaba started the car and scraped the ice off the windows.

"At last she decides to show up," he said, as Atii jogged across the parking area, a piece of toast between her teeth as she fiddled with the utility belt around her waist. She flicked him the finger as she opened the door and sat in the passenger seat.

"You could have given me more warning."

"You could have set an alarm."

"But you had time to shower, shave and oil your bloody head."

"*Aap.*"

"You had time to do all that."

"Because I set an alarm," Gaba said, as he put the car in reverse and backed out of the parking space.

The snow crunched beneath the thick winter tyres as Gaba accelerated onto the road and sped down the hill from the tower blocks of Qinngorput and past the school below. It would take five minutes to drive into the town centre, fifteen in total to the training area. Atii finished her toast and wrangled her wet hair into a ponytail as Gaba drove.

"She was right," she said.

"Who?"

"Petra said you were a bastard."

"Constable Napa," Gaba said. "Did you or did you not have a good night?"

"*Aap.*"

"Was I or was I not a good lay?"

"What?"

"Answer the question, Constable." Gaba slowed at the roundabout by the docks and accelerated out of it. "Was I a satisfactory hump?"

"You were."

"And did you, at any time, regret pleading for me to take you home?"

"Pleading?"

"That's how I remember it."

"I did not plead."

"Well that's not what I will be telling the boys."

"You'd better not," Atii said, as she balled her hand into a fist and thumped Gaba's arm.

"We share everything."

"Bastard."

"I tell you what," Gaba said. "Give me ten perfect groupings with an MP5 on the range today and I will keep my mouth shut."

"Ten?"

"That's right."

"Perfect groupings?"

"Three rounds inside centre circle, ten times. That's thirty rounds, Constable."

Atii muttered as Gaba slowed for a bus.

"What's that?"

"I said *fine*. You're on."

"Good."

"And you're buying dinner. Regardless."

"We'll see about that."

Gaba pulled up beside Miki Satorana's police car four minutes later and waved at the younger policeman. He shrugged when Miki nodded at Atii in the passenger seat.

"We have a deal, Sergeant," Atii said, as she got out of the car. She grabbed her jacket from the back seat and walked across the compacted snow to the training hut.

Gaba winked at Miki and walked with him around the hut to the firing range. He inspected the FBI-style targets Miki had set up thirty metres from the firing line. He nodded and gestured towards the hut.

"Peter, the new guy, is coming later," Miki said. "He had the night shift."

"And Tiguaq?"

"He's sick. He showed up but I sent him home."

"Why?"

"Because he's sick," Miki said. "And I don't want to catch it, whatever it is."

Gaba slapped Miki on the back and followed him inside the training hut. There were four MP5s on the table, and a fifth that Atii assembled as Miki made coffee. Gaba watched her work, nodding as she placed the machine pistol on the table and got to work on loading the thirty-round magazines. Miki handed her a mug of coffee when she was finished.

The SRU – the Greenlandic Police Special Response Unit – was small enough to fit inside the *King Air* twin turboprop aircraft that Air Greenland made available for emergencies all over the country. Usually the emergencies were medical, but if the Commissioner determined that the SRU was required, then they would go wherever and do whatever it took. The last non-medical sortie was when Miki and Gaba had flown to Uummannaq in search of the First Minister. The team was small but well-trained, and Atii, the newest member of the SRU, was a welcome addition, a fact that Gaba reminded himself about, on and off duty. When Atii was finished with the first five groupings, and Gaba had inspected them, he decided to change the rules.

"Twenty groupings," he said. "At forty-five metres."

Atii shook her head and laughed. "Why don't I just tell Miki that we had sex last night and be done with it?"

Miki rolled his eyes and waited for Gaba's signal to fire.

"Fifteen and I won't say how good you were," Gaba said.

"How about this, Sergeant," Atii said. "If you can make a perfect grouping at fifty metres, I won't tell Miki about what I did to you with the..."

"Stop," Miki said. "I really, *really* don't want to hear it." He pointed at the range. "But I'll give one hundred kroner to whoever can put three in a group at one hundred metres."

Gaba stared downrange towards the sea. "Is the range long enough?"

"You see the barrel?"

"Yes."

"That's eighty. The range dips after that. But if we put a target on top of the barrel and move it another twenty, we should just about be able to see it."

"Just about?" Atii said.

"Yeah."

"Alright," Gaba said. "Let's do it."

Constable Peter Iikkila waved from the deck of the training hut as the three SRU members walked back along the range to the firing line.

"What are we shooting?" he asked, as Gaba shook his hand.

"Group of three at one hundred metres," he said, and looked up. "In the snow."

"Is that standard?"

"*Naamik*," Miki said. "But it's the only way I could get Atii to shut up about her sexual exploits with the boss."

"Thank you, Miki," Gaba said. "Welcome to the SRU, Peter. Now grab an MP5 and let's see what you can do."

"It's an elimination round," Miki said, as soon as they were all ready. "You miss with one bullet, you're out. Each bullet on target, and in the circle," he said, tapping the spotting scope on the tripod beside him, "gets you through to the next round. Boss? You first?"

"Alright," Gaba said, and walked up to firing line.

"Wait a second," Miki said and held out his hand. "You want to play, you've got to pay."

Gaba fished a one hundred kroner note from his wallet and slapped it into Miki's hand. He winked at Peter, and shouldered the MP5. Flakes of snow flurried across the range, and Gaba waited for a second, aimed, and fired. Miki checked the scope, sucked a breath of air through his teeth, and then moved to one side as Atii pressed her eye to the eyepiece.

"It was the snow," Gaba said, and slapped Peter on the back. "Your turn."

Atii hid a smile behind her hand and turned away as Gaba stared at her.

Peter's shot went wide and Miki pressed the two notes into his pocket.

"I'm just keeping them safe," he said, when Gaba pointed at him.

Atii pressed her money into Miki's hand and took aim. She shrugged when Gaba checked the shot.

"Dead centre," he said.

"That's not what you said last night," Atii said, and giggled.

"Please," Miki said. "I'm shooting."

The four SRU members took it in turns to check Miki and Atii's shots. None of them heard the car pull up outside the hut. Nor did they notice Police Commissioner Lars Andersen as he stepped out of the hut and onto the firing range.

"Sir," Gaba said when he heard the Commissioner's discreet cough.

"Can I have a quick word, Sergeant?"

"Yes, sir."

Gaba pressed his MP5 into Peter's hands and followed the

Commissioner inside the hut. He sat down at a nod from the Commissioner.

"What's this about?"

"There's no easy way to say this, Gaba, so I'll make it quick. Petra Jensen is dead. It's suicide. Her clothes were found at a hole in the ice in Uummannaq."

"Petra wouldn't..."

"Together with a note." The Commissioner paused. "It was her handwriting, Sergeant."

"You're sure?"

"Simonsen called earlier. He said that Maratse confirmed the clothes are Petra's and the note was written by her hand. There's not much else to go on. According to Simonsen's Constable."

"Aqqa."

The Commissioner nodded. "According to Aqqa, Petra was last seen outside the store in Uummannaq two days ago. Apparently, she struggled with a man, and was taken against her will."

"Then it's not suicide."

"We don't know that."

"Has Simonsen picked up this man?"

"He can't find him."

"Do we have a name?"

"Just wait, Gaba."

"Sir," Gaba said. He stood up. "Do we have a name?"

"It's poor evidence at best. The eyewitness was drunk."

"All I need is a name."

"And if I give it to you?"

"I'll be on the first flight north, sir."

"Well, that's lucky, because I have three seats on the morning flight to Ilulissat tomorrow morning. We change there and fly on to Qaarsut. Simonsen will drive us to Inussuk. They are burying Petra's clothes. A symbolic gesture, I suppose."

"What does Maratse say?"

"He's the one who arranged the funeral."

"He hasn't asked for any details?"

"No, and Simonsen has promised not to give him any. We're concerned that he might take matters into his own hands."

"Might?"

"Listen, Gaba, this is Simonsen's case. He's in charge. The last thing he needs is a retired Constable and the leader of the SRU hunting down a man who may or may not be involved in Petra's death." The Commissioner looked up at a cheer from the firing line. "That's Atii, isn't it?"

"Yes, sir."

"It looks like she won. What was the distance?"

"One hundred metres."

"A group of three?"

"*Aap.*"

"Well, you can console Miki by telling him to pack."

"He's coming with us?"

"I'm temporarily assigning him to Simonsen. Once we're finished with the funeral, he will help with the investigation. Petra meant a lot to me, too, Gaba. I trust Simonsen's judgement on keeping you and Maratse out of the loop. But I also trust Miki to report back to you with regular updates. Until then, pack your bags. I'll see you at the airport tomorrow morning."

Sisamanngorneq

THURSDAY

Chapter 5

Nanna followed Maratse around for most of the day, sitting beside him when he sat on the deck of his house and drank coffee, running alongside him as he strode from the house to the dogs, and holding his hand as he walked up the mountainside to the graveyard overlooking the fjord to one side and the settlement of Inussuk to the other. Sisse, Nanna's mother, joined them in the graveyard, stroked Nanna's hair and fixed her hat so it covered her ears. She lifted Nanna onto her lap as she sat down on the bench beside Maratse.

"I hope Nanna hasn't been bothering you," she said.

"No bother," Maratse said and smiled.

"David, I just don't know what to say." Sisse took Maratse's hand. "It's just so terrible. Petra was such a wonderful woman. And what you had..." She let go of his hand. "I'm sorry."

Maratse nodded. "How is Buuti?" he asked.

"She's busy," Sisse said with a nod.

"I told her not to make a fuss."

"Not to make a fuss?" Sisse laughed softly. "The First Minister is coming to the funeral. And the Police Commissioner. What on earth made you think she wouldn't make a fuss?"

"Hm."

Sisse waited for Maratse to speak.

"I gave money to Nikoline in the store and made her promise not to take any money from Buuti or Karl for the food," Maratse said.

"That's clever, but what if Karl drives into town on his snow scooter to get everything?"

Maratse reached into his pocket and pulled out a set of keys. He placed them in Sisse's hand.

"You can tell him you found them in the snow. He'll be pleased."

Sisse smiled and tucked the keys into her pocket.

"I have to go. I promised to help Klara with cakes for the wake."

"*Qujanaq.*"

"It's the least we can do, David. I only wish I could do something for you."

"You are," he said. "And I have enjoyed Nanna's company."

The sound of the De Havilland Dash 7 approaching the gravel strip airport in Qaarsut made them look up. Nanna leaped off her mother's lap and pointed at the lights.

"Do you think the First Minister is on the plane?" Sisse said.

"*Iiji*. Maybe her secretary too. And Malik Uutaaq."

"We'd better be off then. Come, Nanna. Let's go and help Klara in the kitchen."

Nanna waved at Maratse and then led Sisse down the path to the settlement below. Maratse waited until they were gone before walking over to Tinka Winther's grave. He looked into the open grave beside it. No-one had questioned why he wanted to bury Petra's clothes in Inussuk. Nor did they wonder at the timing, only a few days since her clothes were found on the ice, together with the note. Maratse pulled the note from his pocket and turned it in the moonlight to read it. The writing was thin, the letters scrawled and shaky. Exhibiting signs of stress, according to the report Simonsen received from the forensic expert in Nuuk. Danielsen had told him about it when they drove back to Uummannaq, across the ice. He said that Simonsen wanted to be sure before they told him.

Maratse lowered the note in his hand. The forensic report had come through quickly. Too quickly. The expert had missed something in Petra's signature. Maratse didn't blame him, the man didn't know Petra, wouldn't know how she usually signed her name, and he couldn't know that the only person who called her by her Greenlandic name was Maratse.

Piitalaat.

She had written it for him.

It was what gave him hope. And, as soon as the funeral was over, once the grieving process had begun and everyone had accepted Petra was gone, Maratse could begin his search, and bring her back from the dead.

He grunted at the sound of footsteps in the snow and folded the note back into his pocket.

"Sisse said you were up here," Karl said. He tapped two cigarettes out of the packet in his hand and offered one to Maratse.

"I quit," he said with a smile. "Petra made me."

"Petra? You usually call her..."

"Piitalaat." Maratse nodded. "You're right."

Karl lit his cigarette and puffed a small cloud of smoke over the fjord.

"We dug seven graves before the winter," he said. "Edvard's niece." Karl pointed to the tiny plot for the stillborn child. "Tinka Winther. Piitalaat," he said with a nod to the open grave next to Maratse. "Buuti is so sad. Nukannguaq has to wipe Buuti's eyes as she bakes. We are all sad."

"*Iji.*"

"All of us. But not you, David."

"What do you mean?"

"I mean you look sad, but then you always look sad." Karl grinned behind another cloud of smoke. "But here we are in the graveyard, standing by Petra's grave, and you are not sad. Why?"

Maratse shrugged.

"Okay, tell me something else."

"What?"

"Why is your sledge packed for a long trip? Why are my bearskin trousers in your closet? And why is my rifle oiled? Why does it have a new sling?"

"It needed it."

"When did you take it?"

"I bought oil in Uummannaq when Danielsen dropped me off. Why?"

"I couldn't find it for about a week. I thought Edvard had it." Karl shrugged. "Anything else?"

"You forgot the shooting screen," Maratse said.

"You've taken that too?"

"*Iji.*"

"And where are you going?"

"I need to get away for a while."

"Where?"

"I don't know."

"You don't think she's dead, do you?"

"Karl," Maratse said and lowered his voice. "You can't say anything. You can't tell anyone."

"But if you think she is alive, you have to tell the police."

Maratse shook his head.

"Simonsen has another investigation to take care of. He won't have time for Petra."

"Not for a suicide, but if you think she is alive."

"No, Karl. I need to do this my way. It will be quicker."

The sound of a taxi on the ice below them turned Maratse's head. He spotted the headlights as they snaked between the icebergs frozen into the fjord. Two more cars followed the taxi. Maratse nodded towards the path and led Karl down the mountainside.

"You'll carry the coffin with me?" he asked.

"You mean, will I play my part?"

"*Iiji*, for Piitalaat."

"I'll do anything for Petra." Karl paused at the top of the path. "I can come with you."

"*Eeqqi*. I need to do this alone."

Maratse said nothing more until they reached the bottom of the path. The black sand beneath the snow cast a grey pallor over the well-trodden path to the houses. Maratse could see Buuti in the window, lighting candles. Nukannguaq bustled at the table behind her, while Sisse, Nanna and Klara carried cakes up the steps to the house. Maratse felt a pang of guilt turn in his stomach as he thought about the deception. He stopped and pressed his hand against Karl's chest.

"You can't tell anyone. Not even Buuti."

"She will understand."

"She wouldn't, Karl. No-one will, and no-one must know. I think I know who might have taken Piitalaat. I can't let anyone stop me."

"You're that sure she's alive?"

Maratse glanced at three pairs of headlights as they parked on the ice. The passengers walked up and over the ice foot and onto the beach.

"*Iiji*," he said, and walked down the beach to greet Greenland's First Minister, and the rest of the guests for the funeral of Sergeant Petra Jensen.

There was no church service. The priest from Uummannaq laid Petra's coffin into the ground with all the solemnity the occasion demanded; a coffin with no body, just a set of clothes. It was Nivi Winther's words that caused even the most stoic of the congregation to shed a tear. All but Maratse. He was the last to leave the graveyard. Gaba Alatak met him on the path to the houses below.

"I'm sorry for your loss," he said, and shook Maratse's hand.

"And yours. She was your friend too."

"I'd like to think so." Gaba waved for Miki to go on without him. He walked with Maratse down the path and stopped at the beach. "Before we go inside," he said, "there's something you need to know."

Maratse waited. Karl's house was small, and soon filled with the people of Inussuk and the few guests with their entourage. A group of men smoked on the deck outside, close enough to hear what might be said on a cold, windless night. Gaba plucked at Maratse's elbow and nodded for him to walk further along the beach.

"Simonsen isn't telling you anything, is he?"

"Petra committed suicide. He has closed the case."

"That's what he wants you to think. The Commissioner told me there is a witness. Someone in town. I can find out who it is. Then, maybe we can pay them a visit. We can find out what really happened to Petra."

"Are you staying to help with the investigation?"

"No, but Miki is. You know about the boy who was killed, Salik Erngsen. That's Miki's assignment, but he's going to report everything to me."

"But you'll be in Nuuk."

"I will. But I can fly here..." Gaba coughed. "Anytime," he said.

Gaba's eyes glistened in the moonlight, and Maratse looked away to give the SRU leader a moment. He remembered Petra's outburst about Gaba when she picked him up at the hospital in Nuuk. Something about Gaba's infidelity. That was the first time Maratse had seen her angry. She had a fire in her eyes that burned so brightly. His stomach twisted again, and he could almost feel the tick of the watch on his wrist, thudding through his body. He was wasting time. The charade needed to end now, so that everybody, Gaba included, could drift away and grieve in their own time, and give Maratse the space and time he needed to bring her back. He shoved all thoughts of what Petra might be experiencing to one side. He couldn't think of that. He just had to act, and the sooner the better.

"If there's anything I can do. If you need anything."

Maratse realised Gaba was speaking to him, and he shook his head.

"I'm fine."

"Okay," Gaba said, and nodded towards the house. "We had

better go inside." He paused at the sight of a fully-laden sledge and the dog team chained beside it. "Someone is going hunting," he said.

"*Iiji.*"

"Someone you know?"

"I don't know them," Maratse said, as he walked beside Gaba to the house.

Nivi Winther met them on the deck and Gaba excused himself, leaving the First Minister and Maratse alone.

"I'm so sorry, David. I know that Petra was very special to you."

"*Qujanaq.*" Maratse stiffened slightly as Nivi hugged him, and then he smiled. "Your words were very nice," he said and pointed up at the mountainside. "I think everybody appreciated them."

"It was the least I could do. It was you and Sergeant Jensen who found Tinka for me. You brought her home. I plan on visiting Tinka often, when work allows. I know Tinka will watch out for Petra. They can keep each other safe."

Maratse ignored the twist in his stomach and nodded.

"You must be cold," Nivi said. "Let's go inside."

The tick of the second hand struck hammer blows inside Maratse's body as he shook hands, hugged, and mumbled thanks to the mourners, his neighbours and friends. Simonsen shook his hand and the Commissioner took him to one side. Maratse had to concentrate to hear his words over the thundering of the watch on his wrist.

It was Karl who saved him, as he apologised to the Commissioner and guided Maratse into the kitchen and out of the back door.

"Your clothes are in the shed," he said. "The rifle too."

"I have to wait until they have gone, at least."

"*Naamik,*" Karl said with a shake of his head. "You need to find Piitalaat. Now go," he said, and pushed Maratse towards the shed. "I'll tell people it was too much, that you needed some time for yourself."

"You'll help me apologise to Buuti?"

"Bring Petra back and you won't have to." Karl curled his finger and thumb to his ear. "You'll call me if you need me?"

"*Iiji.*"

Karl nodded. "Good hunting," he said, and closed the kitchen door.

Chapter 6

Sergeant Petra Jensen's breath misted over her body, cooling and beading on the rusted bracelets cuffing her wrists. The tattered jeans she wore were long enough to cover her ankles if she pointed her toes, but too large to provide any warmth around her waist. Her stomach was bare, like her chest, her neck, and her arms. The fine hairs on her skin prickled in the cool air. She rested her head on her arm, felt the pull on her wrists as the bracelets rattled against the chain hooked above her head on a nail bent into the thin wooden wall. She breathed again, another cloud of warm breath, condensing around her body. She looked through the cloud and saw the red eye of the camera staring at her, unblinking, unmoving, penetrating, vibrating slightly to the insistent thump of the diesel generator juddering on the rocks outside. She twisted at the sound of someone kicking the snow from their boots, unlocking the padlock on the door, dragging the chain, one link at a time, through the iron rings on the door and the frame. The freezing air from the ice rushed in to mix with the cold air in the cabin, followed by the man in the parka, his head funnelled and hidden inside his hood like a trunk, and the tools he carried in front of him were the tusks. A hideous elephant, silent but for the thump of its feet and the rattle of the chain.

He ignored Petra, dumping the tools on the floor beside the legs of the tripod before turning the camera off. She heard the click of the back cover being removed, the thick shush of sleeves rubbing against the man's sides as he swapped the SD card in the camera for another. He closed the cover with a click. The camera beeped as he turned it on and Petra held her breath.

The screen glowed for the few seconds it took the man to setup the camera and focus the lens on Petra. A few seconds in which she could see the fibres of the fur ruff lining his parka, the elephantine extension of his head, and the wet sheen of the man's eyes deep within the tubular shadow of his hood.

This was the third card change in a row since he last touched her, when he forced three spoons of sticky oatmeal into her mouth, splashed her lips with water. He would touch her again, the next time he changed the card. The fourth time. Four was important. No matter how much it hurt when he twisted her skin between his fingers, when he tightened the chain, the fourth time was contact, and she dreaded and longed for it, in the tragic way that contact, *any* contact, connected her with the real world, not the dark, solitary, freezing claustrophobia of captivity.

She moved her head as he retreated from the camera, and the screen's glow diffused in the black of the cabin. The floor thumped as he crossed it. The door creaked, the chains rattled, and the padlock snicked, and she was left with the thump, thump, thump of the generator.

Creak, rattle, snick, and *thump, thump, thump.*

Until the fourth time.

It was important to keep track. She bent three fingers of her hand, holding the tips of her frigid fingers against the stiff pads of her palms, hoping she wouldn't relax when she slept; weak, cold, tired, hungry, scared. It was important not to lose track of time, not to lose count.

The fourth time was important.

She needed to be prepared.

As soon as he was gone she stared at the red light on the camera until all she could see was a circle of red. When it filled her vision she replayed the images of her capture, as if she could transmit them, record them on the camera as it recorded her, as if they might be found – clues to her disappearance, evidence to discount her death, and a trail that might lead to her location. She knew it was folly, that the images were trapped inside her head, and that the camera recorded only the dark outline of her captivity, no words or sounds. She glanced at the microphone on the floor beneath the camera – disconnected, discarded, redundant. No-one would hear her scream, not unless he wanted them to.

She thought about him, the elephant man, the rough skin of his hands on her arms, the twist of his fingers on her skin and the jerk of the greasy rope around her neck before he had brought her to the cabin. She had heard him hacking and chipping at the ice as she scratched and thumped at the inside of the car boot the day after she had been taken. She had fought him, but the second heavy blow to her head had dropped her onto the ice. He had bundled her into the boot, tied her hands and noosed her around the neck. He cursed her thumping, and she listened as he chipped at the ice.

When he finally opened the boot of the car, the fishing hole was the second thing she saw in the moonlight that night. The first was the barrel of the hunting rifle he pressed into her cheek. He tied one end of the rope around her neck to a hook he had dug in the ice, and then he forced her to strip, thrusting a piece of paper and a thick pencil into her hand as she shivered on the ice.

He told her what to write, gave her a metal plate to rest the paper on, and pointed the rifle at her. Petra's teeth chattered as her body temperature plummeted. She looked at the hole in the ice between each written word, until he slapped her and told her to be finished, quickly.

"I'm getting cold," he said. His breath was frosted in the fur around the rim of his hood. Her own breath cascaded down her body in puffs and clouds to the ice.

"Sign it and we can go."

Her signature, she realised, was her *affidavit*, notarized and authenticated by the gun. The hunter's law.

But she was not dead. The hole in the ice was not for her, at least not yet.

She added the Greenlandic spelling of her name to her signature.

Piitalaat.

If the suicide note kept her alive, then no matter what the physical or psychological cost, that one name would be enough to save her. *If*, of course, he saw it.

I need you, David, she thought, teeth chattering, as she gave the man the note and the pencil.

"Now get back in the boot," he said.

They were the last words she heard him speak before the cabin, but not the first.

The first time she saw him he was wearing a helmet. The visor was dark, impenetrable. She could barely hear him.

"Are you police?" he had asked, the Danish words scratching through the visor.

"Yes."

"I need help. This way."

She had followed him from the store, past the post office and along the path below the colonial flagpole that reached high above the frozen surface of Uummannaq harbour. There were sledge dogs tethered along the path, and Petra had slowed, cautious all of a sudden, as her excitement about spending her first Christmas with Maratse was dulled by the sense that something was wrong about this man.

The body of a young man slumped on the sledge behind the snow scooter distracted her. She did a quick visual check of his condition, calling out to him, as she shook his shoulder and pressed her fingers to his neck to check for a pulse. His skin was warm and his pulse raced, but the young man, a teenager, was unresponsive.

"Has he taken something?" she said to the man in the helmet.

He responded with a flash of metal, striking a bar into the side of Petra's head.

She remembered the flap of a plastic tarpaulin covering her face, the bump of the sledge runners across the ice, and the medicinal breath of the teenager bound close to her body as they sped away from Uummannaq across the fjord.

Later, in the cabin, between the first and third changes of the camera card, Petra tried to recall what had happened, when they had been moved from the sledge to the car. Was the teenager moved with her? What had happened to him? He had never been in the cabin, had never been filmed, fed, or fettered – at least not with her. She believed he was dead, or perhaps there was another cabin, somewhere else on an island in the fjord.

He could be anywhere, she realised. How foolish it was to believe that a single name added to her signature might lead someone to find her.

"David," she said, forcing herself to stare at the camera.

She remembered their last night in the hotel in Berlin, his warm body pressed against hers. She could almost feel the heat, the light wisp of his beard on her neck, the rough skin of his hunter's hands, the calluses on his fisherman's fingers. He might have been a policeman once, but his body and mind were of the land, the rocks, the sea, and the ice. She closed her eyes, pictured his face, saw the gap between his teeth when he smiled, tried to measure the depths within his eyes – tried to read some of the pain he hid there.

David has survived somewhere and something like this. I can too.

There was a creak on the step.

Petra held her breath.

The rattle of the chain, each heavy link bumping over the iron rings was almost louder than the thump of her heart, but slower. Her heart beat in her chest like the rapid thump of the Arctic hare prepared for flight, or the Little Auk, wings spread, neck pinioned between finger and thumb, paralysed within the grasp of the hunter as he pulled it from the net.

She barely heard the snick in the lock, and the thump, thump of the generator could have been the blood pulsing in her ears.

This was the fourth time.

Petra's eyes widened, fixing on the man as he placed the dirty bowl of oatmeal on the floor, together with a glass of water. He turned his hood towards her for a second, and then he bent down to pick up the microphone from the floor. She held her breath as he attached it to the camera. And then she saw his eyes in the glow of the screen as he changed the card.

The analytical part of her brain determined that he must need more time to set up the microphone. He spent longer than usual behind the screen, and the light from the screen lit his eyes so brightly she thought they were burning; so intense was the energy that charged within them that his eyes might blister and pop from his face.

And then she understood why. She retreated across the dusty floor of the hunter's cabin, as far as the chain would allow, tugging the waistband of the jeans over her hips as she scooted backwards, away from the man, the camera, the microphone, and his intentions.

"David," she said. "David, help me."

"David?" The man's voice was muffled, his words funnelled through the hood. "Is that your policeman?"

Petra pressed her back against the wall, tucked her knees to her chest.

"David is not coming," the man said. "No-one is coming. It's just you and me." He smoothed his hand over the camera body as he took a step towards her. "And some friends," he said.

This was the fourth time.

She thought of the Auk, the hare, she thought of David. And then she stopped thinking. It was best not to think, not about the man, his friends, not even Maratse. If she was going to survive, she could not think.

Chapter 7

Gaba held tight to the handle above the passenger door as Simonsen bumped the police Toyota up and over the welt of ice on the ramp from the sea to the island. Miki hid a grin and the Commissioner smiled at him from the passenger seat. Gaba remembered that the Commissioner didn't get out much, as his job tied him to Nuuk and limited his movements to brief visits, courses, and the occasional meeting in Copenhagen. Driving across the sea ice and past the smaller villages and settlements on Greenland's coast was a welcome break from routine, despite the tragic reason for the visit. Simonsen slowed at the hotel but the Commissioner waved him on.

"You said we could see the body?"

"Now?"

"We fly tomorrow morning. If there's a link between the teenager's death and Sergeant Jensen, however tenuous, I want to know. Seeing the body might help."

"Okay," Simonsen said. He drove past the hotel and parked in front of the hospital.

Gaba could see the hotel dining room from the hospital parking area. There was a good view of the harbour, and he turned to scan the fishing boats frozen into the ice, and the sledges, snow scooters and dogs moored between the wooden hulls.

"What are you thinking, boss?" Miki asked as he joined Gaba.

"Petra wasn't taken from here, not without someone seeing her. Look." Gaba pointed. "The dock is wide open. There's plenty of activity, lots of lights." He nodded at the hotel. "There's a good view from there, and there's traffic on the road, people, taxis, sledges. Petra was too smart to just follow anyone. If she was taken, she must have been attacked somewhere, but not here."

"There's a road that runs around the harbour, past the post office. It's more secluded," Simonsen said. "It could have happened there."

"But you don't think she was taken, do you Simonsen?" the Commissioner asked.

"There are a lot of things I don't know. The note is compelling, but, suicide? I'll admit, it's out of character."

Simonsen lit a cigarette. "On the other hand, snatching a police officer is a little beyond what goes on around here. It's too elaborate a play for a local, too dangerous. The criminal element in Uummannaq is not so..."

"Clever?" Gaba said.

"I was going to say theatrical."

"And yet you've had a spate of *theatrics* of late," the Commissioner said. "Wouldn't you agree?"

"We've been busy," Simonsen said. "Ever since he arrived."

"By *he* you mean Maratse?"

"Yes."

"You're referring to the Tinka Winther case, and the *Ophelia?*"

"Two high profile cases within months of each other." Simonsen flicked his cigarette onto the ground, extinguishing it in the snow with the sole of his shoe. "It makes sense when you consider Maratse's past."

"I don't think that has anything to do with it, Chief."

"No? Maybe not, but it has *everything* to do with what kind of man he is."

"I think you should try to be more objective."

"I have tried. But this thing with Sergeant Jensen, it's just one more black mark against Maratse's name in my book. It makes sense when you put it in perspective." Simonsen caught Gaba's eye and then nodded for them to follow him. "The doctor is waiting," he said.

The storage room was too small for all of them to fit around the examination table. Miki volunteered to wait outside as Simonsen introduced them to Elena Bianchi, the doctor currently in charge of the hospital in Uummannaq.

"You're Italian?" the Commissioner said, as he shook her hand.

"Do you know how hard it is to find doctors willing to work this far north?"

Gaba smiled at the doctor's accented Danish.

"They won't even come on a short-term basis?"

"Sure they will, during the summer, once they have sold their practice and fancy a paid vacation in Greenland." Elena sighed. "I'm sorry," she said. "It's frustrating."

"We're pleased you're here," Simonsen said. "You've made a hit with the people in town and the settlements."

"Thank you, Torben," Elena said. "But, you're here to see Salik, right?"

"If you've got time?" the Commissioner said.

Elena nodded and pulled back the green paper sheet covering Salik's body.

"We don't do autopsies," she said. "And we don't have a morgue or cold storage. The Chief has kept us busy lately, so we have kept the bodies on ice from the fish factory, but..."

"This is Anton Erngsen's son," Simonsen said. "Anton runs the fish factory."

The Commissioner nodded, and pointed at the red welt around Salik's neck.

"It's possible he died from strangulation," Elena said. "But, he could also have bled out." She lifted Salik's wrists. The fingers were bent and bunched into a fist. She ran a gloved finger along the deep cuts on both of the teenager's forearms. "You can see he was bound." She shifted her grip to show the bruising around Salik's wrists. "And at the feet."

"Head, hands, and feet," Gaba said.

"That's right." Elena lowered Salik's arms to the table. She smoothed her hand across the skin and patted the back of his hand. Softly, quickly, but long enough for the men to pause and wait for her to speak. "It's possible he was pulled in this position."

"Pulled?" the Commissioner asked.

"I mean *stretched*. Sometimes I forget the correct word."

The Commissioner smiled. "It's not a problem. Tell me more."

"I think he was stretched in at least two directions. There is bruising on the tops of his feet, as if a rope or chain pressed into his skin, and he couldn't move."

"That would require space," Gaba said. "Outside, with a scooter perhaps?"

"Possibly."

"Which meant the killer had time, and wasn't worried about being seen." Gaba looked at Simonsen. "This happened deeper in the fjord."

"That's likely, but we found the body at the corner of Salliaruseq, the big island just over there, seven kilometres from here. The body was dumped close to the ice road to Saattut. We were meant to find it. Just like we were meant to find Sergeant Jensen's note."

"They have to be related," Gaba said.

Elena waited for Gaba to finish.

"Suicide is just as common here as it is in Nuuk," she said.

"You didn't know Petra."

"Take it easy, Gaba," the Commissioner said. He pointed at a clipboard hanging from the end of the examination table. "What are they?"

"Photos," Elena said. "Of his back."

The Commissioner picked up the clipboard and leafed through the photos.

"These are fish hooks?"

"Yes."

"And threads?"

"Different colours. All of them. The hooks were attached to his body, and then sealed into his skin with a blowtorch. Those are burn marks, not blood, you can see in the photos."

Gaba studied the photos as the Commissioner turned the clipboard towards him.

"And these photos?" he asked. "What's that on the inside of his hands?"

"Inside his fingers." Elena lifted one of Salik's arms and prised the fingers from his palms, straightening them and exposing black bands between the joints in his fingers. "I thought they were bruises or burns at first," she said. "As if he had held something."

"They're tattoos," Gaba said, as he pressed his face closer to Salik's hand. "Stick and poke."

"What's that?" the Commissioner asked.

"A needle or something sharp, poking ink beneath the surface. It's not a tattoo machine."

"It's rough work. Amateurish," Elena said, as she showed Gaba the boy's other hand. "But all of the spaces between the joints are inked. Three on each finger, two on each thumb."

"Did you know him?" Gaba asked Simonsen.

"Reasonably well," he said. "Mostly through his father."

"Anything to suggest he was into something?"

"No more than any of the teenagers here. He drank too much. He smoked and had tried sniffing at some point in his past."

"Sex?"

"What about it?"

"If he was like the other teens in town..."

"You think this is sexually motivated?"

Gaba turned to the Commissioner. "This is pretty weird, sir. The hooks. The coloured threads. I don't know about the bands on his fingers, but something was going on with this kid."

"I agree."

"I don't suppose I am breaking patient confidentiality now that he is dead," Elena said. "But Salik came to see me twice this year. In the summer he complained of sores on his penis. He tested positive for syphilis. There has been a small surge in cases around here recently."

"Also in Nuuk," the Commissioner said. "And the second time?"

"Was when we did a test for tuberculosis, of the whole town. Salik tested positive for latent TB. He was not sick and he showed no symptoms. It's possible that if his immune system was weakened he might develop the disease."

"Weak with syphilis, for example?"

"We treated him for that. It was in the early stages. But if he was sexually active, of course, he could be exposed again." She tapped the clipboard in the Commissioner's hand. "The lab technician is at home with a migraine, and we're waiting on the results of the tests."

"Thank you, doctor," the Commissioner said, and handed her the clipboard. He gestured for Simonsen and Gaba to follow him into the corridor. "I'm leaving Miki here," he said to Simonsen. "Gaba will brief him about Salik."

"Is he reporting back to you?" Simonsen asked.

"He's assisting you, and keeping Gaba and me in the loop, yes."

"I can do that."

"I know you can, Chief, but you're stretched pretty thin. Miki is here to help. Use him," he said. "Now, before you take us to the hotel, tell me who might have done something like this, however unlikely, however *theatrical*."

Simonsen looked at the Commissioner. "You're taking Gaba back with you?"

"Yes."

"Because if we're trying to link the two..."

"Just say it, Simonsen," Gaba said.

"Easy now," he said. "I heard you and Petra were a couple."

"That was a while ago."

"What I don't need right now is for Gaba to go off the rails," Simonsen said. He looked at the Commissioner. "Everyone knows

Gaba Alatak. He's your pit-bull."

"Sergeant Alatak leads the SRU, Chief. I think you should choose your next words carefully. This is an emotional time. We have just buried a colleague. It is in everyone's interest to bring this investigation to a satisfactory close. It won't bring Sergeant Jensen back, but it might help all of us, and those who cared about her, to move on. Sergeant Alatak is responsible for his actions, but he's under my command, as are you, Chief. So, tell us what you know, or what you are thinking, and we can move on with the investigation."

Simonsen glanced at Gaba.

"Alright," Simonsen said. "There's one man, a Dane, who I would like to talk to about Sergeant Jensen's disappearance, and the murder of Salik Erngsen."

"His name?" Gaba asked.

"Aksel Stein," Simonsen said. "There's just one problem, no-one has seen him for over a week. But if we find him, we might find some answers. That's where I would start, after we've talked with Salik's parents." Simonsen sighed. "That's not going to be easy."

Tallimanngorneq

FRIDAY

Chapter 8

The brief period of grey twilight had passed, dragging the memory of Petra Jensen's funeral into the winter night. A fresh wind teased at the light layer of new snow that had fallen since Maratse stood beside Petra's grave, twisting the snowflakes in front of the runners of his sledge as he encouraged the small Greenlandic sledge dog, Tinka, to lead the team with gentle snaps of the whip on the ice. The sledge creaked past the corner of Salliaruseq, past the spot where they had found the body of the teenager, Salik, and on to the fishing hole in the ice. Maratse paused there for an hour, scouring the surface of the ice with a torch, and resisting the temptation to reel in the long line one more time. The crime scene, if it could be called that, was clean, with no further evidence of Petra having been there. But a closer inspection of the wooden legs supporting the drum of fishing line revealed a tiny purple thread of cotton beneath a splinter of wood. It twisted in the light wind. Maratse teased it free, examined it for a moment and then wrapped it around his finger before stuffing his hand back inside his sealskin mittens.

Buuti had sewn the mittens for Karl the previous winter, just as she had sewn each of the items that Maratse wore above his thermal layers. The white cotton anorak he wore above the sealskin top, the polar bear skin trousers, even the *kamikker* he wore on his feet – it was all Buuti's work, all white. With the hood drawn above the white silk ski mask Karl had tucked into the pockets of Maratse's anorak, the only item not handmade. From a distance, Maratse was practically invisible, a ghost on the ice.

The dog team stirred as he walked back to the sledge. They watched as Maratse drifted the torchlight across the frozen surface of the sea, pausing at the tyre tracks furrowed into the ice and leading to the settlement of Saattut. If Petra had been here, if she had been brought by car, then the car must have stopped in the tracks – there was no other sign – about one hundred metres from the fishing hole, a long way to walk with no clothes. If she had been here. If *he* had brought her here at all.

Maratse had a name for *him*. Danielsen had given it to him earlier in the month. There had been a confrontation with an older Dane driving a snow scooter – the man had nearly run over Sisse's daughter, Nanna. According to Danielsen, the man, Aksel Stein, had a history of abuse. His behaviour that day put him at the top of Maratse's list. Aksel's profile – a reclusive man with an attitude and a history of violence – made up for the apparent lack of motive, but Maratse needed a place to start. He took a last look at the ice and walked back to the sledge. At a soft clap from Maratse, Tinka tightened the traces and the team lurched into motion, the sledge grated across the ice to one side of the car tracks towards Saattut.

Saattut was a little over twenty kilometres northeast of the island of Uummannaq. Half an hour by car, perhaps twice that by sledge. Maratse used the time to plan his next move. He knew he was looking for a remote cabin – the one Aksel supposedly occupied throughout the year. One of Saattut's two hundred inhabitants knew where that was, and one of them was going to tell Maratse before the dawn of another dark day in December. Maratse barely felt the wind through the mask covering his face, nor did it penetrate the bearskin trousers, or the thick sealskin covering his upper body, but he was cold, chilled from his stomach at the thought of yet another day that Petra was in danger. If he had revealed his face to any observer they would have seen that chill twist into a fierce determination, a dangerous motivation, and one that held little regard for those obstructing his investigation.

Maratse was on the trail of a monster. A monster who would breach the quiet restraints for which Maratse was known, in order to save the one he loved. He knew now that it was love, and there was nothing he wouldn't do if someone he loved was threatened or in danger. He pulled the rifle from the scabbard slung from the sledge upright and chambered a bullet in the barrel. Tinka flicked her head to look at him as the metal snicked and clicked in the darkness.

"Go on now," he said.

The sledge lurched and creaked as Tinka picked up speed and the team of eight sledge dogs behind her increased the pace. Maratse would have to slow them before the settlement, and, as the lights above the tiny harbour dock grew stronger, he rested the rifle in his lap and used the whip to drive the team to the right of the settlement. He stopped them by a drift of snow half a kilometre from the tip of Saattut island. Maratse dug a loop in the ice and anchored the team. He heard them settle on the snow as he slung the rifle over his shoulder and walked towards the island.

The Christmas stars shone from the windows, casting soft red and orange lights on the snow outside the brightly painted houses. The people of Saattut were indoors, but the local dogs stirred as he whispered past them, their chains rattling across the exposed rock at Maratse's ghost-like image. He stopped by the tiny school building, scanned the neighbouring houses, tilting his head to one side at the sound of seventies rock music thumping through the thin walls of a blue house close to the harbour building. Maratse walked towards it.

He caught a whiff of herbed smoke and slowed at the sight of two men, younger than Maratse, drinking and smoking outside the house. He watched them for a moment, gauging how much they had had to drink, how much they had smoked, with the eye of a policeman used to weekend shifts in the Arctic. If he had to go house-to-house, if he had to rouse the whole settlement, then that is what he would do. But the smell of hashish, the loud music, and the raucous nature of the party indicated that the people in this house might have the answers he needed. Like attracts like, and Aksel, Maratse determined, had more in common with the people partying in the house, than the quiet families in the rest of the settlement.

Maratse leaned his rifle against a large fishing box beneath a drying rack to the right of the house. He tucked the mittens inside the chest pockets of his anorak, unwinding the purple thread from his finger and slipping it inside one of the mittens. He removed his anorak and the sealskin, draping them over the box, before he pushed the sleeves of his thermal top further up his arms.

Then he took a breath and walked towards the house.

"Hey, look," said the shorter of the two men smoking by the front door. "It's *Julemanden*." He passed the joint to his friend and patted the front of his black hoodie. "He needs to eat more."

"*Aap*," said the other man. "He's too thin to be Father Christmas."

Maratse stopped in front of the man in the hoodie.

"Is this your house?"

"Who wants to know?"

"I want to know. Do you live here?"

"*Imaqa*. Maybe. Why?"

"I'm looking for someone."

The man slapped his friend on the arm. "He's looking for someone." He slipped his hand inside the pocket at the front of his hoodie and pulled out a thin knife. "Are you police?"

Maratse shrugged. "I'm retired."

"Pigs don't retire," the man said. He nodded at his friend and thrust the knife towards Maratse's face.

Maratse moved to one side and then stepped towards the man, wrapping his arm around the man's knife arm, and dropping him to the ground with a swift kick to the knee. He gripped the man's chin and lifted his head.

"Drop the knife."

"Piss off," the man said, with a glance at his friend.

Maratse saw the second man flick his joint into the snow and raise his fist. He threw a punch at Maratse, catching him on the shoulder as Maratse turned and twisted the man with the knife onto the snow in front of his friend. Maratse ducked beneath a second swing, grabbed the man's arm and pulled him over the man sprawled on the snow. When both men were on the ground, Maratse stepped around them and walked across the snow to the house.

The music thumped through the walls and vibrated through the door handle as Maratse turned it and stepped inside. Maratse had been called to more than one *after party* in his career. He ignored the couple having sex on the sofa and crossed the floor to the stereo. Maratse glanced at a young woman sprawled in an armchair, a triangle of alcohol stained the front of her top. She shrieked when he pulled the stereo plug from the socket and the music stopped, just as the two men from outside the house lurched through the door, snow scattering from their shoes as they ran towards Maratse.

"He's police," said the man with the knife.

"I'm not here for you," Maratse said. "Just listen for a moment."

The two men from outside drifted to the walls, one on each side of Maratse. The woman in the armchair slid off the cushions and onto the floor, while the couple having sex stopped and stared. Maratse looked at the two young men flanking him, and pointed at the man with the knife.

"I'm looking for Aksel Stein," he said.

"Aksel?"

"*Iiji.*"

The man on the sofa climbed off the woman beneath him and pulled up his jeans. He wobbled as he tightened his belt, and then waved at the two young men to stand still.

"Why?" he said.

"That's my business," Maratse said. "There's a cabin that Aksel uses. Do you know where it is?"

"There are lots of cabins," the man said.

"And he uses one of them."

"*Aap*, from time to time. When he's not here."

"What?"

"This is Aksel's house. He only goes to the cabin when he is going to get drunk."

"He lives here?"

"*Aap.*"

"And all of you live here too?"

"*Naamik*," the man said. "Just me."

"And who are you?"

"I'm Aksel's son."

Maratse took a moment to look around the room. The few pictures in the lounge hung at odd angles, tilted by the bass and the drums beating through the walls. The picture closest to Maratse showed an older Dane with a young Greenlandic woman. He looked at Aksel's son and pointed at the picture.

"My mother," the man said.

"She doesn't live here?"

The man shook his head.

"Where's the cabin?"

"South of here. In the fjord."

"You can show me on a map?"

"*Aap*. But it won't help."

"Why not?"

"He's not there. I haven't seen him for a week."

It made sense that Aksel would be missing, that no-one would know where he was. But, empty or not, Maratse had to see Aksel's cabin. He reached into a pocket sewn inside the leg of the bearskin trousers and pulled out Petra's note together with the stub of a pencil. He pressed the note against the wall and drew a rough map of the fjord on the back of it.

"You," he said and pointed at Aksel's son. "Show me where the cabin is. The rest of you can leave." Maratse glared at the two young men he had fought with. "Leave or I'll call the police." He waited as they drifted out of the room and then gestured for Aksel's son to walk over to him. "I don't have time to waste. Show me where the cabin is."

Chapter 9

The snow settled on the lid of the cardboard box in Qitu's hands as he stepped off the bus on *Aqqusinersuaq,* Nuuk's main street. He walked north past Hotel Hans Egede and east along *Kongevej,* until he reached a low building next to the CrossFit gym. He rested the box on a railing as he fished the keys from his jacket pocket. Once inside, Qitu pushed the box onto a large empty desk and removed the satchel slung over his shoulder. He searched for a plug socket, powered up his *MacBook* and investigated the kitchen. Palu had promised that it would be fully stocked, but the fridge was mouldy, and the cord for the coffee machine was frayed, almost severed, just like Qitu's contract with *Sermitsiaq.*

"You're crazy," his boss had said the day after Qitu's meeting with Palu and the girl.

"I know."

"Then why?"

Qitu remembered shrugging and his now former boss shaking his head. There was nothing more to say. He couldn't explain why he was prepared to swap a promising position as journalist with Greenland's leading newspaper for an unknown future with a start-up media group, but something about Tertu's story intrigued him. It felt more important than reporting the regular news and he realised that ever since working on the Tinka Winther story, he had been longing for a similar story, one that would shake its readers and maybe even make a difference.

The sentimentality and sudden righteousness made him laugh, and he felt the vibration of his voice through the walls around the tiny kitchen. But without coffee, any grand plans Qitu had for a big story would grind to a halt. He checked his calendar on his phone and decided he had plenty of time to visit the store before Tertu arrived. *If* she arrived. While he didn't doubt she had a story to tell, he did wonder if she was willing to tell it. Qitu locked the door on the way out and turned his collar up as the snow swirled about the streets of Nuuk.

Thoughts of a related story drifted through Qitu's mind as he walked towards the town centre. A year ago he had been assigned to research a story about homosexuality in Greenland. He remembered an interview he had arranged with the church. The official comment from the Bishop's office at the time had been one of pity for the gay people of Greenland. Qitu had pressed for a deeper explanation but had left the interview with little more than a promise that the Lutheran Church of Greenland was interested in the spiritual welfare of all the people of Greenland.

"But it's only the gays you pity, isn't that right?" Qitu had asked.

The interview had ended with no further comment, and the quote had been removed in the final edit of the article.

Nuuk was often considered to be a provincial town, a fact that could be seen and heard in the attitudes of many of its residents, both Greenlandic and Danish. The acceptance of alternative lifestyles was more on a par with a small town in Denmark, with some enlightened views and a good measure of ignorance and incomprehension. But Nuuk was a city with all the trappings of an Arctic capital, with grander plans than the size of its population might warrant. To be pitied might even be the enviable alternative to being shunned or ignored. Qitu understood that for a lot of gay men in Greenland, sex and sexuality was linked to alcohol – strong spirits that set them free.

The idea of an underground network for sex suggested something else, and it intrigued him. Greenland is a vast country with great distances between the towns, villages, and settlements. Flying is expensive; there are no roads connecting the communities, and local travel meant a boat in the summer, and a snow scooter, car or even a sledge in the winter. And that is only if the ice is strong enough, if it came at all. A network that provided sex for alternative tastes, that didn't rely on alcohol and after parties would also be expensive and no doubt lucrative for those who controlled it.

Qitu stopped at the door to *Brugsen*, glancing at the drunks clumped on either side of the street. There were plenty of people ripe for exploitation in Greenland. If he could write something that might make a difference, that might change the status quo, then he considered that his duty. The thought buoyed him through the entrance of the store and along the aisles as he searched for coffee.

A hand on Qitu's arm made him turn. He smiled when he recognised an older colleague, one of the Danes who had taken him under his wing when Qitu was just starting out as a journalist. He focused on Jerrik Poulsen's mouth as he spoke.

"You've left *Sermitsiaq*?" he asked.

"Yes."

"Where are you working now?"

"Just off *Kongevej*. Palu hired me to work for Nuuk Media Group. This is my first day."

"Palu Didriksen?"

Qitu nodded.

"That's a curious move." Jerrik frowned as he looked at Qitu. "Everything alright?"

"Yes."

"When did you move?"

"I picked up my things last night."

"Then you haven't heard about the police Sergeant who committed suicide?"

"Who?"

"A woman." Jerrik paused. "A Danish surname. Jensen, I think."

"Petra Jensen?"

"That's the one. Did you know her?"

Qitu gripped the shelf on his left as he processed the news. He liked Petra, and he liked her friend, the retired Constable.

"Maratse," he said.

"What's that?"

"She had a friend called Maratse. This will hit him hard."

"That's not all. They found a body the same day they discovered the Sergeant's clothes and a note."

"What body?"

Jerrik reached into his shopping basket. "This one," he said and handed Qitu a copy of *Sermitsiaq*. "There's not much information yet, but they found the body of a young man, still in his teens. The police have yet to comment; a taxi driver found the boy. He mentioned something about fish hooks and strange markings on the boy's hands." Jerrik took the paper when Qitu was finished with it. "I hope the job with Palu works out, because I think you just missed out on a good story. We haven't heard the last of this, that's for sure." Jerrik tossed the paper into his basket. "Look after yourself, Qitu. Call me if you need anything."

Qitu nodded as Jerrik shook his hand. He waited until the man was gone and then pulled out his phone, unlocking it and searching through his contacts for Maratse's number. He paused before sending a message. What could he possibly write? He settled on a short message of condolence and the promise to help if Maratse needed anything. He stared at the screen for a second, pressed the icon to send the message, and then slipped the phone into his pocket. Qitu added a paper to his basket and went to the checkout, pausing at the shop door to read the story one more time before walking back to his office.

Qitu barely noticed the snow as he considered the details of the article, the speculation, and the reluctance of the police to comment at this time. *Out of respect for the family*, Qitu mused as he fumbled with the keys in his pocket. A shock of pink hair made him start as he pulled out his keys. The tusks, he noticed, were gone, replaced with flat black squares. They were unremarkable and he wondered if she was toning down her appearance, trying to blend in. Then he glanced at her hair. *Not yet*, he thought.

"You're early," he said, as he unlocked the door.

Tertu said nothing. She followed him inside and found a seat in his office.

"Do you want coffee?" Qitu tossed the newspaper onto the desk and waited for Tertu to speak. "I'll make a pot," he said, and walked into the kitchen.

Qitu stared at the cord of the coffee machine as the water heated and started to percolate through the coffee grounds. He didn't know if his sense of smell compensated for his hearing difficulties, but the smell of coffee always calmed him. He waited until the jug was full and poured two mugs, the last drips of water spat and sizzled on the hot plate as he removed the jug. Tertu was standing at the back of the office when he put the mugs on the desk, arms wrapped around her body, shoulders trembling.

"Tertu?"

Qitu caught her eye and followed her gaze to the newspaper on the desk. It was open at page two, the continuation of the story from the front page. Qitu turned the paper towards him and looked at Tertu.

"Did you know Salik Erngsen?" he asked.

She shook her head. He watched as she slipped her hands slowly out of the sleeves of her hoodie and turned her palms towards him. She tapped the two spaces on her finger and nodded at the paper on the desk.

"But you knew *of* him?"

Tertu nodded.

"He's free now," she said. "That's his reward."

"You think he's connected? To your story?"

"*Aap*."

"But are you sure? You said you don't know him."

Tertu walked back to the desk and sat down. Qitu handed her a mug of coffee and she warmed her hands around it. He stared at the Aleut markings tattooed into her fingers and pictured the darker bands poked into her skin on the other side.

"He liked my Aleut tattoos," she said, and lifted her fingers. "That's what gave him the idea to mark people." Tertu turned her palm towards Qitu. "And that," she said, and pointed at the newspaper.

"We need to be sure," Qitu said. "If Salik is linked to your story."

"Then he is the first one to die."

"That we know of."

Qitu sat on the desk and considered Salik's place in Tertu's story. If he could prove there was a connection, then he had the foundations of an investigation. Travel to Uummannaq was expensive, but if he could confirm the link then he could justify the expense, and discover just how deep the Nuuk Media Group's pockets really were. He needed help, someone in the area.

"Maratse," he said.

"Who?"

"He's a friend. A retired policeman. He lives in the area. He might be able to help us."

"Then call him," Tertu said.

"I can't." Qitu sighed.

"Why not?"

"His friend just committed suicide. It's too soon."

"Too soon?" Tertu gripped the mug until her fingers turned white. "Salik is already dead. If I'm found, then I'll be next."

"We don't know that. In fact," Qitu said, "I don't know anything. That's why you're here today, so I can find out more."

"Salik's death changes everything," she said. "You have to call your friend."

Friend, Qitu thought as he looked at Tertu. He knew Maratse only a little more than he knew the young woman sitting in front of him. But what he knew about him, what he had observed and discovered when working with him, was Maratse's moral centre – he would do the right thing, selflessly, if asked, perhaps even in his time of grief, and especially if he knew someone's life was in danger. Qitu took out his phone, opened his messages and stared at the new thread he had started less than an hour ago. It was absurd, heartless, but necessary. He glanced at Tertu, nodded once, and started typing. Time would tell if Maratse could help, if he even saw the message. Qitu looked at the girl once more and wondered how much time she had left.

Chapter 10

"I need you to stay here and mind the shop," Simonsen said, as he stopped Miki at the door to the police station. He pointed at the counter. "Any problems give us a call. We'll be at the Erngsen's house."

"The Commissioner said I was to be a part of the investigation."

"I heard him. But I also heard him say you were working on Sergeant Jensen's case."

"The two could be connected."

"Then why don't you use your superior policing skills and find out. Or don't they teach you how to do that in the SRU?"

Miki bit back a laugh and stared at Uummannaq's Chief of Police.

"Do you want to say something, Constable?"

"*Naamik.*"

"Because it looks like you do."

"I've got nothing to say, Chief."

Simonsen tapped a cigarette out of the packet and stuck it between his lips. He fiddled with his lighter as he looked at the young police officer.

"You know what I think?"

"What's that?"

"I think Greenland is too small for SRU. I think local policing is the key and that the likes of you and your boss..."

"Sergeant Alatak."

"The one with the muscles and the swagger, that's right. He belongs in America, not here."

"But you need us once in a while, Chief."

"That's debatable." Simonsen nodded at the counter. "Mind the shop, and stay out of my office."

"Yes, sir."

Simonsen grunted and walked out of the police station. He lit his cigarette and waved to Danielsen that he was ready. He opened the passenger door of the police car and climbed in, winding the window down an inch to allow the smoke from his cigarette to drift out of the car into the cold, dark night.

"Anton Erngsen will want to know when his son's body will be released," Simonsen said. "But I want you to wait before you tell him.

As soon as he knows that he'll be thinking of the service and the funeral. We need to interview him first."

"Interview?"

"Questions." Simonsen flicked his cigarette out of the window. "His wife, Oline, will be there. If Anton offers us a coffee, I want you to go into the kitchen with her. Talk with her. I can't, her Danish isn't so good."

"Salik is their only son," Danielsen said, as he slowed for a hunter pushing a sledge with a team of dogs to the ice. Danielsen waved at him.

"I know," Simonsen said. "Just be gentle, and see if you can look at Salik's computer or his phone."

Danielsen nodded and they drove the rest of the way in silence.

The front of the house was dark when they pulled up outside it. Simonsen knocked on the door as Danielsen peered inside the kitchen window. It took three more knocks before Anton opened the door and invited them inside.

"Oline is still in bed," he said. "Do you want coffee?"

Simonsen nodded for Danielsen to wait in the lounge. He followed Anton into the kitchen. The sink was full of dishes and ash flowed from a saucer on the kitchen table. Simonsen picked up an empty beer bottle from the counter and slipped it into the plastic crate of empties by the back door.

"When can we see Salik?" Anton asked, as he filled the kettle with water.

"We're waiting to hear from the hospital. If they don't call before we leave, I'll call them."

"Okay."

Simonsen pulled out a chair and sat at the table. Anton lit a cigarette and sat opposite him.

"I usually smoke outside," he said, and shrugged.

"That's okay."

The kettle boiled and Anton poured three cups of coffee. His cigarette burned on the table. Simonsen picked it up and placed it on the saucer.

"Aqqa," Anton called out. He handed Danielsen a coffee as the young Constable came into the kitchen and put the other two cups on the table.

"Does Salik have a computer?" Simonsen asked.

Anton raised his eyebrows, *yes*.

"Does it have a password?"

"Maybe. I don't know."

"Can I have a look at it?" Danielsen asked.

"It's in his room. Down there," Anton said.

Danielsen nodded at Simonsen and slipped out of the kitchen. Anton watched him leave. The cigarette burned in the saucer as the two men drank their coffee.

"You know I need to ask some questions, Anton."

"*Aap.*"

"Are you ready?"

"Sure." Anton shrugged.

"When did you last see Salik?"

"*Marlunngorneq*," he said. "Tuesday."

"Last week?"

"*Aap.*"

"Where was he?" Simonsen waited as Anton lit another cigarette. It burned between his fingers, the smoke mixing with more from the cigarette still burning in the saucer. "Was he with friends?"

"Maybe."

"Who are his friends?"

"Natsi."

"Natsi Hermansen?"

"And Aaju."

"I don't know him."

"Aaju Imiina. He lives up on *Juaarsip Aqqutaa*. The blue house, next to the teacher's house."

"Where's Aaju from?"

"Nuuk, maybe."

"And it was just the two of them, and Salik?"

Anton finished his coffee and stubbed his cigarette out in the saucer. Simonsen looked through the kitchen door and listened to the sound of Danielsen typing on a keyboard. He pulled out his notebook and made a note of the two names.

"Anyone else? Any girls?"

"Pah," Anton said. "No girls for Salik."

"No?"

"You never heard what they say about my son?"

Simonsen had heard the stories. It was hard to be different in a town with just over two thousand people. He remembered when Salik was a happy young teenager, before he became moody and withdrawn in his last year at school. Simonsen lost touch with him then as Salik seemed to vanish. He looked at the names on the list. Aaju was a new one, but Simonsen knew Natsi. The kids called him *Nasty*. Simonsen found out why the first time he put him in jail for the night to sober up. But whether it was Natsi's hygiene, language or sexual preferences that earned him the nickname, Simonsen didn't know. Unfortunately, given that Natsi was the name at the top of Simonsen's list, he realised he might yet find out.

"No-one else?" Simonsen asked. "What about older men? A Dane perhaps."

"When Salik went fishing, sometimes he was gone for a week," Anton said. "Sometimes two weeks. I asked him why he never went fishing with me. Why he never spent time with me? He said he didn't like fishing. So, I asked him why he did something he didn't like. He said it was a job." Anton stared at Simonsen. "I never saw him get on a boat, or drive out to a fishing hole. He always wore jeans. He never had any working gloves. Not even a knife." Anton pointed at his jacket hanging by the kitchen door. "I have a knife. I have gloves." He paused. "You know what I think?"

"What's that?"

"I don't think my son was a fisherman."

"No, Anton, I don't think he was either."

Danielsen knocked softly on the door frame and nodded for Simonsen to come with him. Anton lit another cigarette and they left him in the kitchen.

"In here," Danielsen said.

He led Simonsen into Salik's room. Danielsen pulled out the chair in front of the computer and waited for the Chief to sit down. Simonsen took a moment to look at the pop posters tacked to the walls and the rumpled sheets of Salik's bed. He wrinkled his nose at the smell and Danielsen shrugged.

"It smells of teenager," he said. "You'll get used to it."

"I don't think I want to."

Danielsen leaned around Simonsen and used the computer mouse to click on the screen and open a series of photographs. Each photo was dark and blurry. There were figures in the background, but the eyes were red, the features grainy. Danielsen tapped the screen on each of the photos. The flash had caught the skin of fingers too close to the lens, giving each photo a white glare in the left corner of the image that obscured the background.

"Do you see it?"

"See what?"

"The threads wrapped around the fingers," Danielsen said. "Here." He tapped one of the photos. "And here. Purple and green. This one," he said, as he clicked through two more photos, "is blue."

"Threads, like the ones from the hooks."

"And something else." Danielsen clicked back to the first photo. He tapped the screen. "Look there. In the corner of the photo."

"Is that shadow or..."

"It could be shadow. But I think it is a black band on the inside of his fingers."

"Whose? Salik's?"

"Maybe." Danielsen took a step back. "I can't tell."

"But if it is Salik. Who are they?" Simonsen pointed at the two men in their early twenties in the background. He showed Danielsen the list in his notebook.

"That's *Nasty*," Danielsen said and tapped the image of the man on the left. "He has an afro wig. I've seen him wear it around town."

"And him?" Simonsen pointed at the man on the right. "Is that Aaju?"

"Who's Aaju?"

"I don't know. But he's staying on *Juaarsip*."

Simonsen clicked through the images to the last one in the folder. He fiddled with the mouse and then leaned back as Danielsen enlarged the image. A third figure with long black hair was lost in the shadow of the corner of the room. The same room as the other photos, but a different time – the light outside the window was grey, not black, and the mountains were just visible.

"Where is this taken?" Simonsen said.

Danielsen zoomed in on the window in the centre of the photograph. He stared at it for a minute and then shook his head.

"I don't recognise it."

"And the one with the long hair? Is that a boy or a girl?"

"I don't know."

"*Niviarsiaq*," said a voice from the door.

Simonsen turned to see Oline Erngsen standing in the corridor outside Salik's room. Her finger trembled as she pointed at the computer screen.

"*Niviarsiaq*," she said. "A girl."

"Do you know her name?" Simonsen asked.

Oline shook her head and slid away from the door.

"We need the photos," Simonsen said, as he stood up.

"How? I don't have a USB drive."

Simonsen shrugged. "Take the computer."

"The whole thing?"

"Yes," he said and walked out of the room.

Oline reached for a bottle of beer from the crate on the floor, checking each one to see if it was empty. Simonsen took her arm and pulled her gently to the kitchen table. Anton stared at his wife.

"You can arrange to have Salik moved to the chapel," he said. "Call me if there is anything you remember. Anything at all."

"Are you going to find out who killed our son?" Anton asked.

"I'm going to try," he said.

Simonsen nodded goodbye and left the kitchen. He met Danielsen in the hall and opened the front door as the Constable carried the computer to the rear of the police car.

"Where to, boss?" Danielsen asked, as he opened the driver's door.

Simonsen held up his finger for Danielsen to wait, as he pressed his mobile to his ear. His breath misted in front of him, beading on the front of his jacket in a fine sheen of ice.

"Miki? Take a taxi and meet us at *Juaarsip Aqqutaa*," Simonsen said. He walked around the car and opened the passenger door. "Wait. You still there? Bring the vests and a rifle from the cabinet."

Danielsen grinned as Simonsen closed the door.

"What is it, Aqqa?"

"You told Miki to bring the vests and a gun?"

"So?"

"He's SRU. You told him this morning that we didn't need him."

"You heard that?"

"*Aap.*"

"Things change, Constable." He sighed as Danielsen laughed. "Just shut up and drive."

Arfininngorneq

SATURDAY

Danielsen parked alongside the taxi on the road below *Juaarsip Aqqutaa*. There were three twin houses on the rocks above them. The houses shared twenty wooden steps to the decks at the front of each twin house. Simonsen pointed at the rocks below Natsi's house as Danielsen fastened the ballistic vest over his police sweater and Miki checked the rifle.

"We know Natsi is in Uummannaq," Simonsen said. "And at this time of day he's probably in bed. He won't be up before late afternoon."

"Anyone else inside?" Miki asked.

"Natsi's sister, maybe. And maybe our mystery man Aaju Imiina. He could be on a visit from Nuuk."

Miki nodded and pointed at the rocks behind the house.

"If they run then they will come out the back window. There's no back door on these types of houses. I'll wait there and you flush them out."

Simonsen turned at the sound of Danielsen repositioning the broad Velcro tabs on his vest. He rapped his knuckles on the younger man's chest.

"Wipe that smile off your face, Aqqa."

"Chief?"

"I can see it in your eyes. You're excited, and Miki is talking you up. We're picking up two young men, that's all. They're not bank robbers."

"Then why the vests?"

Simonsen tucked his thumbs inside his belt and looked at Danielsen. "Because," he said, "I don't know Aaju, and I don't like surprises." He threw his jacket onto the back seat of the car and took a vest from Miki. Simonsen nodded at the taxi driver as he tightened the straps at the sides. "The sooner we get a second vehicle the better," he said. "Danielsen, pay Taavi and be sure to get a receipt."

Miki slung the rifle over his shoulder and looked up at the houses. Just like all the houses in the smaller villages and settlements in Greenland, the water and electricity pipes were laid above ground. Like stiff snakes in metal collars, they connected each house to the mains. Miki would have to crawl over them as he worked his way over the snow and ice to the back of the house. The street lights lit the front, but there was a dark patch of shadow beneath the bedroom window.

Miki nodded towards the shadows, "I'll be there."

"Miki, wait," Simonsen said.

"*Aap?*"

"No heroics, okay?"

"With respect, Chief, you seem to have some issues you need to work through."

"Issues? What I have is problems, the kind that we never used to have here. Ever since Maratse turned up, we have had more violent crime in one year than I can remember in the twenty years I have been in Uummannaq. This is the second time this year you have been here, Miki, and I don't like it."

"I'll do my job, Chief."

"I don't doubt it, I just don't like that you have to. Added to that," he said, as Danielsen approached them, "you're a bad influence on him." He gestured towards Danielsen. "We'll give you two minutes before we start walking around the front."

Simonsen resisted the urge to smoke as he watched Miki move into position. Once the SRU Constable from Nuuk waved that he was ready, Simonsen tapped Danielsen on the shoulder and walked to the foot of the stairs leading to the houses on *Juaarsip Aqqutaa*. They passed the first house and continued on to the first step below Natsi's house. The kitchen light shone through the window and lit the deck outside. Unlike the other houses in Uummannaq, there were no Christmas stars in the windows, and little to suggest that the occupants had much to get excited about in the holiday period.

Simonsen knew Natsi and many others like him. Out of work, struggling with a tough family background, and burying all of that beneath a tough facade and alcohol binges that lasted from Wednesday to Monday every week. Simonsen looked at his watch. It was Saturday. He nodded at the kitchen window and listened as the snow on the deck crunched beneath Danielsen's boots. At a shrug from the Constable, Simonsen knocked on the door.

"Natsi? It's Simonsen. Open the door."

They waited in anticipation of some movement inside, and the vibration common in houses built on thick wooden foundations and bolted to the rocks.

"Natsi?"

Simonsen turned the door handle and opened the door slowly. Danielsen peered around it and nodded that it was clear. Simonsen was the first inside. He checked the bathroom on the immediate left as Danielsen walked into the kitchen.

"Natsi?" Danielsen said. "It's the police."

They stopped at the sound of something heavy falling onto the floor in the living room, on the other side of the kitchen door. Simonsen tapped Danielsen's shoulder and followed him through the door. Another thump vibrated through the floor, followed by the squeal of a cold metal window clasp and the sticky creak of the window cracking through a layer of frost as it opened. Simonsen ran towards the spare bedroom, as Danielsen turned to the bedroom on his right.

"Natsi, stop," Simonsen shouted, as he slammed into the bedroom door and caught a glimpse of a someone leaping out of the window. "Miki?"

There was a shout and scuffle on the rocks beneath the window.

"I've got a girl here," Miki said, raising his voice above the screams of a girl he had pinned to the rocks beneath his knee.

Empty bottles scattered across the floor as Simonsen ran to look, pausing at the sudden movement of a body beneath a duvet on the bed.

The bed creaked as a man fought his way free of the twists of the thin duvet, and leaped for the door. Simonsen reached for his arm, but caught a fist in his face as the man flailed out of the bedroom and into the living room, tugging at the boxer shorts sliding down his thighs.

"Danielsen," Simonsen shouted, as he pressed his hand to his nose.

He wiped a bloody palm on his vest as he staggered after the man, glancing at Danielsen as he struggled to restrain a young Greenlander on the threadbare sofa. Simonsen recognised Natsi's scowl and continued into the kitchen. He heard the crash of the front door as it slammed against the side of the house, and the tremble of feet down the wooden steps to the road.

Simonsen slipped on the ice covering the first step, gripped the banister and pulled himself to his feet. He saw the man run towards the steps leading down to the road where the police car was parked and gave chase.

The man slipped on the ice covering the road beside the communal water pump, picked himself up and ran along the road that snaked its way down the mountainside to the heliport. Simonsen climbed into the driver's seat of the police Toyota, turned on the emergency lights and reversed into the road. The man took a shortcut between the bend in the road and ran past the heliport towards the centre of Uummannaq.

Simonsen slowed to match the man's pace, drifting the police car into the middle of the road. The blue emergency lights swirled across the man's skin, and lit his breath misting in front of him. Simonsen tugged a cigarette from the packet on the dash and lit it. He wound the window down and blew out a cloud of smoke as he pulled to the right and drove alongside the young man.

"Aaju Imiina?" he asked, as he leaned his arm on the door.

"Piss off," the man said and continued running.

"Are you cold, Aaju?"

"*Aap.*"

"Then stop running and get in."

Simonsen pulled over to the side of the road and waited as the man slowed to a stiff walk and opened the passenger door. Simonsen offered him the packet of cigarettes.

"Smoke?"

The man shivered as he took a cigarette and Simonsen turned up the heat.

"Where were you going, Aaju?"

Aaju shrugged and took a long drag on the cigarette. The smoke tumbled through his lips as he coughed. Simonsen reached between the seats and dragged his jacket through the gap, dumping it on Aaju's lap. Aaju held the cigarette between his lips as he twisted into the jacket and zipped it to the collar.

"Do you have a ticket?" Simonsen asked, as he hiked a thumb towards the heliport behind them.

"*Naamik.*"

"So you're not flying anywhere today?"

Aaju shook his head.

"Then why did you run?"

"I thought you were him."

"Who?"

"That crazy policeman," Aaju said, as he gripped the cigarette between his fingers. "You know the one? He beat up some friends in Saattut."

"Who did?"

"Some policeman."

"When?"

"Last night." Aaju shrugged.

"And that's why you ran?"

"*Aap.*"

Simonsen turned in the road and drove back to the house, parking at the bottom of the steps. He pressed the packet of cigarettes into Aaju's hand.

"Stay here," he said, and got out of the car.

The impact of his boots vibrated through the steps as he climbed them and Danielsen met him at the door. He looked beyond Simonsen at the car and smiled when he saw Aaju smoking in the passenger seat.

"How are you doing, Aqqa?"

"Come and see."

Simonsen stopped at the sink in the kitchen, found a cloth and rinsed it. He wiped his nose as he walked into the living room, stuffing the cloth into his pocket as he nodded at Miki and then looked at the two Greenlanders sitting on the sofa with blankets around their shoulders.

"You know Natsi," Danielsen said.

"I do."

"The girl won't give her name." Danielsen grinned.

"That's alright," Simonsen said. He smiled at the girl. "Hello, Siki." She glared at him as he turned to Miki. "Sikkersoq Hermansen," he said. "Natsi's sister."

Miki slapped Danielsen on the arm. "You said you didn't recognise her?"

"I've never seen her naked before," Danielsen said and shrugged.

"That's enough," Simonsen said.

He dragged a chair to the sofa, brushed a layer of crumbs from the cushion and sat down. Sikkersoq looked away as Simonsen pulled his notebook from his pocket. The floor creaked as Miki moved to the windowsill and leaned against it.

"I have some questions," Simonsen said. "If you help me with them, then you can clean up and we'll be on our way." He waited as

Natsi nodded.

"Is this about Salik?"

"Yes."

"And what about that crazy policeman?"

"About that too." Simonsen looked at Danielsen. "Go and talk to Aaju. I'll stay here with Miki."

Natsi waited until Danielsen was gone and then nudged his sister. She glared at him and pulled the blanket tighter around her shoulders.

"What can you tell me about Salik?" Simonsen said. "When did you last see him?"

"What are you going to do about the policeman?" Sikkersoq asked. "Answer that and maybe we'll tell you about Salik."

Simonsen lifted his hand as Miki stirred at the window.

"That isn't how this works," Miki said.

"No? You want our help? You help us first."

"Alright, Siki," Simonsen said. "Let's hear it."

"Some crazy guy crashed a party last night. He was mad. Fighting. They said he was a policeman. That's like police brutality or something. It's not right. Our friends were just having a party."

"Did your friends say who he was or what he wanted?" Simonsen scribbled a few details at the top of a blank page in his notebook. "What did he look like?"

"All dressed in white. Like he was hunting, they said."

"Hunting?"

"He was looking for a man."

"Where was the party? Whose house?"

"Our friend's house."

"Who owns the house?"

"That old Dane," Natsi said. "But he's never there. He's always at his cabin."

"The party was at Aksel Stein's house?"

"*Aap.*"

Simonsen sighed as he lowered the notebook. He looked at Miki.

"Maratse?" Miki whispered.

Simonsen nodded.

Chapter 12

Qitu opened his notepad and placed it on his knee. He clicked the top of his pen and watched as Tertu curled into the chair opposite him, placed the toes of her shoes on the coffee table and hid behind her knees. He had tried to offer her coffee the last time they met. Today he had cake. But Tertu, he noticed, brought her own provisions. He spotted the top of the slim can of Red Bull hidden inside her sleeve. She pulled it out, opened it and sipped as he made his notes. Tomorrow he would make sure he picked up a case of it on the way to the office.

"Palu said he put you in a hotel. Which one?" he asked. He tilted his head to see past her knee, giving him a better view of her lips.

"Nuuk Hotel."

"Is it nice?"

Tertu shrugged. "It's okay."

"Why don't we start," he said.

"Did you call your friend?"

"What?"

"The man in Uummannaq. Did you call him?"

"I sent a text. He hasn't replied."

Tertu fidgeted behind her knees and Qitu studied her hair, from the bright pink tips to the black roots. She was wearing the tusks again today. They wobbled beneath her bottom lip as she spoke and scraped the side of the can as she drank.

"I need some background, Tertu," he said. "To put things in context. Can you tell me where you grew up? What it was like at school?"

"I grew up in one of the settlements in Upernavik. My dad was a fisherman." She paused to watch as Qitu looked at her; he wrote without looking at the notepad. "How can you do that?"

"It's better if you just talk," he said. "Tell your story; pretend I'm not here."

"Okay," Tertu said and took a sip from her can. "My dad was away a lot. Mum met him in Denmark. She had problems." Tertu stuck out her thumb and little finger and pretended it was a bottle she raised to her lips. "She didn't work. Dad earned money. Some money. Most of it he drank and she drank the rest. I played outside a lot, and slept at my grandparent's house."

"What about school?"

"I didn't learn much until I moved to Upernavik for ninth grade. I lived at the students' home. I was good at Danish, which made them think I was clever. Only I really didn't know anything. I didn't go to school much, and I didn't show up for my exams."

"You moved back home?"

"*Naamik*. I met a boy and went to stay with him in Maniitsoq."

Qitu lifted his pen from the notepad and Tertu shrugged.

"Sometimes you do what people think you should do, not what your body tells you to."

"You had a relationship with him?"

"I had sex with him. He made me laugh and he had money for beer, so I stayed with him."

"Until when?"

"I met a girl. A nice one who thinks like me. I was seventeen, she was fifteen, I think."

Tertu put the can down on the floor. Her hands disappeared inside her cuffs and she folded her arms across her chest. The coffee table creaked as she trembled.

"She wasn't a lesbian. She just liked sex. She told me about these parties, where you do all kinds of things. She even said you could get money – not like being a prostitute, but because everyone was so wasted that you could take the money from their jackets and stuff."

"So you went to one of these parties?"

"I went to a lot of them. I stole lots of money, until he caught me."

"Who?"

Tertu pressed her thumbs to her mouth and stared around her sleeves at Qitu. The table creaked again and she gasped as her toes slid off the edge and her feet thudded on the floor. The coffee from Qitu's mug sloshed over the side. He mopped it up with an empty page from his notebook.

"Sorry."

"It's okay," Qitu said. He let the paper soak up the coffee and forced a smile. "You met someone at the party. He's important to the story, isn't he?"

She nodded.

"Can you tell me his name?"

Tertu shook her head.

"Maybe later then. Just tell me *about* him."

"He's smart. He knows all about the Internet. But not the regular stuff. He's into something else."

"The Dark Web?"

Tertu nodded. "He said we could make a lot of money. More than I stole at the parties."

"And you believed him?"

"He gave me money. He paid for a room in Maniitsoq. He paid for my food, and beer."

"What did you do for him?"

Tertu shifted position on the seat, tucking her heels beneath her bottom and twisting the cuffs of her sleeves in her fingers. She caught Qitu's eye.

"The first time was fun," she said. "He told me to do things with my friend."

"The fifteen year old? What was her name?"

Tertu continued as if she hadn't heard. "He made the room all dark and filmed it. Then he put it on the net. He had this website where people paid to see my video."

"A pornography site?"

"Maybe. But more than that," she said. "It was more of an *anything* site. He said that this was just the start. He gave us money and said that there was more money when we did what people asked us to do."

"Who asked you?"

"People wrote and told him what they wanted. People from all over the world. He told them how much it would be. Then we did it." Tertu slipped one of her hands out of her sleeve and turned it in the light. "He gave us one of these each time we did what they asked."

"Why?"

"Because what he did hurt me," she said, and showed him the tattoos in the joints between her fingers. "They hurt too, when he made them, but nothing like what we had to do for the camera. He said we only had to do a handful of things – two hands – and when our hands were full, we were done. We never had to do it again."

"Do what?"

Tertu shook her head. She slipped her hands out of sight and stared out of the window. Qitu checked his notes. He glanced at

Tertu. He needed details, but understood that if he pushed her too quickly, he would end up with nothing. No story. No job. He had given up a lot for this. He needed to give her time. But he needed something to work on. He had to have a name or a lead, at the very least.

"Tertu," he said. "You don't want to talk about it. I understand. But can you show me the website? Maybe I can see for myself."

"You?"

"I'm a journalist, Tertu. I know how to access the Dark Web. I have the TOR browser on my Mac."

Qitu stood up at a nod from Tertu. He picked up his *MacBook* from his desk and gave it to her. Tertu's sleeves covered the keyboard, her fingers darting out of the cuffs like painted snake tongues, revealing tiny glimpses of her Aleut-tattooed fingers. She handed him the computer when she was finished.

"I have to pee," she said and walked out of the office.

The website looked like a shopping page, with padlock icons over boxes arranged in rows. Dark shapes moved with strobe-like motions, just visible behind each padlock. As Qitu moved his cursor over them a pop-up text revealed the name of the video and the amount required per minute to watch it. Bitcoin and other cryptocurrencies were the only method of payment. For ten thousand Satoshi, the smallest denomination of the Bitcoin, Qitu could see five minutes of extreme video in High Definition. Each video had the Greenlandic name of a fish, followed by the English translation. Ten thousand Satoshi, or roughly one hundred and forty US dollars, gave Qitu access to *Eqalussuaq*, the Greenland Shark. It was difficult to see, but the strobe movements of figures behind the padlock icon gave the impression of a group feeding frenzy that matched the name. He flipped through his notes and found the name Palu had used to describe Tertu. *Qaleralik*, the flat fish, halibut, a bottom feeder. For another one hundred and forty dollars he could see five minutes of what looked like bondage. But that wasn't what caught Qitu's eye. It was the box at the bottom of the page.

Qitu moved the cursor over the padlocked image on the last row of boxes and stared at the pop-up description: *Kukilik taartoq*, the black dogfish. It was the most expensive video on the page, inviting only the wealthiest of voyeurs. One Bitcoin, over six thousand US dollars, bought ten minutes of what looked like someone in captivity.

The small amount of light that was in the teaser box, hidden behind the padlock, cast a shadow from what looked like a chain and cuffs of some kind, and pale brown skin. A sticker flashed beside the pop-up box with the word *live* in bold letters.

Tertu walked into the office and Qitu closed the lid of his *MacBook*. She sat down and Qitu looked at her eyes, saw the red rims as if she had rubbed them, and the wet sheen of tears.

"I'm sorry," he said.

Tertu shrugged. "It wasn't you."

"But we can stop him. You and me."

"How?"

"We go to the police."

"*Naamik*," Tertu shouted. She stood up. "No police."

"Tertu. What you had to do, what *they* have to do, we have to stop it."

"Palu said no police. Only you."

"There's a video there – it's live. Someone is chained in a black room somewhere."

"No police."

"What if he kills her? What if someone pays him to do that?"

"He'll kill me."

"You're safe, Tertu. She's not."

"I'm not safe. No-one is safe. He'll find me and kill me."

Qitu stepped around the coffee table as Tertu ran for the door. He followed her to the street, chased her along the snowy footpath towards the town centre. Thick snow caught in the headlights of cars coming towards them. One of them was a police car. Qitu barely had a moment to think before Tertu stopped and screamed. The police car slid to a sudden stop and she ran across the open ground to the right of Hotel Hans Egede, racing across the rough building ground as the police officers pressed Qitu to the side of the police car and shouted for Tertu to stop.

"Let me go," Qitu said. "It's not what you think." He twisted in the policeman's grip to see the man's lips.

"Why were you chasing her?"

"I was chasing *after* her. She's upset."

"Why?"

"We were doing an interview," Qitu said. "The questions were difficult for her."

The policeman waited as his partner gave up trying to stop Tertu and walked back to the car. He let go of Qitu and opened the passenger door of the police Toyota.

"Let's start again," the policeman said as he sat in the passenger seat. "What's your name?"

"Qitu Kalia. I'm a journalist. Tertu was helping me with my research."

"Tertu?"

"The young woman." Qitu paused. "We were looking at something. I suggested we had to contact the police and she ran away."

"Is she a criminal?"

"No, not at all. She's a victim. And there are more. We need to find them."

"And she doesn't want to?"

"She's frightened of the consequences. She's involved in something, and she is scared for her life." Qitu wiped snow from his face and looked at the police officer.

"You believe her?"

"Yes," he said. "She needs your help."

Chapter 13

There was a small crowd of officers standing around the IT consultant's desk on the first floor of Nuuk Police station. Gaba spotted the Commissioner standing a good head taller than the officers hunched around the computer. He nodded as the Commissioner waved him over.

"What's going on?" Gaba asked.

"It's a developing situation," the Commissioner said. He pointed at the glass windows of the interview room opposite them. "Do you recognise him?"

Gaba looked and nodded. "That's Qitu Kalia."

"He's researching an article and felt the need to disclose what he had found already."

"And what's that, sir?"

"Some kind of live porn site that Kalia claims has links to Greenland. Kristian Møller, the computer guy, is confirming that now."

"Are we concerned about pornography?"

"This looks far more sinister than that. Kalia suggests it is time-critical, and he has a source who is frightened for her life. I've got people looking for her now."

"In Nuuk?"

"Yes, but this," the Commissioner said and pointed at the computer screen, "is somewhere else. See for yourself and then come find me in my office."

Gaba waited for the Commissioner to leave, and then leaned around his colleagues to look at the images on the computer. Kristian had three screens on his desk. The middle one streamed with code. The one on the left popped with messages. The third screen displayed an enlarged image of the website on the Dark Web.

"This is live?" Gaba asked.

"Yeah, it is. There's a constant stream of data, the size and speed of which indicates it is live. But the stream itself is interesting."

"In what way?"

The police officers standing around Kristian's desk moved back as he turned in his chair.

"Regular Internet users in Greenland don't have the streaming capacity for this amount of content, not without degradation of image. Plus, it's way too expensive. I think, if this is being streamed here, within the country, we're talking about a hi-tech setup using a satellite transmission, piggy-backing a cable connection in another country. It's elaborate and exclusive."

"Explain."

"It requires a high degree of technical ability, and access to expensive equipment."

"So, we're looking at someone in the telecommunications industry? TelePost?"

"Possibly, but more likely someone who studied it, not necessarily working in the industry. Not right now, anyway."

"Why not?"

"This kind of setup requires constant maintenance. Whoever is running it needs to be close to it."

"Close to the equipment or close to that?" Gaba said and pointed at the screen. He frowned as a stray thought passed through his mind at the sight of the victim's naked chest.

"Both. The camera is set up to stream."

"And what about the cost? You said this was an expensive setup."

Kristian tapped the pop-up window on the screen.

"Bitcoin? How much is that in real money?" Gaba asked.

"It costs about two months pay to watch."

Gaba smoothed his hand over his scalp. "Alright, so he's got money. Where is he?"

"It'll take some time before we can answer that," Kristian said. He pointed at the screen with messages cascading, one window on top of the other. "I'm getting some help, but I can't tell you yet. I can say it's somewhere within North America."

"If you get closer than that, I'm your first call," Gaba said, as he took his mobile out of his pocket. "Understand?"

Gaba waited for Kristian to nod, tapping the list of contacts in his phone as he walked over to the interview room. He stared at the journalist as he waited for his call to be connected.

"Atii? You there?"

"Bad connection, but yes. I'm here."

"Get the team together, grab your gear, and meet me at the station."

Gaba ended the call, knocked once on the door and walked into the interview room. He nodded for the two police officers to leave, waited for them to close the door, and then sat down opposite Qitu.

"Now, tell me what you didn't tell them," he said.

"What?"

"Tell me what you're holding back. Anything. Doesn't matter what, just the thing you're thinking about. The answer to the question they haven't asked yet."

"I don't understand."

"Yes, you do. It's the thing you think might get you into trouble."

"I haven't done anything."

"I don't care, either way. Just tell me." Gaba slapped the table. "Don't look at them. This is me you're dealing with now, Qitu."

"I'm not a suspect."

"I don't care."

"This is an interesting technique..."

"It's the way I roll and you're wasting time," Gaba said. He stabbed his finger towards Kristian's desk. "You're wasting *her* time – the girl chained up in that dark place. In my book, that makes you an accomplice to whatever shit is going down with her. It will be on you, unless you start talking."

"I *am* talking," Qitu said. He gestured at the tape recorder between them. "I'm co-operating."

Gaba stopped the tape with a quick stab of his finger. He drummed his fingers on the table and stared at Qitu.

"Okay," Qitu said. "One thing I haven't said yet." He paused as Gaba stopped drumming the table.

"Go on."

"The teenager they found on the ice in Uummannaq. I told your colleagues that he is connected, possibly to the man or woman who runs that website. What I didn't tell them was that I contacted someone to find out more."

"Who?"

"David Maratse. I sent him a text."

Gaba cursed. "Why would you contact Maratse?"

"My source, Tertu, didn't want any police involvement. But she wanted to know if the boy's fingers were marked."

"What kind of marks?"

"Tattoos like bands on the joints of his fingers. I thought

Maratse could find out."

"Because he's a private detective?"

"Because he's in the area."

"That's it?"

"Yes."

Gaba pushed back his chair and stood up. He waved for his colleagues to come in and walked to the door.

"You didn't ask *me*," he said to Qitu. "About the boy's fingers. Of course, you couldn't know I was there." He waited for Qitu to comment, smiling at the furrow on the journalist's brow. "So, here's the answer to the question you didn't ask me. Yes," Gaba said. "The boy's fingers were banded. All the joints on the inside of his fingers."

Gaba walked across the office floor to Kristian's desk.

"You haven't called yet," he said, and waved the mobile in his hand.

"There's nothing to..."

"Work faster," Gaba said, and dialled Atii's number again.

"*Aap?*"

"Forget about coming to the station. Go to the airport. Talk to the Air Greenland desk about getting the *King Air* prepped."

"Where are we going?"

"I don't know yet," Gaba said. He jabbed his finger at Kristian. "But we'll know soon."

"It could take a while," Kristian said, his voice faltering as Gaba glared at him.

Gaba ended the call and strode across the floor to the door. It was five minutes more before the Commissioner waved him into his office. The Commissioner placed the handset of his telephone on the receiver and gestured for Gaba to sit down.

"That was the First Minister," he said.

"She knows about this?"

"No. She was passing on her condolences and wondering if we should do something for Petra. She suggested some kind of initiative or training programme in her name to commemorate Sergeant Jensen's service. I said I would think about it."

Gaba waited.

"There's something else."

"Busy day."

"Yes, but not an easy one. Have you talked to Miki?"

"Not today."

"That's impressive, if Simonsen managed to give me the message before you." The Commissioner smiled. "But that's where it stops being funny. It seems Maratse is taking matters into his own hands. Apparently, Maratse crashed a party in Saattut and beat up a couple of guys," the Commissioner said, as Gaba frowned. "Yes, I didn't believe it either."

"He's a quiet guy. It doesn't fit, sir."

"Simonsen mentioned a man called Aksel Stein. Do you remember the name?"

"Yes."

"It seems that Maratse is looking for him. Simonsen actually used the word *hunting*."

"He thinks this guy has something to do with Petra's death?"

"Possibly. And Simonsen is concerned about what Maratse might do if he finds Stein. To be honest, given what Simonsen told me, and the reaction from the locals, I'm inclined to agree with him."

Gaba stood up and walked to the window. He tapped the glass as he stared at the icebergs in the fjord. The clouds were thinning and the sun had found a few weak spots to shine through the clouds and light the tips of the icebergs. North of Nuuk, at the top of Greenland it was dark, pitch black. Gaba thought of Maratse hunting beneath the black winter sky and wondered if it was grief that drove him, or something else? What answer would Maratse give to the question no-one was asking? Gaba felt another twist in his stomach as he thought about the video on the website, and the two months' police pay it would cost to see it. Who would he see if he could afford to watch?

"You're thinking, Gaba. I can hear you."

"What do you want me to do, sir? About Maratse?"

"He's one of our own, Gaba. We owe it to him to stop him doing something stupid. And we owe it to Petra, too. She was very fond of him."

"Yes, sir."

"This is what SRU trains for. I'm tasking you to stop Maratse before he kills someone."

"He's not a killer."

"He's armed, Gaba, and he's hunting. You need to stop him."

"What if he's right? What if it wasn't suicide?"

"Petra?"

Gaba walked to the map of Greenland mounted on the Commissioner's wall. He found Uummannaq and traced his fingers from the settlement of Inussuk to Saattut.

"It's interesting, sir, that Petra's clothes were found close to the boy's body. Simonsen suggested the two things are linked. What if Petra saw something? Maybe she tried to stop whoever killed the boy. They took her, and killed her, and then they made it look like a suicide, just to throw us off the scent."

"Coincidence."

"I don't think so. Think about Maratse. For a man who loved Petra, he was quick to bury her."

"She's gone. Maybe it helped to move on as quickly as possible?"

"With respect, sir, I know you were fond of her."

"Like a daughter, I suppose."

"But for Maratse it is so much more. I can understand where he is coming from. I talked to him at the funeral, when we walked down the mountainside. I was more upset than he was."

"He's reserved. He hides his emotions."

"It was more than that. It's like he didn't believe she was dead." Gaba rubbed his hand across his scalp. "Now that I think about it, he wasn't sad, he was impatient. Like he had something to do."

"You're making presumptions, Gaba."

"No, sir. It's starting to make sense. He arranged the funeral in a hurry because he needed to get started. Son of a bitch." Gaba laughed. "Simonsen is right. Maratse is hunting. But he's not hunting Petra's killer, he's hunting whoever took her. He thinks she's alive."

"Sergeant," the Commissioner said, as Gaba walked to the door. "I gave you a job."

"Yes, sir."

"Bring Maratse in," he said. "That's your first priority. Don't get caught up in presumptions."

Gaba nodded and dialled Atii's number as he jogged along the corridor to the stairs.

"Get on board. We're going north."

Chapter 14

The prickle of heat teased at Petra's skin, the crack, hiss and spit of wood in the pot-bellied stove worried at her ears, and the smell of smoke wrinkled her nose as she opened her eyes. Petra stared through the sticky film of tears, spit and sweat, and saw him sitting beside the stove. The funnel of his hood was dipped comically low as he read the book on his lap through a tunnel of fur. The book was lit by lantern light and the thick wick twisted black inside the oily flame. Petra could see it if she squinted, a dance of orange inside a smoky glass bulb. The wick crackled, dry like her tongue when she moved it from where it sat heavy and thick inside her mouth. The sucking noise of dry spit lifted the man's head from his book. She saw him rise, heard the chains of her cuffs scrape rusted flakes from the links as she shrank to the wall and he clumped across the dusty floorboards towards her. He tugged something black from his jacket pocket and then the orange flame was gone as he bound Petra's eyes.

"You're awake," he said.

His Danish was strong, but with an unfamiliar stress on the endings. Petra surprised herself with the analysis, wondered if she was getting stronger, or if the will to survive had taken over her senses, searching for details, filtering the dark, dust and despair for something to cling to, some kind of hope.

She heard the zip of the funnel hood, and then his voice, clearer now, as he sat down and the wooden legs of the chair creaked between the spit and crack of wood, the crackle of the flame, and the thump of her pulse.

"I've put your show on hold," he said. "You're quite the little earner. You deserve a break."

"Cold," she breathed.

"Yes, of course. No-one's watching right now."

The chair creaked, the floor vibrated, and Petra felt something heavy draped over her shoulders. A fleece-lined jacket perhaps. She turned her head, felt the chunky plastic teeth of the zip press into her cheek, and smelled the tang of old fish blood. She shivered inside the jacket, and drew her feet beneath her bottom. She could feel her rough heels on her skin, but couldn't remember if she had been wearing jeans once, when, or if, they had been removed.

"I'm sure this is strange for you, Sergeant Jensen. But we all have our part to play, you understand? I *hope* you understand. It's not so very different from what you do in your job. We both provide a service. People are needy, and you and I attend to those needs. Of course, in your work you had physical contact with the people who needed you. But let me reassure you that now, with my help, you are enhancing people's sad lives, giving them pleasure. Like I say, providing a useful service."

"You hurt me," Petra said.

"I hurt you? No," he said. "That wasn't me. *I* didn't hurt you."

Petra flinched as she realised he was close – close enough to smooth his hand through her hair. She moved her head and he let go.

"They told me what to do, and I... I had to do it, Petra. I couldn't ignore them. Why, that would be the same as you ignoring a theft, or perhaps walking over someone who had collapsed in the street. Without us to pick people up, if we don't listen to their needs, they will suffer, Petra. You do understand?"

"What you did..."

"I did it for them."

The floorboards creaked as the man kneeled in front of her. He coughed, and his breath rattled and wheezed through his lungs. Petra heard the man unscrew a bottle, and she smelled fruit and artificial sweeteners, but there was no fizz. The soft drink was flat, like she felt. The man cleared his throat. She felt him tug the tail of the jacket and pull it over her knee.

"They like watching you, Petra." He laughed. "You're a policewoman and that seems to give them a kick. I don't know why I didn't think of it before. Of course, I had to prove you were police, so I kept your ID card. Everything else is on the ice." He caught another cough in his throat and took a drink. "The note you wrote was a nice touch. It was generous of you. Now we have plenty of time. We... we can make a lot of money."

Petra moved, just a tiny bit, and felt something run from her ear. It splashed on her chest. She flinched again when the man pressed a greasy thumb onto her breast and wiped away a spot of liquid.

"Blood," he said. "It got a little rough last time. I'm sorry, of course I am, but the numbers... the numbers doubled. We had more viewers than last time."

The floor creaked as he stood up. Petra turned her head at more noises, desperate to identify them, to be sure that the twist of metal was a lid not a tool of some kind, that the bubbling of water was for coffee, and that he cursed because he dropped something, not because she screamed and bit at him – *that* she did remember – and that the soft words that followed did not disguise a sudden fleck of pain.

She smelled coffee.

She felt her body ratchet down from red alert to something more like regular fear. She recognised the sounds of spoons striking ceramic mugs, and the splash of coffee, the hiss of water on the hotplate. But then the sounds were obscured by a rush of energy and she tilted from fear to a state of terror as he freed one of her arms and stretched it to her left. The jacket slipped off her shoulders and she cried out, her breath stalling in her mouth as he fastened her wrist again.

And then he let go.

"Coffee," he said, and she heard the soft thud of the mug on the wooden floor. "Lower your hand. You should just be able to reach it."

Petra felt the rim of the mug with the tips of her fingers. There was just enough play in the chain to lift the mug to her lips, if she bent her head down, if she tilted the mug. The coffee stung her lips. The sudden rush of caffeine surged through her body and she thought about dropping the mug and ripping the blindfold from her eyes. But to what end? She was bound. Stretched. She wasn't ready for this. She wasn't prepared for someone like him.

"It's good, isn't it?" he said. "That's one of the things about this cabin, unlike the others; it's well-stocked with those little comforts that make it all worthwhile. I mean, we can work here, undisturbed. The conditions are perfect. And, with a little ingenuity, the technical challenges associated with the service can be solved."

Petra struggled with the last of the coffee as she tried to tilt the mug at the limit of the chain and the limit of her neck. The last third of the mug splashed over her lips and chin, and she lowered the mug, placed it on the floor, and wiped her chin on her shoulder.

"You want more?" he asked. "I'll make some more."

Petra listened to the now familiar noises as the man talked.

"You know this is actually rather nice. My usual co-workers are less..." he paused, tapping a spoon on the can of coffee grounds as he thought. "Well, they're not as educated. Let's leave it at that. But there is one thing they understand – it's something we agreed on, a contract of sorts. I thought about making the same contract with you. What do you think? Should we formalise this? Should we have a contract?" He waited a beat. "It's up to you, of course. But it might make it easier for you to provide the service. What do you think?"

Petra lifted her head. She heard him move, followed him with bound eyes, straining to see through the black cover tied around her head.

"Yes," he said. "Let's do this. Let's make a contract."

"What are you doing?" Petra said, as the man unhooked the chain attached to her hand. He pinched her wrist between the floor and his knee.

"It's something I learned from a friend."

Petra jerked at her hand and he pressed harder.

"Stop that, it will spoil it."

"Spoil what?"

The smell of paint or thin spirits pinched the air beneath her nose. She twisted at the sound of something being bound to what could have been a stick – hollow and dull.

"I have to use a hook," he said. "One of the thick ones they use on the boats. You know the ones I mean? I've straightened it."

"Please stop," Petra said. She gasped at a prick of metal in the skin between the joints of her little finger.

"Don't move."

She held her breath at more pricks, like tiny wet teeth biting into the first layer of her skin, and a tapping, a *tick tick tick* of fish teeth, spiny and sharp. The man splayed her fingers, his breath soft, concentrated, as he tapped the hook into the three gaps between her joints.

"You were such a star," he said, as he worked, "that I have given you three tokens on your contract."

"I don't know what you are doing. I want you to stop. Please stop."

"Shush, Petra. This is good for you. Each token I give you, each mark, is one step closer to your freedom. When your fingers are full, you are free."

She felt him wipe at her fingers, a soft cloth. And then he gripped her wrist and bent her hand towards her face. He pushed one side of her blindfold up with his thumb, angling her head in his grip so that she could only see her fingers. Petra blinked at the black bands between the joints of her little finger. Pricks of blood were creased into her skin, but the bands were solid. The man tugged the blindfold into place and fastened her wrist to the chain hooked into the wall.

"I was in Thailand," he said. "I saw some tattoos, but they were done with a machine. Then I met my friend – pretty, like you, with such pretty hands. Thin blue lines and diamonds all tapped into her skin. It gave me the idea, and I... I think it works. It's a good contract. This is iron gall ink. You can't break a contract written in ink like that."

Petra bent her finger. It pulsed beyond her view. She could still see the bands, purple-black, thick squares, and irregular rectangles. He had hurt her during the fourth change of the card, and in the first change after it; he had tagged her, made his mark. Her lower lip started to tremble and she bit it, bit it until it bled.

"You said I would be free?"

"Yes. Yes, that is the contract. And I will honour that."

"As soon as my hands are filled – all my fingers marked?"

"That's right."

Petra licked the blood from her lip, tasted copper in her mouth. She thought about being free, and then a sound from outside the cabin made her think of something else. It wasn't the sound of freedom, more like a shush and grind of ice. It reminded her of something that sounded like escape, and she pictured a man on a sledge, and bit his name into her lips, soft enough that the man would not hear, but strong enough to ignore the pain in her body, the bands on her fingers, and the fear of unfamiliar noises.

This wasn't unfamiliar.

It was hope.

Sapaat

SUNDAY

Chapter 15

Maratse saw the glow of the cabin lights and slowed the sledge with soft commands. The metal runners scraped to a stop and the rear of the sledge shimmied until it bumped against a clump of old snow, leached of moisture by the wind. Spindrift swirled across the surface as Maratse fought back a yawn. He had not slept since leaving Inussuk he'd barely rested, and he couldn't remember when he last ate a full meal, not since the funeral. He stepped off the sledge and pulled a brick of frozen *ammassat,* capelin, out of the sledge bag strung between the uprights, breaking off two or three fish for each dog. Maratse chewed on the last fish as he kneeled beside Tinka and watched the cabin.

He dug an arch in the ice as the dogs ate, looping the traces through the arch and securing the team. Maratse untied the white canvas shooting screen from the sledge and attached it to the wooden frame. He pushed the rifle through the gap in the canvas and lashed the barrel to the frame. Then he dressed, pulling the white anorak over his sealskin smock, and tugging the silk ski mask over his head. Maratse waited for the moon to slip behind the clouds, picked up the rifle and walked across the ice towards the cabin.

Hunters used the shooting screen to approach a seal on the ice. From a distance, the hunter would appear to be nothing more than an iceberg. The hunter would inch his way towards the seal, soundlessly, just as Maratse inched his way across the windblown snow beneath the cabin. The light flickered inside. Maratse watched it, searching for shadows between each increment of movement until he was at the wall, beneath the window, to the left of the door.

The wind dropped, stealing the sound from the land, stilling the snow and bursting Maratse's ears with silence. He moved to the door and opened it.

The rifle on its frame was clumsy in his grasp, and he lowered it to see the light dancing in the oil of the large soap stone lamp in the middle of the cabin. The oil was nearly spent. It must have burned for days. Maratse crossed the floor and stood beside it. He lowered the rifle and examined the cabin's only room.

The empty tins suggested it had been occupied for some time. The lamp burned but the cast iron stove was cold. There were footprints in the ashes and curved striations that could have been the tips of raven wings if Maratse hadn't seen the fish hooks and multi-coloured threads scattered beneath the stove. He bent down for a closer look, traced the marks in the ash, his fingertips a needle's breadth above the story in the soot, the marks in the ashes, the hooks beneath the fire. The shelves dipped beneath the weight of glossy literature – pornography, peeling at the edges, the models mostly male. Men with men. Men alone. Maratse put the rifle down and looked at the mattress. Soiled with grease and age, it was raised above the cabin floor on a tabletop sitting on four plastic milk crates. There was barely enough room for one sleeper, but the used condoms suggested there had been at least two.

Maratse sat down on the chair by the window. He peeled the ski mask off his head and stuffed it inside the pocket of his anorak. Once the mask was removed the scents of the cabin flooded in to his unfiltered nose. It was the smell of men, old, and young, unwashed, uncaring. A triangle of brushed wood above the door caught Maratse's eye. He studied it, standing on his toes and gripping the top of the door frame to peer at the triangular shape surrounded by old, blistered varnish. He pressed his finger into the remains of a tacky residue. Glue, fatigued by the cold. Maratse turned to look back at the bed. Whatever had been stuck on the wall above the door would have pointed right at it. There was a hole through the wall and Maratse opened the door to follow it. Four soft holes in the wood suggested something had been mounted on the outside. A sensor perhaps. But the cabin had no electricity, and it made no sense to have a sensor outside and a light within. The holes might have supported a battery box, with a lead to something inside. A camera, Maratse realised, would have a perfect view of the bed. But a battery box mounted outside the cabin would be drained by the cold. Maratse walked around the cabin, studying the walls, finding nothing.

He stopped in front of the door, lifted his foot to enter, and then paused. The snow was fresh but something had scratched at the surface to get at what lay beneath. Maratse brushed the snow to one side and revealed a patch of dark blood. He brushed more snow further from the door, until he was two metres from the cabin at the beginning of a trail. Maratse stopped brushing. He walked back to the cabin and picked up his rifle. The last of the oil burned as he left, plunging the cabin into darkness as Maratse picked up the trail and resumed the hunt.

The thump of the second hand on his watch diminished as he allowed thoughts of Petra to recede from his mind so that he might better concentrate on the trail of blood. It twisted around the rocks, was lost – black blood on black lichen – where the snow had been blown to one side, only to reappear beneath the frantic claw marks of hungry foxes. Maratse followed the trail up towards the ridge overlooking the glacier in the next fjord.

Was it seal blood or the blood of a man, he wondered. And why did the trail lead up the mountain to the ridge? There were no reindeer here, and if there were, if the hunter had dragged a reindeer to the cabin, there would have been fur pinched between the stiff flowers of lichen, or trapped between the sharp clefts of rocks and splintered boulders. The trail led Maratse across and around all these things, but upwards, up the mountain towards the ridge.

He stopped beneath a sharp rise and slid the smooth base of the shooting screen frame – two lengths of wood-like fat sledge runners – onto the snow. He tucked the rifle butt against a rock as he pulled on the ski mask and lifted the hood of his anorak. Maratse gripped the rifle and slid it slowly over the lip as he crawled behind it. He stopped when he was flat, lying still as he scanned the ridge, a thin plateau before the steep climb down to the fjord. The blood trail was exposed, a dark swathe leading across the top of the rocks. Maratse tucked his head behind the shooting screen and slid across the wind-smoothed snow.

Hi grandfather, his *ata*, would have smiled.

"Qilingatsaq?" he would ask. "What are you doing?"

"Shush, *ata*. I am hunting."

"The screen is for the ice."

"*Iiji*, I know."

"But you are on a mountain top, Qilingatsaq. There are no seals here. There are no bears. You cannot hunt here, Qilingatsaq. Not like this."

"Shush, *ata*, you do not understand."

"It is you who does not understand." His grandfather laughed. "I will call you David."

"Why?"

"Because it is a Danish name. You are hunting like a Dane, Qilingatsaq."

"No, *ata*, I am not hunting *like* a Dane, I am hunting *for* a Dane."

"Then stand up," he said, "because Danes don't hunt like this. They don't have the patience."

Maratse frowned as the voice of his grandfather brushed against the snow beneath his rifle. He let out a soft laugh as he pushed himself onto his knees, and then stood up. Petra didn't have time for him to be patient. Maratse cradled the rifle in his arms and jogged across the ridge to the other side. At the bottom of the mountainside, perhaps three hundred metres below Maratse, the sea ice fused with the land. Maratse followed the direction of the blood trail and saw a dark shape on the ice, with another one hundred metres from the land. He unlashed the rifle and left the screen and frame on a large black rock. He picked his way down the mountain, slipping the soft soles of his sealskin *kamikker* across the exposed rocks and through the pockets and pillows of snow, all the way to the ice foot.

He lifted the rifle to his shoulder and centred the sights on the middle of the dark shape. It was too far to see. He climbed over the ice foot and walked along the ice, shushing the soles of his feet across the surface with reckless impatience.

The blood from the cabin led here. There were answers here. Maratse was meant to come here. He knew this, and the body of the man splayed on the ice behind the snow scooter confirmed it.

Maratse stared at the entrance hole of the rifle bullet in the middle of Aksel Stein's forehead. But the bullet had not killed the man. Maratse leaned over him, saw the ragged knife wound in Aksel's stomach, and looked back up the mountainside towards the ridge, beneath which was the cabin. Aksel was naked, his clothes strewn across the ice, frozen in acts of escape, as the wind teased at the flaps before the snow hardened and secured the corners. It reminded Maratse of the scene at Petra's suicide spot and he wondered for a moment if that was significant. Was there something he should be considering, beyond the hunt for the Dane, now that the hunt was over? Was there a message hidden here? What was it? Who left it? Who was it for?

Maratse ignored the clothes and examined the snow scooter. He slung the rifle over his shoulder and opened the compartment beneath the seat. Maratse found a camera attached to a triangular mount beside a box with four screws, one in each corner. The camera battery was dead, and the box contained a battery pack that looked like it could be attached to a more robust supply of power, like a generator. There was an SD card inside the camera. Maratse thought about taking it, but he would need a computer, to see it, and the nearest computer was one night away by sledge.

His watch reminded him of moments passing, as the thump of the second hand grew stronger.

Petra was running out of time.

Maratse put the camera inside the seat compartment and closed it, securing the clasps to seal it from the snow. This was evidence, someone was meant to find it, he just wasn't sure it was meant to be him.

He was hungry, cold and tired. Maratse warmed up on the climb back up the mountainside. He picked up the shooting screen, carried it across the ridge and past the cabin. The interior was dark, the soap stone lamp extinguished, and the stars pricked at the night sky. Tinka was the first dog to react as Maratse crossed the ice to the team. He greeted her with a soft pinch of her ears before he walked to the sledge, pulled a chocolate bar from the sledge bag, and dug into his gear to find his mobile phone. He slipped a cold hand inside his sealskin smock and teased the slim battery for the mobile from a pocket Buuti had sewn inside the smock. He powered up the phone and cast a hopeful glance at the stars, that this area of Uummannaq might be blessed with good service. Two bars out of four were better than he had hoped. Maratse fumbled through the short list of contacts Petra had keyed into his phone and selected one of them.

"Karl," he said once the dial tone ended and a short brush of static crackled on the line. "I need your help."

Chapter 16

A stream of families and youth groups shushed past the cultural centre. Qitu watched them, stunned for the moment that he could hear the legs of their salopettes rubbing, the soft thuds of mittens on duvet jackets, and the occasional shriek of laughter as a father chased his young son, or a sister chased her brother. Children were having fun, on their way to the shopping centre to see Father Christmas. Qitu plucked his hearing aids out of his ears and pocketed them. He walked down the steps from the police station and turned right out of the parking area, following the broad, snowy road to the sea.

He sat on the bench beside the *qajaq*s. The statue of Sedna was coated in snow, and the little wall at the base of the statue did little to deter the tiny growlers of ice bumping at the sculpted mammals and fish swirling around her naked body, twisting into her hair, teasing her. Qitu pressed his hand to his mouth and stared through Sedna to a much darker place where another naked woman was twisted into positions he tried not to imagine. Gaba Alatak called him an accomplice, and even the most rational part of Qitu's mind couldn't convince Qitu otherwise. He *felt* responsible, as irrational as that may be.

Qitu pressed the tips of his shoes into the snow beneath the bench. He stared at Sedna, tried to plug into the mother of the sea as if she might have the answer. *Any* answer. He felt responsible for two women, and no matter what he might achieve with the publication of his article, he couldn't write fast enough. This would be an *expose* of the underground Greenland sex industry with international links. In reality, he had yet to write a single word. He knew that words alone wouldn't save Tertu, or the woman in the video. He needed facts, something to work with, to analyse and dissect for details, perhaps even a location. He could waste time looking for Tertu, or he could wait for her to come to him. In the meantime, he could make an effort to locate the woman in the video. He tasted bile at the thought, swallowed and stood up. Qitu took one last look at Sedna, and walked back towards the town centre.

He caught the bus to his apartment, packed a bag and picked up the charger for his phone. He emptied the cupboard of coffee, bread and noodles, took cheese and reindeer meat from the fridge. If Tertu was going to find him, he had to be in the office, for as long as it took the police to find the woman. He locked the door and caught the next bus on its loop back into town.

It was snowing, harder now than before. The road outside the NMG office was dark and empty, with only a handful of people visible through the window of the CrossFit gym. Qitu kicked the snow from his boots and opened the door.

He sent a text to Palu as he cooked the reindeer meat, slicing it into thin steaks and pressing it into the slices of white bread. He felt the incoming text vibrate through the counter and checked Palu's response. Qitu's mouth stretched forgotten muscles into a smile – his first since he had met Tertu in the café. Palu's text suggested that the Berndt Media Group had a very guilty conscience because of what happened in Berlin. His request for funds had been approved with the proviso that Qitu could link his expenditure to the investigation. He texted that he could, but wondered how he would document his spending, and if that documentation might put him behind bars.

There's no other way, he thought, as he carried his sandwich into the office and typed the password into his computer. He wondered for a second if he should have eaten, if it wasn't better to work on an empty stomach. Qitu pushed the sandwich to one side. Once he had created an account, bought two Bitcoins, and opened the TOR browser, he forgot all about being hungry.

The website contained a string of code that identified Qitu's screen capture software. A pop-up window over a blank screen advised him to turn it off before he continued. Qitu grabbed his mobile, plugged in the charger, and held it front of the screen. The image of the website flickered until the camera in his mobile compensated. Qitu taped his mobile to the arm of the desk lamp, clicked on the padlock covering the black dogfish video and entered the details required to transfer the payment. He paused before the final click, pressed his hand to his mouth and took a moment. He reasoned that it was necessary, that he had to do this. He was an investigative journalist, this was his assignment. The thought that exposure to such material might affect him crossed his mind. He snorted at such concern, reminding himself that he was in no danger, that it was the woman in the video who was suffering. Watching her didn't make him an accomplice. He would be abandoning her if he didn't. And it was not as if the police would be paying to view the content. They didn't have the budget.

Qitu confirmed the transaction with a click.

The padlock icon faded and the video window drifted to the edges of Qitu's screen. Living in a world with limited sound required an extra step to remember that it was available. Qitu reached for the hearing aids in his pocket and stopped. He swallowed, his tongue dry, as the camera zoomed in on the face of a woman, her long black hair taped to the sides of her head to reveal her face, as a gloved hand smeared thick lipstick across her lips and onto her cheeks. A cursor flashed in a live chat box beneath the image. Qitu read what was going to happen next. He grabbed the waste paper basket beneath the desk as the bile turned to vomit and he emptied his stomach.

Qitu clutched the basket to his chest and walked around the office, glancing at the top right corner of the screen to see how many minutes remained before the padlock returned and he was kicked off the session. He had two minutes. Another glance at the main image drew him closer to the screen as the camera shifted to focus on the woman's fingers. Her little finger was banded with three tattoos, just like Tertu's. The camera image wobbled as if the operator was pulling it closer. Qitu saw what looked like an industrial fish hook, bent straight, harpoon-like. He watched as it was dipped into a dark liquid and then something obscured the camera again as the man shifted his hands and Qitu saw a flash of white as someone tapped the hook into the joints between the woman's fingers. The image paused as the padlock faded into focus. The woman had three more bands on her fingers.

It was over, Qitu realised. At least it was for him. He clicked out of the TOR browser and checked his mobile. Qitu started the transfer of the video to his *MacBook* and then made coffee in the kitchen. Strong coffee. He pushed his hearing aids into his ears, waited for the coffee machine to finish spitting and spluttering, and then took the whole can and a mug into the office. Qitu drank two mugs of coffee while he waited.

He removed his hearing aids after the first minute of video. He closed the lid of his *MacBook*, took a breath and pulled out his notebook. He would start with the text, transcribing it onto paper before typing it up. Focusing on the text removed the intimacy. It read like a poorly-scripted porn movie, full of bad spellings, bad grammar and bad intentions. Qitu almost laughed at the child-like English language. Almost. He focused on the sound next, adjusting his hearing aids and tilting his head to one side to capture as much detail as possible. He filled his notepad with an audio description that turned the porn movie into a chilling horror film.

Qitu took a break, emptied his bladder, emptied the waste paper basket, made more coffee, cleaned the sink and started on the mould in the fridge.

"Stop," he said. "Just get it done."

He filled his coffee mug, wondered if he could muster a casual approach to watching the video – a professional objectivism, and then realised he couldn't. Qitu sat down and played the video for the third time, pulling his eyes away from the live chat to actually look at what was happening on screen.

Behind the lipstick, beneath the tears on her cheeks, the tic of muscles around her eyes, Qitu saw a face he recognised. He reached for his mobile, dropped it and bent down to pick it up. When he looked up he saw Sergeant Petra Jensen, her face pressed to the camera, and a dull distant look in her eyes.

This can't go on, he thought. *It has to stop.*

Qitu opened the thread of texts he had sent to Maratse and wrote one more. The urgency of each message increased from the first to the last. But it was hopeless, of course, even if Maratse looked at his mobile, even if he read his messages, where would he go? How would he find her? He read the last message one more time and pressed *send*.

PETRA IS ALIVE.

For the moment, at least. She had six bands on her fingers. Qitu looked at his hands. The thumbs had space for two bands each, and three on each finger. Petra had six bands already. If he filled a finger after each... Qitu struggled to find an adequate description. He settled on *session*. Petra had eight sessions left, before her hands were full and she was free.

But what kind of freedom? According to Gaba, the fingers of the dead teenager were fully banded. Loyalty was slavery and freedom was death. Petra was going to die.

Qitu closed the lid of his *MacBook* and stuffed it into his satchel. He pressed his notes into the sleeve in the back, and tucked his mobile into his pocket. He scribbled a note for Tertu and taped it to the office door on his way out.

He took the pedestrian street between the shops on his way to the police station, bumping shoulders with parents and dodging children. They carried paper bags full of sweets from Father Christmas, swapping treats and pressing toffees into their mouths as they walked. Qitu tucked his arm around his satchel and jostled his way to the side of the street. With his head down he didn't see Greenland's First Minister as she touched him on the arm. He recoiled into the wall of the supermarket and stumbled. Nivi Winther steadied him with her hand and he turned to look at her face.

"I'm sorry, Qitu. I startled you."

Qitu leaned against the wall and took a breath.

"Are you alright?"

"I'm alright," he said. "But..."

"What's wrong, Qitu? You look pale. Are you sick?"

"It's Petra."

"Petra Jensen? Yes, I know. I'm so sorry, Qitu. Did you know her well?"

"No, I mean..." Qitu stuttered.

How much did she know? he wondered. Did she have some kind of briefing from the Police Commissioner, or did she just read the police reports the following day? Qitu smoothed his jacket and repositioned his satchel, thinking of the consequences of bringing the First Minister into a police investigation. The image of Petra, lipstick smeared across her face, her fingers banded and bruised, the horror soundtrack and the immature grammar of torture and pain set his jaw and he made a decision.

"I am on my way to the police station," he said. "Petra is alive."

Chapter 17

They flew through the night. The SRU team was quiet. Peter tried to sleep. Atii cast furtive glances at Gaba as the team leader mulled over his responsibilities and tried to identify the parameters within which the mission success might be measured. Maratse had to be stopped, for his own protection. The Commissioner had been vague about how, but you don't send the SRU to talk softly. You send Gaba and his team to act – hard and fast, to respond to any given situation in which violence is likely. The SRU was trained to be flexible, disciplined, but effective. Maratse had been identified as a threat, a fact that no doubt pleased Simonsen who would feel vindicated at last. Uummannaq's Chief of Police was also in charge of the investigation, although Gaba retained operational command. But how would Maratse react?

He remembered working with Maratse in Nuuk a long time ago, years before the Tinka Winther case. Maratse was investigating a missing persons case, and Gaba just happened to have stumbled upon a person of interest in a drug bust. Petra was there too. She was just a Constable back then. She was the one to talk Maratse down when the suspect played hard to get. Maratse had a temper, or, rather, he had the potential for violence, if you pushed the right buttons. If Maratse had an idea who might have abducted Petra – if she had been abducted – then it was safe to assume that Maratse's buttons had been well and truly pressed.

If he was right, Gaba thought. *What then?* What was the appropriate SRU response? What was his own? Hadn't Gaba insinuated that he and Maratse could help each other, just as soon as Miki discovered a lead? Clearly, Maratse had leads of his own, and his own method of finding more. That was what was getting him into trouble and forcing Gaba and Maratse on a collision course.

Atii tapped his knee.

"Are you alright?"

"I'm fine, just thinking," he said.

"I met him you know."

"Maratse?"

"Yep, at the airport in Nuuk. Petra was meeting him there. She'd just broken up with you." Atii paused. "We weren't all that close, but I miss her, you know?"

Gaba nodded.

"Anyway, Maratse got off the plane. He was with Nivi Winther. I think she hired him."

"She did."

"Is he like a private investigator or something?"

"I think people want him to be," Gaba said. "But he doesn't solve things as such; they just seem to evolve around him. I think that's what bugs Simonsen so much."

"And now? Who's he working for?"

"No-one. And that's what makes him dangerous."

"So, we're going to stop him?"

"*Aap*," Gaba said. The decision was made. He would operate within the law, to the very letter of the law, and stop Maratse before he did something stupid. He owed Petra that at the very least.

"We're landing," Atii said. She turned in her seat, tightened the belt around her lap and took Gaba's hand.

"Constable?"

"Flying is alright," she said. "But I don't like landing. There's too many things that can go wrong. Like wind shear," she said, as the small twin-turboprop engines surged in the wake of a sudden gust, the tail end of a catabatic wind from the mountains above the gravel landing strip in Qaarsut.

She held Gaba's hand until they landed, and the pilot taxied the *King Air* to the airport building. Danielsen met them at the plane and helped them carry the gear to the back of the police car. He yawned as he climbed in behind the steering wheel.

"We're on a budget," he said. "So, I'm driving to Uummannaq. Don't fasten your seatbelts," he said and grinned. "There's a few leads opening up in the ice."

Gaba glanced at Atii.

"What?" she said.

"Leads in the ice? That's open water, Atii."

"So? We're in a car." She slapped Peter on the shoulder and dipped her head towards Gaba. "He thinks I'm scared."

Peter said nothing, but Gaba saw him fiddle with the seatbelt. *We need to* focus, he thought. The sooner they were briefed the better.

"Is Simonsen in the office?"

"He said I should take you to the hotel. He'll brief you first thing tomorrow."

"And Miki?"

"Waiting at the hotel."

Danielsen sped across the ice, slowing only at the spot where the leads had formed a ridge in the road as the plates of sea ice fused, cracked and froze in pressure ridges with the changing of the tides. He bumped the police car over the ridge and accelerated towards Uummannaq. Ten minutes later he parked outside the hotel. Miki helped them unload, and gave them the keys to their rooms.

"Get some rest," Gaba said, with a nod towards the stairs. He waved as Danielsen got into the car and then steered Miki into the dining room. "Catch me up," he said, and poured a cup of coffee.

"We still can't connect the two investigations," Miki said, as he sat down at a table by the window. The street lights turned the snow into the colour of brushed peaches. Teenagers walked in groups beneath the lights. They would be late for school the next morning, or they would sleep in class. Miki watched them pass.

"Miki?"

"Sorry," he said. "We picked up three people yesterday. A brother and sister from Uummannaq and a guy from Nuuk."

"Name?"

"Aaju Imiina. I don't know him. He's sleeping in one of the cells. The sister kicked him out of her bed."

"I'll talk to him tomorrow," Gaba said.

"Simonsen won't like that."

"Then you'll distract him."

"Sure." Miki nodded.

"What about Maratse?" Gaba almost said *Petra*, but he caught her name on his tongue before it slipped out.

"Sikkersoq, the sister, said something about a policeman beating up people at a party. Danielsen confirmed it with a phone call and was given a description that matched Maratse. We have the location of a cabin that Aksel Stein is known to use, and Simonsen has chartered a helicopter for first thing tomorrow morning. No expense spared."

"Good," Gaba said. "What do we know about Stein?"

"He has a history of abuse – alcohol and physical. His kids were taken away from him, twice, from two different partners. The oldest of the kids was the one Danielsen talked to. He's living in Aksel's house. He hasn't seen his dad in over a week. It's not unusual, apparently. And he didn't think to go looking for him. He doesn't want to see him when he's drunk."

"Anything else? Other vices we should know about?"

"There was some mention about boys, or young men, but nothing confirmed. We'd have to pick him up to find out. So..."

"Tomorrow. Sure."

Gaba walked across the room and returned with the coffee pot.

"What do you think about Maratse?" he asked, as he sat down.

"Do I think he's after Stein? Yes. Definitely."

"Should we let him?"

"Sir?"

"If Maratse is looking for Petra's killer, maybe we should just give him a chance. Turn a blind eye for a moment. What do you think?"

Miki twisted in his seat. He looked at the door for a second, and then back at Gaba.

"Is this a test?"

"Maybe." Gaba topped up his coffee.

"I don't know," Miki said. He glanced over his shoulder at the bar. "If you were asking me over a beer..."

"So, get a beer."

Miki drummed his fingers on the table. He looked at the bar and laughed.

"I don't need a beer," he said. "I would stop him, *before* he did something stupid. Petra wouldn't want him to do anything like that. We owe her."

"And if she's alive and he's onto something. Would you stop him then?"

"This is all hypothetical, right? I mean, Petra committed suicide."

"You really believe that? That Sergeant Jensen would crawl through the ice?"

Miki shook his head. "No."

"Neither do I. But I'm struggling with this, Miki. I need you to be the check and balance to my decisions these next few days. If we're in that position, and we can see – clearly, mind you – that Maratse knows something or has a lead that might lead to Petra, I need to know that if I look at you..."

"We stop him if we have to, Gaba. We do what's right."

Gaba made a fist and rapped his knuckles softly on the table.

"Okay," he said. "Now get some sleep."

"Yes, boss," Miki said. He paused at the bar on his way to the door. "Did I pass the test?"

"Sure," Gaba said.

Miki nodded and walked to the door, it creaked as he opened it. Gaba listened to him thump up the stairs. He finished his coffee and refilled the cup. He felt his mobile vibrate inside his pocket. He pulled it out and clicked on a new message. Kristian Møller was working late it seemed. Gaba called him.

"Yes?"

"Gaba?" Kristian said. "There's been a development. The journalist paid to access the video. He has made a positive identification of Sergeant Jensen."

"What?"

"The woman in the video. It's Petra Jensen. The First Minister has confirmed it too."

"Nivi Winther?"

"It's a long story. Apparently they bumped into one another and..."

"Kristian."

"Yeah, sorry. We've got ten minutes of video. Qitu recorded it on his phone. We're processing the audio for any clues as to location."

"What about the video?"

"It could be anywhere. It's too dark. The audio is our best bet. But the quality isn't great." Kristian paused. "He transcribed the chat messages. I can send them to you in a mail. The audio and video is too big to send with standard connection rates. You won't have broadband in Uummannaq."

"Send it to my mobile," Gaba said.

Petra is alive.

"You're sure? That's going to be expensive."

"Kristian, let's be clear about this, if you're not uploading it the second we're done talking..."

"I understand."

"What about the Commissioner?"

"He's on his way in."

Gaba thought about the *King Air*. The pilots said they were close to their maximum flying time. They would rest at Qaarsut. Gaba needed to keep them there if Kristian discovered the location and they needed to fly. He almost laughed. Of course they would need to fly. He had to keep the plane on the ground, just in case.

"Listen, you need to get the Commissioner to give us the plane. We have to have priority. No medical emergency take precedence. Not right now."

"I'm not sure..."

"Just give the Commissioner the message. He can work it out."

"Right."

"One last thing – you don't leave your desk."

Gaba ended the call and pushed his chair back. He grabbed his travel bag from the corridor and pounded up the stairs.

"Miki?" Gaba shouted, as he paused between the two wings of the hotel.

"What's up?"

"We're meeting in the dining room in five minutes. Get everyone downstairs."

Gaba brushed past Miki and opened the door to his room. He flung his bag on the bed and pulled the phone charger from the inside pocket. He stopped to take a breath. With little or no rest on the plane, the team was tired. But they needed to stay on top of this. He would brief them while the video uploaded to his mobile. A message from Kristian confirmed it was uploading, but the two bars of service on his phone suggested it was going to take some time. Time they could use to plan. Maratse just dodged a bullet, maybe even literally, as his status was de-prioritised. But then, if he was already on the trail of the man responsible for taking Petra, Gaba might have to split the team to find him. He searched for Simonsen's number in his list of contacts. It was time to wake up the Chief.

Chapter 18

Something was ticking. Petra could hear it, but it was far away. She tried to turn her head but a dull ache in the base of her skull stopped her. She tried to swallow, drawing her tongue to the centre of her mouth. It stopped in the middle, like a truck jamming the highway, wheels dry with raw rims, the tread of the tyres almost gone, the metal poking through the rubber, dull slivers of steel. The ticking continued, and then paused, only to start again. She could feel it now. A pricking on her fingers. Petra opened her eyes. Her eyelashes, thick and heavy, scratched against the blindfold. It was bright, and the light in the cabin pressed through the black cloth. She moved her eyes; saw the shape of something, *someone*, hunched over her arm. She could feel a weight pressing on her wrist and she knew it was him, that she was being marked, and she closed her eyes. Petra sighed at the thought of freedom, her soft breath, barely audible, pushed past her broken down tongue. He was marking her, counting down her freedom. If only she could see her hand, she would know she would soon be free, that he would let her go. He was the only one who could set her free. *No-one else.* Not even Maratse. She felt a twinge of something – anger perhaps. It tremored through her body and it turned the man's head.

He must be finished, she thought, as the ticking stopped and she heard the air rattle in his lungs as he took a breath before speaking.

"Petra," he said. "You're awake. Let me help you."

She felt his hands on her bare arms, a brush of something wet on her skin before he thumbed it away. It might have been ink. *Freedom*, she thought, as he helped her sit up.

"You're weak," he said. "I'm not surprised. That was a tough session. You are probably sore, all over. Let me find something to warm you up."

Petra listened to him clump across the floorboards. She drew her left hand to her body. It was free. She pulled it all the way to her lap. Then she tested the chain on her right hand. Petra almost laughed as she felt the rough scratch of the floorboards on her knuckles. There was no chain. She rested her palms in her lap, pressed the tips of her fingers into a light touch. Euphoric. That's how she felt. To feel one's own touch after so long. She would have smiled, if her bruised lips didn't hurt quite so much. She looked up at the sound of the man returning, and smiled at his shadow as he draped a thick blanket around her shoulders.

"Thank you," she whispered, her voice hoarse – that damn truck, parked in the way of everything.

"Do you want to see your hands?"

Petra's breath caught in her throat.

"Yes."

She understood that there were things after the pain, there was something after that. Her hands were free, and then it went dark as he leaned around her, his arms on each side of her head, rough fingers tugging at a thick knot of cotton that caught in her hair and pressed into her skull. Perhaps it was that causing her head to ache? Petra didn't know, but a second later she didn't care, as the knot loosened and the blindfold slipped over her face, tickled her nose and hung around her neck. She realised his face was not hidden and she dipped her head quickly, averting her eyes.

"You can look at me, Petra," he said. "You've earned that."

"Not yet," she whispered.

"Of course." He took a step backwards. "Your hands."

Petra started to shake; her breath lumped in her throat, pressing past her tongue from both sides, in and out, short breaths as she looked down at her fingers, saw the fresh pricks of blood and ink tracing the thin lines on her skin. She flattened her hands against her thighs, palms up. She gasped when she saw the bands on her fingers. All of them.

"Your thumbs," he said. "They are always tricky, so I left them 'til last."

"Last?"

"Yes, Petra. One last session, and you're free."

Petra felt a shiver grip her shoulders. It rippled down her arms and made her hands shake. She curved her back and lowered her head, felt her hair tickle her skin as it slipped from her shoulders. She tried to draw her knees up to her chest, but found that she ached in other places too, like her hips, as if they had been pressed. Her legs were sore. Her whole body was sore. It crumpled her, but he was there to help her. Somehow he helped her to her feet and they moved slowly, so slowly across the floor to a bed.

"I'm sorry," she said. "I'm so slow."

"It's okay," he said. "Let me help you."

The sheets on the bed were soft and warm, as if someone had just crawled out of it. She let him help her onto the bed, felt the blanket slip from her shoulders, and then he pulled the sheets over her body, tucking the edges around her neck. Petra slipped her hands up through the sheets and stared at her fingers as he draped the blanket on top of her.

"Tattoos are powerful things," he said, as he walked away from the bed and sorted things in the small kitchen area. "Symbolic. I only wish I was better at doing them. You deserve better. Of course, I'll get better over time."

Petra stared at her thumbs.

One more session. The last one.

"I was telling you about my friend. Do you remember? The one with the tattoos on her fingers. She had them done in Alaska and then more here at home." He filled a pan with water, splashed oil into a saucepan. He coughed for a moment and then continued. "She never said exactly what they meant, or what significance they had. That's part of the magic," he said, as he cracked two eggs into the pan. "You must be hungry. I have bacon too."

Petra heard him twist the cap off a carton of orange juice. He carried it over to her, stepping around the camera. She noticed the red light was on as he held the glass to her lips. She winced as the tart juice stung her lips, but it loosened her tongue.

"Better?"

"Yes," she said.

She looked into his eyes, a deep brown like her own. He had a strong jaw peppered with a light stubble, black like his thick brows and the neatly cut hair on his head. He smiled. Petra looked away as something started spitting on the hotplate.

"Eggs," he said. He placed the glass on the floor and thumped across the floorboards to save the eggs. The water started boiling and he slipped two more eggs into the pan. "I like to dip bread into mine," he said.

Petra saw him flick his head towards the window. The glass was hidden behind heavy curtains. She watched as he walked to the window, lifted one corner and peered out. The sky was dark but not black. Petra felt the midday twilight tug at her eyes, and she stared past him. She continued staring as he let the curtain fall and walked back to the kitchen area.

"I'm sure you'd like some fresh air," he said, as he lifted the pan to slide the eggs onto a plate. "But it's too dangerous right now."

"Dangerous?" Petra felt her skin tighten as she frowned.

"Yes. I need to do something before we can go outside."

"Will I be able to go out?" she asked. "When I am free?"

"Of course. Everything will be sorted by then." He turned and smiled at her. "Are you hungry?"

Petra apologised when she spilled the food on her chin. The fork shook in one hand and the plate wobbled in the other. It all felt so unfamiliar, as if she hadn't eaten before, or as though her body had forgotten how to move the fork from the plate to her mouth. He helped her again. She felt his light touch as he took the plate from her hand, cut the bacon and egg and bread into pieces, and lifted small forkfuls into her mouth.

"Thank you," she said, as she licked yolk from her swollen lips.

Her tongue, at least, was behaving. He smiled as he pressed the fork into the last mouthful. She saw him glance to one side, and followed his gaze to the camera. She felt her stomach cramp. Felt the food rise up to her mouth.

"Don't mind them," the man said. "They can wait. You need food. You need to sleep. And soon you will be free." The fork scratched across the plate as he chased an errant piece of bacon fat. "Open wide," he said. "Last piece."

He started coughing as she chewed, and suddenly the camera was forgotten. He was ill. She could see that. The bed shook as the cough took hold of him and he struggled for breath. Petra watched, eyes wide. He needed help. She could almost feel the joints of her fingers weep as the ink settled and mixed with the blood beneath her skin. Petra glanced at the camera, her body tense, and then the man stopped coughing, pressed his hand on the bed to steady his body, and she felt the press of his fingers on her leg.

"I'm alright," he said and smiled.

"What's wrong with you?"

"I have a cold. It might be the flu. I've been coughing for weeks. I sweat at night too," he said and twisted a corner of the bed sheet in his hand. "You can probably feel that. I'm sorry."

Petra knew what he had. A part of her brain clicked out of her body, removed itself from the cabin, the pain, the red light of the camera, and the bands of ink tapped into her fingers. He had tuberculosis. She was sure of it. He was sick, just like so many people in Greenland, especially in the settlements.

"You need help," she said.

"I'll be alright."

"No." Petra tried to straighten her back, but the pain in her stomach and her hips stopped her. *Why do I have to be so weak*, she thought.

"It's you we have to worry about," he said. "Sleep now. Get your strength back."

"What about you?"

"I'll be fine," he said. He wiped his hand across his mouth and frowned at the spot of blood on his skin. "Get some rest."

Petra lay back on the pillow and watched as he put the plates on the counter and crossed to the window. He lifted the curtain once more and she heard him curse. There was a soft crack, like wood tearing, and a dull thud that could have been something heavy pounding or flattening something. Petra had a strange thought of the neighbours throwing things into a skip, tidying up the house. The image blurred as she closed her eyes, ignored the pain in her stomach, and turned her head to one side, brushing her nose beneath the white sheets. White like the snow quilting the ice, and a figure somewhere in the distance, out of reach, fading. She heard the neighbours break another piece of wood and then let the mattress tug her body into sleep as she searched one last time for the figure in white.

What was his name?

Ataasinngorneq

MONDAY

Chapter 19

The hotel dining room buzzed with activity. Simonsen moved to one side as Danielsen bumped past him carrying a large flat-screen television. He watched the young Constable position the television on a table at one end of the room, pulling leads and power cables out of a shopping bag, as he hooked the screen up to a computer. Simonsen thought he recognised it.

"Is that my computer, Aqqa?"

"*Aap.* I took it from your desk."

"Why?"

"Because it's faster than mine."

"And the flat-screen? That looks like yours."

Aqqa grinned. "Don't tell my girlfriend?"

"What girlfriend?"

Danielsen winked and pulled another handful of cables out of the plastic bag. Simonsen wasn't finished. He took a step towards him and stopped when Gaba called his name.

"You're late," he said.

"I had to let Aaju out of his cell."

"You let him go?"

"We had nothing on him." Simonsen waved his hand at the activity in the dining room. "What's all this?"

"This is the situation room," Gaba said. "Your police station is too small."

"And this is too public and expensive," Simonsen said, as the hotel owner held the door of the kitchen open for a member of staff carrying a tray of refreshments to the table. "I don't have the budget for this."

"Relax. Nuuk is paying."

"Because of a video?"

"Because Petra is in the video, Chief." Gaba pointed at Danielsen. "Once we've got the screen up we'll run it through there. There's about seven minutes before it downloads."

"And Maratse?"

"Was right. Petra's not dead."

"If he was so sure, then why the hell did he arrange a funeral?"

Gaba sighed. "I would have done the same," he said. "Just to get you and everyone else off my back."

"It was a distraction. He knows more than he's saying. He might even be involved somehow."

"You don't believe that, Chief."

"No," Simonsen said. "But we need results. This," he said and gestured at the SRU officers helping Danielsen hook up the computer, "is all very elaborate. You'll have the whole town looking through the windows."

"Listen, Chief. I don't care about how this looks. Petra is out there somewhere, alive and in trouble. The only *result* I'm interested in right now is her safe recovery. If that means we let Maratse run rampage through the settlements. Fine. So be it. If it means he busts a few heads in the process. I can live with that. But I won't let you slow this down because of how it looks. I have tactical command for situations like this. Are we clear?"

Simonsen glanced at Miki as he hovered by Gaba's side. He saw the start-up screen of his computer blink onto Aqqa's flat-screen television, just as the kitchen staff set up the breakfast buffet. He patted the pockets of his jacket and found his cigarettes, sticking one between his lips as he tapped his lighter against his thigh.

"Just remember, I've chartered a helicopter. Whatever happens here, I'm sending Aqqa to Aksel's cabin and I want your team with him. It's the one lead we've got, and whatever else you discover in this situation room of yours, is secondary to the cabin."

"Unless new evidence..."

"If you can confirm a location from the video, the chopper's yours, Sergeant. We're clear on that."

"Thank you," Gaba said. He nodded at Miki.

"The video has downloaded. We're ready to see it."

"And you can run it through the Chief's computer?"

"It's on your Micro SD card and Aqqa has an adapter. We're good to go, boss."

"Alright." Gaba took a breath. "Let's do it."

Simonsen caught the kitchen staff loitering by the buffet bar and waved them into the kitchen. He locked the door to the dining room and cursed the lack of curtains.

"We're ready," Aqqa said and he gestured for Simonsen to join them.

The six police officers stood in a semicircle around the flat-screen, obscuring the image from anyone looking through the windows from the street below, and blocking the view from the kitchen if a curious member of staff looked through the tiny square of glass set in the door.

"There's no sound," Danielsen said. "I forgot the speakers."

"That's alright, Constable," Gaba said. "Just play it as soon as you're ready."

As the image clicked onto the screen, the only sound in the dining room was the whir of the computer fan and a series of low gasps between them as the image of Petra flickered into focus.

"Motherfucker," Gaba whispered.

Simonsen felt the cigarette fall from his lips as the camera captured images of Sergeant Petra Jensen and the shadow of a man twisting and pulling her in different directions with different implements like a deranged puppeteer, cavorting to some demonic dirge that only he could hear.

"Chief," Danielsen said, and then again, louder. "Chief."

"What?" Simonsen pulled away from the screen and looked at the young Constable.

"Your phone."

Simonsen heard it then, and pulled the phone from his pocket. He caught Gaba's eye and then walked away from the screen. Simonsen unlocked the dining room door and took the call outside.

"Simonsen," he said, as he took in a breath of cold air outside the hotel entrance.

"You need to come."

"Who is this?"

"You need to come to the dock, now, Chief."

The caller hung up and Simonsen jogged to the car. He glanced at the hotel as he backed onto the road. He wasn't sure he could cope with much more of the video, and Gaba knew how to reach him. Simonsen looked at his watch, saw that there was a little less than an hour before they had to be at the heliport, and then drove to the docks.

A man wearing the plastic overalls they used in the fish factory waved as Simonsen drove onto the dockside. Simonsen slowed and wound down the window as the man pointed at one of two trawlers moored at the dock. The hull was frozen into the ice.

"Hurry," the man said.

Simonsen drove along the dock and parked beside the second

trawler, the one moored at the very edge of the dock. There were people on the deck, more men wearing factory overalls. A single woman was among them, hugging one of the men. She looked up as Simonsen climbed over the railings, pointing with one hand as she cradled the man's head with the other.

"Up there," she said.

Simonsen looked up, following the shrouds up the trawler's mast until he saw the body of a woman, neck bent, hanging from the last rung of the ladder welded to the mast. Simonsen cursed as he recognised the face of Oline Erngsen, her blue cheeks and enlarged eyes shone stiffly in the glare of the sodium lights mounted on the cabin. Simonsen knew then who the woman from the factory was consoling. He crossed the deck and laid a hand on Anton's shoulder.

"Come on, Anton," he said. "Let's get you inside." Simonsen stepped back as the woman guided Anton across the trawler deck. "Put him in my car," he said. "And stay with him."

Simonsen waited until he heard the click of the car door opening and shutting, before asking the three men from the factory to help him cut Oline down. Once they had her body on the deck, one of the men covered her with a tarpaulin as Simonsen called the hospital. His next call was to Gaba.

"I've got a suicide here, down by the docks," he said. "I'm going to be a while." He paused for a second. "You okay?"

The crackle of static on the line did little to disguise the rage in Gaba's voice, and Simonsen was impressed by the Sergeant's control.

"It's going to take some time," Gaba said. "Atii said she will stay and look at the video. I can't watch it again."

"I understand."

"I'll take Miki and Peter with Aqqa on the helicopter. But I'm sending Miki by himself to Marmoralik."

"The mine? Why?"

"We had another call since you left. The security guard at the mine said there was a polar bear busting into the huts. The guard was scared to go outside. So, we'll fly to the cabin and Miki can pick us up on the way back from the mine." Gaba paused. "I don't want to waste any time, Chief. The sooner we investigate the cabin, the sooner we can get back to work on the video. If we learn anything new at the cabin, it might open up some leads. We need to act on them as fast as possible."

"Okay," Simonsen said. "Keep me informed."

He ended the call and slipped his mobile into his pocket, just as a snow scooter slowed at the harbour entrance. Simonsen waved as he recognised Karl Nielsen from Inussuk. *Maratse's neighbour*, he recalled. Karl stopped on the ice below the deck of the trawler and Simonsen called down to him.

"Have you spoken to Maratse recently?" he asked.

"*Naamik.*"

"Have you seen him?"

"Not since the funeral."

"And you would tell me if you had?"

"Sure."

"Okay." Simonsen waved, as Karl accelerated away between the hulls of the smaller fishing boats frozen at their moorings.

He watched as Karl powered up the ramp onto the island and then drove along the road, past the hotel, until he lost sight of him up the hill between the Nukissiorfiit utility company local offices and the hospital. Once Karl was out of sight, Simonsen saw the ambulance leave the hospital. He walked back across the deck to hear the details surrounding Oline's death. Simonsen was pretty sure he knew why she had chosen to take her own life.

The hospital porter doubled as the ambulance driver. Simonsen helped him coordinate the men from the factory to lift Oline's body onto a stretcher. They carried her off the trawler to the back of the ambulance – a small transit van with a medical bag tucked beneath the driver's seat. One of the factory workers removed the tarpaulin. It crackled between his fingers as the porter draped a blanket over Oline's upper body.

"I'll be right along," Simonsen said, with a nod to the porter. He waited until the ambulance had turned and then opened the back seat of the police car. Simonsen climbed in beside Anton and took the man's hand. "I'm sorry," he said. "Do you want to go to the hospital?"

Anton shook his head. "Take me to my sister's."

"Okay."

Simonsen thanked the woman from the factory and then drove Anton along the docks and through the town. There was nothing Anton could do for Oline, but at least he could be with family, those he had left. Simonsen struggled to link the different pieces of the puzzle surrounding Salik's murder and Petra's disappearance, but however they were linked – *if* they were linked at all – events were taking their toll on the people of Uummannaq. These were his people, his responsibility and they needed a break, a lead, anything to bring this to a close, and they needed it soon.

The tyres crunched into the drift of snow outside Anton's sister's house. Simonsen got out of the car, helped Anton out of the back seat, and supported him by the arm as they walked to the front door. He turned his head at the sound of a snow scooter braking as it came down the hill. It was Karl with a passenger. Simonsen wasn't sure, but in the few seconds it took for Karl to pass him, he thought he recognised the passenger as Natsi Hermansen.

Chapter 20

Maratse checked the dogs' feet, teasing clumps of ice from between their toes, running his fingers along the harnesses, frowning at the areas that had frayed a little and inspecting them closely as he clamped each dog between his knees and smoothed the ice from their canine beards when he was done with them. But the distractions didn't help; he couldn't erase Qitu's messages from his mind, especially the last one, the one that said Piitalaat was alive. Knowing it instead of just believing it, didn't make the waiting any easier, or the thudding of the second hand on his wrist any softer. Things were moving too slowly, and when the leads ended in dead ends and dead bodies, Maratse knew he couldn't continue without something stronger to work on.

He looked up at the sound of Karl's snow scooter approaching the old school house in Uummannatsiaq. Maratse waited by the dogs as Karl bumped the snow scooter from the ice to the land and stopped beside the schoolhouse. Karl told his passenger to wait inside, glancing at the hulk of an older snow scooter as he walked across the snow to shake Maratse's hand.

"He's a distant relation," Karl said, as he lit a cigarette. "The police raided his house. He knows people, David, but I don't think he'll tell you anything."

"We'll see."

"He's suspicious."

"*Iiji,*" Maratse said. He saw the young man stare at him from the schoolhouse window. "Did you take his mobile?"

"*Aap.*"

"Without a fuss?"

"Natsi is the son of my second cousin. He's scared I will tell his mother the truth about what he does for money."

"Scared enough to help me?"

"I don't know," Karl said. He blew a cloud of smoke from his lungs, noticing that Natsi had moved away from the window. "I think he's more frightened of the man who murdered Salik."

"Qitu thinks there is a connection."

"Who?"

"A journalist in Nuuk. Here," Maratse said, as he handed Karl his mobile.

"David," Karl said, as Maratse walked towards the schoolhouse. "What are you going to do?"

"Wait here."

"Maybe I should help."

The snow crunched beneath his boots as Karl took a step forwards. Maratse stopped him with a flat palm. He patted the older man softly on the chest.

"Stay here. Enjoy your cigarette. This won't take long."

Maratse let go of Karl and walked away.

"How do you know it won't take long?"

Maratse said nothing. He kicked the snow from his *kamikker* and stepped inside. The lantern lit the white walls with a flickering glow, casting shadows between the dark beams above the eating area of the kitchen. The tables had been pushed to one side. Maratse looked at Natsi as the young man perched at the end of a table, tapping the ends of his fingers as Maratse removed his mittens and tossed them onto the table opposite Natsi. He removed his anorak and the sealskin beneath it.

"It's warm in here," he said, as he rolled up the sleeves of his thermal top.

"No, man, it isn't," Natsi said.

"Man?"

"Yeah, *man*. You think you're some kind of hunter? Is that it? My dad's a hunter. The bastard."

"What's his name?" Maratse asked. He crossed the stone floor to the kitchen and picked up the dog whip from the counter. "Your father," he said. "What is his name?"

Natsi watched as Maratse coiled the whip into his fist. The sealskin cord was as wide as his thumb at the end that was bound tightly to a wooden shaft the length of Maratse's forearm. The cord tapered gradually over the six metre length until it was the same breadth and depth as the tip of his little finger.

"Why do you want to know?" Natsi swallowed as Maratse took a step towards him.

"Maybe I know him."

"I don't think so."

"Tell me anyway."

"No, man. I won't tell you anything."

Maratse dipped his head for a second as he gripped the coil and the first fist length of the shaft. The table creaked as Natsi took a step backwards.

"I'll call Karl."

"Karl is my friend."

Natsi slid along the table towards the door.

"He'll call the police if you touch me."

"I am the police," Maratse said.

"What?"

"Retired," he said, as he struck Natsi across the side of his face with the wooden shaft. Natsi fell to the floor and Maratse pinned him there as he looped a length of sealskin cord around both of Natsi's wrists. He cinched them tight, tossed the whip to one side of the room, and pulled the sealskin cord through an iron fitting bolted to the wall. Maratse dragged Natsi across the floor, tied the cord in a knot, and then pulled the cord attached to the opposite wall, stretching Natsi until he was on his knees, with his arms stretched tight. Natsi hunched forward with his shoulders just higher than his neck.

"Are you gonna hurt me, *man*?"

Maratse picked up the dog whip and placed it on the counter.

"There's nothing you can do to me that he hasn't done already." Natsi laughed as Maratse reacted to the word *he*. "You heard me. Salik had it coming. It was just sex for him, but the man – he wanted more. Salik should've known. He should've listened. Maybe he wouldn't be dead. Stupid, dumb *qaleralik*." Natsi spat. "I had nothing to say to the police. I've got nothing to say to you."

Natsi twisted at the sound of the door opening.

"Karl," Maratse said. "Please leave."

Karl shook his head.

"I was thinking about it. I need to see this, if I am going to look his mother in the eye."

"You have to get out, Karl."

"Yeah, *old* man," Natsi said. "This party isn't for you. You don't have the stomach for it." He glared at Maratse. "And neither does he."

Maratse leaned over the counter and reached for a plastic bag. He placed it beside the whip. He ignored Natsi as he lifted a metal bucket of water from the kitchen floor and put it in front of Natsi.

"You're going to waterboard me, man?"

"You know what that is?"

"I've seen the movies. I'm not ignorant."

"Okay," Maratse said. He turned his back on Natsi and pulled the snow scooter battery from the bag. He put it on the floor next to the bucket of water and fiddled with two leads which he attached to the battery contacts. A spark flashed brighter than the lantern light, shining in Natsi's eyes and the young man paled.

"Hey," he said. His voice crackled and he coughed to clear it.

"You've seen the movies, Natsi," Maratse said. "So, you know what I am going to do with this, and the water. Right?" Maratse glanced at Karl. "You're sure you want to stay?"

Karl nodded.

Maratse kneeled in front of Natsi and gripped his chin. He pressed his face to within a few fingers of Natsi's face.

"I have a friend. She's in trouble," he said. Maratse tugged Natsi's chin and forced him to look at the battery and the water. "I would do anything to find her. I think your friend knows where she is. So, you're going to tell me where I can find him, or..."

"I can't tell you," Natsi whispered.

Maratse let go of Natsi's chin and stood up. He took a step back and peeled off his thermal top. He tossed it onto the table and picked up one of the lanterns. He held it close to his body and shone the light over his chest. Natsi stared at him. He swallowed as Karl let out a soft gasp.

"A Chinese man did this," Maratse said, as he traced the large blistered welts on his skin with his finger. "He used metal paddles with wooden handles. He had a generator. It was fast. The pain was intense, but quicker." Maratse lowered the lantern. He shined the light on the water and the battery. "This will take a lot longer."

Maratse lowered the lantern to the stone floor and kneeled again. He looked at Natsi as he picked up the leads and struck the ends to create another spark. There was a ladle in the bucket. Maratse filled it with water and splashed it over Natsi's head.

"David, wait," Karl said, as Maratse picked up the leads.

"I'm sorry, Karl. I don't think you'll be able to look in his mother's eyes."

"Wait," Natsi said.

"But we can start with the eyes," Maratse said. "Left or right, Natsi?"

"His name is Jaqqa Ujarneq," Natsi said. The water dribbled through his greasy hair. It spluttered from his lips as he spoke. "He's at the mine. He's always at the mine. That's where we go."

"What mine?" Maratse dipped the ladle into the water and lifted it.

"Marmoralik. The marble mine."

"He's there now?"

"*Aap.*"

"You're sure?"

"Yes, I'm sure."

Maratse tossed the ladle into the bucket and reached for his thermal top. He grabbed the dog whip from the counter and stepped over the cord securing Natsi's arm, stopping to pull on his sealskin.

"I'm coming with you," Karl said.

"*Eeqqi,*" Maratse said, as he pulled the anorak over his head. "But I need your snow scooter."

"What about the police?"

"Give me two hours, and then call them. You can take him back on the sledge."

"Two hours? What about Petra?"

"If he's there, he'll hear the helicopter. He'll kill her before they land."

"You don't know that."

"I can't risk it."

Maratse pressed the whip into Karl's hand and opened the door. Karl ran after him. He stopped by the snow scooter as Maratse slung his rifle over his chest and pulled a broad knife from beneath a cord on the sledge. He slid the knife between the bungee straps Karl had added to the snow scooter and climbed on.

"You were never going to hurt him," Karl said. "Were you?"

Maratse looked him in the eye as he turned the key in the ignition. The engine growled, belching a small cloud of smoke into the snow behind it.

"Not with a bucket of water and a scooter battery," Maratse said.

"But if he hadn't talked?"

"I would have used my bare hands," he said. Maratse revved the engine, pulled his ski mask over his head and nodded at Karl. "Two hours," he said.

Karl stepped back as the snow scooter lurched forwards. He

watched Maratse until he reached the ice, and, losing sight of him as the snow scooter sped around the point of Uummannatsiaq, Karl turned back towards the schoolhouse, lit a cigarette and sat on the bench beside the front door and pictured Maratse tearing across the ice as he smoked. He wished he had made him promise to call or text if he needed help. Karl swore as he patted his pockets and realised Maratse had forgotten his mobile.

"Forgotten?" Karl whispered. "I wonder?"

It seemed unlikely. The more he got to know the retired Constable, the more he realised that despite his quiet and slow manner, there was little that Maratse forgot. The man was an enigma, and a thorn in the side of Uummannaq's Chief of Police. Despite all that had happened since Maratse had arrived in Inussuk, Karl liked his new neighbour.

He turned his head at a shout from Natsi. The thought crossed his mind that he could untie him.

"Two hours," he said, and lit another cigarette.

Chapter 21

The helicopter flared on the ridge above the cabin, the skids pressing into the snow covering the rocks as Gaba yanked the side door open and leaped out. Atii followed, with Danielsen and Peter jumping out of the other side. Miki waved from his seat next to the pilot and then the red Air Greenland Bell 212 lifted off in a white tempest, filling the folds and creases of the police officers' jackets and trousers with snow. Gaba waited until the snow had settled and the thunder of the rotor blades receded, before issuing his orders.

"Danielsen and Peter, I want you to work your way down to the ice," he said and pointed at the dark shape they had seen from the helicopter. "Atii and I will take the cabin. I want status updates on the radio every five minutes. Use your mobiles if there is interference." He gestured at the mountains. "The helicopter will be back in about thirty minutes. I want us on it within two hours."

Gaba waited for Danielsen to lead Peter down the mountainside, and then tapped Atii on the shoulder. He nodded as she tucked the MP5 into her shoulder and moved ten metres to his right. Despite the terrain she stuck to the distance as if they were connected with a length of elastic. Impressed, he nodded once and then worked his way off the ridge towards the cabin. The midday twilight gave plenty of light, enough to see that the cabin looked empty, with little sign of recent activity in the snow around it, other than a regular scuff of snow revealing old blood beneath it. Gaba stopped to inspect the first two scuffs. Despite the light layer of wind-blown snow covering it, he could see that it had been cleared with something about the size of his hand. Someone wearing mittens, perhaps. Atii scanned the area around the cabin as Gaba crouched by the blood. Someone had followed the trail either to or from the cabin.

"Maratse," he whispered.

A sudden gust of wind pressed beneath the lip of his ballistic helmet. Gaba tightened the straps, tugged the thin fleece hat beneath the helmet over his ears and waved for Atii to continue.

"Approaching the cabin," he said with a click of the radio attached to the shoulder of his bulletproof vest.

Atii moved in close, pressing her left hand on Gaba's shoulder as she aimed around him. Gaba opened the door, raised his MP5 and stepped quickly through the door frame. Atii followed, covering the right of the cabin as Gaba covered the left.

"Clear," she said.

"Clear." Gaba lowered his MP5 and let it hang on the strap cinched around his chest.

He tugged the small LED torch from his belt and lit the cabin with a powerful beam of light. Atii did the same. Starting from the ceiling, they searched the walls, the shelves, the furniture and the floor without taking another step. When Gaba saw something of interest on the floor he shone his light at it and Atii moved closer to investigate.

"Fish hooks and coloured thread," she said.

"Like on the boy's body."

"Sir?"

Atii's professionalism, regardless of their relationship, brought a thin smile to Gaba's face. Coupled with her skill with the MP5 and the way she crossed the terrain and entered the cabin, Gaba decided she was a serious contender for Miki's role as his number two. *A little professional competition within the SRU is no bad thing*, he thought.

"Salik had fish hooks with coloured threads in the skin on his back." He pointed at the dust and ash beneath the stove with the beam of his torch. "If this is Aksel's cabin, or if he was here, we have a link to Salik's death right there."

Atii lit the mattress with her torch and pointed. "Condoms," she said. "Used."

"But not much else," Gaba said.

"Gaba?" Peter's voice crackled through the radio.

"Go ahead."

"We've found Aksel's body. Danielsen has identified him."

"Dead?"

"A rifle bullet in the head. He's naked. His clothes have been tossed around the ice. Danielsen says it looks just like Sergeant Jensen's crime scene. The place where she committed suicide."

"Supposedly."

"*Aap.*"

"Okay. Start documenting the scene. Oh, and Peter?"

"*Aap.*"

"Tell Danielsen to call it in to the Chief."

Gaba pulled out his phone and started taking pictures of the cabin interior. Atii did the same, starting with the hooks and thread, the condoms, even the magazines on the shelves. Gaba pulled on a pair of thin plastic gloves and collected the fish hooks into a clear plastic bag. He tucked it into the chest pocket of his vest, and found another bag for the condoms.

"If this was Aksel and Salik's love nest," he said, as he sealed the condoms inside the evidence bag, "we can start joining the dots."

"What about Aksel? The rifle bullet in his head..."

"Could be Maratse's. He's mirrored what happened to Petra."

"You mean Aksel did that to Petra?" Atii pointed at the condoms as Gaba secured the bag inside another pocket. "It doesn't make sense, if Aksel was screwing Salik. Why would he take Petra?"

"Danielsen said they found photos on Salik's computer. I want you to look at them when we get back. Compare them with this place," Gaba said. He checked the signal on his phone and swore. "How's your phone?"

"No service."

"Miki was supposed to call." Gaba pressed the transmit button on his radio. "Peter, any word from Miki?"

"He's at the mine. He was just about to meet with the security guard. The helicopter is on its way back." Peter paused. "I think I can hear it."

"Right. Tidy up the scene and cover the body. You can't carry it up the mountain. Simonsen can arrange to have it picked up later." Gaba nodded at Atii. "We're leaving."

They moved quickly through the snow to the ridge above the cabin, sheltering just beneath the ridge as the helicopter landed. Their breath clouded the interior of the helicopter as they waited for Danielsen and Peter to return from the ice.

"Did you see the bear?" Gaba asked the pilot.

"We did a circle of the mine. Saw some damage to some of the huts. Your officer..."

"Miki."

"Right. He said to leave him there. The security guard had a rifle. He said they would be fine."

Gaba nodded and then opened the door for Danielsen and Peter. The pilot started the engines, and the helicopter whined and shuddered into life. The view through the windows was obscured in a cloud of white needles until the pilot took off and they escaped the snow on the mountain. Normally, Gaba might have enjoyed the view of the moonlight lighting the snowy peaks of the mountains. He would have looked as the pilot pointed out the coloured houses and buildings of the settlement of Saattut, or marvelled at the way the twin peaks of Uummannaq mountain really did look heart-shaped, just before the helicopter slowed to a hover above the landing pad. But the job wasn't done, they hadn't found Petra, and the one man they wanted to question was dead.

Convenient, he thought, as the pilot settled the helicopter on the landing pad and shut down the engines. Gaba was the first out of the door, striding across the pad towards Simonsen and the police car parked at the heliport gates.

"Aksel is dead," Gaba said, as he tossed his helmet and vest into the boot of the police car.

"How?"

"Rifle bullet to the head. Danielsen has the photos. You'll need to pick up the body."

"Later," Simonsen said. He watched as Danielsen and the SRU officers removed their helmets. "You're corrupting my Constable, Sergeant," he said, with a nod at Danielsen. "Don't fill his head with gung ho SRU delusions. I need him here."

Gaba shrugged and climbed into the passenger seat. He started giving orders as soon as everyone was inside and Simonsen pulled away from the gates.

"Danielsen and Atii, I want you to go through all the photos. Peter will start processing the physical evidence."

"Lucky for you," Atii said and thumped Peter on the arm.

"I'll check in with Nuuk."

"No need," Simonsen said, as he slowed to a stop outside the hotel. "Your tech guy called. They've processed the video, the audio. About the only thing linking the video to Greenland is Sergeant Jensen." Simonsen turned off the engine. "She's still alive," he said. "The Commissioner has agreed to buy another ten minutes of video, but he's waiting for confirmation from Denmark. The tech team there is also on the case." Simonsen paused and looked at his watch. "The media have got wind of the story. There's a press conference scheduled for about twenty minutes from now."

"Press conference?" Gaba said, as he got out of the car.

"Live. Together with the First Minister. I've got a television set up in the dining room."

Gaba excused himself as his team sorted the gear and Danielsen briefed Simonsen on what they had found on the ice. He heard Simonsen curse as he pounded up the stairs to his room. Gaba realised he didn't care if Maratse had killed Aksel, what bothered him, what really pissed him off, was the thought that Maratse knew something, and that he was withholding information that could help them find Petra.

"Why?" he said, as he stared into the bathroom mirror.

Gaba called Miki, frowning as the call was diverted to voicemail. He finished up in the bathroom and joined the team in the dining room just as the *KNR* news anchor announced the start of the press conference. Gaba recognised the line-up, with Nivi Winther standing beside the Commissioner and Malik Uutaaq.

"What's he doing there?"

"He's pegged for a ministerial post," Simonsen said with a shrug. "I don't understand either."

"Who's the girl standing next to Qitu? The one with the pink hair?"

"No idea."

Gaba listened as the Commissioner explained the situation concerning the disappearance of Sergeant Petra Jensen. He fielded questions regarding her supposed suicide, before deferring to the First Minister. She introduced Qitu and talked about an ongoing investigation into an underground culture of sex and violence. Then she beckoned Qitu to the microphone.

"Gaba," Atii said.

"In a minute."

"You'll want to see this now," she said and placed a hand on his arm.

"See what?" Gaba followed Atii to where Danielsen sat at the computer.

"These are the photos from Salik's computer." Atii tapped the screen. "This is the window in the photos. We've cleaned it up as best we can. Do you see the line stretching from one side to the other?"

"Yes."

"It's on all of the photos. The same window. The line is too thick to be a washing line, or a rope. It looks more like a cable."

"At an angle?"

"*Aap.*" Atii waited as Simonsen joined them. "These are Salik's photos. We're pretty sure he was involved in some kind of extreme sex or violent acts. They need somewhere private for that."

"Like the cabin," Gaba said and leaned closer to the screen.

"*Aap*. But there's only one window in Aksel's cabin, and no cable outside."

"There's all kinds of cables and wires in the settlements," Danielsen said. "On boats and hanging from cranes."

"In Nuuk too," Atii said.

"But they usually hang straight down," Danielsen said. "This one is at an angle. It looks like it is pretty far away, but it's still thick."

"Tell me what it is, Constable." Gaba rapped the table with his knuckle.

"I think it's the cable for a cable car," he said. "And if it's in this area, then there's only one place it can be."

"Marmoralik mine," Simonsen said.

Gaba swore and pulled out his mobile. "We need the helicopter," he said with a look at Simonsen. He swore again when he heard the voicemail message on Miki's phone.

"Just a second," Simonsen said. "Even if Salik and friends were at the mine, how do we know Sergeant Jensen might be there?"

"It's deserted in the winter," Danielsen said. "There's just one guard for the whole winter. He lives there."

"Do we have a name?"

"Jaqqa Ujarneq."

"What?" Simonsen said, as Karl walked into the dining room.

"The guard's name is Jaqqa. He's at the mine now. Maratse told me to tell you."

"Maratse?" Simonsen gripped the back of Danielsen's chair.

"And where is Maratse now?" Gaba said.

"He's on his way to the mine." Karl looked at his watch. "He should be there by now."

"And so is Miki," Gaba said. He clicked his fingers at Peter. "Gear up," he said. "Everyone, now."

Chapter 22

The plates in the sink rattled and the walls of the cabin shook. Petra rubbed at her eyes and stared around the room. The grey light behind the curtains drew her out of the bed and she wrapped the sheet around her as she walked across the floor. The rattling increased as a familiar *thud thud thud* triggered a rush of adrenalin through her body. It spread like fire to her fingertips, the ink bands in the joints of her fingers pulsed with energy and, for the moment at least, she ignored the ache in her hips, the sore patches of skin and the stiffness in her muscles. She pressed warm fingers to her lips and almost smiled at the touch. Petra drew back the curtain and saw the big red helicopter descend to the landing pad. She struggled to take it all in – the helicopter, the cabins, and the tube-like metal cab hanging from a thick cable. The orange paint on the cab was blistered like her lips.

The helicopter's blades thundered just beyond the cabins. Petra looked around the room for her clothes – any clothes. She considered running out in the sheet, but anything more than a walk turned the warmth in her body to fiery needles, slowing her down. Perhaps the helicopter would wait? But the rattling of the plates increased as did the pitch of the rotor blades, as the Air Greenland helicopter lifted up and away from the landing pad. She glimpsed the bottom of it as it passed the window.

Petra gripped the window sill, pressed her head against the cool pane of glass, and felt the adrenaline seep out of her body. She started to shake as her body chilled. She should have run to the helicopter.

I can't. My legs, my muscles, everything hurts.

She should have tried at least while she had the chance.

Petra felt the sheet slip from her shoulders. She grabbed at it, caught a corner in her fingers, and winced as a broken nail was tangled in the threads. And then her knees buckled and she slid down the wall to the floor, her hand slipping from the windowsill, as the distant roar of the helicopter diminished and she was alone again.

But I'm not alone, she thought.

Her body shook with a sudden rush of fear.

Did he leave on the helicopter? Was she alone? And what about them?

What if the man left her alone with them, the ones who forced him to do what he did to her? If she was truly alone, then who would stop them? Who would set her free?

"He promised," she whispered, as she looked at her banded fingers. Petra clenched one fist and thumped it softly against the wall. "He promised."

She looked back at the bed; saw the camera on its tripod and the glow of the screen pointing towards her, the lens fixed on the mattress. They were still here, watching, forcing him to do the things that hurt. Would he hurt her if they didn't tell him to?

"No," she whispered. "He's sick. And now he's gone."

The air between the cabins sank in the wake of the helicopter, and, as it settled, the wind began to chatter, gusting shouts at the glass, brushing words against the cabin walls. Petra pressed her ear against the wall, catching her hair in the flecks and splinters in the wood. The wooden wall amplified the voices until she could understand the words, Danish with the occasional Greenlandic exclamation.

"It was over there."

Petra's heart spasmed with an extra beat at the sound of *his* voice. *He's still here*, she thought.

"Just stand still for a minute. Let it come to us."

The second voice was familiar, but distant, as if she knew it once, but couldn't place it. And then it was gone, hidden beneath a bestial huffing and the crash of metal. An oil drum, perhaps? Petra reached for the windowsill and pulled herself onto her knees. The energy she felt when the noise from the helicopter had tugged her out of bed had been sapped with the roller coaster emotions of abandonment and fear. But the voices, two of them, gave her just enough energy to peer out through the window, past the ice flowers decorating the inside of the glass. Petra scraped at the flowers, pressing a film of ice beneath her broken fingernails. She made a hole, enough for one eye to see the space between the cabins, the man with a hunting rifle in his hands, and a second man, wearing black. Her brow creased as she tried to process a burst of familiarity – there was something about his jacket, the black trousers, and black boots. She knew this man. Not as well as some, but enough to realise he was important. He could help her.

"Hey," she said. She cleared her throat and tried again, a spot of blood bursting beneath the scab on her lips as she tried to shout. "Hey."

Petra tried to knock on the window. If felt loud in the confines of the cabin, but not loud enough to compete with the huffing of the beast and the shouts of the men. She saw it then, a large bear, ranging towards the man in black. She shuddered at the *crack crack* of the weapon in the man's hand. She saw the burst of orange flame from the barrel. Petra heard the bear roar. And then there were more cracks, and a loud bang. She saw a puff of smoke cling to the air around *his* head. She heard the other man's voice.

"Wait there," he said.

Petra watched him walk towards the bear, the gun in his hands tucked tight into his shoulder, the muzzle pointing at the bear lying on the ground, its creamy fur striped with deep red blood, like rust. Petra heard the snick of the rifle as *he* worked the bolt and aimed at the bear. He was helping the other man, she was sure of it. And then he pulled the trigger and the man in black slumped onto the bear.

Petra couldn't breathe. She didn't feel the frost on the window cooling her fingers, or the soft scratch of the sheet as it slipped from her shoulders. She watched him walk towards the man in black and drag his body off the top of the bear. Then she saw him struggle, lifting the bear's head with one hand as he tried to drag the man in black beneath it, just his head, so that when he let go of the bear, its jaw covered the dead man's head. The man pointed the rifle at the bear's head, adjusted the angle, and then fired again. Then he turned towards the cabin, fiddling with something he had strapped to his head as he slung the rifle over his shoulder and walked towards the cabin. Petra heard him kick the snow from his boots and then he opened the door.

"You're up," he said, as he leaned the rifle against the wall and removed his outer clothes. "I thought you were going to sleep all day."

Petra clung to the wall. She watched him as he removed the camera from the strap around his head and placed it on the counter in the kitchen area. He filled the kettle with water, watching her as it bubbled and spat. Petra said nothing. She didn't move. She just watched him. The man made two mugs of tea. He placed one in front of her and then drew up a chair. He nodded towards the window.

"You saw what happened?" He sipped his tea. "It's okay," he said. "Tragic, really, but that's what they wanted." He turned to point at the camera on the counter. "It's a GoPro camera. High Definition but no sound." He shrugged. "It's probably best without the sound. They'll have to use their imagination."

"Who was he?"

"Him? He was a policeman, Petra. Oh," he said, nodding his head. "Perhaps you knew him. I don't know his name. I just called and asked for help with the bear. Of course, I could have killed it with the rifle, but since working with you, well... I realised there is a lot of money to be made when working with the police. So, I asked for help." He rested his arms on his knees and warmed his hands around the mug. "Now, I admit, it's a little risky. Bit of a game changer, but the game has to change if we want to make the big bucks, as they say."

"I don't understand."

"Of course not. Um, let me think," he said, and paused. "Things are moving quite fast, and you'll soon be free." He pointed at her hands. "And as we've only got a short time together now, I may as well explain a few things. First, just so we're clear, I never realised how much people hate the police. I mean, they," he said, and pointed at the camera on the tripod, "they want to see people like you get hurt. They'll pay for it. I've got enough money put aside now for a good long time. But, now we have to step things up a gear. We have to move fast."

He sipped his tea, watching Petra over the rim, his eyes flicking from her hair to her shoulders, to her bare chest, her skin cooling, goose bumping.

"It won't be long before they come," he said. "They'll see that it was an accident, that the bear attacked that poor policeman and that I tried my best to kill the bear, but I missed." He held up two fingers. "Twice. It is tragic and there will be consequences. I'll be charged of course, but..." He shrugged. "A fine. Manslaughter at the very worst. But we have to clear up all this," he said with a wave that took in the whole room.

He coughed, pressed the back of his hand to his mouth, and looked at the blood speckling his skin. Petra shivered as she watched him.

"It's TB," he said. "I didn't know Salik was sick." The man sighed as he wiped the blood from his hand on his trousers. He pulled a coloured thread from his pocket and twisted it around his finger. "He's free now, though, Salik. I thought I loved him. You know what I mean? It's complicated, but I had to let him go. It became too personal, too much to handle. It's so much easier with you," he said. "Of course, I should thank you too. Without you I wouldn't have been able to set Salik free."

Petra wrapped her arms around her chest and pressed her fingers into her skin. She tried to stop the shivering, tried to control her tongue, to form the words, to ask about her freedom. The man smiled, as if he knew what she wanted to ask.

"It's all planned," he said. "Every detail. Do you want to hear it?"

"Yes," Petra whispered.

"Well," he said and stood up. He walked to the camera and turned it off. He opened a packet of batteries and replaced the dead ones in the camera as he talked. "It's genius really, but to start from the beginning. I took you from Uummannaq. Do you remember? You travelled with Salik on the sledge."

Petra caught the image of the young man, his face pressed against hers beneath the tarpaulin.

"You see, Salik died. Very sad, very unfortunate, but fact. I knew people had seen me with Salik, but they didn't know he had been with someone else too. An old man," he said and sneered. "They thought I didn't know, but I know everything. I even filmed it. Not for money, you understand. I filmed it because I had to. It was all part of the plan. I left the camera with the old man's body. He's free too. Do you see? I freed Salik, and I freed the old man. But you have freed me, because you gave me the chance to walk away."

"How?"

He picked up the GoPro camera and sat down, replacing the batteries as he talked. "I was in town the day the old man – Aksel – had a run-in with your friend, the retired policeman. What was his name?"

Petra tried to remember. The shivering stopped as a deeper cold settled on her body, pressing her into the floor as she realised she had lost time, had forgotten things, she had forgotten him. But the cold grip seemed to squeeze a new resolve from sudden hidden depths, and she saw him again, all in white, just the eyes – those soft brown eyes – she could see them, and she knew his name.

"David," she said.

"That's right. Constable David Maratse." The man laughed.

"When I heard about their confrontation, I knew Maratse would not forget Aksel. And then it all clicked into place. Once Salik was free, I took you because I knew your Maratse would come looking for you, and that he would start with Aksel. With the video and those awful fish hooks, well... the police are so predictable. They will link Salik's death with Aksel. When they find Aksel's body, they will assume Maratse killed him – an act of revenge, you see. For you." He paused to close the camera case. "Now, we really must hurry, because I have heard that your friend has discovered where you are."

Petra pressed her hand over her mouth. The shivering stopped.

"Oh," he said. "That pleases you? Well, that's good. Of course, the poor policeman outside, he is insurance, you see. When I heard the bear I realised I had another play to make. Maratse will come looking for you; the police will come looking for their colleague." He stood up and walked to the bed. He lifted the mattress and pulled out a ski suit, socks and a hat. "I can see some of the details puzzle you," he said, as he dumped the clothes on the floor beside Petra. "The bullet in Aksel's brain isn't from just any rifle. Do you know Karl? I took his rifle last week and returned it when I was finished with it. Maratse's rifle is old and I knew he would borrow Karl's. So, the evidence is planted, along with the motive. Now we just have to see who comes first? Maratse or the police. But you'd better get dressed. We have to go into the mine. It's time to set you free."

Chapter 23

Maratse turned off the engine and let the snow scooter drift to a halt on the sea ice, two hundred metres from Marmoralik mine. He stepped off the snow scooter and felt the wind beat at his anorak. It was nothing compared to the wind blasting his cheeks on the ride across the fjord. He pressed his fingers around his face, felt the hard skin, the flesh solid to his touch. Maratse lifted the seat, wrapped a wire around the battery and bound it around the handle next to the start switch. He removed the rubber grip with his knife. Once he was finished, he studied the living quarters, the mess hall, the satellite dish and the office buildings clustered around the base of the mine, right beside the helicopter landing pad. It had passed him as he sped across the fjord. He had seen it again on its return, just ten minutes later. He was curious as to who might have visited the mine, concerned that they might cause problems. The second hand thumped from his watch into his wrist. He took it off and fastened it around the handlebars of the snow scooter. Time was of little consequence now. He had arrived, and now he had to act.

Maratse tugged the rifle from his chest and worked a bullet into the chamber. He left his mittens on the seat of the snow scooter and tugged the silk ski mask onto his forehead, like a hat. Maratse crossed his arms, hugging the rifle to his chest as he walked across the ice towards the rocks below the mine.

Close to the rocky shore the ice was soft, and Maratse slowed to pick a dry route onto the land. He skipped onto a small floe of ice bobbing in the water, and then further onto the land, holding the rifle in one hand as he grasped a pointed rock with the other. He paused for a moment, studied the light and wondered if he should wait until it was dark. A quick glance at the halogen lamps scattered around the buildings suggested it wouldn't matter either way. If Jaqqa decided to turn them on.

Jaqqa. He had a name but no history, no motive. But none of that mattered. This man had Piitalaat. He was sure of it. It had to be right; this had to be the place. She had to be here. He felt the weight of the rifle in his hands and wondered what he would do if she wasn't. Could he live without her? Would he even try?

"No time for that" he said and climbed up the rocks to the accommodation block.

The area was flat, blasted smooth with rubble around the perimeter. The cabins linked with insulated wires and pipes. Empty oil drums covered in dents and rust – the ubiquitous gargoyles of the High Arctic – gathered in groups, or stood alone, beside cabins. The oil drums peopled the deserted mine with stoic figures, some painted, others naked, bitten into splinters by the frost and the wind, shadows of the last human activity before the onset of winter. Maratse worked his way around the cabins, until he saw the bear.

Maratse paused at the sight of it, saw the body – head tucked beneath the bear's jaw – and scanned the surrounding buildings. The windows were dusted and flowered with ice. No witnesses. No-one watching. Maratse walked to the bear and kneeled beside the body. He shoved the bear's head to one side and sighed as he recognised Miki, the young SRU officer. Maratse wasn't much for riddles or games. He preferred the more straightforward cases – someone missing and needing to be found, an opportunistic but typically dumb robbery, even a drunken brawl. But this, like the body of Aksel on the ice, naked with clothes strewn to all sides, it suggested a plan of sorts. A scheme within which he had a part to play; and he had to play by rules that he didn't understand, rules that changed the minute Jaqqa had taken Piitalaat. He must have known that. And if he didn't then, he must surely know now.

The bark and shudder of a large diesel generator startled Maratse away from the bear and Miki's body, as he moved behind an oil drum and scanned the buildings for movement.

Nothing.

Only the generator, and then the grind of a large cable around a drum. An orange capsule, like a small bus without wheels, swung into view as it rose up from behind the cabins and ticked along the wire towards the dock bolted to the mountainside above the camp. There were two faces in the windows. Maratse ignored the man, and focused on the woman instead.

"Piitalaat," he said and stood up.

She pressed a small hand against the window as the man gripped her by the hair and lifted her head. Maratse saw the barrel of a rifle pressed into the soft skin beneath her chin. He held his breath until the cable car stopped at the dock above, and Jaqqa forced Petra onto the rocks leading into the entrance of the mine. Maratse started to pick a route between the rocks, wondering if he could climb so high, if his legs would finally give up the charade of overcoming his previous injuries, and simply quit working on the rocks, failing him and failing Petra.

Maratse slung the rifle around his chest and jogged to the rock face. He stopped at the sound of the cable car lurching away from the dock with a metallic thud, ticking down the cable towards the camp. It was part of the game, Maratse realised. The grander scheme. Jaqqa wanted him to play his part.

Maratse waited for the empty cable car to swing to a stop and opened the door. He gripped the handle, pausing for a moment at the sound of something beating against the wind, somewhere in the distance, beyond the fjord. It could have been a helicopter. If Karl had given his message, then it was probably the police. If Miki was here, then the chances of Gaba and his team being on the helicopter was high.

I should wait, he thought. But the next thought was of Petra and Maratse closed the door.

Jaqqa had left a trail from the cable car dock leading into the mine. If it hadn't been for the sight of Petra, Maratse might have stopped to consider what it meant, what Jaqqa intended to do. Maratse ignored the fish hooks hammered into the wooden rails. The brightly coloured threads twisted in the wind, losing momentum and colour, sapped of energy the closer Maratse got to the entrance of the mine. The air inside the mine was denser, it lay thick in the entrance, like treacle tugging at Maratse's *kamikker*, and clinging to the thick hairs of his polar bear skin trousers. Maratse peered into the mine, found a long thread attached to the last of the hooks and teased it between his fingers as he followed it inside.

"I knew you would come." Jaqqa's voice echoed around the walls.

"Why?"

"It was just a matter of time."

"Hm," Maratse said, as he followed the thread deeper into the mine.

"We've been waiting for you," Jaqqa said. "And now you're here."

Maratse reached the end of the thread. He stopped as it slipped through his fingers. Something clicked to his right and then a powerful beam blinded him as Jaqqa turned on the interior lights.

"Welcome to Marmoralik," Jaqqa said, his voice loud, theatrical, the words echoing up the walls, curving around the low ceiling. "Smile for the camera, Constable Maratse."

Maratse crumpled to the rocky floor as a bullet slammed into his thigh. The boom of the rifle repeated like a machine gun, but only one bullet hit Maratse. The polar bear hairs of his trousers turned crimson in the harsh light and he winced at the pain. It was deep, but Petra's scream went deeper still, lancing through his body like a harpoon, the tip breaking off as she drew another breath. Maratse shielded his eyes and scrabbled on the floor for his rifle.

"Self-defence," Jaqqa said. "That's what they'll say. You were armed. You rushed to attack me, while I tried to defend this young woman, to protect her from you."

"What about Miki?"

"Who's Miki?"

"The policeman you shot by the bear," Maratse said.

"More self-defence. An unfortunate accident. I have it all on film. Step closer Maratse. I want to show you something."

Maratse stumbled towards the light, with slow steps. They reminded him of that time, after the Chinaman, when he had forced himself to walk, and Petra had taught him to live again. She was here. She was alive. Just past the lights.

But Petra wasn't behind the lights, she was above them.

Maratse used the rifle as a crutch and looked up at a small gantry. He could see Petra's feet, he could almost reach them. Her hands were tied, her mouth gagged. Jaqqa stood beside her on the gantry, one hand on the railing and the other tugging the noose above Petra's head.

"We faked it last time," he said. "This time it should be real."

"I don't understand," Maratse said.

"No? Look at her fingers. I'm going to set her free."

There was blood on Petra's thumbs, dark, like ink.

"And if you look over there," Jaqqa said and pointed to a second gantry. "Look at the camera. I left an iPad at the entrance; it's all connected to a satellite phone. Expensive, but don't worry, it's all covered. I remember someone once said you have to make as much money as you can, when you can. Well, the time is now, Maratse. And this is the end. You might think I am a demon, but I'm just a storyteller. My viewers – they gave me the script, they told me what to do." Jaqqa coughed. He wiped the blood from his hand on Petra's ski suit. "Petra knows that. She understands."

"Piitalaat," Maratse said, as he caught her eye. He lowered his rifle. "It's going to be okay."

Petra's eyes, wide and black in the dark, stared back at Maratse. Her feet twitched as Jaqqa tugged at the noose, her socks sliding on the gantry's wooden plank.

"It's touching, of course, but it's all part of the plan." Jaqqa nodded at the camera. "It's a real cliffhanger, if you'll pardon the pun."

"I'm going to help you, Piitalaat."

"Oh, I'm counting on it," Jaqqa said. "As soon as I let her go." He kissed Petra on the cheek and brushed the hair from her eyes. "You really were wonderful to work with. *Qujanaq*," he said, and pushed her over the edge.

Maratse slipped as he leaped, cursing the wound in his leg as he gripped Petra's legs, pressed his hands beneath her heels and lifted her feet. She twisted above him, bumping against the side of the gantry, fingers splayed, mouth open. Petra gasped as the noose tightened and Maratse stumbled beneath her. Jaqqa hovered in front of them. He steadied the GoPro camera on his head as he circled them, laughing once as he retreated down the mine towards the entrance.

Maratse grunted with the pain from his leg and the weight of Petra above him. It wasn't her bodyweight that he struggled with; it was the thought of letting go, of losing her that bore down on him.

"I won't let go," he said. "Not ever."

His leg twitched with the effort, and Maratse began to wonder just how deep the wound was. Was this how it would end? Petra hanging at the end of a rope as Maratse bled to death beneath her?

"You are free," Jaqqa shouted from the mine entrance. "Both of you."

Chapter 24

The slow moving high pressure air beneath the rotor blades of the helicopter pushed the aircraft into the faster, low pressure air above, as Gaba clicked the microphone on his headset and read the email on his phone to his team. The pilot dipped the helicopter's nose and increased speed towards the mine at Marmoralik.

"Jaqqa Ujarneq," Gaba said, "is twenty-eight years old. He was born in Denmark. Lived most of his life just outside Copenhagen. He moved back to Greenland two years ago. His circle of friends in Denmark includes a hacker and others known to the police. The tech teams in Nuuk and Denmark believe Jaqqa may have had help from his hacker friend, and other associates, to set up and access the tech needed to stream and sell his videos." Gaba slipped his phone into his pocket. "Honestly, we don't care about that. We know he is an evil son-of-a-bitch and we are going to take him down today. The email from Nuuk suggested he has some mental health issues which make it difficult for him to empathise with people." He turned in the co-pilot's seat to look at Atii, Peter and Danielsen sitting on the seats behind the cockpit. "Let's be clear about this. There's no sympathy or empathy from us today. We find Petra and then we take him down. He stays alive until she is found. If we plug him, I don't care if we have to set up an on-the-spot blood transfusion, he stays alive. As long as he can talk then he can tell us where she is. We'll let the detectives in Nuuk find out the rest. Are we clear?"

"Clear," Atii said.

Peter nodded.

"Danielsen?" Gaba tapped him on the knee. "You understand?"

"*Aap.*"

"Simonsen didn't want you to come. He thinks you're easily impressed by this," Gaba said with a wave at the two heavily-armed and armoured SRU officers sitting either side of Danielsen. "He thinks we might be a bad influence. Is he right?"

"Yes, Sergeant."

"Good," Gaba said and smiled.

"What about Miki?" Atii asked. "We haven't heard from him."

"I know," Gaba said. "Something's not right. What I said before, about keeping Jaqqa alive – obviously, that applies to Miki too."

"Two minutes," the pilot said.

"Peter, you're our medic. Danielsen stays with you."

"Got it."

"Atii?"

"*Aap?*"

"You're on point. I'll be right behind you. According to the map we've got thirty buildings to search. That will take time. We stack-up outside each building, Atii first, me second, Peter third, and Danielsen stays outside. Every time. Same procedure. Each building."

Gaba paused as the pilot turned into a slow circle above the mine. Atii was the first to spot the polar bear and the dark shape partly obscured beneath it. She called it out and pointed.

"Over there," the pilot said. "The cable car is moving."

"There's a man inside," Peter said.

"Put us down now," Gaba said, as he unbuckled his seat belt. "New plan," he said, with a quick look at his team. "Move fast to the cable car and surround it."

"What about Miki?" Atii asked. "That could be him under the bear."

"Danielsen checks him on the way, the rest of us move, move move."

Gaba opened the door as Atii and Peter slid open the side doors. The helicopter skids barely kissed the ice on the landing pad as Gaba leaped out and ran up the narrow road towards the cable car. He heard Atii's light step to his right, and the heavier pounding of Peter's boots behind him. Gaba ran right past the bear and the body beneath it. That was Danielsen's responsibility. The rest of the team had only one objective: secure the cable car and the occupants before they could get out, or start the return journey back to the mine.

"On the ground," Gaba shouted as a man opened the sliding door of the cable car. "Now," he said, as he slowed, MP5 extended, the sling taut, and the sights trained on a man with a small camera strapped to his head.

"I give up," the man said.

"Jaqqa Ujarneq?"

"Yes."

"Get on the ground." Gaba closed the gap, circling Jaqqa as he walked towards the cable car. "Atii?"

"Got him," she said, as she slammed her knees into Jaqqa's back.

Peter covered her with his MP5 as Gaba entered the cable car.

"He's secure," he said, as Gaba came out again.

"Get him up."

Jaqqa grunted as Atii and Peter pulled him onto his knees. Atii gripped the ties binding his hands behind his back and lifted his arms, forcing Jaqqa to swear as Gaba stood in front of him and gripped him by the chin. Gaba waited until Danielsen joined them. He swore when Danielsen nodded.

"It's Miki," he said.

Atii swore and gripped Jaqqa's hair, pulling back his head as Gaba leaned closer.

"Jaqqa Ujarneq," Gaba said. "Where is Sergeant Petra Jensen?"

"Aren't you going to arrest me?" Jaqqa asked. "Don't you have to look at your watch and say the time, and..." he paused to cough and Gaba let go of his chin and stepped back as Jaqqa spat a stream of blood onto the snow. "You have to arrest me."

"Why?" Atii asked.

"Then I'll be in your custody."

"You already are," she said.

Jaqqa twisted to look at her. "You have to make it official."

"Jaqqa Ujarneq," Gaba said.

"Yes?"

Gaba raised his hand and slapped Jaqqa across the mouth, splitting Jaqqa's lip and smearing blood on his glove. Gaba made a show of looking at his watch. "The time is 16:34, and you are under arrest for the kidnapping and torture of a police officer, amongst many, many other things."

"What things?"

Gaba hit him again. He pressed his fingers around Jaqqa's throat and lifted him onto his feet, turning him to look down the short road to the landing pad.

"That man," he said and pointed at Miki, "was a good friend of mine. You had something to do with his death. I'll find that out later. Right now, you're going to tell me where Petra is."

"You're too late."

"No," Gaba said. "That's not the right answer." He kicked Jaqqa's knees and dropped him to the ground. Gaba shifted his grip to Jaqqa's hair and pulled his head back. "Try again."

"I said you're too late. She'll be dead already. They both will."

"Who?"

"Maratse and your Sergeant. They're in the mine."

"Peter," Gaba said, as he kicked Jaqqa onto the ground. "Watch him."

Atii and Danielsen followed Gaba into the cable car. Gaba pushed the button to climb back up the mountain as Danielsen closed the door.

"Miki?" he asked.

"He was shot twice. Once through the bear. Maybe the bear caught him by surprise?"

"Unlikely." Gaba tapped his leg. "Come on, come on."

Atii was the first out of the cable car. Gaba and Danielsen ran after her, faster when they heard her shout. Gaba watched her climb the gantry and ordered Danielsen to help her as he ran to Maratse. He was at least a head taller than the retired Constable, and he gripped Petra's legs, shoving them straight up as Maratse slumped against him.

"Cut her down, Atii," Gaba shouted.

He looked up at Petra, saw the gag in her mouth. Her hair covered her eyes. He couldn't see if they were open.

"We have to pull her up," Danielsen said.

"Do it." Gaba lifted her feet, pushing her soles above his head as Danielsen and Atii pulled her up and over the side of the gantry. "Status?"

"Unconscious. We've got a pulse. Slow, thready," Atii said. "She's breathing."

Gaba sank to his knees and gripped Maratse by the shoulder. "She's breathing," he said. "She's okay."

"*Iiji.*"

"What about you?"

"I'm okay."

"You're bleeding." Gaba lay Maratse down and inspected the blood pooling in the hairs of the polar bear skin trousers. He pulled a folding knife from his utility belt. "I have to take a look," he said.

"*Eeqqi,*" Maratse said, and placed a hand on Gaba's arm. "Buuti will kill me."

"She can blame me," Gaba said, and grinned.

Maratse lay down as Gaba slipped the tip of the knife into the hole torn by the bullet. He cut a patch in the trousers and tossed the bloody patch of bearskin to one side.

"Piitalaat?" Maratse said.

"She's alright," Gaba said. "We'll get her down in a second." He looked up at the gantry. "I need some bandages," he said.

"Danielsen," Atii said, as she removed the noose from Petra's neck. "Bandages in the back of my vest."

Gaba caught the bandages from Danielsen and continued to cut away at the trousers. When he could see the entry and exit wound, he rolled Maratse onto his side, pressed the dressing over the wound and bound it tight.

"We'll get a stretcher. Danielsen will stay with you."

"I can walk," Maratse said.

"I know you can, but..."

"I'll walk."

Gaba nodded. "You're a stubborn bastard."

"*Iiji.*"

"Rest for a minute. I'm going to help them with Petra."

The ladder to the top of the gantry was thin with rusted rungs. Gaba climbed halfway as Danielsen and Atii lowered Petra into his arms. She was lighter than he remembered, thinner, her skin bruised, black in places. Gaba gripped her body with one arm, and with her head over his shoulder, he climbed down the ladder. Maratse helped him at the bottom, peeling Petra from Gaba's arms as he lowered her onto the ground. Gaba stepped back as Maratse pulled Petra onto his lap, brushed the hair from her face, and kissed her brow. She opened her eyes at his touch, jerked her hand up his chest and splayed her fingers on his cheek.

"Piitalaat," Maratse whispered. "I'm going to take you home."

"Yes," she said.

Gaba nodded for Danielsen and Atii to step to one side.

"We're going to need photos," he said. "Once we get them to the helicopter, I need you both to stay here. Document everything."

"You're taking them back on the same chopper with him?" Atii whispered. "With Jaqqa?"

"No," Gaba said. "I think we can stretch Simonsen's budget just a little more. Besides," he said with a firm twist of his jaw. "I can talk to Jaqqa while they fly back."

"Do you have him?" Maratse said. Gaba hesitated as Maratse looked at him. "Gaba?"

"Yes," he said. "We have him."

Maratse looked at Atii. "Will you stay with her?"

"Of course," she said, as Maratse helped Petra into Atii's arms.

"David?" Petra said. "You can't leave me."

"It's okay, Piitalaat. I won't be long."

"What are you going to do?"

"Don't think about it, Petra," he said. Maratse raised his arm and Gaba pulled him to his feet.

He looked at Petra as he found his balance and then stumbled across the rocky floor to pick up his rifle.

"Maratse," Gaba said. "This isn't a good idea."

Gaba swore and followed Maratse as he slung the rifle over his shoulder and took slow steps towards the cable car.

"We have him in custody," Gaba said. "He'll be tried, and convicted. We have plenty of evidence. Hey, listen to me." Gaba gripped Maratse by the shoulder as they reached the cable car dock. "He'll get life. That's fifteen years, minimum."

"He doesn't deserve life," Maratse said.

"Stop."

"You're going to stop me?" Maratse looked Gaba in the eye.

"I can't let you do it. You're a police officer."

"I'm retired." Maratse brushed free of Gaba's grip and stepped inside the cable car.

Chapter 25

Maratse gripped the handrail as the cable car reduced speed to a slow swing above the dock at the camp. He nodded as Gaba took his arm and guided him over the gap between the car and the wooden dock. Maratse took small steps towards a figure kneeling on the ground.

"Peter," Gaba said, as he walked around Maratse. "Take the car back up, and help them bring Petra down."

"Sure," he said with a glance at Maratse.

Maratse ignored him, concentrating on one measured step after another until he stood in front of Jaqqa.

"You're alive," Jaqqa said, as he lifted his head.

"And you're free to go," Maratse said.

"No." Jaqqa twisted on the ground. He frowned at Gaba as the SRU Sergeant pulled out his knife and cut the plastic ties binding his wrists.

"They're not pressing charges," he said.

"But I'm in your custody."

"Not anymore, you're free to go." Gaba closed the knife and waved as Peter watched from the cable car.

The clank and loud tick of the cable turning in the drums made it difficult to talk. Maratse stared at Jaqqa until the drums slowed and the sound stopped. The cable car had reached the entrance to the mine. It would be returning soon. Petra would be with them. Maratse nodded at Gaba.

"Now," he said.

"Now *what?*" Jaqqa rose to his feet.

"It's time for you to go."

"Go where? On the helicopter?"

Gaba shook his head. "That's for Sergeant Jensen. You'll have to make other arrangements."

He leaned to one side and stared out onto the frozen fjord. Almost black against the ice, the snow scooter cast a shadow in the moonlight. It was just visible. Jaqqa looked in the same direction. When Maratse slipped his fingers around the sling of his rifle, he started to run. Gaba waited until he was past the first building before he spoke.

"Did you kill Aksel?"

"*Eeqqi.*"

"I didn't think so. There was a video camera. We haven't seen much, but Salik was in it."

Maratse worked the bolt of the rifle to check the bullet in the chamber. When he looked up Jaqqa was scrambling down the rocks. He watched him leap onto the ice. Maratse took a slow, painful step forwards.

"You'll never catch him," Gaba said.

"Maybe not."

"And you know it's life if you do. Who will look after Petra?"

"So long as he lives," Maratse said, "she'll never recover."

"So, you're doing this for her?"

"*Iiji.*"

Gaba sighed. "I'll have to arrest you."

"Call Simonsen," Maratse said. He almost smiled. "He'd like that."

"We'll see," Gaba said. He flicked his finger towards the ice. "How good a shot are you? He's almost at the snow scooter."

Maratse shrugged and took another painful step forwards. Jaqqa slowed as he reached the snow scooter. Maratse leaned against the last building in the camp before the rocks and the ice. He caught his breath as Jaqqa slid his leg over the seat and sat down.

"Christ, Maratse," Gaba said, as he ran to the building. "Show me the keys or shoot him. I can't let him get away."

"Just watch," Maratse said, as he lowered the rifle.

There was no cry, or scream, Jaqqa said nothing as his body flipped backwards off the snow scooter as a short burst of lightning blazed into his body.

"Wait here," Maratse said, as he stumbled down the rocks and onto the ice. He walked around the softer ice, winding a longer route to the snow scooter than the one he had taken on the way in. He heard the cable car start its descent as he closed the distance between him and Jaqqa.

"What did you do?" Jaqqa said, as Maratse leaned against the back of the snow scooter.

"I once knew a Chinaman," Maratse said. "He liked electricity and did some things to me that I'd like to forget. But I see the scars in the mirror, feel them in my legs, and remember them in my dreams." Maratse grimaced as he shifted his weight from one leg to the other.

"Why are you telling me this?" Jaqqa said.

"Because the hardest thing for me is not the scars, not even the pain, it's wondering if he will ever do it again. As long as he is alive, there is that chance. I can't let that happen to Piitalaat. Do you understand?"

"You're not going to let me go, are you?"

"*Eeqqi*," Maratse said and shook his head.

Maratse and Jaqqa turned at the sound of shouting in the camp. Someone had found the switch to turn on the halogen lights. The buildings reflected the light onto the snow between them, and the light from the lamps closest to the ice caught the reflective stripes of Petra's ski suit as she slipped down the rocks and splashed through the water at the edge of the ice. Maratse started towards her, stopping as he saw Gaba leap onto the ice and pull Petra into his arms. She kicked at him, her heels thumping softly on his shins as she jabbed at his vest with her elbows.

"David," she screamed. "Don't, David."

Jaqqa kicked at Maratse's wounded leg, throwing him off balance. Maratse grunted as he sprawled on the ice. The rifle skittered out of his grasp. Jaqqa lunged for it, kicking at Maratse's hands.

"David," Petra screamed. She threw back her head and caught Gaba in the nose. He dropped her and she scrabbled to her feet, slipping across the ice in wet socks until she found her footing, and her strength. Petra ran towards them.

"You should have left me in custody," Jaqqa said, as he stood up. He pointed the barrel of the rifle at Maratse's chest. "You could have killed me with that battery trick." Jaqqa laughed, and then turned his back on Maratse and aimed at Petra, shifting his aim slightly as Petra slipped on the ice.

"No," Maratse said, as he pushed himself onto his feet. "This isn't how it ends."

"Quiet, old man," Jaqqa said.

Maratse heard three things – the slap of Petra's feet across the ice, the first click of the trigger tightening in Jaqqa's grasp, and his grandfather's voice on the wind.

Now, Qilingatsaq.

Maratse gripped the knife from the scabbard lashed to the scooter and thrust it into Jaqqa's side. Jaqqa dropped the rifle and Maratse pulled the knife out. He stabbed him again and again until

Jaqqa stopped squirming and his blood pooled on the ice. Petra froze at the sight, dropped to her knees, and pressed her hands to her face.

"It's okay, Piitalaat," Maratse said. "He can't hurt you anymore."

Maratse closed his eyes. He could feel the vibration of feet pounding along the ice. He felt hands on his body, and he tried to open his eyes, but he was weak. He heard Gaba's voice, and then another, the new man, Peter, perhaps. Something about *loss of blood* and *very weak*. He could have told them that.

He felt something else, thin fingers tugging at his own as Gaba and Peter lifted him and carried him across the ice to the mining camp. *Piitalaat.* They were her fingers. There for a moment and then gone, and then he was lying down on a seat. There was a scratch of metal. He tried to open his eyes, but it was white, just white, and then the whining and the roaring began. He lifted his hand, heard the man's voice again. *Was it Peter?* And then he searched for her, found her fingers and gripped them. He would never let go. Never again. She was back. They would be together, always.

Maratse woke inside a white room, a tiny ward off the main corridor of Uummannaq hospital. He could smell tobacco. Old smoke. He searched the room and saw Simonsen leaning in the corner. The Chief of Uummannaq police was smiling, and Maratse felt a twinge in his stomach that had nothing to do with being shot in the thigh. He started to speak but Simonsen shushed him.

"Just a second," he said, and turned up the volume on the radio.

He watched Maratse as they listened to the news broadcast in Greenlandic first, followed by a Danish version. Maratse understood both. He was one step ahead of the Chief, but he realised it was likely to be the last time.

Maratse couldn't remember ever hearing Malik Uutaaq speak Danish in public, but his accent and pronunciation were perfect, although he declined to comment when asked about his personal thoughts on diversity in Greenland.

"You've heard the official statement," he said, his voice booming through the radio, his tone strong and commanding, defying the radio host to press him any further.

"Can you believe it?" Simonsen said. "Uutaaq's has been given a ministerial position in Nivi Winther's government. It's a mistake." Simonsen laughed. "She must be mad. "

"Or clever," Maratse said.

"Well, you would know all about that, eh?" Simonsen sat at the end of Maratse's bed.

"Where is Piitalaat?"

"She's next door. She's waiting to see you." Simonsen paused. "*Piitalaat.* That's how you knew. Isn't it?"

"*Iiji.*"

"And you couldn't just tell me?"

Maratse thought for a moment, and then he remembered the watch on his wrist, the second hand thudding for every wasted moment. "There wasn't time," he said.

"Well, you're going to have plenty of that for a while," Simonsen said. "You killed someone, Maratse." he lifted his hand. "Extenuating circumstances, I will agree, but you obstructed justice and took the law into your own hands. Do you remember Natsi Hermansen? He says you tortured him. He's pressing charges. As are the two men you beat up in Saattut."

Maratse closed his eyes. He had forgotten about them.

"I did what I had to do," he said.

"You did. Like you always do."

The wheels beneath the bed squealed as Simonsen stood up.

"I have two funerals to go to. Anton is burying two thirds of his family." He sighed. "It makes no sense."

Maratse nodded. He waited until Simonsen was at the door.

"How long?" he asked.

"What do you mean?"

"Before you arrest me?"

Maratse had the impression that Simonsen would have spat, if they had been outside. "You still have friends in high places. The Commissioner has pulled some strings, again. You'll be under house arrest until the case is ready for court." Simonsen shook his head. "I'll be watching, Maratse. Closer now than before. You don't leave that house. Do you understand?"

"*Iiji.*"

Maratse waited until he was gone, and then threw back the sheets. He held his breath as he swung his legs over the side. The floor was cold beneath his feet. He saw a pair of slippers beside the bed and squirmed his feet into them. The grip wasn't quite as firm as the soles of Buuti's *kamikker*, but they would do. Maratse shuffled to the door.

There was a small crowd in the corridor, faces he knew. Maratse felt a tiny hand clasp his and looked down at Nanna; her blonde hair tickled his skin as she tugged his hand to her face.

"Gently, Nanna," Sisse said. She pressed her hand against Maratse's cheek and collected Nanna into her arms. "We'll see you later," she said.

Buuti was next. She wrapped her arms around Maratse's body, hugging and squeezing with a sense of urgency that could have been therapeutic or disciplinary. The look on Karl's face suggested it was best not to ask.

"Buuti," Karl said, as he placed his hand on her shoulder. "We can see him later. There are others..."

Buuti wiped her eyes on Maratse's hospital gown and pressed her hand against his chest.

"Come home soon," she said. "Both of you."

"*Iiji.*"

Karl pointed at the door to the next room and Maratse shuffled towards it. He almost turned around at the sight of a pink-haired young woman. She had studs beneath her bottom lip. In the soft light of the room, Maratse thought they might have been tusks.

"This is Tertu," Qitu said, as he crossed the room to shake Maratse's hand. "We're here for Salik's funeral. She and Petra have been talking. When you're ready, we'd like to talk to you too."

"Are you writing an article?"

"Yes. Tertu wants to tell her story," he said, as Tertu nodded. "She feels she can tell it now, thanks to you."

"Hm," Maratse said.

The woman hugged Petra, and then took Qitu's hand, pulling him out of the room. The door closed softly behind them, and they were alone.

Petra fiddled with the drip taped to the back of her hand, brushed her hair behind her ears and smiled.

"It's okay, David," she said. "I'm alright."

He sat down on the bed and took her hand. The weave of the dressings was rough to the touch and there were spots of blood seeping through the white bandages. Her hand trembled.

"You're sure?"

"Yes," she said. "With your help, I'll be okay. But it might take some time."

THE END

Author's Note

Greenland is the largest island in the world, but with roughly 56,000 inhabitants, its population is smaller than the city of Galveston, Texas. The capital of Nuuk has a population of roughly 15,000 people. Some settlements have fewer than one hundred residents. There are no roads connecting the towns, villages, and settlements. Transport to and from the inhabited areas is predominantly serviced by planes with short take off and landing capabilities, helicopters, and boats. In the areas where the sea ice is thick enough, Greenlanders can travel across the ice in cars, and by snow scooters and dog sledges.

Constable David Maratse's fictive Greenland is affected by the same limitations of the real Greenland. His fictive stories are inspired by some events and many places that exist in Greenland. Most place names are the same, such as Nuuk, and Uummannaq, but used fictitiously. The settlement of Inussuk does not exist, although observant readers looking at a map will be able to take a good guess at where it might be found.

Chris
November 2018
Denmark

Acknowledgements

I would like to thank Isabel Dennis-Muir for her invaluable editing skills and feedback on the three manuscripts.

While several people have contributed to *Seven Graves, One Winter*, *Blood Floe* and *We Shall Be Monsters*, the mistakes and inaccuracies are all my own.

Chris
January 2019
Denmark

About the Author

Christoffer Petersen is the author's pen name. He lives in Denmark. Chris started writing stories about Greenland while teaching in Qaanaaq, the largest village in the very north of Greenland – the population peaked at 600 during the two years he lived there. Chris spent a total of seven years in Greenland, teaching in remote communities and at the Police Academy in the capital of Nuuk.

Chris continues to be inspired by the vast icy wilderness of the Arctic and his books have a common setting in the region, with a Scandinavian influence. He has also watched enough Bourne movies to no longer be surprised by the plot, but not enough to get bored.

You can find Chris in Denmark or online here:

www.christoffer-petersen.com

By the same Author

THE GREENLAND TRILOGY
featuring Konstabel Fenna Brongaard
THE ICE STAR
IN THE SHADOW OF THE MOUNTAIN
THE SHAMAN'S HOUSE

THE GREENLAND CRIME SERIES
featuring Constable David Maratse
set in Greenland

SEVEN GRAVES, ONE WINTER
BLOOD FLOE
WE SHALL BE MONSTERS

Short stories from the same series
KATABATIC
CONTAINER
TUPILAQ
THE LAST FLIGHT
THE HEART THAT WAS A WILD GARDEN

THE DARK ADVENT SERIES
featuring Police Commissioner Petra Jensen
set in Greenland
THE CALENDAR MAN
THE TWELFTH NIGHT

THE SIRIUS SLEDGE PATROL SERIES
featuring Sirius Patrolman Mikael Gregersen
set in Greenland
PITERAQ

THE JON ØSTERGÅRD SERIES
featuring Wildlife Biologist Jon Østergård
set in Denmark
PAINT THE DEVIL

Printed in Great Britain
by Amazon